GIFFORD PINCHOT

Forester–Politician

GIFFORD PINCHOT

FORESTER ✦ POLITICIAN

M. NELSON McGEARY

PRINCETON, NEW JERSEY
PRINCETON UNIVERSITY PRESS
1960

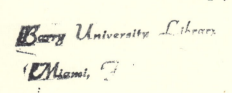

Publication of this book has been aided
by the Ford Foundation program to support publication,
through university presses,
of works in the humanities and social sciences

Printed in the United States of America by
Princeton University Press, Princeton, New Jersey

TO JANE

GIFFORD PINCHOT had two careers—one in forestry and the other in politics. Although my original purpose was to write a political biography, it soon became apparent that Pinchot's two careers were so closely interlaced that an account of his political life must by necessity deal also with his career as a forester and conservationist. The famed Ballinger-Pinchot controversy, for example, was as much forestry as politics. This volume, therefore, tells how Pinchot became America's first trained forester, and at the feet of his idol, Theodore Roosevelt, took the leadership along with the President in promoting the great conservation movement. Many statesmen of a national reputation gain experience in government at the state level and then move on to the national political scene. Pinchot, working in reverse, first became nationally prominent in Washington as the dynamic administrator of the United States Forest Service, and then, as Governor of Pennsylvania, emulated TR by installing a "little square deal" in Pennsylvania.

One of Gifford Pinchot's characteristics was better suited to his career as a forester than to his political career. His reluctance to compromise was almost indispensable to him in accomplishing his goals in conservation. In politics—which has been defined as the art of compromise—his unbending attitude helped to explain his inability to satisfy his strong desire to be returned to Washington by the vote of the people.

In most of his activities Pinchot was a highly controversial figure. Few of his associates spoke of him in neutral terms—some placed him on a pedestal and others despised him. The purpose of this volume is to try to show what kind of person he really was, what he was striving to accomplish, and what methods he used to attain his objectives. Endeavoring to treat him as objectively as possible, I may satisfy neither his worshippers nor his detractors.

I have placed heavy reliance on the papers that Pinchot deposited in the Library of Congress before he died in 1946. Apparently having assumed early in his life that his correspondence might someday be valuable, he carefully preserved it. Since he was a prodigious letter writer and speech maker, it has been estimated that his papers form the largest individual collection in the Library. Partly because he corresponded with many nationally prominent persons, the collection contains a wealth of interesting and useful material. His personal diary was most helpful in revealing his attitude on some key questions and events, although many days and important events are not covered.

I have also used the collections in the Library of Congress of the papers of Albert J. Beveridge, Mira Lloyd Dock, James R. Garfield, William John McGee, Frederick H. Newell, Amos R. E. Pinchot, Elihu Root, William Howard Taft, Thomas J. Walsh, William Allen White, and Woodrow Wilson; the papers of John M. Phillips; and material in the National Archives from the Forest Service and the Department of the Interior.

In conversations I had with a great many people, some of whom knew Pinchot intimately, I gained useful background information to supplement the written material available. I cannot begin to list them all, but am especially indebted to the following: David Cushman Coyle, Samuel T. Dana, George B. Galloway, Maurice K. Goddard, W. Brooke Graves, Frederick P. Gruenberg, Ralph Hetzel, Thomas Kennedy, John L. Lewis, Edward Martin, George Wharton Pepper, Stephen Raushenbush, William A. Schnader, Anna Jane Phillips Shuman, P. Stephen Stahlnecker, Roy Wilkinson, and George H. Wirt. These people are, of course, in no way responsible for any mistakes I may have made.

I should like also to thank Neal Riemer and my wife for having read the entire manuscript and offered valuable suggestions for improvement. In addition I wish to express appreciation to Kent Forster, who read selected chapters; to Dolores Hovick, Harold T. Pinkett, R. Miriam Brokaw, Elizabeth Smedley, Charles D. Bonsted, and Bruce Harding; and to the staff of the Manuscripts Division of the Library of Congress, including Katharine E. Brand, Robert H. Land, and C. Percy Powell.

Parts of Chapters 15 and 16 are rewritten versions of articles that appeared in the *Pennsylvania Magazine of History and Biography* for July 1957 and July 1959.

Quotations are reprinted by permission of the publishers from

Elting E. Morison, editor, *The Letters of Theodore Roosevelt*, Cambridge, Mass.: Harvard University Press, Copyright, 1951, 1952, 1954, by The President and Fellows of Harvard College.

Finally, I wish to express my gratitude to the American Philosophical Society and the Administrative Committee on Research of the Pennsylvania State University for funds which enabled me to conduct the research.

M. NELSON McGEARY

CONTENTS

CONTENTS

PART THREE
ACTIVE LAST YEARS

GIFFORD PINCHOT

Forester–Politician

"MY own money came from unearned increment on land in New York held by my grandfather, who willed the money, not the land, to me. Having got my wages in advance in that way, I am now trying to work them out."[1] Gifford Pinchot, candidate for United States senator at the age of forty-eight, revealed one of the underlying motives behind his remarkable career in this letter to a friend in 1914. Little that happened in Pinchot's childhood gave any hint of the calling he would follow. Certainly the climate of his early upbringing encouraged acceptance of things as they were.

On his father's side Pinchot's family was distinguished for success in business. Gifford's great-grandfather, Constantine Pinchot, who was mayor of Breteuil in Picardy, raised and equipped a company of soldiers just prior to the battle of Waterloo and put his son, Cyril C. D. Pinchot, Gifford's grandfather, in command. Failing to arrive in time for the battle, the company turned back after the surrender. Cyril Pinchot, expelled from France after the restoration of the Bourbons, came to America with his parents and settled in 1816 in Milford, Pennsylvania, located in what came to be called the Pocono Mountains. Before railroads reached the vicinity, the grandfather became a leading merchant, running a line of freight wagons across to the Hudson River, where goods were shipped to and from New York.

Gifford's father, James W. Pinchot, born in Milford in 1831, left the village of Milford for New York City. Starting as a clerk in a drygoods store at the age of nineteen, he soon formed a partnership called Pinchot, Warren & Co., located at 6 Cortland Street. Success came so fast that he was reluctant to reveal the amount of business he did because it "was so much out of proportion with the amount of capital invested."[2] So hard did he work, in fact, that in 1859 he broke down with "hemorrhages of the lungs." The treatment—strange by medical standards of the present time—was a protracted vacation in the form of a tour on horseback through a number of southern states. His survival to the age of seventy-six proved that the prescribed medicine was effective.

Returning to the business, James Pinchot continued to prosper. Four years later, in 1864, he married Mary Jane Eno, a member of a wealthy family. Partly because of his own prosperity, and also because of the generous dowry of his wife, he was able to retire eleven years later at the age of forty-four. With a stern face wreathed in sideburns, he already had all the appearances of a country squire.

For the next quarter century James and Mary Pinchot maintained homes in both Milford and New York City. Midway in this period James constructed a large home, Grey Towers, on his estate just outside Milford, which in future years was to be the scene of innumerable political palavers called by his son Gifford.

Patron of the arts, James Pinchot counted among his most intimate friends a number of artists. For one of these, the painter Sanford R. Gifford, he named his first son.

James loved France and her people. His numerous trips to Europe took him more often to Paris than any other city. Vitally interested in developing friendly feeling between France and the United States he served on the committee in charge of the erection of the Statue of Liberty. Grey Towers, significantly, had the appearance of a French chateau.

But of more lasting importance to Gifford Pinchot than his name or the French influence on his childhood was his father's fascination with the forestry which was practiced in Europe. Although forestry had developed to maturity in France and other European nations in the 1880's, it remained in its infancy in the United States. Timber in America had been so abundant that there was little incentive to save it. The creation of the American Forestry Association in 1875, however, showed that a few persons were beginning to think of the future consequences of timber exploitation. Those who took the leadership in forestry, however, were either professionals in related fields (such as botany), or laymen, or men born and trained in other countries. James was one of the outstanding laymen who was vitally concerned over the rapidly disappearing forests. Author of various articles on the subject, and onetime vice-president of the American Forestry Association, he suggested the profession of forestry to his son and eventually influenced him to enter it. Up to this time no American had chosen such a career.

James Pinchot unquestionably helped to launch the practice of forestry in the United States. But no conservation historian would go so far as his proud son in designating him "the Father of Forestry in America."[3]

James was a staunch Republican and member of numerous clubs including the Union League. He sincerely regretted the defeat of Benjamin Harrison for President in 1892. Gifford, it is clear, was reared in a climate where "gentlemen" were Republicans.

The elder Pinchot, not the kind of father to teach a son how to swim by throwing him in the water, was ever ready to proffer detailed advice on how Gifford should handle his affairs. Even after Gifford was graduated from Yale, the fond father found it difficult not to be oversolicitous.

Because Gifford had some trouble with his eyes and was a highstrung individual, it is not surprising that James often cautioned him about using his eyes or energy to excess. But on other occasions he gave advice well beyond the amount to be welcomed by an average, mature boy. When Gifford went to Europe after college, for example, his father wrote that he wanted him to return by "one of the good Cunard ships with one of the old captains,"[4] since the voyage would be in the stormy season. At another time he urged his son while abroad not to "sleep in bad air nor near bad drainage."[5] Moreover, when Gifford had reached thirty-five years of age and had had considerable experience in camping and hunting, his father still begged him to take care of himself on a trip into the woods and to "take no risks by separating yourself from your party."[6] If Gifford ever rebelled inwardly at such parental solicitude, it is not apparent in his letters to his father. If he suffered, he suffered in silence.

Gifford's grandfather on his mother's side, Amos R. Eno, began his career as an office boy in Hartford, Connecticut. From there he went to New York City, where he amassed a fortune, the bulk of it in real estate investments. In 1859 he built the Fifth Avenue Hotel, one of the finest hostelries in the country, which was later sold by his estate for $7,250,000. His son-in-law, James Pinchot, commented somewhat casually when the hotel suffered a bad fire, "If Mr. Eno has lost a million of dollars which I presume probable he has several more left."[7]

As befitted the daughter of a wealthy and prominent family, Mary Jane Eno, Gifford's mother, was a leader in the social world. Described by a newspaper interviewer as the "ideal *grande dame*,"[8] she played a dignified, nonobtrusive role in society. She and her husband counted among their acquaintances some of the most celebrated persons in the nation. One of their close friends, and a traveling companion in Europe, was General William T. Sherman. On several occasions they were guests of President Harrison at the White House. Indeed, Gifford Pinchot later in life was proud to have known all the Presidents from Grant to Truman.

When Mrs. Pinchot at the turn of the century built a home at 1615 Rhode Island Avenue in Washington, D.C., she and her husband moved there from New York City, although they continued their frequent visits to Milford. Gifford, now a government employee, lived with them and later inherited the home. For some fourteen years, Mary Pinchot, who outlived her husband by six years, served as a gracious Washington hostess. Congressmen, senators, Presidents, Supreme Court justices, foreign emissaries, and other Washington notables were frequent guests. So regularly did the Pinchots entertain that when on occasion the family ate alone, it was unusual enough for Mrs. Pinchot to enter in her diary, "No one at dinner."[9]

The unbounded energy which Gifford Pinchot displayed throughout his life must have come partly from his mother. At least in the entertainment of guests, she seemed untiring. Even in her later years she continued her social activity. At the age of seventy-four, in 1911, she had some 300 guests to tea and it was not surprising that the next day she complained of feeling "poorly." And two years later, under her own close supervision, she received about 800 guests at a splendid reception.

The Pinchot homes were "proper" homes. Both the father and mother displayed a warm kind of old-fashioned courtesy, but each scrupulously followed the rules of decorum and etiquette. Neither of them was attracted to innovations or passing fancies in the world about them. Mary, for example, strongly disapproved of the tight skirts which women were wearing in 1912. "They are the fashions of the Empire, when most women were not proper," she lamented. "If women persist in wearing those short, scant skirts, they should learn to walk. If they only realized how perfectly ungraceful they appear, as they hobble along, . . ."[10] Such new styles were very different from her own wedding dress, which included hoops and a total of twenty petticoats.

But Mrs. Pinchot's conservatism with respect to dress did not mean she was a reactionary concerning social and economic problems. Developing a high admiration for Theodore Roosevelt, whom she visualized as a good antidote to McKinley and later to Taft, she saw a need for change. Although always a Republican, she noted in her diary when the Democrats captured the state of Maine in 1910, "Good news from Maine. Democrats in power again—a protest against stand pattism."[11]

His father's influence on Gifford was fundamental if for no other reason than that he persuaded his son to enter forestry. But it was his mother's attitude of mind which helped to explain the son's later ardor for championing the "little" man. Mrs. Pinchot's humanitarianism is revealed in a comment she once made concerning her hobby of collecting lace. With the widespread use of machinery in the twentieth century, she bemoaned the gradual passing of the finest quality lace. But, as she explained, although she "deplore[d] it artistically" she "rejoice[d] from a humanitarian standpoint" since the lace had so often been made in "damp, dark cellars by poor laborers, whose very lives were sacrifices for their art."[12]

A member of the Daughters of the American Revolution, her energies in that organization were directed toward preventing waste of the nation's natural resources. At one time, appropriately for the mother of a famed forester, she served as chairman of the D.A.R.'s conservation committee.

James and Mary Pinchot were the parents of four children (the fourth, a daughter, died of scarlet fever at the age of two). Gifford, born August 11, 1865, at his grandfather Eno's summer home in Simsbury, Connecticut, made a striking appearance. Better than six feet tall, his slim, trim frame tended to accentuate his height.

7

His thick and spreading moustache was a boon to cartoonists. His highly masculine and handsome face—with its prominent nose, stern mouth, and strong chin—was well suited to the broad-brimmed, soft hats which he delighted to wear. Both his features and manner portrayed an individual confident of his own capacities. A stranger needed to see him only briefly to realize that here was a man of immense vitality, enthusiasm, and purpose. Some persons spoke of his shining brown eyes as those of a determined crusader, but others detected in them also a quizzical expression which seemed to reveal an inner warmth.

Antoinette Eno, born three years after Gifford, became Lady Johnstone, wife of the Honourable Sir Alan Johnstone, British minister at Copenhagen. Tall like her brother, her height was conspicuous in a woman. Her only son became a Liberal party member of the British House of Commons. Through the years Gifford and his sister continued an intimate and frank correspondence.

Amos Richard Eno, born in Paris in 1873, was the youngest of the three. Amos never seemed to get his feet planted firmly on the ground. As a practicing attorney in New York City, he was for a while an ardent supporter and leader of Theodore Roosevelt's Progressive party. His political ambitions led him to run for Congress in 1912, but without success. If Gifford's political and economic beliefs placed him somewhat left of center, then Amos was a little left of Gifford. Although in the earlier Progressive days the two brothers saw eye to eye on most issues, in later years Gifford dismissed some of Amos's ideas as impracticable. No actual rift developed between them, but a mild drifting apart did occur.

Mary Pinchot was fond of all her children and they of her. All three affectionately addressed her throughout her life as "Mamee." Equally devotedly, but less elegantly, they sometimes referred to her as "the mouse." But beyond much doubt, Mamee had a favorite, and he was Gifford. "I record as the paramount blessing of my life," she said in her latter years, "the fact I am Gifford Pinchot's mother and in a way one who helped to form his ideals, who has always ardently sympathized with all that he hoped to do."[13] "No one was ever so blessed as I," Mrs. Pinchot wrote in her diary concerning her relations with her children. And here again, a little special adulation was reserved for her first son, "My children have grown more than I. G[ifford] has more than one could have imagined."[14]

In a red brick house at fashionable Gramercy Park in New York City, Gifford Pinchot began his life—the very image of a coddled son of privileged parents. During his first six years the family frequently took him on extended visits to the Eno homes in New York and Simsbury. One summer, with a French governess, he lived in a Newport, Rhode Island, hotel.

When he was six the family sailed to Europe for a visit of three years, although the father shuttled between his family and his business in New York. After a summer in England, the Pinchots crossed to Paris in 1871 where they viewed the ruins following the "dreadful commune,"[15] as Mr. Pinchot described it.

Later the children traveled with their parents around France, Italy, Switzerland, and Germany. From France, James wrote his father that Gifford was "a real good boy," although Nettie (Antoinette) "was pretty hard to manage."[16] In Nice, France, the family's friend and part-time traveling companion, General Sherman, "delighted" Gifford by taking him on a ship; the same evening the General and the son of the President of the United States, Lieutenant Grant, dined with the Pinchots.

While the Pinchots were in Paris, Gifford had a French lesson each morning until he came to speak the language about as well as English. In Paris also he went to day school and both he and his sister attended dancing classes.

From the time that Gifford returned to the United States at the age of nine until he entered Yale, his formal education was of high quality but decidedly helter-skelter. At various times he attended at least three different private schools in New York City.

When he was fifteen he again sailed to Europe. His complaint that on the trip across the water "there were no pretty girls at all" suggested that he was developing into a normal young man. This time he was left alone in England, where for a period of three or four months he lived with and was tutored by Canon Angelsmith of Canterbury Cathedral. A report to the father by the tutor praised Gifford for his memory and his ability to understand explanations

9

quickly.[17] Outside of his studies, Gifford was happy to be jumping horses "over low barriers."

The young student also found time to do some fishing—a hobby which was to mean so much to him in later years. Even as mild a sport as this brought expressions from his mother of some fear for his safety. "I don't think," he wrote to her, "that you quite understand about our fishing. We don't fish on the banks of a stream, but from a boat in a pond, and so I hope that you will not object to it."[18]

London did not impress him. For one thing, it was dirtier than New York. He objected, moreover, to the "snobbish crowd" around the city. If "a fellow carries a bundle out of a cab into a store, . . . they may lose all respect for him."[19]

A year later Gifford found himself enrolled in the class of 1884 at Phillips Exeter Academy in New Hampshire. Since he was accustomed to close supervision by his father and was now on his own more than ever before, he found the adjustment somewhat difficult. "[It] is very hard," he wrote "to keep my manners and my bearing what they should be when there is no one to caution me when I go wrong."[20]

As was true also in college, he showed a marked interest in religious matters. He wrote from Exeter, for example, how much he enjoyed reading Farrar's *St. Paul*. Periodically he referred to meetings of the "Christian Fraternity," and he told his mother of his decision to join the Presbyterian Church in New York.

At Exeter, too, Gifford displayed an interest in insects, just as in earlier childhood he had been overjoyed at finding specimens of bugs and beetles in the woods. Such a hobby seemed to point toward a scientific career. Indeed, at one point he explained to his father that he probably would not play baseball because he wished to keep his hands "in proper condition for scientific work."[21] Although not for the same reason, incidentally, he pleased his mother and father by giving up football and, at some prodding from his father, agreed to drop pistol practice.

James Pinchot without doubt was gratified at the comments from a member of the Exeter staff concerning his son's "generosity and purity of spirit."[22] But Gifford, not at all used to routine, was unenthusiastic about his preparatory school life. He complained, moreover, that his eyes were bothering him. All through his life, as a matter of fact, his eyes periodically tended to ache and burn, and were a recurring source of worry to him. At times he feared he might eventually go blind. But doctors in general were always reassuring, provided he did not use his eyes to great excess.

When Gifford threatened to give up Exeter during his second year, his father urged him to hang on, reminding him that the doctor had said his eyes were satisfactory. Gifford for the time being submitted to parental urging, but before the year was out wrote his mother that he had "almost come to the conclusion that I had better take a year out of my school life and go into business. If the present condition of my eyes lasts, it will be almost impossible for me to enter Yale next fall."[23]

He did in fact stay out of school for a year, although he did not seek a job. After taking entrance examinations for Yale, he was admitted with five conditions, but was able to work them off before classes began in the fall of 1885.

In view of the sheltered and pampered life which Pinchot led before entering college, it is remarkable that he was not seriously spoiled. Sometimes he did have an air of stiffness about him which bordered on snobbishness. The year before going to Yale, for example, he was disturbed when his sister's governess called him Gifford. "I am afraid," he wrote his parents, "that I haven't yet been dignified enough myself, for Miss Miller has already taken to calling me by my first name. I will try to be more so in the future."[24] His attitude seemed somewhat mellowed by 1886 when he reported to his mother that the workmen who were building the new family home at Milford, "know me already well enough to call me by my first name, which I don't at all object to."[25]

Pinchot came to Yale in 1885 with a seeming determination to counteract any possible feelings by fellow students that he was a Little Lord Fauntleroy. He went out of his way, as if in reaction against his earlier life of ease, to emphasize his own vigor and virility. In a "frosh-soph rush" he was conspicuously in the front, where he "lost nothing except a few buttons and the integrity of my trousers."[26] He became a halfback and captain on the freshman football team, and complained that the Princeton freshmen were afraid to play the Yale squad. Despite his height he weighed only 161, hardly the right build to make the varsity. He was, nevertheless, proud of serving, even though only as a substitute, under the great coach, Walter Camp. He took further pride in the results of a physical examination which showed him to have the second highest lung capacity of all members of his class—perhaps a bright omen, although not realized at the time, for a future politician.

Try as he might, however, Pinchot had difficulty in shaking loose from a family somewhat oversolicitous for his welfare. In his senior year, for example, a skating accident cut a small piece of skin away from his cheek and caused two or three scratches on his face. With a tone of disgust he related to his father how one of his uncles had been sent to New Haven by "grandpa" to see how serious the injury was, and his aunt had written offering him a room to "lie in bed in." "People," wrote young Pinchot, "seem to enjoy making other people anxious."[27]

All through life he was inclined to advertise his rugged side. His genuine love of the outdoors fit in well with this pattern. Sleeping on the ground in the woods thrilled him. He frequently boasted of his long and fast walks; companions of average energy sometimes felt like puppies trudging along beside him. The same kind of spirit was revealed in his later habit of campaigning, in all kinds of weather, in an open car with the top down. His reputation as a spartan became legendary and led to such apocryphal stories as his preferring to sleep on a wooden rather than a feather pillow.

Although he joined a fraternity, Psi Upsilon, at Yale and served on the junior prom committee, he could hardly be called a college social light. In his senior year, for example, he took a trip to Hartford only "in obedience to Papa's instructions to go out more in 'sassiety.' "[28]

As a leader in his class, Pinchot entered into a variety of campus activities. But the one which not only took the most time but gave him the greatest satisfaction was the religious work on the campus. For four years, Samuel Fisher, Edward L. Parsons (who later became Bishop of San Francisco), and Pinchot worked together as deacons of the class of '89. As such, they had responsibilities for the religious activity of the class, including the conduct of both Sunday and week-day prayer meetings. In addition Pinchot took a turn at teaching an off-campus Sunday school class. The three deacons remained the closest of friends for over fifty years.

After college Pinchot continued to display an interest in various church affairs. At one time, for instance, he served as chairman of a Commission on the Church and Country Life, of the Federal Council of Churches. During most of his post-college life, he did not regularly attend church. An obvious carry-over, however, from his interest in collegiate religious matters was the moralistic tone that permeated many of his later activities in conservation and politics.

Upon graduation Pinchot was offered the position, for a year, of general secretary of the Yale Y.M.C.A., at a salary of $750. Although its acceptance would have delayed his forestry work, he seriously considered the idea. There is no question that he had a kind of missionary zeal. As he told his father while trying to decide whether to accept the offer, "I might, and I think should, do some good here at Yale."[29] In the end, however, he decided to pass up the opportunity.

It was hardly surprising that Pinchot as a junior earned a prize in French. Probably more satisfying to him personally was a medal he won at graduation time in a speaking contest. Although the orations by the six finalists were said to be far above the average, the judges selected Pinchot the winner for his discussion of "The Quakers of the Seventeenth Century." In view of the political career which Pinchot eventually chose to follow, it is interesting to note his explanation of the choice of his oration subject. At first he considered speaking on "The Industrial History of the English Revolution of 1680 and the Rise of the *Bourgeoisie*," but finally offered the substitute because the original "must necessarily deal very largely with Political Economy, of which I am not very fond."[30]

The economic and political views of Pinchot the student differed radically from those in later years of Pinchot the chief of the United States Forest Service and Pinchot the Governor of Pennsylvania. He was destined to become a leading proponent of government controls over business, especially over monopolies, and an advocate of requiring business to operate in the public interest. But at Yale he

13

tended to consider as paramount the interest of the owners of a business. He was indignant, for example, over government regulation of railroad fares, "The railroads own the tracks and the cars don't they? Then why shouldn't they charge what they please?"[31]

Further evidence of Pinchot's early style of thinking appears in an undated theme found among his college papers. Entitled "Education for Citizenship," it stressed the political responsibility of educated men for "guiding and controlling the uneducated masses." He bemoaned the power of political bosses like Tweed in New York; to his mind the true shame was that the failure of educated men in the cities to assume the trust which was properly theirs had "made it possible for the bar-keeper to control many times more votes than the manufacturer." Pinchot once admitted that he was born a reactionary, but no one would have applied that label to him when he died. By the end of his four years in college, however, he still was not far removed from the conservative pole of politics.

Twenty years following graduation, after many bitter fights in the Forest Service for "the public interest," he concluded that the Yale faculty as a whole were on the other side of the fence. "The Faculty of the University," he wrote his friend, Yale professor Irving Fisher, "is more nearly uniformly wrong on all public questions than any other possible body."[32]

In spite of some later reservations, however, Pinchot developed a strong affection for Yale. The longer he stayed at the university the more he enjoyed the life. "This last year at college," he wrote his mother, "is as much better than any other as good eggs are better than bad."[33] Several of his classmates and other Yale men became his close associates in governmental work both in Washington and Harrisburg. When Pinchot had so won the confidence of Theodore Roosevelt that the President often sought from him the names of persons qualified to fill various government posts, Pinchot once felt impelled to half apologize to Harvard-man Roosevelt when he proposed a name for the office of federal judge in Alaska, "You will notice that this is again a Yale man, but that is almost the only kind I know."[34]

When Pinchot came to Yale he had already accepted the advice of his father and tentatively decided to follow forestry as a career.

14

But he still knew very little about the nature of the field and the opportunities. He had been in college three months before he learned that a Forestry Division actually existed in the federal government. Indeed, so new to the subject was he that in some of his letters the word appeared not as "forestry" but as "forrestry."

The eager freshman obviously wanted to learn more about the field before making a firm decision. Early in the year he had a long talk with one of his professors who explained that no science of forestry existed in the United States and that Pinchot's proposed venture would certainly take him into unexplored territory. But the boy was unabashed by the prospect of having to break new ground. "[It] seems to me," he wrote his mother, "that I shall have not only no competitors, but even a science to found. . . . This is certainly as good an opening as a man could have."[35] That Christmas he was particularly pleased to receive presents of books on forestry.

Nothing happened at Yale to make him change his mind about his career. Although his college education was of a broad liberal nature rather than professional, he made it a point, when he had a choice, to select courses which had some relationship to forestry, such as those in botany. In his senior year he also prepared a special report on forestry for one of his classes. Gifford astounded his friends at Yale when he announced that he was going into forestry. To many of them it was hard to believe that this able young man, who seemingly could have anything he desired, wished to plunge into the relatively unknown. Yale professor William Lyon Phelps, who was a fellow student of Pinchot's, once asked him, "What are you going to do after graduation?"

"I am going to be a forester," replied Pinchot.

"What's that?"

"That's why I am going to be a forester."[36]

Sometimes, undoubtedly, questions arose in Pinchot's mind concerning the wisdom of his choice. Much of the advice which he received was discouraging. The chief of the Forestry Division in the Department of Agriculture, Bernhard E. Fernow, for example, believed it inadvisable for Pinchot to place all of his eggs in one basket. A German by birth, and trained as a forester in his home-

15

land, he believed that at that time forestry was impracticable in the United States. He therefore advised the student to straddle the future by preparing primarily for some associated career, such as landscape gardening or nursery work, and to consider forestry only as a secondary activity. As if to fortify himself, Pinchot had a long interview with one of his professors at the beginning of his senior year; the advice he received to stick to his original purpose of studying forestry obviously pleased the young man. Apparently discontinuing any further debate within himself, Pinchot assured his father, "I don't see that I can be more useful in any other way or so successful and happy. These reasons seem to me sufficient."[37] Pinchot again had some doubts when further unfavorable opinions of the wisdom of his choice were expressed. Sometimes he thought of medicine or other scientific work as more desirable. Shortly after graduation, however, he informed his father that he was determined to study forestry, at least "for a year or so," even though he might be forced, because of the lack of any opportunity, to give it up at the end of that time.

PART ONE

Forestry and the Rise of Conservation

CHAPTER I

AMERICA'S FIRST TRAINED FORESTER

HAVING MADE UP HIS MIND, Pinchot, after a summer of ease, sailed early in October 1889 from New York to Europe to learn more about the forestry profession, of which he knew so little thus far. Armed with gifts from his father of a watch and $600 he landed at Liverpool with the intention of talking with some foresters, buying some books on the subject, and returning home.

After enjoying himself and absorbing some information on forestry in England and France, Pinchot, by a fortuitous chain of circumstances, had an opportunity to go to Germany to meet Sir Detrich Brandis. Dr. Brandis, already retired, was perhaps the outstanding forester in the world. Among his foremost achievements was the introduction of forestry in India. The youthful and eager Gifford and the elderly master quickly formed a sincere attachment for each other. Brandis had a more profound influence on Gifford both as a forester and as an individual than anyone except his family and Theodore Roosevelt. One of the best sources of information on Gifford Pinchot's young manhood is the multitude of letters which he wrote to Brandis throughout the years until the latter's death in 1907—asking advice on forestry matters and informing the old gentleman on events in the United States.

Brandis, sternly Prussian in appearance and in many of his manners, demonstrated a warm kindliness toward the young American. Although Pinchot had encountered little but discouragement in his own country toward forestry as a career (except from his father), Brandis and other European foresters were enthusiastically reassuring. When Brandis endorsed the suggestion of a French forester that the young man enter the French Forest School in Nancy, Pinchot hastened to enroll.

Pinchot began his classes with a gleam in his eye. No student was ever more eager to learn. Probably no pupil ever went farther beyond the minimum requirements of a school to amass a knowledge of his chosen field.

While at Nancy he performed in a truly enthusiastic manner. Impatient at the emphasis placed on lectures rather than work in the woods, he made it a point to supplement his classroom study by spending every spare moment he could find in the forests. With this lust for information it is not surprising that he looked with disdain on most of the other students as loafers. Even in this energetic drive for knowledge, however, Pinchot showed a distaste for routine work—a characteristic which clung to him for the rest of his life. Always eager to be on the go, he was restless at a desk or in a classroom. He could not be called lazy, although he sometimes misinterpreted his feelings to be just that. "A kind of dislike for work bothers me,"[1] he noted in his diary at Nancy.

Unlike the regular students at Nancy, Pinchot, with the help of Dr. Brandis, withdrew temporarily in the middle of the term in order to spend one month at a city forest in Zurich, Switzerland.

After a total period of some six months at the Nancy school, Pinchot was given the unusual opportunity of accompanying a group of English students who were being trained for service in India on a tour conducted by Dr. Brandis through German and Swiss forests. In an effort to learn everything possible on the trip, Pinchot hired a tutor to help him improve his spoken German. By such foresight he was able to participate in conversations with local foresters and to squeeze out of the trip far more useful information than would otherwise have been possible.

On long walks and carriage rides with Dr. Brandis, Pinchot saw many of the best managed forests in the world and absorbed an immense amount of professional information. Small wonder that he wrote, "What I should be as a forester without Doctor Brandis makes me tremble."[2] Almost equally invaluable were the many suggestions that Brandis offered on how the young man should conduct his general living. Sir Detrich with almost uncanny perception observed characteristics in the young man which he felt might develop into weaknesses and offered advice on how to guard against them. Pinchot, accepting the advice in a serious manner, religiously copied down in his diary the Brandis maxims. He never forgot, for example, that Sir Detrich, believing Pinchot had a tendency to "run off at a tangent," strongly urged the young man to discipline himself to stick to his job. Decades later, moreover, Pinchot remembered, although by then he may have forgotten the source of the original advice, Brandis's charge, "Never punish or rebuke a man or defend yourself in anger."

A piece of Brandis counsel which in future years Pinchot had difficulty in following was, "Always be loyal to your superiors no matter what fools they may be. A man disloyal to his chief is not trusted."[3] A request for complete loyalty to a superior might be expected from a Prussian, but any sort of blind loyalty did not suit Pinchot's personality. Aggressive and zealous in most activities which he entered, he was not averse to battling lustily against a superior with whom he disagreed.

An element of intolerance crept into some of Pinchot's thinking and writing at this time. Before this trip to Europe, he had not, in reality, seen how the other ninety-eight per cent of the people lived. He had, as it were, been running with blinders. When people differed from the pattern to which he was accustomed, he was too prone to criticize. Shortly after arriving in England, he visited Cambridge where he found the students "hospitably inclined . . . cordial, polite, and in general very good fellows."[4] But the students on the Brandis trip were not as acceptable to the young American as were the Cambridge scholars or his former associates at Yale. "There are several nice fellows among the Englishmen," he told his mother, "but also a large proportion of muckers . . . they are as fresh and wearisome a crowd as I ever fell in with . . . infantile behavior."[5] When one of them began to "curse [Brandis] for an old fool," Pinchot immediately sprang to his mentor's defense, "I told them very plainly what I thought of their conduct, there has been no more of it since."[6]

Unquestionably a part of his feelings against some of the European students was based less on snobbishness than on distaste for what seemed to him their loose morals. He often showed a curious tendency to correct in others the habits he deemed undesirable or inappropriate. In later years some of his friends as well as enemies occasionally resented his tendency to preach to them. One of his elders, apparently recognizing this inclination in Pinchot as a youth, cautioned him at the time he entered college not to become a missionary nor to remonstrate with fellow students who got drunk or went around with the wrong kind of women.

There is no evidence, aside from his general work as a deacon, that Pinchot made any overt attempts to place individual fellow students on the straight path at Yale, but when he got to Europe he seemed impelled by some such urge. His "disrespect of the Roumanians and the other extremes of the school," he told his parents, "increases. Their conception of happiness seems to consist chiefly in smoking and drinking . . . these scarecrows."[7]

His greatest disgust was reserved, however, for the French students at Nancy. His early attitude was a kind of paternalism toward them and even a feeling that he might do something to convert them. Indeed, while still at Yale he and a friend had considered the possibility of living in Paris in order to "reach" French students "in a religious way."[8] But after a month or two at the French Forest School he confessed to his mother that "the longer I am here the truer your remark about the impossibility of foreigners helping Christian work among Frenchmen seems."[9] After another six weeks he appeared to be thoroughly disillusioned. With a note of despair he wrote his father that "the average French student has no more moral sense than a bull frog." Pontificating that his own "principles [had] the sanction of the bible," he complained of a society "where what we take for vice [is] so universal . . . and where the man who does not take part in it is regarded as simply an ass."[10]

Gifford's early trip to the Folies Bergère in Paris demonstrated, however, that he did not completely shelter himself from French variations on the life to which he was accustomed. His diary makes no comment on his reactions. But when a man in a little shop on the Rue de Rivoli showed him "the filthiest lot of photos imaginable," Pinchot was genuinely shocked and "awfully sorry" he had gone in.[11]

After thirteen months of cramming information on forestry into his receptive head, Pinchot decided it was time to go home. Almost all the professional advice that he received, both in Europe and from America, urged him to continue his studies in Europe for another year or two. Dr. Brandis, for example, wrote Pinchot's father of the importance of two additional years of study. Since in the opinion of Brandis all persons who had had something to do with forestry in America (except Dr. Fernow, chief of the Forestry Division) were either timber merchants or amateurs, he stressed the high desirability of enough training to make Pinchot a master of his profession.[12]

Pinchot, however, became convinced that the law of diminishing returns would set in if he stayed longer, especially since he felt that European forestry methods were not entirely transplantable to the democratic United States. With a generous portion of self-assurance, moreover, he had told his parents early in the year that Brandis, in urging a longer period of training, had "not counted with Yankee push and Yankee woodcraft."[13] While in Europe, Pinchot became painfully aware as never before of how little he knew about his own country. Not once had he been west of the Alleghenies. "I see more and more how foolish I have been," he wrote, "not to get more fully acquainted with America."[14] Determined to fill the gaps, he returned home at the end of 1890.

A few years later he admitted to Dr. Brandis some misgivings over having failed to continue his formal work until he had acquired a Ph.D. in forestry, "The time has come, as you foretold it would, when I begin to feel the scantiness of my preparation."[15] But at the end of his career, when he could look back in perspective, he was convinced that his decision to go home had been a wise one.[16] Even his severest critics generally admitted that he knew forestry.

Pinchot left Europe with some firm convictions about forestry. He had learned to his own satisfaction that trees are a crop. It was commonly understood in America that the cutting of trees destroyed a forest; Pinchot brought the gospel that forestry was the art of using a forest without destroying it. If cut in a scientific manner, some forests could be made to seed themselves and to keep on producing endlessly. He was satisfied as a result of his European observations that forest lands could be made into paying commercial projects without destroying them. The average American believed that the only way to preserve a forest was to keep out the axe; "woodman spare that tree" was symbolic of the thinking. Pinchot preached that through the use of proper methods a forest could be both harvested and preserved. He was certain, furthermore,

that such practices could be assured only through government control of private cutting. Pinchot was not the first person in the United
States to refer to trees as a crop, but he was the first with a determination to prove that such scientific handling of a forest could be
made profitable.

When Pinchot was a senior at Yale he went to Washington, D.C.,
to make a "provisional proposition" to Dr. Fernow, chief of the
Forestry Division in the Department of Agriculture, about going
to work for him during the coming year without compensation.
According to Pinchot, Fernow accepted gladly.[17] But it was this
same Fernow who had strongly discouraged Pinchot from choosing
forestry as a career.

Pinchot's decision to study in Europe, of course, eliminated his
proposed work with the Forestry Division. He was pleased, however, to receive while in Europe a letter from Fernow offering him
the new position of assistant chief of the Division at $1,600 a year,
and suggesting the likelihood of eventual succession to the position
of chief.[18] Fernow asked for a reply by cable. Pinchot first consulted
at length with Dr. Brandis and also his mother, who happened
to be in Europe at the time, before wiring his acceptance. In a
follow-up letter he requested permission not to begin work for
about six months—until after the Christmas holidays.[19]

No sooner had he accepted than he received a letter from Charles
S. Sargent advising against taking the position. Sargent, who was
the famed director of the Arnold Arboretum at Harvard University,
had for several years been consulted by Pinchot concerning his
proposed career in forestry. Like Fernow, Sargent had counseled
against it; again like Fernow, he had urged Pinchot once he began
studying to remain with it for another two years in Europe. Now
he cautioned Pinchot to avoid the position offered since the standing
of the Department of Agriculture, of the Division, and of Fernow
was not sufficiently high.[20]

Pinchot's father also was displeased that his son had accepted so
quickly. He admitted to "distrusting" Fernow and to feeling that
he was "posing and insincere."[21] Pinchot, beginning to have doubts
of the wisdom of his decision, cast around for a chance to back out.
He even hoped that Fernow would refuse to grant the six months'

delay, in which case Pinchot could ease out of the commitment gracefully.[22]

But he was startled and somewhat mystified when Fernow wrote again stating his belief that Pinchot was headed for the top and advising him against interrupting his European studies by accepting the position.[23] It was "queer," thought Pinchot, "that Fernow should have offered me the place if he does not want me to take it."[24] A second letter from Fernow a few days later promised to keep the position vacant until Pinchot was more fully prepared to take it.[25]

Pinchot's reputation as a budding forester reached his home shores even before his ship landed. Almost before losing his sea legs he was invited to deliver a paper at a national forestry meeting. Friends looked upon him as already an expert forester—a fact which irked him somewhat, ". . . people seem to think I have distinguished myself. Which is nonsense."[26] Home less than a month, he obtained his first job—examining and making recommendations for use of timber lands in Pennsylvania owned by the Phelps, Dodge Company.

By this time, however, he was certain of two things. First, he must spread his wings and travel throughout the United States in order to get to know both the people and the forests. And secondly, in accordance with advice from Dr. Brandis, he must find an opportunity to manage a large tract of forest and prove that it could be made profitable. Brandis had suggested that Pinchot might be able to persuade his grandfather to invest a half million dollars in buying a wooded area which Gifford could use for demonstration purposes.[27] But grandfather had not taken to the idea.

Twice within a year Pinchot had chances to quench his thirst for travel. Dr. Fernow graciously invited him along on a trip to view some woodlands in Arkansas. On this journey, however, the first indications of a basic personality clash between the two men developed. Fernow, like Pinchot, was a domineering individual and, in addition, inclined to be highly critical. As they saw more and more of each other, Pinchot grew "pretty weary" of the man; "Runs everybody down with tiresome uniformity," and tries to take "credit for everything," he complained.[28]

Hardly had Pinchot returned from Arkansas before he received a second assignment from Phelps, Dodge to make recommendations on land in Arizona. Although his expenses were paid, he received no salary. Since money was one of the least of Pinchot's worries, he made the trip by way of a circuitous train route which took him to Niagara Falls, Grand Canyon, Yosemite, and parts of Canada. Sometimes in the woods he had a chance to use the rifle and revolver which he took along. Keeping his eyes wide open and his pad full of notes, he truly increased his knowledge of trees and people.

Home again at the beginning of summer, he was both thoroughly tired from the trip and impatient to be doing something important. Sometimes feeling "rotten," he began to fret. His aunt was trying to get him married. He was "wasting time awfully."[29] Playing tennis at Milford and trying without much success to follow his father's suggestion of writing a book on forestry to be used in the schools, he restlessly made such diary entries as, "A useless day, of which I am greatly ashamed."[30] Sometimes he referred to his "blues," which a few days before Christmas had become "bad blues."[31]

Meantime Dr. Fernow, wondering when he would have an assistant, kept writing to Pinchot to learn his plans. And Pinchot kept stalling. Nor was his attitude toward Fernow softened by the latter's bluntly derisive opinion that Pinchot's idea of a schoolbook on forestry was preposterous.[32]

It was a full year after his return from Europe that an end came to Pinchot's indecision and restlessness. He was invited to supervise about 5,000 acres of land as a demonstration of practical forest management on the Biltmore estate of George W. Vanderbilt near Asheville, North Carolina. The first experiment of this kind in the United States, it had been suggested by Frederick L. Olmsted, a noted landscape architect whom Vanderbilt had hired to help develop Biltmore into the finest country estate in the nation. Pinchot had already seen the project and met Vanderbilt—a "simple minded pleasant fellow."[33] Here was the kind of opportunity Dr. Brandis had continually envisioned and Pinchot did not hesitate to accept. The salary was $2,500 plus subsistence and traveling expenses; in addition he had his own home and a horse. Had Vanderbilt wished to bargain, he might well have obtained his manager for no salary at all. It was understood that one of Pinchot's duties at Biltmore was, in conjunction with Vanderbilt and the state of North Carolina, to prepare an exhibit on forestry for the Chicago World's Fair.

When Pinchot, hardly reluctantly, wrote Fernow of his decision to take the Biltmore position, he explained that for the present at least he would have to give up any idea of entering the government service. "There having been no obligation on either side . . . I felt myself entirely free to accept Mr. Vanderbilt's offer."[34] But Fernow was highly irritated. While conceding that Pinchot had no legal obligation to come to Washington he made it clear that he felt Pinchot had reneged on a bargain. Taking the occasion, moreover, to tell Pinchot of his doubts of the wisdom of the young man's plan, he offered his opinion that the Biltmore experiment was a kind of impracticable fad.[35]

Both Fernow and Pinchot deserve important niches in the hall of fame of those who promoted forestry. Some persons refer to Fernow as the father of forestry in the United States, a title which has also been bestowed on Pinchot. Their conceptions of forestry were so different, however, and their personalities collided so forcibly that each lost respect for the activities of the other. Pinchot was impatient to accomplish things in a hurry; Fernow was in favor of moving more gradually. Jealousy undoubtedly contributed to their attitudes. When Pinchot published a little book on white pine, Fernow wrote a severe criticism of it in *Garden and Forest* magazine.

In spite of considerable disagreement with Fernow, Pinchot had an appreciation of his abilities. When Fernow was being considered as dean of the faculty of forestry at the University of Toronto, Pinchot wrote the acting president that "His brilliancy, knowledge, and gift as a teacher are not excelled by any man in forestry whom I know." But Pinchot's reservations overbalanced the praise. Fernow had, in Pinchot's opinion, so mismanaged a tract of land used for demonstration at the New York State College of Forestry that he was "mainly responsible" for the closing of the school. In spite of "his remarkable native ability," wrote Pinchot, he lacked the capacity to work well with other people and was "intolerant of other men's opinions."[36] Notwithstanding Pinchot's letter, Fernow got the job.

The depth of Pinchot's feeling was revealed when a friend asked him to write Fernow when the latter, in bad physical shape, retired from the deanship at Toronto. "As to Fernow," replied Pinchot, "I find myself in a difficult situation. I believe that Fernow did more to retard American forestry than any other man that ever lived. . . . On the other hand, I do not want to seem to hold off because of an ancient quarrel."[37] In the end he wrote no letter. This comment on Fernow was an example of an unhappy tendency, which in a sense plagued him throughout his career, to express an opinion in stronger language than his feelings actually warranted. On more than one occasion, for example, he referred to individuals as "yellow dogs," a term which obviously could engender deep bitterness. But Pinchot used the word so casually sometimes that he obviously did not mean to imply its full connotations. Sometimes his impetuous use of language more extreme than actually intended caused unnecessary ill will. When Pinchot portrayed Fernow as having held back forestry more "than any other man," it probably was a distortion of his true opinion of the man.

January 1892 was a month of high excitement for Pinchot. At last he had a chance to make his dreams come true. Fully aware that Biltmore would present the sternest of challenges, he was stoutly bolstered by his own supreme self-confidence.

CHAPTER 2

GETTING ESTABLISHED

GIFFORD PINCHOT arrived at Biltmore on ground-hog day in 1892 and embarked on his work with characteristic gusto. Following a thorough study of the wooded estate he set out to prove that scientific management of the forests could produce both a financial profit and a sustained yield of trees.

One of his most difficult tasks was to convince the resident lumberman of the necessity for saving the young trees which would furnish the next crop. On Pinchot's orders, Mr. Vanderbilt's forest land, contrary to prevailing practices throughout the country, was not stripped. Only trees marked by Pinchot were felled and they were dropped in the direction which would do the least damage to the young seedlings. Moreover, larger trees were saved at regularly spaced intervals to provide seeds for future crops.

These outdoor days in the North Carolina hills were a glorious adventure for Pinchot. Not only did he roam the forests of the estate, but, in company with Vanderbilt's lumberman or his real-estate agent (and a cook), he made numerous scouting trips to observe additional forest lands which Vanderbilt was considering for purchase. Sometimes, in order not to reveal the interest of his employer in the land, he traveled incognito as "Mr. Gifford."

On some of the trips he and his companions slept in the cabins of friendly, although sometimes suspicious, mountaineers. He reported with amusement in his diary about spending the night in a one-room cabin with two other beds and a shakedown full of women and children.[1] On other trips he camped out, at the beginning with a companion, and later, for the first time in his life, by himself in the middle of the deep forest.

At the end of the first full year of forestry management of the Biltmore tract, Pinchot satisfied himself that the project was paying. According to the simplified accounting of the local lumberman, the total expenditures were $10,103.63. The income in dollars was $4,616.19, but the value of the cut wood on hand (most of which was used on the estate) was $6,708, showing a "Balance our favor" of $1,220.56.

In the course of another two years Vanderbilt, on the recommendation of Pinchot, purchased an additional tract of some 80,000 acres which came to be known as Pisgah Forest. By this time Pinchot, with other irons in the fire and characteristically beginning to tire of the routine at Biltmore, persuaded Vanderbilt of the need for a resident forester at Biltmore. Since no second American had yet been thoroughly trained in the new profession, Pinchot called for help from his old guide, Dr. Brandis, who recommended another German, Carl Alvin Schenck.

Once Schenck was installed, Pinchot's status was changed to a nonresident consultant at a new salary of $1,000 a year. Although for a while there was some tension between Pinchot and Schenck over the question of which one was to direct the forest policy, Pinchot eventually won the point that he was to supervise the technical side of the work.[2] Both men, however, made great contributions in introducing the practice of scientific forestry in the Big Creek portion of the Pisgah Forest.

Some forty-five years later the United States Forest Service took a look at the tree plantations started on Vanderbilt's properties. In an article in *American Forest* entitled, "Biltmore—Fountain-Head of Forestry in America," a senior silviculturist attested to the importance of these early experiments. "Although commercially the plantations have not fulfilled the expectations of their founder," he reported, "they have set up for foresters a notable object lesson of success and failure in forest planting."[3]

If Pinchot was satisfied and happy over his work in the outdoors of North Carolina, the same could not be said of his efforts to prepare the exhibit for the Chicago World's Fair. Always an avid exponent of the value of publicity, he spent much time and effort in getting a display arranged. But he believed that the state of North Carolina was failing to carry out a promise to help support the project. He found it necessary, for example, because of delays, to advance some of his own money for the undertaking. Several times he was on the point of resigning from the display work. "I would give sixpence to throw the whole thing up," he wrote his father, "but that would hardly be fair at the present moment."[4] He did send an actual letter of resignation, but kept on working. His mother, however, would have been happy if he had quit: "I do hope those old bores of North Carolina State Commissioners will keep on in their hatefulness, and then you will resign, and then we can have you more at home."[5] Mr. Pinchot, from a more practical standpoint, felt the whole affair was good experience for his son.[6]

Eventually, however, the exhibit was completed and shipped to Chicago. Primarily it showed the accomplishments of forestry management in Europe and explained what was being done along these lines at Biltmore. Pinchot himself prepared a pamphlet, distributed free at the exhibit and mailed to thousands of newspapers, giving details and pictures of the first year of operations at Biltmore. It was, incidentally, the first of a long line of publications to come from his pen, many of them dealing with forestry, but others covering a wide range of subjects from fishing to traveling—even autobiographical writing.

At the time Pinchot was resident forester at Biltmore, his contract did not ban him from engaging in other activities away from North Carolina. He found it possible in December 1893 to set up an office as consulting forester on Twenty-second Street in New York City. Persons seeking his advice on forestry by no means beat a path to his new door. At first, unpaid work kept him considerably busier than paid, but gradually he began to gain a respectable number of clients and his reputation grew. "Contrast the career of this Yale graduate," wrote Kate Fields in a syndicated column, "with that of certain young men of Gotham who flatten their noses against club windows in the morning, and soften their brains with gossip, champagne and the unmentionables at other periods of the day and night."[7]

Two events that occurred in 1894 had a profound effect on Pinchot's later life and made this a momentous year. The first was his final decision to continue in the field of forestry. His grandfather, Amos R. Eno, had never been enthusiastic about this work with trees. Undoubtedly recognizing in the young man, still in his twenties, a vast amount of ability, Mr. Eno had urged him to go into business. Now, in the summer while Pinchot was visiting in Simsbury, his grandfather talked long and hard about the young man's future. The climax of the talks was an offer by the old gentleman to take Gifford into his own office and pay him a starting salary of $2,500 a year.[8] The kind of work that his grandfather had in mind was not exactly clear to Pinchot, but the prospects for advancement were good. The young man understood, certainly, that if he refused he was turning down a chance to accumulate greater wealth than he would inherit. He did not give his final answer immediately. In the long discussions with his parents on this decision, there is no record of his mother's point of view, but it can safely be assumed that his father opposed any divorce from forestry. The final decision, which Mr. Eno perhaps anticipated from his zealous grandson, was a polite "no." Pinchot's idealistic attitude was perhaps best expressed in a little book he wrote, "No man can make his life what it ought to be by living it merely on a business basis. There are things higher than business."[9]

The second major event that took place in 1894 was a tragedy. When he first went to Biltmore to look at the estate, preparatory to accepting the position, he had been introduced to Miss Laura Houghteling of Chicago, who was living temporarily near Biltmore. Attracted to her from the very first, he saw her frequently in North Carolina. Explaining to his mother that Laura and he "have always been very good friends, and especially so of late," he considered her "one of the most intelligent and sincere women I have ever met."[10] Although he knew she was not strong, he was hardly prepared for the news, received one evening upon his return from a trip in the woods, that she might not live, and if she did, might be an invalid for the rest of her life. As the months went by and Pinchot looked forward to her getting "stronger," he developed the deepest affection for her. Admitting his love, he begged his parents, in a letter from Chicago, where she was now living, to come there to see the World's Fair "but chiefly to see Laura."[11]

James and Mary Pinchot, however, not happy over their son's infatuation, made clear to him their worry about the effect of a marriage on his career. Pinchot regretted upsetting his parents and wrote, "I am dreadfully sorry that I have caused you so much pain."[12] By way of assurance, he reminded them that "the best and most refined people in Chicago are her best friends."[13]

But on February 2, 1894 Pinchot's mother noted in her diary, "Laura worse." Four days later it was "Dear Laura worse—My poor G[ifford]." And on the eighth, "Laura died—poor G[ifford]."[14]

Pinchot was crushed. For years, he made notes in his diary about "My Lady." Many days were described as "hard." But at other times the curtain of sadness would rise and it was as if he were seeing and actually talking to her. Time and again, when she seemed far away he would note that he had a "blind day." Other times he would register his happiness because of a "clear day" and the feeling that his "Lady" was near and speaking to him. Normally a self-confident extrovert, Pinchot, during the period of despair immediately after Laura's death, bordered on losing some of his assurance. Analyzing himself in his diary, for example, he confessed, "I am so small inside, and do my work so meanly."[15] Such a statement was not typical.

There is no question that the loss had a profound effect on Pinchot. A few years later, he spoke in a church on "the unity of our life here and hereafter."[16] After testifying at a Senate committee hearing in 1906 he went home and jotted down, "I felt today my Lady's help."[17] For twenty years he continued to note anniversaries in his diary; on August 8, 1913, for example, appeared "19 years and 6 mos today." His slow recovery from the shock undoubtedly helped to explain his continued bachelorhood until the age of forty-nine.

Pinchot's profound imprint on American forestry resulted not only from his own broad pioneering work but also from his ability to fire others with enthusiasm for entering the field. His most important convert was Henry S. Graves, who in 1910 would succeed Pinchot as head of the U.S. Forest Service after serving as dean of the forestry school at Yale. Graves and Pinchot were drawn together in college when they served as deacons of their respective classes and were rivals for the quarterback position on the Yale football team. While Graves was teaching school in 1893, having practically decided to be a chemist, he chanced to meet Pinchot in New York City. Falling under the spell of the earnest budding forester, he decided to follow in Pinchot's footsteps as the second American to choose forestry as a career.[18] Going first to Biltmore to study the work being conducted under Pinchot's direction, he then became the first student of forestry, however limited the offerings, at Harvard. As Pinchot began to accumulate more business in his consulting office in New York, he was able to use Harry (as Pinchot called him) in the field work. Finally, as the result of arrangements made by Pinchot, Graves went to Europe to study forestry with Dr. Brandis. When Graves returned to the United States, Pinchot was willing to concede that the second forester's "professional equipment" was ahead of his own.[19]

For at least a full century, Americans thought that forests were as inexhaustible as the water in the seven seas. In the early days of the country there was nothing vicious about denuding the land. To pioneer settlers a growth of trees was a positive nuisance—a hindrance to farming—which needed to be removed as soon as possible. Settlers continued to take their toll, but after about 1850 exploitation of the country's forests by lumber companies reached new heights of destruction and devastation.[20] Under a procedure which has been described as "chop and run," slashing axes and ripping saws completely leveled vast areas of virgin timber and left nothing but desolation.

The forest which managed to escape the settler or the lumberman, moreover, still ran the very real risk of falling prey to fire. In the total absence of fire protection activities, miles upon miles of forest land were burned over by fires which ravaged unchecked through both winter and summer. Cattle and sheep from private ranches, furthermore, caused additional devastation as they fed on the tender seedlings in the forests without restriction.

The situation was not improved by the federal government's attitude toward the land it owned. Of the total of 1,500 million acres included in the original public domain (excluding Alaska), about 550 million were timber land. But Washington sometimes seemed intent on disposing of it as quickly as possible; by 1904 only about a third of the original total public domain remained in government hands.[21] Millions of acres of land were donated to the railroads; such gifts could honestly be justified as encouraging the development of the country. Indeed, much of the legislation affecting the public domain was generally laudable. The famous Homestead Act of 1862, for example, which granted a citizen 160 acres of land if he lived on it for five years, was of immense benefit to individuals and contributed mightily to building the nation. Similarly designed to aid the little man was the Timber and Stone Act of 1878, which permitted an individual to obtain, at $2.50 an acre, a maximum of 160 acres of land containing either timber or stone.

Much of the enforcement of such legislation, however, was so loose that it encouraged wide abuse. Violations of public domain laws were common practice. The citizen or corporation who stole from or cheated the government was little frowned upon. Government officials winked at abuses. If, as a requirement for obtaining government land, a citizen had to swear he had constructed a house on the property, he might ease his blunted conscience by placing a small toy house on the land; one inspection by the Land Office of 180 squatters' claims in northern Idaho uncovered over 100 cabins built of unchinked logs, without floor or chimney or window.[22]

One of the worst subterfuges was used by some business concerns or speculators in obtaining valuable timber sites. A lumber company, for example, might induce a man to purchase from the government, at $2.50 an acre, 160 acres of lush forest land which commercially was easily worth $50 or even $100 an acre.[23] Although the purchaser was required to swear he would not allow title to his new property to pass to any other person, the land would somehow end up in the possession of the company. This procedure, multiplied over and over, resulted in the accumulation by some companies of vast timber holdings. Although this practice was clearly in violation of both the intent and the letter of the law, easygoing and understaffed government agencies often failed to notice the abuses.

Some of the legislation, too, was defective. Thus, one law authorized the Secretary of the Interior to issue a "free permit" for the right of cutting timber upon government land, but did not allow him to sell the timber.[24] As a result, large sawmills, even though willing to pay for logs if the law permitted it, were supplied with gratuitous timber.

Not until about a decade before the Civil War was there any awakening to the seriousness of what was happening to the nation's forests. For about a generation thereafter, interrupted only by the war, there was much talk about the need for preservation of timber, but very little action in the woods themselves. Time was needed for the warnings to seep into men's minds.

Government forest work in the United States can be said to have begun in 1876 when Congress authorized the Department of Agriculture to make a study and prepare a detailed report on forests and forestry. Franklin B. Hough, chosen for the task, was not a technically trained forester; as an expert on trees, however, he was one of the small band of pioneers who deserve so much credit for their efforts in convincing Americans of the necessity of preserving their wooded wealth. In a half dozen years Dr. Hough produced three bulky reports containing much significant information on the existing forests in America, the various forest-products industries, and forestry practices in Europe. At the same time he organized a tiny unit in the Department of Agriculture which in 1881 became the Division of Forestry, the forerunner of the Forest Service which later grew to such high stature under Pinchot.

During the 1870's and 1880's lonely voices were raised urging that if an eventual timber famine was to be avoided the national government must set aside forested areas of its public domain to be retained as forest preserves. Although Congress at first paid little attention to the warnings, it enacted in 1891 a law which Pinchot later called "the most important legislation in the history of Forestry in America."[25] By a fortuitous set of circumstances Congress passed a rider to a bill, without any debate on the floor, authorizing the President to reserve forest lands in the public domain. President Harrison promptly used the new legislation to set aside 13 million acres of forests.

This first withdrawal of forest land into government reserves was a major forward step. But it was not enough. Congress had not yet made any provision for administering the reserves or for keeping them in good shape. Timber which needed to be cut could not be sold. Unrestricted grazing in the reserved forests continued unabated. With few or no rangers to protect the reserves, thieves often found it easy to cut and remove some of the finest timber.

The American Forestry Association, which had been founded in 1875, kept pounding away, at first without any success, at getting Congress to take further action. Two of the most persistent advocates of properly administered government forests were Pinchot and Dr. Charles S. Sargent, professor of arboriculture and director of the Arnold Arboretum at Harvard University.

Sargent was one of the most eminent of American experts on forests. As publisher of a magazine, *Garden and Forest*, he had contributed much toward arousing the public to the importance of stopping the waste of the nation's heritage. Like Hough and the other American forest experts of the time, however, he was not trained in forest management. Looking at trees more from a botanist's viewpoint, he was inclined to emphasize the *preserving* of forests. He was a strong advocate, therefore, of the establishment of additional forest reserves, and of the banning of grazing within them. Pinchot, on the other hand, laid more emphasis on *using* the forests, but using them in such careful ways as to permit a sustained yield of lumber.

Sargent was a man of strong will and firm convictions. When Pinchot at the end of college went to him for advice, the expert questioned whether either of them would live to see a practical system of forest control in America.[26] Warning that there would be little money in it for any man devoting himself to the study of forestry, he nevertheless admitted that there was perhaps an opportunity "to do some good."[27] It will be recalled that Sargent advised Pinchot against accepting the position offered him by Dr. Fernow in the government service.

Sargent, Pinchot, and two men representing magazines, at a meeting called by Sargent in New York late in 1894, agreed to push a bill in Congress to create a commission to study and report on government timberlands. Failing to gain much response in Congress, however, the group fell back on a substitute plan suggested by Dr. Wolcott Gibbs, head of the National Academy of Sciences. The Academy, Gibbs explained to Sargent and Pinchot, had been created by Congress to perform scientific studies requested by government departments. It was agreed that the Secretary of the Interior, Hoke Smith, be asked to request a study by the Academy on the subject of forests. An employee of the Interior Department, friendly to the cause of forestry, was delegated to sound out the Secretary. To the joy of the little group of arrangers, Smith agreed to make the request. Pinchot helped to draft the letter which Smith finally signed and sent to the Academy on February 15, 1896. That the feasibility of forest conservation was still far from an accepted principle is indicated by the nature of one of the questions which the Academy was asked to study and answer: "Is it desirable and practicable to preserve from fire and to maintain permanently as forested lands those portions of the public domain now bearing wood growth, for the supply of timber?"

The National Forest Commission, set up by the National Academy in response to Smith's letter, had Sargent as chairman and Pinchot as secretary. Pinchot was not only the youngest man on the seven-member commission but also the only nonmember of the Academy. Although he planned to "keep rather quiet" on the Commission and "not attempt to direct the course to be pursued,"[28] he entered into the work with such enthusiasm that he assumed anything but a retiring role. Making a point of talking with influential people on the subject of forestry, he even managed a half-hour's conference with President Cleveland, who, he reported, was "anxious to do everything in his power to help the plan of forest reform."[29] Inasmuch as Cleveland would be leaving the White House in March of 1897, Pinchot begged the Commission to work fast in order to send the President by November 1 the outline of an organization for managing the government's existing forests. Cleveland himself had suggested that the Commission take up first the organization of a forest service before turning its attention to the advisability of establishing additional forest reserves.[30]

Sargent was not one, however, to be pushed into hasty action. Preferring to proceed slowly, he led the Commission at a cautious pace. It soon became apparent that the chairman and the secretary had opposite viewpoints on most Commission matters. Pinchot, keenly disappointed by their first meeting, had the clear impression that Sargent was "indifferent" if not "hostile" to the methods of practical forestry. The Harvard professor emphasized instead a protective scheme for the government's forests which was to be administered by the Army. Pinchot vowed to do his "level best to prevent" the carrying out of Sargent's general plan.[31]

As was proved repeatedly in later years, Pinchot was a man of action. His father once described him as always being in a feverish haste. In this instance, fretting at the Commission's delay in starting an inspection trip to the western forests, Pinchot set out on his own a full five or six weeks before the other members—at his own expense. As fellow observer and companion, he took along the man who had become a kind of protégé, Henry Graves.

Once again Pinchot was in his beloved outdoors and learning more about American forests. With the help of guides he and Graves penetrated into some of the wildest government and private lands. Since he was paying his own way, he did not hesitate to sweeten the trip by several sessions of hunting and fishing.

After meeting the other members of the Commission in Montana in the middle of the summer, he accompanied them on an extensive tour for another two or three months. The group as a whole, as might be expected, did not tend to wander as far from comfortable bases as did Pinchot. The gradually widening rift between Sargent and Pinchot was hardly alleviated when the latter learned that the chairman neither hunted nor fished nor knew "anything about the mountains." "He tried," Pinchot sneered, "to take 36 cans of condensed milk for [a side] trip, but was headed off. . . . We used 6 or 7."[32]

After the members of the National Forest Commission returned home it became increasingly clear that their report would not be ready before President Cleveland left office. To try to capitalize on his sincere interest in protecting timber, the Commission approved a kind of interim report in the form of a letter, written a month before Cleveland's exit, proposing the establishment of thirteen additional forest reserves with a total area of about 21 million acres. Some idea of the revolutionary flavor of this recommendation can be gained from the estimate that up to this time the government had set aside total reserves of only 17½ million acres. While Pinchot favored the new reserves, he believed the Commission erred in failing to propose, at the same time, a definite plan for their administration and use.[33]

In accordance with a recommendation from the Secretary of the Interior that the Commission's suggestions be followed and the new reserves proclaimed on George Washington's birthday, Cleveland issued the proclamation only two weeks before leaving the White House.

The reaction to Cleveland's proclamation was instantaneous. An avalanche of protest almost smothered Congress. Small men and large corporations joined in the complaints. For all they knew, these millions of acres of forest were to be withdrawn permanently and entirely from any use. Pinchot, looking back on these events some fifteen years later, maintained that the fundamental mistake of the Commission had been to "pass through the Western country without allowing the Western people to know what was being done."[34] Because the proclamation was a complete surprise to the people of the West their bitterness was accentuated. A reading of the Commission's interim report would have been somewhat reassuring to doubters. The members recognized that the boundaries of the reserves would have to be modified in order to remove from them any land better suited for agriculture than for forestry. They also agreed on the desirability of permitting some cutting of timber and extracting of minerals in the reserves.

But the sudden proclamation set the West aflame; protests were sounded and demonstrations were staged. In the Black Hills of South Dakota, for example, men dressed themselves as Indians and whooped around railroad trains to protest what they felt was a move to stop the development of the West and to turn it back to the red men.[35] For the next several weeks Pinchot had a hectic initiation into the workings of the United States Congress. In endless personal talks with both doubting and approving congressmen and senators he stoutly defended the forest reserves.

Meantime the Commission was working on its final report. Sargent and Pinchot continued to conflict at many points. Basically, Pinchot was fighting against any scheme that would lock up the government's forests. Stressing the desirability of the fullest legitimate use of forests, he insisted that protection without use was but little less desirable than use without protection. Moreover, he was unalterably opposed to Sargent's idea of bringing troops into the forests for protective purposes; trained foresters, not trained soldiers, were the real need in the woods. Although Pinchot frequently found himself alone or in the minority on the Commission, he fought hard for his principles and was able to win sufficient support to gain a number of modifications to Sargent's ideas in the final report.

Although the report provided for Army protection of the forests at the beginning, it also recognized the need for more scientific management in the future. Pinchot agonized over his decision to join the rest of the Commission in signing the report. Although disagreeing with many parts of the main report, he acknowledged that it contained "a great deal that is valuable."[36] Looking at the problem in perspective, and painfully aware of the attacks that had been made on the Commission as a result of Cleveland's proclamation, he saw the need for an undivided Commission and decided against writing a minority report. In a spirit of compromise, therefore, he signed along with the others.

The real value of the National Forest Commission stemmed from its help in publicizing the need for forest reform. At the time its final report[37] was submitted to the legislature by President McKinley, Congress, in response to heavy western pressure, was completing action on a law which for a period of about nine months would reopen to private acquisition all but two of the forest reserves established by Cleveland. Partly as a result of the report, however, the Senate and House added an amendment providing for the management, preservation, and use of existing and future reserves. This amendment, sometimes referred to as the Magna Charta of national forest administration, gave sweeping powers over the forest reserves to the Secretary of the Interior.

No sooner did the President sign this law than the new Secretary of the Interior, Cornelius N. Bliss, offered Pinchot a position with the department as special agent at $1,200 a year. Pinchot was interested in the job, but complained that such positions in the past had been "cheap pol[itical] rewards."[38] When Bliss changed the title to "special forest agent," Pinchot accepted with the understanding he would be paid ten dollars a day for each day worked plus subsistence and travel expenses. The new government employee himself drew up the instructions which were issued to him later; he was directed to make a general study of the suspended forest reserves, to recommend modifications of their boundaries, and to submit a proposal for the organization of a forest service. For this last assignment Pinchot was well prepared as a result of his studies while a member of the Commission; he had received from Dr. Brandis, for example, a detailed twenty-page handwritten outline of the requirements for such a service.[39]

Pinchot's acceptance of this position was to Professor Sargent a clear expression of bad faith. The Commission's chairman evidently felt that Pinchot had turned traitor by accepting a strategic post where he could see that his own ideas rather than those presented in the Commission's report would prevail. In a bitter letter to Brandis, Sargent accused Pinchot of throwing over his old friends for immediate political position. Declaring he had always expected Pinchot eventually to take a prominent place in national forestry, he now feared that his usefulness was nearly at an end. It particularly annoyed Sargent that the young forester had taken the position without consulting "his friends" in the Academy,[40] although in reality he had discussed the matter with two members of the Commission who had looked with favor on his proposed acceptance.

Dr. Brandis, in turn, was greatly disturbed by the rift between these two able men. He was already aware that Pinchot and Fernow frequently did not see eye to eye, and also that Fernow and Sargent sometimes were at odds. Sitting in his study in Germany, Brandis feared that forestry in the United States would be retarded by the cat-and-dog fights among the leaders in the field. Pleading with Pinchot to patch up the break, he stressed that Sargent had "fought the battle of Forestry" in America for over twenty years. Assuring Pinchot that he believed Sargent was wrong in supposing Pinchot had thrown over his former colleagues on the Commission, he nevertheless reminded that "The appearances . . . are against you."[41]

Although Pinchot did write to Sargent offering "to be of assistance, if necessary, in order to clear up your evident misunderstanding of the situation,"[42] the gesture had no effect in calming the storm.

A measure of Sargent's feeling was his curt reply that because their standards of conduct were so different it was useless to discuss the subject further.[43]

The breach between these two proud men was never closed. Pinchot admitted that Sargent had rendered great service to the cause of forestry in America, but he continued to believe that the contributions of a "forest botanist" could only be limited. Several years later when Brandis suggested that Pinchot recruit Sargent to make a forest study for the government, Pinchot maintained that "the reappearance of Prof. Sargent in that work would do only harm."[44]

Pinchot completed his survey of the reserves in the summer and fall of 1897. Much of the land had never been viewed by a forester. Seven years before, his mother had counseled him that he must "help make a public opinion which will force the Government to do what ought to be done."[45] He never forgot her advice. Now between excursions into the forests, he sandwiched many interviews and discussions with newspapermen and other leaders in nearby areas. Determined to avoid what he believed was a mistake of the Forest Commission, he everlastingly pounded home his assurance that the practice of forestry in these lands did not mean their withdrawal from use.

Once again Pinchot enjoyed his work to the utmost. With a rifle and bedroll as constant companions, he spent many days and nights in the wilds. Since he was being paid only for the days he worked, there was no reason for not devoting a day now and then to hunting big game. This he did sometimes with his brother Amos, who accompanied him on the trip, and also with his old friends the Henry L. Stimsons, whom he met in Montana.

Pinchot's final report came in on time in spite of his interludes of relaxation. In addition to an analysis of the eighteen reserves that he visited, it included his recommendation for the organization of a governmental forest service to take charge of the reserves. The heart of the proposal was the need for the permanent employment of technically trained forest officers. Pinchot drafted a proposed budget which at the beginning was to entail a total expenditure of $70,000 a year.[46]

43

Sargent's Forest Commission had proposed the establishment of a bureau of forestry in the Department of the Interior. In addition a law of 1897 had given broad powers over the forests to the Secretary of the Interior.[47] The Secretary in turn had designated the General Land Office to administer the law. But if the legislation was now adequate, there was an absence of technical know-how in the Interior Department for putting it into effect. The General Land Office, in other words, now had some forests but no foresters. The two or three foresters now employed by the United States government were with Dr. Fernow in the Division of Forestry in the Department of Agriculture. This Division, however, had control of no forests.

Pinchot's report to Secretary of the Interior Bliss made no mention of the department in which he believed his proposed forest service should be located. The more he learned about the Department of the Interior, however, the more distrustful he became of the general philosophy of its personnel. As the months and years passed he became convinced that, with exceptions here and there, the Interior Department tended to be more interested in methods of giving away government land than in protecting it for the general use and welfare.

According to Pinchot, Secretary of the Interior Bliss had told a mutual friend that if he could get Congress to appropriate $100,000 for forestry work he would put Pinchot in charge of it.[48] Since Pinchot's critical attitude toward the Department was only a slight suspicion in his mind in 1897-1898, he probably would have been willing to accept the task, if offered, of creating a forest service in the Department of the Interior. The money, however, was not voted.

He could hardly have guessed when he completed his survey for Secretary Bliss, that another department would soon be bidding for his services.

CHAPTER 3

TR AND A DREAM COME TRUE

A FEW WEEKS after the publication of Pinchot's report on the forest reserves to Secretary of the Interior Bliss, Dr. Fernow resigned as head of the Forestry Division to organize a school of forestry at Cornell University. James Wilson, who was Secretary of Agriculture under President McKinley (as well as Roosevelt and Taft), decided that Pinchot was the best man to succeed to the post. When Pinchot was informed of the offer, however, his first reaction was to refuse, partly because of his feeling that the Forestry Division to date had been singularly ineffective and partly because of a kind of horror of mere office work. But Wilson was insistent. Particularly pleasing to Pinchot was the promise that he could appoint all his own subordinates and would have a free hand in running the Division as he saw fit. Wilson was even willing, if necessary, to hold the position open for Pinchot for three years.

It did not take a great deal of coaxing thereafter to win Pinchot's acceptance of the headship of the Division of Forestry, with the special title of Forester, at a salary of $2,500.[1] Now he had a chance to put into effect some of the proposals he had made to the Secretary of the Interior—provided the forest reserves were removed from the Interior Department to the Division of Forestry. From the very first day he took office in 1898, therefore, Pinchot never lost sight of his major target of instituting a transfer.

Even at this early date the tiny Division of Forestry was under civil service, which meant that new employees, including the director, were required to take examinations to prove their qualifications. Inasmuch as no one in the government seemed competent to draft such an examination for Pinchot, he and Secretary Wilson agreed that he would have to compose his own. Pinchot conscientiously prepared ten comprehensive and stiff questions, such as, "Discuss the rise and progress of forest policy in any two countries of Europe"; and "Describe briefly and from personal experience, giving localities, the forests in the Olympic Mountains, the Sierra Nevadas, the Coast

Range of California, the Cascades, the Rockies, the Adirondacks, and the forest conditions of the arid regions."[2] But before he had a chance to answer the questions, Secretary Wilson obtained the approval of President McKinley to waive the examination in this one instance.[3]

As might have been foreseen, Pinchot chose as principal assistant his close Yale friend and frequent associate, Henry S. Graves. Pinchot was delighted that Graves passed the examination, which Pinchot had drafted, with a grade of 98 per cent.

Three Yale classmates also found their way into the Forestry Division. Burly George W. Woodruff, after obtaining a law degree and coaching the University of Pennsylvania football team, became the Division's first legal officer. It soon became clear that he and Pinchot had much the same conception—the proper role of government was to take positive steps to promote the general welfare. Each man developed the highest admiration for the other. Woodruff probably was Pinchot's closest and dearest lifelong friend. The latter was instrumental in getting him an appointment as Assistant Attorney General. And when Pinchot became Governor of Pennsylvania he selected his friend as Attorney General of the state and afterwards as a member of the Public Service Commission. It was Woodruff, moreover, who handled many of Pinchot's personal affairs and drafted his will.

The two other classmates who came into the Division were Herbert A. Smith ("Dol" to Pinchot) and Philip P. Wells. Smith spent nearly forty years of his life with the Division, watching it grow into a Bureau in 1901 and later into the U.S. Forest Service. He was in charge of editorial and publicity work. Wells, drawn away from an instructorship in the Yale law school, assisted Woodruff in Washington and later in Pennsylvania. Both Smith and Wells gave considerable help to Pinchot in writing the story of his early forestry career.

The new Forester, at the age of thirty-two, was embarking on his first attempt at administrative work. It soon became apparent that he was a master executive. Alertly sure of himself, he set out to build his little group of eleven persons, including himself, into an agency to save the nation from the catastrophe of the lumber famine toward which he believed it was racing. His crusading zeal was so highly infectious that he was able to instill in the agency an *esprit de corps* rarely matched.[4] Men who worked with him testified that he made no idle boast in writing that he "never appointed, refused to appoint, promoted, demoted, transferred, or dismissed a single person on political grounds."[5] Contrary to some Washington administrators, job patronage played no part in his thinking; he rated men as good or poor government employees entirely apart from any political connections they might have.

Pinchot became an idol to many of his men. A man's man, he could "outride and outshoot any ranger on the force."[6] He expected hard work from them, just as he himself worked long and intensively. When they produced, they could be sure of his support. To men in the field, who were constantly running into bitter opposition by individuals who stood to lose from forest preservation, it was a strong booster of morale to know that the boss would back them to the hilt.

During the early months in his new position, Pinchot was bogged down with far more details than a chief should have to perform; the work had to be done, however, and he was willing to do it. Because of a lack of stenographic help, for example, he was unable to dictate much of his mail and had to write his letters in longhand. Before hiring Dol Smith, he himself handled all the publicity for the Division. He was fully aware, however, of the necessity of ridding himself of the detail as quickly as possible in order to devote more attention to promoting acceptance of his plans by congressmen and senators and the general public.

The real administrative help which Pinchot especially needed came in the person of Overton W. Price. As a tense and idealistic young man interested in becoming a forester, Price had spent some time at the Biltmore forest school. Pinchot, impressed by his ability and enthusiasm, induced him to study with Dr. Brandis in Germany. Price was literally thrilled, therefore, to receive while in Europe a letter from Pinchot offering him a position with the Forestry Division.[7] Showing a flair for administration, he finally became associate forester in general charge of the entire unit. Price, the organization man, and Pinchot, the public relations man, supplemented each other well. They acted as a team in the Forest Service until both were fired by President Taft in 1910.

As Pinchot was able to persuade the Secretary of Agriculture and

Congress of the need for substantially larger funds for his agency, it became increasingly evident that the lack of trained foresters in the country was a growing handicap. Although the Division was not in control of any government forests, there was rapidly developing a demand from private owners of wooded lands to have the Division manage their forests. Pinchot had worked out a plan, as a means of demonstrating the benefits of practical forestry, by which the Division would provide such help if the owners would supply the traveling and subsistence expenses of the government's employees. The demands for such assistance consistently kept ahead of the available supply. Moreover, Pinchot in his own heart was certain that eventually he would be successful in obtaining a transfer of the forest reserves. Already the Interior Department was asking the experts in the Forestry Division for advice on how to handle the forests which, somewhat awkwardly, were under its care. Secretary of the Interior Hitchcock, in fact, had expressed a willingness that the transfer be made, although there was much opposition to it within his own Department.[8] If and when such a transfer came about, there would be an immediate need for more trained foresters.

Although a few forestry schools had sprung up in the country, they all provided only undergraduate work. Pinchot, seeing a need for more advanced study in the field, approached his father concerning the possibility of helping to finance a graduate school. After much deliberation the Pinchot family as a group contributed $150,000 to a university—Yale, of course—for the purpose of starting a forestry school. The Yale Forest School, as a result, opened its doors in the fall of 1900. Gifford Pinchot appropriately was appointed as a member of the governing board. Pinchot's father also provided space at Grey Towers (his Milford, Pennsylvania, home) for the Forest School's summer school and field work; this arrangement continued for over twenty-five years. Yale, in 1905, gratefully conferred an honorary M.A. degree on James Pinchot.

In future years various members of the Pinchot family continued to contribute money to the school until they had doubled the original endowment. Gifford was so enthusiastic about the project that somewhat impetuously he arranged for a will giving everything to the Yale Forest School except a few small bequests to his family. James

Pinchot, however, learning of his son's intentions, told him in no un-certain terms that it was "not right" to let so large a sum of inherited money go out of the family.[9] Gifford finally acquiesced in his father's wishes.

It was of course Pinchot's sincere hope that the best possible man should be put in charge of the new school, and that man seemed to be Henry Graves. Although badly wanting Graves to remain in the Division of Forestry, he concluded that his assistant would be even more valuable to "the cause" in New Haven. Graves therefore became the first dean of the school. Pinchot's connection with the school was always close. For a number of years, in fact, he delivered a series of annual lectures at Yale in the official role of professor of forestry.

In view of the number of Yale men whom Pinchot brought into the Division, and the fact that the Yale Forest School began provid-ing him with some of the best foresters in the country, it was under-standable that the Division (and the succeeding Forest Service) sometimes was referred to as "the Yale Club." Of the fifty-five men who passed the civil service examination for the Bureau in 1905, twenty-four were Yale men.[10]

When Pinchot agreed to accept his position with the Division, he made it one of the conditions that he would not be held to the strict routine of office hours expected of the ordinary government employee. As has already been said, he could turn out as much work as any man, and usually did; but he was not the kind of person who worked well under a schedule requiring the same number of hours each day. For some months, however, his work was steady and seemingly unending. The only major interruption to his routine was a rush trip to Puerto Rico to bring home his brother, Amos, who was suffering a serious fever as a soldier in the Spanish-American War.

As soon as Pinchot got his Division to the point where it could run smoothly in his absence, he appeared less and less at the office. Throughout his forestry career he insisted that responsible men at headquarters should get out in the open frequently and see the for-ests. This rule, he felt, applied as much to him as to any of his subordinates. Although the Division was still without its own forests, its representatives were working in private forests and, at the request of the Department of the Interior, were preparing reports suggesting working plans for the harvesting of timber in the government reserves controlled by that Department. Pinchot's visits to his men in the woods often were an inspiration. His passionate love of the outdoors and his seeming concern for every single tree in the forest, helped to create a loyalty and admiration for "the boss." Avoiding the mistake of trying to tell his foresters in detail how to handle each individual problem, he preferred to select capable men and allow them, like a good riding horse, to pick their own way along rough ground.[11]

Not all of Pinchot's time away from the office was spent in the woods. Some of the things he was trying to achieve could be only partially accomplished at a desk or in a forest. To obtain, for example, a transfer of forest reserves to his Division, or to win his constant battle with Congress for increased appropriations, he needed public acceptance of the urgency of forestry management. The Division of Forestry under Fernow had laid the groundwork for Pinchot's activities in "selling" forestry to the nation. It deserved credit for having pounded away at the necessity for preserving our wooded heritage. But if important results were to be achieved, it now seemed that a more intense and ardent drive was needed. The time was ripe for action.

At the same time that Pinchot was proving himself to be an able administrator, he demonstrated his adroitness at manipulating public and congressional opinion. The ability which he showed over a period of eight or ten years to get what he wanted has seldom been equalled by a government official in this country.

"Practical Forestry in the woods, through which alone the forests can be saved," was a slogan given wide circulation by the Forestry Division. No government agency had ever made such extensive use of handouts of stories for the newspapers and magazines. Few of the releases attempted to inflate the agency itself. But each one, sometimes openly, sometimes subtly, got across the forestry gospel. Two or three decades later, when many Washington agencies employed skilled publicity agents, much of the huge bulk of handouts to the press reached the wastebaskets. But at the turn of the century it was a new device. The press welcomed the canned material and used it extensively.

Pinchot was tireless in his efforts to awaken public interest in forestry and to drum up support for his ideas. Although not a silver-tongued orator, he was an interesting and attractive speaker who received many requests to tell his story. Any influential organization anywhere which asked him to speak could count on his acceptance unless prior commitments made it utterly impossible.

No pressure group, then or since, has had a more active or effective lobbyist with the Congress. The opposition which he faced was severe. Many congressmen and senators, especially from the West, reflected the antagonism of their constituents to any form of conservation. Some of the most influential legislative leaders, such as the Speaker of the House, "Uncle Joe" Cannon, had nothing but scorn for Pinchot's ideas. However, with his enthusiasm and ability Pinchot was able to win an increasing number of the legislators to his point of view. He *did* talk sense and he *was* persuasive. Moreover, he was adroit at fostering friendships with the right people. When William E. Borah, for example, was first elected to the Senate from Idaho, Pinchot, knowing him only casually, wrote that he looked "forward with great pleasure to . . . working with you for the interests of Idaho through the development of the forest reserve system."[12] Redfield Proctor, the chairman of the Senate Committee on Agriculture and Forestry, a committee especially concerned with matters of Pinchot's prime interest, was one of his principal supporters; the fact that the chairman was an avid fisherman forged a bond between the two which Pinchot used to the full.

Throughout his public life Pinchot widened and deepened his acquaintanceship over his own dining table—with amazing regularity he invited guests for lunch or dinner, or both. During his early days in Washington he had only limited facilities for such entertaining, but by 1900 he was living in the large home built by his mother at 1615 Rhode Island Avenue, on Scott Circle, not far from the center of Washington.

Pinchot's mother, who lived part of the time in Washington, frequently acted as his gracious hostess. A stream of invitations went from the 1615 residence to an increasing number of senators, congressmen, government administrators, and other influential people who either lived in or visited the nation's capital.

Pinchot also kept his contacts with legislators alive by appearing on Capitol Hill. He paid visit after visit to the offices of both senators and representatives in order to peddle his views. Before committee after committee he testified in the interest of building up the work of his Division. Letter after letter he wrote to friends urging them to bombard congressmen. A true crusader, he was determined to keep pushing until his immediate goals were reached.

Pinchot's pressures on Congress for substantial additional funds for his Division bore fruit. During his first year as Forester, he had what he described as only "a little toy"[13] unit, with a total appropriation of $29,000. Although the figures were not large, the rate of expansion of the appropriation was spectacular. In the first four years that he presented budgets for his agency he won the support of the Secretary of Agriculture and Congress for percentage increases of 70, 82.4, 109.4, and 57.3. When for the fifth year he asked for $83,000 more, he belittled it as an increase of only 28.5 per cent, "less than half as great [a percentage] as for last year."[14] At the time the Division became the Bureau of Forestry in 1901 its personnel had swelled from 11 to 179.

Pinchot's attempts to bring about a transfer of forest administration to his own Division, however, were at first exceedingly frustrating. Never doubting his ultimate success in this matter, he nevertheless frequently became exasperated at the delay. The opposition was enormous. Timber grabbing and forest devastation had become so much the accepted practice in the West that any attempts to impose restrictions were bound to encounter defiance. Even though legislation now made it possible to curb the plunderers, the execution of the law by the General Land Office in the Department of the Interior was hardly aggressive. Those who stood to gain by unmolested sawing and cutting and grazing, sensing that forests under Pinchot would be more vigorously protected than forests under the General Land Office, strained every muscle to defeat the transfer. Battling also the apathy of much of the public and of some congressmen, Pinchot faced a formidable task in winning support for the switch.

Only a portion of his opposition came from essentially greedy people. Many average Westerners felt, with understandable conviction, that conservation practices were discriminatory against their part of the country. They correctly maintained that in the East the trees had been slashed with no thought of preservation. Now that the frontier had moved westwards they could not see the justice of the Easterners' sudden awakening to an alleged need for interfering with unrestrained tree cutting or grazing. If the East had not thought of the future, why should the West? Such reasoning, even if not accepted, could arouse sympathy.

For more than three years Pinchot pressed toward his goal of transfer of forest administration with only limited success. Sometimes his hopes rose momentarily, but Congress obviously was not ready for the change. The major assistance in achieving his goal—after another four or five years of hard work—came from President Theodore Roosevelt. This does not mean that President McKinley opposed Pinchot's plans. Actually, McKinley's interest had pleased Pinchot and he had been told that both the President and his Secretary of the Interior were in favor of the transfer.[15] But McKinley was not interested to the point of working for it. Roosevelt was.

It is difficult to tell how long the Pinchot family and the Roosevelt family were friends. As early as 1894, while Roosevelt was a member of the United States Civil Service Commission, a note in Gifford's diary mentions that his family had the Roosevelts to dinner in Washington. It is clear that Gifford and TR quickly developed an ardent fascination for each other. In some ways they were alike. Although in later years they had some differences in politics, both were supporters of the thinking that brought about the Bull Moosers. Each was a lover of the outdoors and proud of his own virility and endurance. Each had come from families of high social station; one had gone to Harvard, the other to Yale.

It was on the nomination of Roosevelt that Pinchot in 1897 was elected to the Boone and Crockett Club, an organization of sportsmen who had proved their prowess as big game hunters. But the two did not get to know each other intimately until Roosevelt became Governor of New York in 1899. TR, beginning at that time to show an interest in preserving the state's forests, found Pinchot a willing and enthusiastic adviser on the policy to be followed; many of

Pinchot's ideas became Roosevelt's recommendations.[16] Their mutual friendship and admiration blossomed. The two men, who were to relax and exercise so regularly together during Roosevelt's presidency, had their first boxing and wrestling match on one of Pinchot's trips to Albany.[17] Pinchot in later years would chuckle at the memory of himself at thirty-four knocking the future president, seven years his senior, flat on the floor.[18]

By the time Roosevelt had assumed the vice-presidency the two had become intimate enough for him to write Pinchot, apparently with enthusiasm, "I am looking forward to seeing you at Washington, and playing with you there."[19] But neither man could have begun to guess how much they would be drawn together during the coming seven years. Less than two months after the writing of this letter, McKinley had been assassinated and Roosevelt was President.

Even before the new President was able to move into the White House, Pinchot and F. H. Newell (an engineer in the U.S. Geological Survey who was also a champion of forests) called on TR at the home of his mother. Newell's primary interest at this time was irrigation, which dovetailed nicely into Pinchot's proposals for conservation of the forests. Both men pleaded their causes before Roosevelt, who asked them to prepare a few paragraphs which he could include in his first message to Congress. Newell and Pinchot, with the help of three or four others, worked for the better part of two weeks in drafting five pages of material.[20] Roosevelt, using the material with a minimum of changes, appealed to Congress to set up a Bureau of Reclamation (the reclamation act was passed in about six months) and to place in the Bureau of Forestry the full responsibility for administering the government's forests.

Thus began a long series of proffers of advice from Pinchot to the President. Roosevelt came to have almost unbounded confidence in Pinchot's judgment. Few important decisions which Roosevelt made on matters relating to the Departments of the Interior or Agriculture were taken without prior consultation of some kind with Pinchot.[21] Along with Elihu Root, William Howard Taft, and James Garfield, Pinchot became one of the principal ghost writers for TR.[22] Messages to Congress, speeches, letters, and reports were frequently composed by Pinchot and largely accepted by the President. Nor was it uncommon for the President to give Pinchot free rein to speak for him officially. For an irrigation congress in El Paso, for example, Pinchot prepared and presented a message in Roosevelt's name, with full assurance from the Chief that "he would stand for whatever [Pinchot] said."[23] Pinchot, indeed, was markedly impressed by Roosevelt's readiness, once he had confidence in an adviser, to adopt "recommendations almost as a matter of course."[24] At the time of TR's death, Pinchot publicly referred to his characteristic of "so much willingness to be advised."[25] Certainly Roosevelt, as long as he was President, demonstrated complete confidence in Pinchot.

Roosevelt often was effusive in his praise for Pinchot, and admitted that he eagerly sought the younger man's advice. "I have one friend," he wrote in a personal letter to Ray Stannard Baker, ". . . in whose integrity I believe as I do in my own. This is Gifford Pinchot. . . . I have relied greatly on his advice."[26]

When in the following year Pinchot was searching for money for the Yale Forest School he asked for a letter of introduction from Roosevelt to Andrew Carnegie. The President wrote to Carnegie with little restraint, "There was no need for his doing any work, as the world commonly understands need. But he had the right stuff in him and was not content to be an idler on the earth's surface . . . having rendered literally invaluable service [to forestry]. He is gifted with the utmost energy and . . . zeal . . . excellent judgment and sound common sense. I know very few men indeed about whom I can write as I write about him."[27] Pinchot, curious concerning the content of the letter, requested and received a copy from the President's secretary. One of his most prized possessions was the original, which Carnegie graciously forwarded to him.

When Roosevelt left the presidency, he assured Pinchot, with more than a touch of sentiment, "I am a better man for having known you. I feel that to have been with you will make my children better men and women in after life."[28]

It was remarkable that Roosevelt and Pinchot worked so closely together for the greater part of two presidential terms with practically no friction. Although Roosevelt, after he left the White House, sometimes lost patience with Pinchot, there is almost no evidence of any annoyance while they worked together in the service of the government. One exception occurred when plans were being laid for an arrangement by which Pinchot would have become the head of forestry within the General Land Office of the Department of the Interior, while at the same time retaining his post of Forester in the Department of Agriculture. Secretary of the Interior Hitchcock was willing, but a snag developed when Pinchot learned that any letters he would write in the Interior Department would merely be initialed by him but signed by the head of the General Land Office. Although this initialing was the usual procedure in government departments, Pinchot insisted on the right to sign. Roosevelt, in obvious exasperation, sent him a letter marked "personal" and addressed to "Mr. Pinchot" rather than the more familiar "Pinchot" which he had been using. Assuring Pinchot that he would have "an absolutely free hand" to do what he wished in the position, he tabbed the objections as "utterly unimportant" and "really trivial."[29] The President implied that Pinchot was motivated by a desire for publicity, but the latter insisted that his balking was explained only by a thorough distrust of the head of the General Land Office. Although Pinchot heeded the President's request and agreed, "under the conditions" of Roosevelt's letter, to accept the position,[30] the plan was dropped.

As was proved both before and after the Roosevelt days, Pinchot was not an easy man to work with in a superior-subordinate relationship when Pinchot was the subordinate. But Roosevelt's implicit faith in Pinchot, his readiness to accept Pinchot's suggestions, and his willingness to allow Pinchot to perform his duties without close supervision, all meant that he was handled in the way best suited to his personality. Pinchot was the kind of person who thrived on recognition and needed to feel important. Roosevelt, indeed, showed so much deference to Pinchot—who, in reality, was merely a bureau chief—that he was perhaps spoiled for any future subordinate work, either in public or private life.

Be that as it may, no executive ever had a more loyal assistant than Roosevelt had in Pinchot. And no boy ever had a greater hero than Pinchot had in Roosevelt. Pinchot's loyalty was not of the blind variety that caused him meekly to acquiesce in everything the Chief said. He frequently argued his position against that of the President. But the adulation for TR was always there, and the strength of it was shown, if in no other way, when as Governor of Pennsylvania he repeatedly tried to handle problems the way he thought TR would.

Vigorous support from the White House was what Pinchot and forestry needed more than anything else, and is exactly what they got from Roosevelt. Pinchot, sensing the value of a professional organization for the rising vocation of forester, organized in 1900 the Society of American Foresters, with seven charter members. The meetings, which were regularly held at Pinchot's new home, were a major factor in developing a sense of comradeship and an *esprit de corps* among the foresters attached to the Bureau of Forestry. Discussions by the group, and the reading of papers, were followed invariably by a supper of gingerbread, baked apples, and milk. The meetings received their greatest boost when Pinchot, without much effort, persuaded President Roosevelt to come to his home one spring evening in 1903 to address the members. In customary fashion, Pinchot wrote the speech.

Roosevelt's strong support for forestry aided Pinchot in his battles again and again. The President and the Forester together planned their strategy and executed it with finesse. The month before a convention of the National Lumber Manufacturers Association, for example, Roosevelt invited Frederick Weyerhaeuser, who had amassed a fortune as a result of cutting the timberlands of the Northwest, to the White House for a conference with him and Pinchot. Roosevelt, wanting the movement for forest preservation to come from lumbermen themselves, managed to gain the support of Weyerhaeuser for the reserve policy. Following the convention of the lumbermen, Pinchot reported somewhat overoptimistically to TR that "practical forestry has arrived, thanks to your action, as a live issue in the minds of the great lumber manufacturers."[31]

Roosevelt continued to recommend to Congress that activities pertaining to forest reserves be consolidated in the Bureau of Forestry, but he preferred not to push the matter until there was at least some indication of western support for the move. He proved himself willing, however, to cooperate in helping to gain that support.[32] On at least one occasion, for instance, he invited members of Congress to lunch at the White House in order to "give [Pinchot a] chance at them" on the transfer bill.[33]

As a subtle method of attack Pinchot persuaded the President to create a Committee on the Organization of Government Scientific Work for the purpose of recommending how the government might be reorganized for more effective work in this field. Appointed to the Committee were five persons suggested by Pinchot, including himself and two close friends, Charles Walcott (the chairman), and James R. Garfield. Pinchot was designated as secretary. It was in no way surprising, therefore, that among the recommendations of the Committee was a proposal that the "custody and care of the National Forest Reserves" as well as of the National Parks be entrusted to the Department of Agriculture.[34] Inasmuch as the report was never printed or made public, however, it had less propaganda value than Pinchot had hoped.

Pinchot was not one to allow things to simmer. To keep the transfer issue boiling he shortly recommended to the President the appointment of another commission, this time to study the public lands and the laws governing them and to make recommendations concerning their management and use. Pinchot later acknowledged having in mind the ulterior motive of revealing the forests to have been mismanaged by the Department of the Interior.[35] So disrespectful was he of the employees whom the Department had recruited through the spoils or patronage system and sent into the forest reserves, that he referred to them as "human rubbish."[36] He earnestly hoped that a commission study would, among other things, make clear to the country and to Congress the high desirability of placing the forest reserves under the expert supervision of the Bureau of Forestry in the Department of Agriculture. The order creating the Public Lands Commission, which Pinchot drafted, was signed by Roosevelt late in 1903. Two of the three members were pro-Pinchot—F. H. Newell, and Pinchot himself who again was secretary. The two reports of the Commission carefully avoided casting direct aspersions on the Department of the Interior—the chairman was the head of the General Land Office in that Department—but the implication of a need for more aggressive administration of the reserves was made plain to the reader.[37]

Meanwhile, the tireless efforts of Pinchot and others were beginning to bear more fruit. As early as 1898 the American Forestry Association had passed a resolution urging on Congress the "wisdom and economy" of a unification of forest work in a single bureau. Gradually, often at the personal urging of Pinchot, dozens of various associations passed resolutions urging the transfer of the reserves to the Department of Agriculture. Roosevelt's letter to Pinchot promising to push the transfer if there were western backing for it, "filled Pinchot with the keenest satisfaction."[38] As if to convince the President of the existence of the support, Pinchot began to work on some of the toughest western leaders. On a trip to Wyoming, he discussed practical forestry with Congressman Frank W. Mondell, afterward Speaker of the House, who was a leader of the opposition. Pinchot's note to Roosevelt declaring he thought he had succeeded in getting Mondell "to change his mind on the subject"[39] proved to be no idle boast. The reluctant Congressman in the end voted for the transfer.

Meanwhile Pinchot had been accumulating support from another surprising source. One of the bitterest issues of the time concerned the grazing of livestock on government forest land. Government regulations for controlling this activity were poorly enforced. Theoretically, all citizens had the right to use government property for grazing, but a large portion of the land had been parceled out by tacit agreements among the various users. Such understandings, however, were frequently violated, and the resulting land feuds not uncommonly ended in shootings or other forms of violence. Cattlemen, increasingly resentful of "encroachments" on their territory by sheepmen and by small homesteaders, resorted to all kinds of deceptions and distortions to repel the "invaders." Not infrequently they erected illegal fences to shut out competition.[40]

Such feuding inevitably led to a chorus of outcries against the cattle "barons," and a swelling demand that all forms of large-scale grazing be banned in the national forests. Pinchot joined in publicly denouncing big stockmen, but at the same time sought and obtained their support for the transfer. Since Pinchot championed the use of forests for grazing and was also a leading proponent of the legalizing of fences, his plans carried considerable attraction for the "barons."[41]

Once again in 1904, however, as had regularly occurred in previous years, the transfer failed to get through Congress. If Pinchot was discouraged, he did not show it, but he did have qualms about the inordinate amount of time he was forced to devote to matters other than the strict pursuit of his profession. Writing to Professor Brandis in Germany, he complained that "So much of my time is necessarily given to the political side of the subject, to looking after the appropriations of the Bureau, trying to convince Senators and Representatives that forestry is to their advantage, and addressing public meetings of lumbermen and others, that I am almost beginning to fear that I may cease to be a forester altogether."[42] Here, then, were early signs of a danger which was to plague him later in life—being lured to politics at the possible expense of forestry.

The climax of Pinchot's resourceful campaign to obtain jurisdiction over the forests came early in 1905 when he organized a meeting of the American Forest Congress in Washington, D.C. Billed as a kind of parliament for representatives of groups interested in forests, the Congress convened for five days. Among the delegates were influential foresters, lumbermen, miners, railroad men, wool growers, and men representing the grazing and irrigation interests. Pinchot, designating Roosevelt as honorary president of the Congress, induced his boss, Secretary of Agriculture Wilson, to act as president, and his father, James Pinchot, as first vice-president. The meeting, packed with persons favorable to forest conservation, was primarily a propaganda device for demonstrating to Congress and the country the sizable amount of support that had been built up for practical forestry. With the aid of the astute publicity unit of Pinchot's Bureau, news releases concerning the meeting were circulated throughout the nation. The *Brooklyn Daily Eagle*, for example, on the day before the Congress met, devoted an entire page to the meetings and to the general subject of forestry.[43] Readers of the *Eagle* and of many other newspapers were reminded that if the current rate of timber cutting continued, the nation's forests would be exhausted in about sixty years.

Among the resolutions passed by the American Forest Congress was one supporting the transfer and this unquestionably had an effect on the United States Congress. The bill for the consolidation of forest administration in the Bureau of Forestry speedily passed both houses, and on February 1, less than one month from the opening day of the Forest Congress, was signed by President Roosevelt.

After a struggle of almost seven years against great odds, Pinchot now had his victory. Overnight he was transformed from a man with some foresters but no forests, into a man with 86 million acres of forest land. Fortunately for Pinchot, he was soon presented with two useful tools for performing his new and difficult tasks: he was permitted to retain in his bureau all money received from the sale of products grown in the government's forests, as well as all fees for the use of the forests; and his rangers were permitted to make arrests within the forests.

Related to the transfer were also two name changes. The Bureau of Forestry soon became the United States Forest Service, and the forest reserves acquired the title of "national forests."

To supplement the law passed by Congress, there was need for a directive from the Secretary of Agriculture to Pinchot laying down the principles to be followed in administering the government forests. Pinchot characteristically was ready with a draft of a letter of instructions to himself, which Secretary Wilson signed on the same day that Roosevelt signed the act of Congress. The letter directed, as Pinchot had always maintained, that "all land is to be devoted to its most productive use for the permanent good of the whole people, and not for the temporary benefit of individuals or companies."[44]

In a ten-page letter to Dr. Brandis in Germany, Pinchot explained how his dream had come true and how he now hoped to accomplish for the United States what Brandis had done for the forests of India. Although admitting that he was "rather used up" by the strenuous winter's work and might need the summer to get back in good physical condition, he was certain that "the game was worth the candle."[45]

Lest it be surmised that Pinchot devoted every hour of every day for seven years to administering his Bureau of Forestry and bringing about the transfer of government forest lands, it should be said that he found many additional ways to use his boundless energy. As a sideline of his profession, he served on the staff of *The Forester*, the magazine published by the American Forestry Association, and on occasion contributed articles of his own. Pinchot firmly believed that the Association should exert more force and influence than it did. At one point, in an effort to make it more effective, he solicited some of his friends to join him in contributing $1,000 each to pay traveling and office expenses of a new secretary.[46] But a year later he was impatiently complaining to the secretary about the slow growth of the Association (by this time up to 2,228 members) and the fact that it was "of no use whatever" when public land and forest matters came before Congress.[47]

During these years he also kept plugging away at writing the *Primer of Forestry*, upon which he had embarked at the suggestion of his father. With the continual interruptions, it was painfully slow work, but by 1899 the first of two parts was finished and published as a government document which eventually gained a distribution of more than a million copies.[48]

Markedly high-strung, Pinchot had recurring indigestion worries, and on occasion was told by doctors that he was in danger of nervous prostration. With the best of intentions he made a New Year's resolution in 1904 to "Take good care of digestion," and also promised himself not to "hurry."[49] But the two goals went the way of most such resolutions. It was while working under high pressure as Forester, however, that he fully realized the benefits of a temporary retreat to some favorite fishing grounds. His ability to find relaxation on such a trip probably added years to his life. As he wrote a friend while working in Washington, "I have reached a point where I had rather go to Florida in the fishing season than into the mountains after bear, and that is saying a good deal for me."[50]

After Pinchot had whipped his Bureau of Forestry into such shape that it could run without his presence, he received an invitation in 1902 to go to the Philippine Islands. Captain George Ahern, who was an able forester, although not technically trained, sent a call for help to his friend Pinchot to assist in drafting plans for a bureau of forestry in the Philippine government. With the eagerness of a schoolboy wanting to see new sights, Pinchot started out in an easterly direction with a letter of introduction signed by President Roosevelt explaining that he was going abroad to study forestry in other countries. Money for an extended trip was of only limited concern; the difference in his financial status from that of the average bureau chief can be ascertained from one notation in his diary, "All day with Father counting securities and cutting off coupons."[51] A month's visit in the Philippines, therefore, was expanded into a four months' circling of the globe. Moreover, he took along a secretary.

Landing in England early in September, he remained in western Europe only long enough to see his mother, who was already there. Eight days later he was in St. Petersburg, Russia, ready for a great adventure in strange lands. With a friend from New Haven as a companion, he boarded the trans-Siberian railroad for a long trek which ended in Shanghai. Inasmuch as the speed of the train varied from five to fifteen miles an hour, he had ample opportunity to see not only the forests but also the people along the bleak route. Impressed by the "admirable" woods, he had mixed reactions to the Russians and the passengers on the train. Struck by the poverty which he saw, he nevertheless declared that the "Russians are kindlier travelers than any other people I have ever seen." But a kind of autocratic stripe was evident in his comments concerning an Englishman and his courier in the same car, "The Englishman is a very nice fellow, but the courier is the most complete beast I have had the pleasure of seeing in many long years. Having had some few words with him, he now touches his hat and calls me 'Sir' on all occasions."[52]

Another potential annoyance on the train was an American girl who was traveling with her mother. "It has never been my misfortune," Pinchot wrote home, "to see any one before who was so utterly abandoned to the vice of endless gabble." He explained, however, that he and his friend were having "no end of fun" over her.[53] This ability to laugh, and frequently to make others laugh, distinguished him from many other zealots with a cause. Pinchot was a crusader, whose brown eyes shone with an intense gleam, but his sense of humor often saved him from excessive rigidity. His was not the earthy kind of humor that flourished in a locker room or a political club. But it was delightful and, although at times somewhat sophisticated, was appreciated by the common man.

When Pinchot arrived in the Philippines, he was almost overwhelmed by the kindness of the Governor General, William Howard Taft. Although the two had been acquainted previously, their friendship was cemented during the month's visit. Taft made available to Pinchot a 1,400-ton gunboat which the Navy had turned over to him; in the company of Ahern, Pinchot made a tour around the islands and was able thereby to get a solid picture of the forestry problems.

On his return to Manila, Pinchot was the guest of Mr. and Mrs. Taft at dinner. While riding in a carriage afterwards to the theater, Taft won Pinchot's high respect when he nimbly helped to stop the horses which started to run away. So impressed was Pinchot that he wrote Roosevelt, "It was perfectly stunning to see the fresh, snappy, almost boyish, spirit with which he jumped into the work. I was so pleased I haven't got over feeling warmed up yet, and I wanted to tell you about it, knowing how you feel about the Governor." But Pinchot's praise was not limited to Taft's agility with horses. "On every side I hear nothing but unanimous praise for him and his work."[54]

Significantly, Pinchot's letters were addressed more often directly to the President than to the Secretary of Agriculture. From Russia, for example, he sent Roosevelt three statements in the hope they would be used in the President's coming message to Congress.[55]

Bidding farewell to Pinchot, Taft asked him to deliver messages to both the President and Secretary of War Root, and again proffered the gunboat to Pinchot for the journey to Japan (by way of Formosa) where he could catch a steamer to the States. Ahern, who was returning home, and Pinchot worked together on the boat preparing a report with suggestions for handling the Philippine forests. Six months later Pinchot sent Taft a copy of a proposed forestry law for the Islands which was the basis for legislation finally adopted.[56]

During the four months he was away from Washington, Pinchot

kept in as close touch with his Bureau of Forestry as possible. Many hours of the trip, moreover, were spent in laying plans for the future of his unit. Upon his return to the capital, therefore, he was able to step immediately into the administrative routine. Overton Price as assistant forester had kept the wheels turning. On the morning that Pinchot's train was to arrive in Washington at 8:30 a.m., he was scheduled to appear before a hearing of the House Agriculture Committee. Although the train was two hours late, Pinchot was so well prepared that, accompanied by Price, he went directly from the station to the hearing and talked for nearly two hours about the work of the Bureau and the need for more money.[57]

Although the far-eastern trip brought him pleasure and excitement, nothing gave him more gratification than his chance, at home in Washington, to relax with President Roosevelt. A believer, like Roosevelt, in the value of regular physical exercise, he took a special delight in his outdoor companionship with the President. The sports-loving chief executive had a number of friends with whom he especially liked to relax, but none stood higher on the list than Pinchot. Often they rode together, or went to Cathedral Hill near the outskirts of the city to chop wood—a vigorous form of exercise to which Pinchot introduced TR. Less regularly they tossed a medicine ball.

The two men frequently played tennis, sometimes singles, more often doubles with such officials as James Garfield, Leonard Wood, Alford Cooley, or the French Ambassador. Pinchot once described the President as a poor player; on more than one occasion he beat TR four straight sets. But both men thoroughly enjoyed the games. Sometimes continuing their matches far into the winter, they once played six sets on a bitterly cold day in January. The President, while on the court between games and sets, frequently discussed important state matters with Pinchot and asked his advice.[58]

Walking was one of the activities in which Roosevelt and Pinchot could best display their physical prowess. Sometimes their walks developed into rugged hikes on a straight line from one point to another. Both men were brisk walkers. Pinchot, with his long legs, although often having to extend himself, always made it a point to stay abreast of TR. Other persons with shorter legs and less endurance found it difficult to keep up the almost trotting pace.

After one such hike Pinchot expressed sympathy for a companion who was "too stout to stand the pace" and had to drop out;[59] but deep down there was pardonable pride in his own ability to match the Chief. Because Roosevelt frequently walked unaccompanied by Secret Service men, Pinchot on such excursions formed the habit of carrying a gun.

One afternoon when Roosevelt, Lawrence O. Murray, Assistant Secretary of Commerce and Labor, and Pinchot were about to start a tennis game it began to rain. The President proposed a walk instead. After the three had plodded through a downpour for some three miles, Roosevelt suggested they run home to the White House gate. Once more Pinchot ran neither ahead nor behind the chief executive.

One of the most spectacular of Pinchot's many hikes with Roosevelt occurred late one afternoon after a telephone call from the President suggesting a walk. Pinchot went from his office to the White House dressed as he was. The third member, Robert Bacon from the Treasury Department, a former banker, appeared in a derby hat, patent-leather shoes, and a cutaway coat.[60] Because it had been raining hard, they soon found themselves wet to their knees as they walked along the Potomac River. When, with darkness coming on, their path was blocked by a canal, the President suggested that Pinchot and he swim it; but Bacon protested at being left behind. All three placed their wallets and other valuables in their hats, put the hats on their heads, and swam across. Pinchot and Bacon both held umbrellas in their left hands. "And then," said Pinchot, "we walked back to the White House with much merriment." As soon as Pinchot reached home the comment of Mary McCadden, his childhood nurse, proved that such escapades were not uncommon. As his sleeve brushed her hand she quickly exclaimed: "Drenched! You've been out with the President."[61]

For a period of several years there is no indication that Roosevelt tired of Pinchot's companionship. Indeed, it seemed as if the President was never able to see enough of him. Pinchot was one of a small group of "Sunday nighters" frequently invited to the White House on Sabbath evenings. In both 1903 and 1904 he spent the Fourth of July at the Roosevelt home in Oyster Bay; on the latter occasion

Mr. and Mrs. Roosevelt and Pinchot took an all-day picnic in a row-boat. The same year he had Christmas dinner at the White House.[62]

On walks or family picnics Pinchot and Roosevelt sometimes had long and confidential talks. Unfortunately, only snatches of them are preserved in Pinchot's diary. Sometimes the two men talked about Roosevelt. When TR spoke of the element of luck in his career, Pinchot expressed his belief that it was the work of Providence.[63] During one hike the President confided that, if it were possible, he would cheerfully serve as Secretary of State or War or Navy under either William Howard Taft or Elihu Root as President.[64] After another outing Pinchot recorded the President's agreement with his suggestion that perhaps the most important and lasting result of Roosevelt's work would be the "entire change" it would make in "the attitude of people toward government service."[65]

Because of his unusually close relationship to the President, Pinchot was of course able sometimes to impress his opinion on Roosevelt in opposition to those of his colleagues in the government departments. A typical example of the way he worked was shown when he learned that the Secretary of the Interior was about to send to the President an opinion on a current matter. Pinchot wrote to Roosevelt's secretary explaining his complete disagreement with the Interior Department's point of view and asking for a chance to see the opinion in order to prepare an answer.[66] At other times he helped to keep the President informed on derelictions in the Administration. Thus, disturbed by the inattention of the Department of the Interior to a request by Roosevelt for the creation of some forest reserves in Alaska, he dutifully reported to the President that the order "has not yet been complied with, nor, so far as I can ascertain, have any steps been taken to that end." And he added his own conviction that the reserves were "exceedingly desirable."[67]

Roosevelt once described Pinchot, before he knew him intimately, as being no more interested in politics than were the Harvard astronomers.[68] At least as early as 1903, however, Pinchot was a member of the Madison Square Republican Club in New York, although in that year he merely signed a proxy for his vote rather than attend the annual meeting. As the election of 1904 approached, and Roosevelt went to the country for a vote of confidence in his Administration,

Pinchot became more active politically. At the Republican primary that year he was elected as a delegate to his party's congressional district convention. Upon sending a campaign contribution of $3,000 to the chairman of the Republican national committee, he admitted that part of his motivation was "pure selfishness" because if Roosevelt won, "my forest work will prosper."[69]

As the result of some gentle pressure from Roosevelt, he actively participated in a political campaign for the first time. "TR said he hoped I would go on the stump in Indiana," he wrote, "and, of course, I will."[70] A few days before the election he also delivered two addresses at New Haven. One of them was staged in a theater after a talk by Senator Platt and a "superb" two-hour speech by William Howard Taft. "I spoke," he recorded, "to the back of the great crowd as it left." He managed, however, to hold about half the audience.[71]

Pinchot spent election evening at the White House, where he shared with the President the pleasure of hearing the returns roll in. Jubilant when a landslide electoral vote for Roosevelt over Parker was assured, he wrote in his diary, "Everything lovely."[72] The only aspect of the vote which troubled him, "a thoroughly bad thing," was an apparent split between a solid South and a solid North. But on the whole, he felt, the election was "An amazing vote of confidence in honest frankness."[73] His winning a Dunlop hat in an election bet with his conservative Uncle Amos was also gratifying.[74]

CHAPTER 4

THE BITTER WAR FOR FORESTS

THE TRANSFER in 1905 of the national forests to the care of the Forest Service was a great triumph for Gifford Pinchot. The move, however, did nothing to silence the opposition to him and his ideas of forest management. The antagonism, which was still enormous, was intensified by persons, large and small, who stood to lose from a policy aimed at administering the forests for the ultimate benefit of all the people instead of for a limited portion of the population. Pinchot, of course, for some years had been strongly urging the practice of forestry, but there had been little he could do about it on government lands. Now that he had the power to put his ideas into effect, some persons shuddered.

For almost a half century before the forests were given to Pinchot to administer, the avowed policy of the government was to dispose of the public domain to bona fide settlers. The Public Lands Commission had complained, however, that "a larger proportion of the public land is passing into the hands of speculators and corporations than into those of actual settlers who are making homes."[1] The two reports of this Commission, which Pinchot had a large hand in drafting, called attention to the pressing need for new land laws, for plugging holes in the existing "antiquated" laws, and, at least by implication, for tighter enforcement of the laws and regulations relating to public lands.

Undoubtedly, Pinchot would make use of his new opportunity. A man of action, he liked to quote Theodore Roosevelt's statement that a man "may make a mistake if he takes action but he is certain to make a mistake if he refuses to act at all."[2] Upon assuming control over the government's forests, he was thoroughly convinced of the need for hurry. There was no time to be lost in protecting the remaining one-third of the original public domain from the kind of exploitation that he felt had occurred too often in the past.

Some of Pinchot's first moves were in the direction of charging fees for the use of the national forests and the natural resources within them. The Public Lands Commission had called attention to the extensive damage done to public lands by excessive grazing of cattle and sheep. Indeed, grazing rather than lumbering was the number-one problem of the national forests. Although the General Land Office had issued regulations for grazing in the forests, the rules had been poorly enforced; cattlemen and sheep herders used the government's land with little interference.

This uncontrolled grazing in the national forests often became overgrazing; excessive eating and trampling of forage damaged both the forests and the supplies of water within them. Some persons believed the solution was nothing short of an absolute ban. Pinchot, however, drafted new regulations for control of grazing, not its prohibition, and, after first obtaining an opinion from the Attorney General that he was on solid ground, instituted the requirement that all persons using the forests for grazing should obtain a permit and pay a fee.

The opposition to the regulations, and especially to the fee, was fierce. The very thought of governmental restriction aroused deep resentment by homesteaders. Many settlers, having endured the hardships of the frontier, and in some cases having fought the Indians, felt strongly that they were entitled to use the public land as they saw fit. Bitter protests to Washington charged that eastern theorists had concocted "impossible" rules. When the regulations governing the forests were assembled for the field force in a Forest Service manual entitled *The Use of the National Forest Reserves*, the booklet quickly came to be known among the foresters as the "Use Book." But among those being regulated it was dubbed the "What's the Use Book."

Sheepmen likewise objected vehemently. Typical of many resolutions of protest was that passed at an annual convention of the Wyoming Wool Growers Association condemning the administration of the national forests and complaining that the "fees charged for the grazing of sheep in the National Forests are excessive and oppressive."[3]

Although some cattlemen also protested, a significant number lined up behind Pinchot. Having looked upon both homesteaders and sheepmen as intruders, they had concluded that their interests would best be served by Pinchot, who had made it plain that he favored grazing in the forests as well as some use of fences to bring order out of the confusion.

Despite Pinchot's repeated assertions that he was fighting for the little man against the big man, many of the larger cattlemen were supporting his program.[4] But there was no denying his sincere interest in the long-range goal of seeking from the nation's forests the greatest good for the greatest number. If he could obtain assistance which he believed would help to achieve that ultimate goal, he was happy to receive it, whether it came from little men or big men.

In the face of all the opposition to the grazing rules, the Forest Service was realistic enough to proceed cautiously with rigid enforcement. At least at headquarters in Washington, they realized that practices of long duration in the forests could not be stopped instantaneously. A form letter to forest officers in the field counseled them "to arrest grazing trespassers when necessary, as directed by The Use Book"; but, it further directed, "this power should be used with great caution and, except in flagrant cases, the circumstances, with the names of the witnesses by whom they can be proven, should be reported and instructions asked, before arrest."[5]

This requirement for central office approval before action was taken was in direct contradiction to Pinchot's basic belief that people in the field should be allowed to make their own decisions. He had been so successful in instilling into his field force a sense of mission, however, that in some instances he was forced to guard against an overzealous enforcement of the laws and regulations. Like any good driver of fast thoroughbreds he sometimes had to hold his horses in check. Rarely did he do more than tighten the reins a little.

But if drastic action were needed, he was the kind of administrator who would take it. Thus, with characteristic frankness in such matters, he removed one of his field men from an assignment because "you have shown your complete inability to get on with the western people, have absolutely not recognized your position as a tenderfoot, and have behaved in a dictatorial and overbearing manner." It may be added that in this case Pinchot was willing to give the chagrined officer another chance, with the reminder that there were "many good men in the Service who made mistakes to begin with, but no good men who have persisted in making mistakes after they have been called to their attention."[6] As an executive here and in later years Pinchot displayed a fairness in his disciplining which evoked warm support from his staff. He was not the kind to modify discipline as a result of political pressure. When, for example, a United States senator asked Pinchot to remove charges from the record of a man who had been dismissed, Pinchot bluntly wrote that the firing was "wholly justified. . . . I should be most happy to act on your request if I could see my way clear to do it."[7]

Every kind of hurdle was thrown in the path of the Forest Service in its efforts to control grazing. Included in the fight against the regulations was a challenge of their constitutionality. The opposition maintained that the rules were matters that could be prescribed only by an elected Congress rather than by an appointed Secretary of Agriculture. The Supreme Court by a unanimous opinion in 1911, however, found no constitutional objections.[8] Once again Pinchot got what he wanted.

Although big grazers, as well as big lumbermen, sometimes marched arm in arm with Pinchot by approving his rules for the forests, some of their ruthless tactics which Pinchot witnessed in the next half decade had a pronounced impact on his thinking. Up to now he had displayed a curious ambivalence—well-nigh snobbishness coupled with an interest in the well-being of the common man. During this period, however, he became a more definite champion of the underdog. A generation later when observers wondered, in view of his family background, at his blistering attacks on "concentrated wealth," "overrich" magnates, and monopolies, they could have found a basis for these attitudes in the strong-arm methods and deliberate cheating employed by some of the "vested interests." After a trip to the Black Hills to study the "sheep question," for example, Pinchot lamented to his mother about "Big men turning sheep on to small men's lands. . . . It was one of the best cases I ever saw of the routine way some big men oppress some small men. I know where I stand in that matter."[9]

Years later, describing his work as Forester, Pinchot related how one settler, living on a desirable piece of public land in the midst of the range of a "great cattle king," had his fences torn down, his cabin burned, and his life threatened by the cattleman's cowboys. He told how big mining outfits jumped the claims of the little miners, and how big lumbermen appropriated the forest land belonging to the small men. Decrying the violence he had seen, he also deplored the unfairness, the "buying up of legislatures and courts," and the twisting of the laws to help "the man who was already rich" to get richer.[10] Although spoken in the heat of an election campaign, the statement expressed an attitude of mind which persisted through the latter half of his life. In view of his experiences in the government service, he had difficulty in believing that any man who accumulated great wealth could do so without oppressing some of his fellow men.

A second problem, along with grazing, to which Pinchot devoted much attention as soon as he gained control over the forests was water power. Long distance transmission of electric power, which began in the United States prior to the turn of the century, had by 1905 helped to catapult electricity into a rapidly growing industry. Various electric companies, to meet immediate needs and to fortify themselves for the anticipated expansion of the industry, were busy acquiring sites along rivers where dams could be built and plants constructed for generating electricity. Many of the best sites in the nation were on government land, and a large proportion of these were in the national forests.

Before the days of Theodore Roosevelt, permits for the use of such sites were practically given away by the Department of the Interior with a minimum of questioning—on a "first-come first-served" basis. Because the states owned the water, the national government lacked authority to dispose of all the resources; but the power companies had little difficulty in acquiring from the states a title to the water. Even though, in theory, title usually could not be obtained until the company was actually ready to use the water, in practice the annual turning of a few shovels of earth would enable a speculator to hold water rights for future development. Thus through a combination of generosity by the states and the national government, some of the power companies acquired immensely valuable rights.

It was the Roosevelt Administration which first began applying brakes to the giveaway program. And in the vanguard of the forces which helped shape Rooseveltian policies on water power was Pinchot. Fighting side by side with him were other stalwarts of conservation such as James R. Garfield, son of the assassinated President. Garfield, who had progressed from membership on the United States Civil Service Commission to director of the Bureau of Corporations to, in March 1907, Secretary of the Interior, had, like Pinchot, risen in high favor with Roosevelt. Brought together in the President's "tennis cabinet" Jim and Gifford became fast friends and, at least as long as they served under Roosevelt, remained staunch supporters of each other's ideas and activities. While Garfield was Secretary of the Interior, Pinchot, probably for the only time in his life, had complete confidence in the Department.

Roosevelt and Pinchot and Garfield and Newell (of the Reclamation Service), plus Philip Wells and George Woodruff (the two Yale classmates whom Pinchot had brought into the Forest Service) were the persons who had most to do with charting the Administration's course in regulating water power. W. J. McGee, a self-educated anthropologist and geologist, also deserves mention; according to Pinchot, McGee was the one who first convinced him of the great danger of monopoly to conservation.[11] All these men sensed a danger of monopoly in water power. Although Roosevelt himself had definite ideas on the subject, there is no question that Pinchot, Garfield, and Newell, but especially Pinchot, exercised strong influence on his thinking. Wells and Woodruff, in turn, were the source of a good many of Pinchot's ideas on power.

An early indication of the way the wind was blowing was Roosevelt's veto in 1903 of a bill passed by Congress granting permission to a group of persons to erect a dam and construct a power station at Muscle Shoals in Alabama. In a veto message that sounded markedly as if Pinchot had participated in drafting it—although there is no definite evidence that this was so—Roosevelt pleaded the need to retain this site (future location of the Tennessee Valley Authority) until a policy could be evolved for granting such permits in the best interests of the public.[12] Parenthetically, it may be added, the opinion has been expressed that without the long-term fight by Pinchot for preservation of water power there never would have been a T.V.A.[13]

Two years after the veto Pinchot received authority, by an agreement between the Interior and Agriculture Departments, to issue all permits for water power development in the forest reserves. As will be seen, some of the government's best water power and mineral sites, having been "withdrawn from entry," were not available for disposal by gift, or lease, or sale. But electric companies still could obtain leases for dam and power plant sites elsewhere in the forests. From their point of view, however, there was the serious drawback that the permits were revocable at the pleasure of the Secretary of Agriculture (in reality, Pinchot).

The companies therefore made a concerted drive to have such permits granted in perpetuity. Pinchot recognized the injustice of a system under which a power company could invest large sums of money in a project only to have its permit suddenly withdrawn. But he also was convinced of the unfairness to the public of a permit that would continue forever. He proposed, therefore, a new kind of permit which would be irrevocable, except for cause, for a definite term of years. At first he suggested a one-hundred-year period, but, after consultation with Secretary of Agriculture Wilson and others, changed it to fifty years. This did not mean that a power company necessarily would lose its permit at the end of the half century, but only that the government would review the matter and decide whether to issue a renewal and under what conditions. But Congress was not yet ready to allow an irrevocable permit, even though it could be canceled for cause. Thus, although the fifty-year limit was established by the Forest Service for all dam sites in the national forests, the permits could be revoked at the will of the Secretary. When the fifty-year rule was instituted, many of the affected interests squealed loudly, but they wanted the sites and some of them signed Pinchot's new type of agreement.

A terminal date in the permits, however, was only the beginning of the rules that the power companies had to follow in order to obtain permission to operate in the national forests. By gradual steps a code was worked out which was designed to protect the public interest. To prevent speculative holding of undeveloped sites, a

75

company was required within a reasonable time to begin and complete construction of power facilities on the site. Moreover, to guard against artificial scarcity of power and resulting high prices to consumers, a plant had to operate continuously at a designated percentage of its full capacity. Other stipulations in the permits were aimed at avoiding monopoly.[14]

All of these requirements naturally found disfavor with an industry which so far had been subject to little in the way of regulation. The provision that created the greatest furor, however, was the charging of rent for the use of government property. If, reasoned Pinchot, lumbermen had to pay for timber from the national forests, and stockmen for grazing permits, and hotel keepers for hotel permits, etc., "many of these being men of small income," he could not understand why "power companies, most of which are wealthy and powerful corporations, should not pay a fair price for what they get also."[15] Since the water in the rivers belonged to the states, the federal government could not charge for it. But, Pinchot argued, if it were not for the land around the rivers there would be no water power. The forests, after all, helped to conserve and regulate the flow of the water. The land, moreover, provided the fall to the water, which in turn was the basis for the power generated at the dams. Why therefore, asked the Forest Service of the Attorney General, could not an annual "conservation charge" be levied against power companies for the use of sites within the forests? So sure was Pinchot of the legality of the charge that, without waiting for the opinion of the Attorney General, he instituted a flexible fee based on electrical output.

Late in 1906 the Stanislaus Electric Company, for example, agreed to pay an annual fixed rental for a site plus "such reasonable charge for conservation from the beginning of productive operation of the plant as shall be fixed from time to time by the Forester."[16] The Attorney General eventually sanctioned the new practice and the Supreme Court, when the matter was later referred to it, gave its full approval. Pinchot's victories before the Supreme Court, it may be noted, were unbroken. On nine different occasions the opposition carried to the highest tribunal complaints concerning government activities that were performed while Pinchot was in office.

In all nine instances the Court (eight times unanimously) upheld the Forest Service's practices.[17]

In spite of the avalanche of opposition that pounded down on Pinchot and the Forest Service from power companies and their sympathizers, a counteracting wave of public opinion began to form among persons who saw the essential justice of the abandonment by the government of its free and easy way of handing over valuable sites to private individuals with little or no remuneration to the government or protection of the public interest. The president of the Chamber of Commerce of a California county, for instance, after having the conservation charge explained to him, assured the Secretary of Agriculture that the new policy was in line with the wishes of the people in that area.[18] The American Mining Congress, to cite another example of public approval, voted five to one for a resolution opposing the granting of rights to water power sites in perpetuity.[19]

Although Pinchot, through his authority to convey sites, had the means of controlling water power development in the national forests, he kept warning Roosevelt of the need for a similar program of protection on the public lands outside the forests. Pinchot had little respect for the opposition. "The waterpower men are trying to get away with the public property in perpetuity," he wrote to his friend Newell. "They demand nothing less. You cannot compromise with a thief who is trying to take your watch."[20]

He was happy to enlist on his side all the help he could muster, regardless of political party. When William Jennings Bryan, in response to his request, agreed to write an editorial against monopolies, Pinchot sent him a résumé of his suspicions. Pointing to lists of corporation directors, Pinchot was of the opinion that "the General Electric Company and the Westinghouse Company are securing control of water and power development over very extensive areas of the country." Admitting a lack of "legal proof" of monopoly, which he believed could be obtained only from the books of the corporations themselves, Pinchot counseled that if the government waited for positive proof "the monopoly will be riveted upon the people" so securely as to make its removal most difficult.[21]

Attempts were made early in 1908 to get representatives of some of the power companies and the government to agree on what the

Administration's attitude toward power development should be. Following a February conference at Pinchot's home and a series of subsequent discussions, he was at first optimistic. Happily he wrote to Wells that the representatives and lawyers of the power companies were beginning to agree that the position of the Forest Service was reasonable. "The plutocrat," he boasted, "will be alone in his glory before long."[22] But three weeks later his optimism had changed to indignation. He became convinced that "most" of the lawyers who were representing the power people "were here to get everything they could, and to yield nothing."[23]

While the talks were in progress, Roosevelt began moving toward a policy that water power sites outside the forests would be handled in much the same fashion as those within. Eventually he announced his decision to sign no more bills passed by Congress which granted water power rights without providing specifically for a fee and for a limitation on the length of the lease.[24] If Congress had any ideas that the President might be bluffing, they soon learned he was in deadly earnest. In two veto messages, undoubtedly written by or with the help of the Forest Service, Roosevelt insisted that grants be made only under conditions essentially the same as those drawn up for forest sites.[25]

Both Roosevelt and Pinchot were indispensable to the establishment of a policy of protecting the public interest in granting the use of dam sites for power development. There needed to be a Forest Service with an aggressive and dedicated director to try out the new ideas. And there needed to be a sympathetic and strong President to offer the necessary support in high places to get the program started. Without both of these ingredients there would have been no program. Because Congress was not yet ready for a departure from tradition, only a resolute executive branch could have accomplished much at this time.

Around the time that Pinchot entered the government service in 1898 there were 19 national forests with a total area of close to 20 million acres. Sizable additional forests were set aside under both McKinley and Roosevelt. When Roosevelt left office in 1909, there were 149 national forests with a total area of about 193 million acres.[26]

A good many Westerners, dismayed at seeing large tracts of their best forest land placed under the wing of the national government, began to rebel. Some were speculators who saw their chances for easy profits disappearing into thin air. Some were lumbermen or mining men whose opportunities to acquire natural resources with a minimum of financial outlay were being curtailed. Some believed in speedy development at any cost. And some were ordinary citizens who could not see the justice of having Easterners prescribe the rules under which the West could be developed. Every step that Pinchot took toward conservation was bound to arouse antagonism. The restlessness of persons pinched by "Pinchotism" began to mount.

The temper of an Idaho senator, for example, rose to the boiling point when the President established new reserves in 1905. He protested angrily not only to Roosevelt but also to Pinchot for making the recommendations, "What little of Idaho remains to constitute a state will still afford fighting ground upon which to stand against the violation of the contract of statehood and the infringement upon the rights of citizens to select their own homes . . . an outrage has been perpetrated."[27]

The rising chorus of complaints, added to those of the disgruntled water power people and the grazers, inevitably had its effect in Congress. The first heavy legislative blow was struck by an Oregon senator who was angered by the steady increase in the number and size of national forests; he offered an amendment to an agricultural appropriation bill transferring from the President to Congress the authority to establish such forests in the six states of Colorado, Idaho, Montana, Oregon, Washington, and Wyoming.[28]

No sooner had Congress passed the bill than Pinchot was at the White House, where Roosevelt and he, almost gleefully, concocted a scheme for avoiding some of the crippling effects of the amendment. During the ten days preceding the final date on which the President could sign the bill, members of the staff of the Forest Service worked day and night preparing plans and proclamations for new forest areas which Roosevelt could create before the deadline. In the haste to get as many tracts as possible approved, boundary lines sometimes were not drawn with precise care.

Secretary of Agriculture Wilson, who had to sign the papers for the new forests, was a little skittish over the whole procedure. Would the Department and the Forest Service, he asked Pinchot, be regarded as seriously breaking faith with Congress? As was customary in his dealings with Pinchot, however, he left the decision to him. After signing some of the papers, Wilson merely uttered a word of caution, "Have you thought this over carefully?" If Pinchot had done so and believed they should go ahead, "Then let the matter go."[29] There was not the slightest question in Pinchot's mind concerning the proper course of action.

Just before signing on March 4, 1907, the bill which took away his power, President Roosevelt issued proclamations creating a whole series of "midnight forests" comprising 16 million acres. The coup was a success. All the opposition could do was protest. And protest they did as they never had before—not just against the new forests but against the whole Pinchot system. Almost all the senators and congressmen from the forest reserve states, reflecting the opinions of many of their constituents, were decidedly hostile. An Idaho senator laid the blame for higher prices of lumber and coal on the government's policy of withdrawals of forest lands. Each time that an appropriation bill for the Department of Agriculture was before Congress, it was a signal for the opposition to open fire on the Forest Service. In March 1908, for example, a blistering attack was made in the House of Representatives against the Service and against Pinchot personally.[30] As he proved so frequently during his life, Pinchot's skin was sufficiently tough to avoid serious penetration. Indeed, seeming to relish the fight, he blandly wrote his sister that the attacks in Congress "failed completely, and we are stronger than if they had not happened."[31]

Pinchot's quality of resiliency, by which he could nimbly bounce back after being unmercifully pounded, was one of his most useful attributes. At the end of most battles, even when defeated, he was able to visualize some gains for himself or his program. Thus, when Congress, in the same law which took away Roosevelt's power to create forest reserves, also abolished the practice of letting the Forest Service keep the income from the sale of timber in the reserves, most men would have considered it a seriously crippling statute.[32] Pinchot, however, saw the fight for such legislation doing "more good than harm" because it "brought to public attention . . . the importance of forestry as a national question."[33]

Illustrative of the quiet calm with which he could take criticism was his advice to his associate forester, who was perturbed over the attacks on the Forest Service. "[D]on't let this matter worry you at all," he wrote, "for it does not in the slightest degree worry me. . . . The thing for us to do is to keep perfectly still, let the Secretary make all the statements, and possess our souls in complete tranquility and peace."[34]

Some of the deepest resentment against Pinchot's forest policy stemmed from the inclusion of good agricultural land within the reserves. Not only when the "midnight forests" were created, but also in other withdrawals, the government sometimes leaned in the direction of preserving too much rather than too little. In the absence of careful surveys of some of the western land, the Forest Service often could not be positive of the exact boundaries of timberlands. If agricultural land were scooped up along with the forests and placed on reserve, it was always possible at a later date to put the farm land back in circulation for homesteaders. Thus, Roosevelt assured the Governor of Washington that "If it shall appear that any of the reserves we have made . . . include agricultural land, that land will be restored to entry."[35]

Senator Robert La Follette, however, although making a bow to Pinchot's conservation activities, offered the opinion in his autobiography that the "only well-grounded opposition" to conservation was caused by the inclusion within forest reserves of "purely agricultural lands, thus retarding agricultural development in some of the western states."[36] Senator Borah declared himself a firm believer in the conservation movement, but opposed to inefficiency and waste in its name. His prime example of waste was the 3 million acres of "good agricultural lands" in the forest reserves located in Idaho. Under the law, he maintained, the homesteader could take up agricultural land in the forest reserves, but under the rules and regulations of the Forest Service "he cannot as a practical proposition."[37] Actually, not a great deal was done under Roosevelt to remove these farm lands from the reserves.

No state was more critical of Pinchot and his methods than Colorado. Some of its individualistic citizens felt strongly that representatives of the Forest Service were both incompetent and arbitrary. So widespread was this opinion that in the election of November 1908, the Colorado Democrats, to the embarrassment of the Republicans, made the Forest Service a lively campaign issue. One piece of party literature, printed in newspaper format, was entitled the "Rustler Supplement." Featured on the front page were two cartoons of autocratic-looking, mounted "Pinchot Rangers." Alongside was a headline, "Pinchot Forestry Landlordism Robbing Miners, Ranchmen and Cattlemen." Farther down the page was another headline, "Pinchot's Policy a Crime."[38]

When the Colorado Democrats won the elections, a good many Republican fingers were pointed accusingly at Pinchot. Even his supporters agreed his program had hurt the Republicans in some areas. A lawyer friend from Denver, in a letter to Pinchot marked "personal," admitted that the campaign attacks on the Service in the mountain regions of the state had gained much support for the Democrats.[39] Another admirer from Idaho warned Pinchot that many persons looked on government inspectors and rangers as enemies, and believed the government's policy was to treat every citizen as dishonest; he quoted the Governor of Idaho as asserting that every single individual originally in favor of the forestry policy was now against it.[40]

Pinchot manifestly needed a strong dose of self-confidence in order to withstand the criticism, and sometimes downright abuse, which continued to be heaped upon him. A congressman from South Dakota showed him a petition signed by 318 residents of the Black Hills National Forest containing a long list of grievances and expressing the opinion that the Forest Service seemed "to be determined to carry on their war of extermination of the miner and prospector within the forest reserves."[41] A Coloradian complained to the Secretary of Agriculture about the forest rangers, assuring him that he loved the American form of government but objected to government by bureaucratic masters in Washington and their two-dollar-per-day hirelings in the field.[42] Other critics sometimes referred to "carpet-bag rule."

Utter disgust toward conservation was shown by many persons who were not interested in providing for future generations if such a policy interfered with the present. Their feelings were succinctly expressed in a letter in the *Northwest Mining News*, "Some of the people are beginning to believe that they may be asked to conserve the air they breathe for future generations if the pace is kept up. There seems to be a complete disregard for the people now living."[43]

A rallying place for some of the more rabid opponents of conservation was the National Public Domain League. In announcing its first annual meeting to be held in Denver in July 1909, the *Denver News-Times* carried the headline, "League Will Fight Pinchotism in the West." Congressmen Mondell of Wyoming and Martin of Colorado were listed as charter members. The president of the organization was quoted as stating that "Everyone who has been up against Pinchotism will want to be a member." The sympathetic newspaper informed its readers that the object of the new organization was to "plan methods of developing the public domain by the people and for the people rather than by the government for the aid and benefit of office-holders."[44] Congressman Martin, unable to attend the first meeting, sent a sarcastic letter to be read to the assembled delegates, "I hesitate to think what might happen to the forest service if in the course of human events it should lose the services of the genius from whose imperial imagination this stupendous federal structure has issued like Minerva from the brow of Jove."[45]

Pinchot's ability to shake off criticism did not mean that he was unwilling to answer it or do something constructive about it. Although in the first year of the Forest Service he had counseled that its officers sit back and let the Secretary of Agriculture reply to the critics, he could not long endure such a passive role. Taking note of the strong criticism emanating from Colorado, Pinchot composed an eleven-page letter to the president of the Colorado State Forestry Association guaranteeing that the Forest Service would not "show an obstructive, litigious, or unfriendly spirit towards those who are entitled to their claims."[46]

In such fights as the one in which Pinchot was now engaged, there was sometimes the danger, paradoxically, of his becoming overoptimistic of the success of his maneuvers. A case in point was a report to his associate forester, Overton Price, on a two-hour conference with Governor Goodling of Idaho. "[We] agreed," he boasted, "on all essential points in dispute. . . . Our troubles, therefore, are at an end. . . . This disposes of the last scrap of organized opposition to the reserve policy anywhere in the West."[47] In the same vein he told Roosevelt, "I think we may fairly say . . . that organized opposition to your forest policy in the West is completely at an end."[48] Nothing could have been farther from the facts. But the letters reveal his trait of overvaluing his power of persuasion and overestimating the points of agreement between himself and others in a conference.

An old friend and associate, Professor Holmes, who knew Pinchot well enough to realize his inclination toward undue optimism, wrote to Price expressing fear that Pinchot was receiving from his many friends in the West a distorted view of the general situation. Assuring Price, as he had Pinchot, that part of the criticism against their field workers in Colorado was justified, he pleaded, as a friend, that the Forest Service send to Denver for a few months a judicious member of the staff who could handle complaints to the satisfaction of members of Congress, the governor, and the public.[49] Pinchot and Price sent a trouble shooter as suggested.

Pinchot was never much impressed by lumber companies as a group. He saw so much forest devastation in the early years that he tended to think of lumbermen as plunderers. "You and I know," he later wrote to his successor in the Forest Service, "that the lumbermen have systematically played with the Forest Service for years, and have directed their policy very ably toward getting all they could from the service, and giving nothing in return."[50]

He sometimes encountered a lumberman, however, who, he felt, was sincerely endorsing forestry. Such a convert he believed was F. E. Weyerhaeuser, of the famed St. Paul lumber company which had accumulated vast timberlands in the West. Although this company was symbolic in some people's minds of selfish land-grabbing, Pinchot was satisfied that it had reformed and that it was honestly trying to cut its timber in accordance with the better practices of forestry. When Mr. Weyerhaeuser once informed Pinchot that his interest in forestry had been aroused largely by him, he graciously replied by calling him a "progressive [lumberman] in the question of forest preservation."[51]

Pinchot easily perceived the value to the forestry movement of having such an influential lumber baron on his side, and was more than pleased that Weyerhaeuser was a member of the American Forestry Association. When Senator Heyburn, an avowed enemy of Pinchot and his forest-preservation ideas, derisively pointed out that "the largest land grabber [Weyerhaeuser]" was a vice-president of the Association, Weyerhaeuser told Pinchot of his intention to resign in order to avoid hindering forestry work. Whereupon Pinchot pleaded with him to stay on as a member: "While there is a strong feeling against great holdings of timber lands in private ownership, . . . it is so clear that forestry can not succeed unless it has the support of great timber owners that I think it would be a very real misfortune for you to draw out."[52]

Senator Heyburn's comment, indeed, reflected an opinion—held by some proponents as well as opponents of forest preservation—that Pinchot's forestry rules actually were playing into the hands of large lumber operators. As additional tracts of forest land were set aside by the government and the prescribed procedures for cutting government timber became more difficult to meet, the advantages held by the large and established lumber companies seemed to increase. For these reasons giant lumbermen not infrequently marched in step with the Forest Service and proclaimed their support of its policies.[53]

Pinchot's successful campaign to have control of the government's forests transferred to the Department of Agriculture had provided him with valuable training in the ways and means of molding public and congressional opinion. As soon as his Forest Service was established, he began to put his experience to use in selling forestry to the nation. He knew the job would be difficult, but from the beginning he had one tremendous asset, without which his efforts might have proved largely futile—the strongest kind of support from a

President who was thoroughly convinced of the desirability of saving the forests for public use.

Once again Pinchot demonstrated his ability as a promoter. He was an "operator" who made use of every conceivable kind of persuasion; he pursued every angle of publicity to the utmost. Pinchot's salesmanship activities were not confined to trying to convince the country of the value of practicing forestry. With almost equal emphasis he urged the preservation of water power for the benefit of the public, the prevention of exploitation of minerals on the public domain, the regulation of grazing on government land, and the irrigation of arid lands.

For the first year or two of his directorship of the Forest Service, however, Pinchot thought of such subjects as independent problems —each important in its own right. He was riding in the Virginia hills near Washington one day early in 1907, as he remembered it, when he suddenly realized that all these matters were parts of one big problem: making available to the people as a whole the God-given resources of the earth. Here was an idea that he felt would catch the imagination of the country and could be "sold" more easily in one attractive package. After pondering with some of his friends on a name for the new movement, Overton Price (to the best of Pinchot's memory) suggested "conservation." Although Pinchot's recollection of the entire series of events was somewhat hazy, he was always certain that the original conception of a unified policy was his own brain child. He was just as quick to admit that the name was suggested by Price and that W. J. McGee provided the real brains for defining the movement.[54]

The word "conservation" was not a new one. It had been used in connection with forests as a synonym for preservation or protection at least as early as 1875. In the same sense it had been employed to describe activities aimed at saving water power, minerals, etc. But up to this time it had not denoted an entire movement. At least one encyclopedia did not recognize it in its new use until 1911. Pinchot is authority for the statement that when he took the conservation idea to Roosevelt, the President quickly saw the desirability of adopting the new word and movement. Certainly Roosevelt lost no time in incorporating conservation as one of the major planks of his program.[55]

Pinchot tried to explain his conception of conservation in a little book published in 1910.[56] The term, he said, stood for three principles: the "development of our natural resources and the fullest use of them for the present generation"; the "prevention of waste"; and the development and preservation of resources "for the benefit of the many, and not merely for the profit of a few."

These principles had broad appeal. They were subject, however, to such varying interpretations that a wide variety of persons joined together under the label of "conservationists." Conflicting ideas concerning the best use of specific resources sometimes led to bitter quarrels among them.

In his own special field of forestry, for example, where Pinchot was not primarily interested in saving the woods for future use, he clashed repeatedly during his career with conservationists who were basically devoted to *preserving* the trees. Not much interested in saving the woods for scenic beauty or romantic purposes, he had no sympathy with a provision of the New York state constitution which prohibited any cutting whatever in a state park. With few exceptions, when timber was mature he thought it should be scientifically cut and not allowed to stand until it deteriorated. Nor was he enthusiastic about turning forest reserves into national parks or game preserves. Such attitudes were in line with his support of grazing (controlled of course) in the government forests.

Other conservationists—naturalists, park enthusiasts, and wildlife groups—sometimes looked at Pinchot and his practices with sincere shock. Proponents of parks, and persons especially concerned with "the promotion of public beauty," found it hard to understand Pinchot's approval of the disfigurement of a portion of Yosemite National Park by the construction of the Hetch Hetchy dam to provide water for the city of San Francisco. And still others, appalled by his lukewarm concern for the preservation of wildlife, questioned his sincere interest in what they regarded as "true" conservation.[57]

Beginning in 1907, with a broad and imaginative new movement to promote, Pinchot proceeded to intensify still further, if such were possible, his efforts to awaken the nation to the need of conserving its resources. In an effort to popularize the new movement he directed his staff to try to include in all letters prepared for his signature the phrase "conservation of natural resources."

Gradually the Forest Service built up an extensive, classified mailing list of persons at whom a steady barrage of circulars and letters containing information on forestry and conservation was directed. By 1909 the list had reached a total of 781,000 and was divided into such categories as: engineers, 16,000; lumbermen, 56,000; newspapermen, 22,000; farmers, 321,000; educators, 111,000, etc. One of the publications most widely distributed by the Service was a twenty-four page pamphlet entitled *A Primer of Conservation*, which explained the origins of the movement and quoted statements on the subject by a number of prominent people.[58] In addition an unending stream of news items prepared by the Service were distributed to the press. Pinchot once estimated that in this way information about forestry was inserted in from 30 to 50 million copies of newspapers every month. The "careful system of publicity," he believed, was "mainly" responsible for "saving" the Service despite the repeated attacks which it suffered.[59]

And so he worked, taking advantage of every possible opportunity to broadcast his message. When an editor of *Collier's* magazine showed interest, Pinchot asked him to publish an article showing the value of forest protection.[60] When Senator Dolliver made what Pinchot considered a "most admirable speech" on forestry, he persuaded the Senator to pay for a reprint of 100,000 copies to be sent to some of the names on Pinchot's mailing list.[61] Traveling widely throughout the West, he worked in the same way as an evangelist to win converts in the very centers of opposition. At the end of the summer of 1907 he acknowledged to his parents that he was doing "much better speaking" and that he was certain the trips had "done good."[62]

One of the most important appearances he made was in Denver at the Public Lands Convention. Called by the Governor of Colorado, this conference was sponsored by persons opposed to the federal government's conservation policies. Roosevelt designated Pinchot and Garfield, as well as Newell of the Reclamation Service and Richard

A. Ballinger, new director of the General Land Office, to present the official viewpoint of the Administration to the convention and to quiet some of the exaggerated rumors about the government's policies and plans.

Envisioning a need for further support at the convention, Pinchot wrote a number of friends of conservation urging them to attend. When the inevitable fight developed on the floor it was clear that the conservation sympathizers were in the minority. One prominent Montana stockman protested that the way the government officials were treated by the convention "was nothing less than shameful"; they were, he complained, "bullied" by the chairmen and not always allowed to speak as long as were the opposition representatives.[63] But Pinchot's report to Roosevelt on the results of the convention was in no sense defeatist. "The congress was intended to be packed and was packed," he wrote, "and that fact became so evident as to destroy altogether its capacity to do harm." Rather, he stated his conviction, which once again was the result of somewhat wishful thinking, that "the forest policy is now a dead issue. No one thinks seriously of attacking it any more." Bubbling with pleasure at the gains he saw for the general conservation movement, he continued, "The general idea of the conservation of natural resources is taking an astonishingly rapid hold on the West."[64]

So incessant was the publicity on conservation that poured forth from Pinchot's office that his friend and supporter, Senator Beveridge, felt impelled to suggest that perhaps Pinchot should soft pedal his activity for fear of unduly annoying the public. But Pinchot, seeing little danger of such a consequence, assured the Senator that he "was not going to keep bothering the people to the point of irritation," but simply to "remind them from time to time" that his organization was busy.[65]

Some other members of Congress, however, were worried about the publicity activities for another reason. It was becoming increasingly apparent that this drive to win the nation's mind was having an effect. Although the opposition to the Forest Service and to Pinchot was substantial, senators and congressmen, with ears trained to detect variations in the sentiments of voters, began to sense a ground swell of opinion favorable to conservation practices. It was, in fact, a compliment to the publicity's effectiveness that Congress began asking questions about it. A Senate resolution, for example, required Secretary of Agriculture Wilson to send to that body a statement showing the attendance of members of the Forest Service at meetings and conventions during the entire year 1907.[66]

When Pinchot himself was asked by the friendly chairman of the House Committee on Agriculture for a statement on the "educational work" which the Forest Service conducted through the newspapers, he went into considerable detail to describe and justify its scope. The work was undertaken, he explained, because the "most important immediate task" of the Service was to inform the American people on forestry, an object that could not be accomplished "through the distribution of official publications alone." He acknowledged that such publicity, "if not scrupulously confined to its legitimate field of education" might easily become "an altogether improper form of activity." It would not be fitting for the Forest Service, he recognized, to use its press releases to put itself in the most favorable light before the public or to advocate special laws which it was the duty of Congress to pass upon. He invited inspection by the congressmen to confirm that his agency did not engage in such inappropriate activities. One of his strongest talking points in support of the contention that the news releases were not aimed at glorifying either Pinchot or the Forest Service was the diligent effort that had been made to avoid mention of the name of the Forest Service.[67]

The upshot of the squabble, however, was the enactment by Congress of an amendment to an appropriation bill that no part of the money be used for the preparation of newspaper or magazine articles.[68] Judging by the amount of newspaper publicity for forestry which continued to appear throughout the country, the prohibition was singularly ineffective.

CHAPTER 5

ROOSEVELT'S FAVORITE COMMISSIONER

MANY PERSONS disagreed with Gifford Pinchot's policies. Few, however, would have taken exception to the statement that he was a superlative administrator of the Forest Service. A born leader, he once offered the opinion that the "distinction between men was much more in their will than in their ability."[1] Based on this conviction he concentrated on building the morale of his men and firing them with enthusiasm for the work they were doing. Employees caught the feeling that they were engaged in an undertaking on which the whole future of the nation depended. The high *esprit de corps* of the Forest Service went far to explain its very real accomplishments.

Pinchot demanded high-quality work, and gave recognition when he received it. Things were expected to be done, and done promptly; he was especially concerned about answering letters on time. While on a trip in the field he wrote to the associate forester that the "greatest fault" of the Forest Service was "lack of promptness, and we ought to get after it very hard." To help speed the process he ordered "every letter the answer to which is delayed," to be placed on his desk daily.[2]

It was a hard and fast rule of the Service that promotions of men in the field were made only after an inspection of their work. Pinchot insisted that the men stationed in Washington, including himself, get out in the woods to see the problems and the men on the spot. He had a refreshing frankness in expressing his judgments of employees; the man who was efficient would receive the warmest kind of pat on the back. The incompetent employee might find himself colorfully characterized by Pinchot: "I found him all tangled up and generally making an Ass of himself, with splendid success."[3]

Pinchot's interest in the broad subject of administration was reflected in his work with the Committee on Department Methods, popularly called the "Keep Committee"—the first presidential commission ever appointed to make recommendations for increasing the efficiency of the executive branch of the federal government. James Garfield, then head of the Bureau of Corporations, and Pinchot originated the idea of such a committee. Both had had enough experience in government to see the need for improved methods. These two Roosevelt favorites, after discussing the project with the President, prepared for him an outline of the matter to be covered in such a study and offered a suggested list of names, including their own, of persons who might be appointed to the committee. While they were in conference with Roosevelt he dictated a letter instructing a committee of five persons to make the study.[4] This letter, which made use of the material Pinchot and Garfield had prepared, showed such insight into administrative matters that it has been called a model of instructions for such a reorganization commission.[5]

Roosevelt, as suggested, appointed both men to the committee; Charles H. Keep, Assistant Secretary of the Treasury, was chairman. Pinchot's influence on the Committee on Department Methods was felt throughout. His associate forester, Overton Price, became secretary of the group. After some seventy departmental officials were appointed to subcommittees of the main committee, the entire group was invited to an evening meeting at Pinchot's home where President Roosevelt talked to them for nearly an hour on his ideas concerning departmental reform.[6]

Although the Keep Committee reported that the Forest Service was one of the most efficient of government agencies, Pinchot's opponents in Congress were naturally skeptical of such pronouncements by a committee so much under his influence. One senator even remarked on the Senate floor that the Forest Service was "the worst organized department of the Government." Less vulnerable to attack, however, was a report by a House committee which undertook to investigate and evaluate the Service at about this time. In direct contradiction to some of the charges being made in the Senate, the House group concluded that "the Forest Service has been administered honestly and with great administrative, executive, and business ability." Garfield had told the House group about the Keep Committee's unanimous belief that "the efficiency in [the Forest Service] was so much greater than we found in the other [bureaus] that we used many of the methods we found in vogue there as a basis for recommendations for changes in other branches of the Government service."[7]

It has already been explained that, contrary to his basic beliefs, Pinchot at first required his eager but relatively inexperienced forest officers in the field to obtain approval from Washington for a number of their activities and decisions. Secretary of Agriculture Wilson, on a tour through the West in 1907, was unhappy to find that district foresters had to telegraph to Washington for permission to spend more than $300 to fight a fire. Nor could they sell more than $100 worth of timber without approval from central headquarters. In vigorous terms Wilson let it be known that be believed the Service needed a thorough overhauling in order to place more responsibility upon field officers. Pinchot did take major steps to decentralize, and thereby to follow the dictates of his natural inclinations. Beginning in 1908 a district forester had discretion to sell as much as 25 million feet of timber.

Secretary Wilson, apparently, was beginning to smart under some of the criticism of this bureau for which he ultimately was responsible. When associate forester Price asked him for permission to hire a New York firm of consultants to examine and report on the organization and business methods of the Forest Service, Wilson somewhat heatedly turned down the request with the sarcastic comment that he thought the Service already had some of the ablest men in the nation on this subject. Since the study was made, it can be assumed that Pinchot, as sometimes happened during his career in both national and state government, reached into his own pocket to take care of at least some of the expense.

Gunn, Richards and Company, consultants, of New York City, after studying the Forest Service, pointed to some weaknesses in its organization and methods. But they did not report an excess of centralization. Somewhat to the contrary, they found that "Expressions or signs of discontent, either with the administration of the Service or the quantity or character of work assigned to the several branches . . . were rare, and this is the best evidence of good administration."

The report, in general, was notably laudatory, and a compliment to Pinchot's administrative ability. It paid unusually high tribute to the quality of the men whom Pinchot had assembled and molded into an effective working organization: "We cannot praise too highly the personnel of the Forest Service, and we have much pleasure in stating that in our rather extended experience in commercial enterprises where the opportunity for financial reward is unlimited, we have rarely, if ever, met a body of men where the average of intelligence was so high, or the loyalty to the organization and the work so great. The volume of the business transacted compares most favorably with that in commercial practice and is worthy of the highest commendation."[8] Critics of Pinchot scarcely could have charged that such comments by an objective consulting firm were those of a prejudiced friend.

A few years previously, Pinchot had proposed to Roosevelt the creation of presidential commissions partly for the purpose of paving the way for transfer of the forests to Pinchot's control. Now he began to employ the same device for helping to create a public demand for conservation.

Roosevelt credits Pinchot with suggesting to him the Inland Waterways Commission.[9] Pinchot was not certain whether he or W. J. McGee first had the idea, but, regardless of the source, these two men worked together closely in creating the Commission, as well as following through on its work. They were the ones who prepared the letter, approved and signed by Roosevelt with only slight changes, setting up the body and making appointments to it. The President directed the Commission to prepare a "comprehensive plan for the improvement and control of the river systems of the United States"; matters to be considered included water transportation, flood control, water power development, irrigation, and soil conservation.[10]

The chairman and three other appointees to the nine-man Commission were members of Congress. Also included were Pinchot, McGee, and F. H. Newell. McGee, who was elected secretary at the first meeting, wrote the final report.

Although the Commission had no funds to hold hearings or hire an expert staff, it was able to serve the purpose of helping to popularize the Administration's views on conservation. Conducting inspection trips on the Mississippi and Missouri Rivers and on the Great Lakes, the Commission held a total of thirty formal discussion sessions.

The report of the Inland Waterways Commission, which dealt with general principles, was limited to 18 pages, but almost 700 pages of statistics, maps, and studies (many of them prepared by experts employed in various government agencies), formed a valuable appendix. Roosevelt, in transmitting the report to Congress, called it "thorough, conservative, sane, and just." Eight of the nine members agreed that every river system was a single unit to be treated as such; no river should be developed primarily for one purpose, such as navigation, at the expense of, for example, power—"every waterway should be made to serve the people as largely and in as many different ways as possible." Twenty-five years later the nation was to hear the same principle espoused in support of the Tennessee Valley Authority. The President cited with approval the portions of the report that urged the conservation of timber and water power. "Forest protection," said Roosevelt in typical Pinchot terms, "without which river improvement can not be permanent, will at the same time help to postpone the threatened timber famine." He called special attention to the Commission's warnings against the danger of the control of water power by monopolies.[11]

The Inland Waterways Commission, however, is primarily remembered not for its pleas for conservation as such but for giving birth to an idea for placing the conservation movement even more dramatically before the eyes of the nation. At a meeting of the Commission in May 1907, on board a boat in the middle of the Mississippi River, F. H. Newell proposed that it stage in Washington, D.C., a gigantic conference on conservation.[12] The idea so appealed to the Commission that they asked the chairman, Representative Burton, and Pinchot to notify the President of their intention to take such action. During the entire summer of 1907, Pinchot, McGee, Newell, and Senator Newlands worked to prepare a suggested program for the conference.

As plans began to take shape it was agreed that the conference should be built around the governors of all the states. It seemed appropriate, therefore, that Roosevelt should make the first announcement of the meeting at an October gathering in Memphis of the Lakes-to-the-Gulf Deep Waterway Association which would be attended by about half the governors. Pinchot and McGee accordingly prepared and sent to the President some material to be included in his speech.[13]

As part of the showmanship to advertise the need for waterway development, it was agreed that the President, the members of the Inland Waterways Commission, and the score or more governors would travel down the Mississippi River to Memphis on river steamers. From the time they left Keokuk, Iowa, on October 1, until they reached Memphis on October 4, the President and the flotilla attracted huge cheering throngs along the banks of the river. On at least one occasion during the trip, three or four members of the Commission, including Pinchot, were closeted with Roosevelt in his cabin on the U.S.S. Mississippi. On the third day, all the members of the Commission met with him formally; the next day the President announced his intention of calling the conference. In the middle of November formal invitations were sent to all governors for the meetings to be held at the White House on May 13-15, 1908.

The day after the President's Memphis speech the Commission met to appoint a committee to confer with Roosevelt and make arrangements for the conference. Pinchot was appointed chairman, and Newell and McGee members. With their eyes always trained primarily on the publicity potential of the meetings, the committee quickly selected a newspaper and publicity man, Thomas R. Shipp, as secretary of the conference. With the same kind of flair for promotion that now goes into a Hollywood production, the committee and Shipp set out to build up the meetings. Almost every morning, from October to May, they met at the Cosmos Club in Washington to plan and handle the innumerable details connected with the staging of such a conference. Sometimes they gathered in the third floor den of Pinchot's home.[14]

Long hours of consultation preceded the selection of persons to be invited. First and foremost, of course, were the governors. Never before had all the chief executives of the states been brought together in one place. A total of thirty-four were able to attend; the other twelve sent representatives. Each governor, furthermore, was asked to bring three citizens of his own choice. The Inland Waterways Commission was of course included. Invitations also went from the President to all members of Congress, the Supreme Court and the cabinet. A generous sampling of the press was also invited. Roosevelt, in addition, approved the sending of bids to leading scientists and the presidents of organizations interested in natural resources. To add further lustre to the list of celebrities attending the conference, five outstanding lay leaders in the country were added: William Jennings Bryan, steel magnate Andrew Carnegie, ex-President Grover Cleveland, railroader James J. Hill, and labor leader John Mitchell. The four who attended—Cleveland was unable to be present because of illness—delivered major addresses. Each governor was given a chance to express himself, either as a scheduled speaker or in the course of discussion from the floor.

This Conference on the Conservation of Natural Resources, as it was called, was indeed an impressive gathering. Never in the history of the country had so many important government officials and scientific men been brought together. The meeting was clear proof to the country of the high importance of conservation in the mind of the President. The official printed program of the Conference nowhere carried the name of Gifford Pinchot. Every delegate was aware, however, that Pinchot was one of the main pillars on which the meetings were built. President Roosevelt, in his opening remarks to the group, took the opportunity to bestow special credit on "the initiative, the energy, the devotion to duty, and the far-sightedness" of Pinchot. "If it had not been for him," said the President, "this convention neither would nor could have been called."[15]

Some of the social life for the delegates was, like the meetings, centered at the White House—the night before the opening session they were entertained at dinner, and at the end of the sessions the delegates and their wives attended a garden party on the White House lawn. During the Conference a reception was held at the Pinchot home for the state governors, federal government officials, and foreign diplomats. Pinchot's mother, in all her grace and charm, received about one thousand guests at this reception.

There is no way of telling how much the Conference cost Pinchot out of his own pocket. Since there was no regular appropriation for the meetings, the amount was probably considerable. Secretary Shipp later revealed that Pinchot took care of many of the expenses—even the rubber tips placed on the legs of the golden chairs in the East Room in order to reduce the noise.[16]

When Roosevelt first invited the governors to the Conference on the Conservation of Natural Resources, he stated in his letter—originally prepared by Pinchot and McGee—that "the conservation of our natural resources is the most weighty question now before the people of the United States,"[17] and his remarks to the delegates were an elaboration of that theme. Roosevelt and the original committee on arrangements, Pinchot, McGee, and Newell, gave subtle guidance to the proceedings of the Conference; this was not always apparent but was ever present. Not that it was necessary to change the attitude of the governors. Generally speaking, the chief executives, with a dissent here and there, were in sympathy with the conservation ideals expressed by the President. But the committee saw to it that any existing sympathetic attitudes had every opportunity to be expressed before the governors. According to Pinchot, McGee wrote a good many of the addresses which the speakers delivered as their own.[18]

There is no doubt that the governors as a whole were impressed, even startled, by some of the things they heard about America's vanishing resources, and were in a mood to adopt unanimously a strongly worded set of principles.[19] Declaring their "firm conviction that this conservation of our natural resources is a subject of transcendent importance," they recommended that each state create a conservation commission to work with like commissions in other states and in the federal government. The memorable declaration ended with the exhortation, "Let us conserve the foundations of our prosperity."[20]

The basic purpose of the White House Conference had been to bring the conservation of natural resources dramatically to the public's attention. Measured by this goal, the meetings were stirringly successful—newspapers throughout the nation carried detailed stories of the proceedings and conservation became the most-talked-about subject in America. The wide interest was exactly what the Inland Waterways Commission and Roosevelt had hoped for. Pinchot exuberantly wrote a friend that he was "as pleased about [the Conference] as a hen that has laid an egg."[21]

Along with his satisfaction over the success of the Conference Pinchot must also have realized that his own prominence and prestige in the country were enormously enhanced. After all, he did not, at least on paper, hold a high position in the government. But rarely has there been a mere bureau chief so much in the public eye.

At this opportune moment when interest in conservation was at its height, Roosevelt appointed a National Conservation Commission.[22] This move was made at Pinchot's suggestion and was in line with the recommendations of the Conference. The National Conservation Commission, consisting of half a hundred members drawn from the government, industry, and science, was asked to work with similar bodies in the states and to prepare a report on the condition of the nation's natural resources. Simultaneously the President directed the various departments and agencies of the government to give the Commission as much help as it requested.[23] No one was surprised when Pinchot was made chairman. Moreover, four of his closest associates (McGee plus three past or present officials in Pinchot's Forest Service) were placed on the executive committee and designated to the key positions of secretaries of the four divisions dealing with water, forests, land, and minerals.

This clearly was Pinchot's Commission. Partly because of this fact, some members of Congress were cool toward it. Although Roosevelt asked for a $50,000 appropriation, Congress failed to provide a single dollar. The Commission, nevertheless, went ahead with the compiling of an inventory of United States resources. With the generous help of sympathetic experts throughout the country, and especially with the assistance of many departments and bureaus of the government, the task was completed in the remarkably brief period of six months. For the first time there was available, in the three volumes produced by the Commission, careful estimates, rather than mere rough guesses, of the amount and adequacy of the nation's natural resources.[24]

Pinchot's deft propaganda hand could be seen when the Commission focused attention on its report by convening a Joint Conservation Conference in Washington. Here, with Pinchot the prime arranger, a score of governors together with delegates from various national and state conservation groups met in the Belasco Theater, listened to a talk by the President, and considered and approved the report. The President, in referring the report to Congress, showed his high satisfaction by describing it as "one of the most fundamentally important documents ever laid before the American people."[25]

In Pinchot's mind this compilation of a resources inventory was only a first step. Much remained to be done. But in the course of only a few weeks, as the result of Congressional action, the Commission found itself helpless to carry on. Representative Tawney, of Minnesota, introduced an amendment to a bill which struck a responsive chord in Congress. Those members of both houses who resented Roosevelt's expansion of executive power, those who believed the Administration had gone wild in creating commissions, and those who were generally opposed to conservation and Pinchot— all rallied around the amendment which provided that no money appropriated by Congress could be used to pay the expenses, directly or indirectly, of any commission not specifically authorized by Congress. With one blow, therefore, Congress killed the National Conservation Commission and all such executive boards. Congress had found that Pinchot gave 20 per cent of his official time to the National Conservation Commission and 15 per cent to the Inland Waterways Commission.[26] In the future this kind of activity would not be permissible.

During his later life when he was active in politics, Pinchot always thought of himself as a friend of the farmer. Only an excessively cynical person would hold that his interest in agricultural matters was adopted for the purpose of winning votes. Although he loved the outdoors, he was more a city boy than a farm boy. But through the years there were numerous indications that he developed a genuine concern for the rural population.

Pinchot's sustained interest in the problems of farmers began as a result of his work with still another Roosevelt commission. When Sir Horace Plunkett, a friend of Roosevelt's, came to the President early in 1908 spilling over with ideas for bettering the farmer's lot,

Roosevelt suggested he talk with Garfield and Pinchot. Plunkett, an Irishman, had been instrumental in encouraging the growth of co-operatives among the farmers of his native land. In their discussions he and Pinchot developed a mutual admiration which brought them together as lifelong friends. The Irishman, with his many ideas, and Pinchot, with his proved ability to sell ideas, worked together to plan a Country Life Commission for drawing the country's attention to the hardships and limited rewards of farm life.

Once again Roosevelt was enthusiastic. At the end of June, Pinchot sent him a proposed draft for a letter setting up the Country Life Commission, and suggested names for appointment.[27] Closely follow-ing the suggestions, Roosevelt created the Commission, his sixth such executive agency, with a Cornell professor, L. H. Bailey, as chairman. The two best known of the seven members were: Walter Hines Page, editor of *World's Work*, and future Ambassador to Great Britain; and Henry C. Wallace, a future Secretary of Agricul-ture and the father of Henry A. Wallace, who was later also Secre-tary of Agriculture. Inasmuch as Pinchot suggested his own name for membership, it was somewhat amusing that he wrote Roosevelt stating his willingness to serve and expressing "great pleasure" at "the honor you have done me by the appointment."[28] On this Com-mission began another of Pinchot's long-standing friendships—that with Henry C. Wallace, whom he always addressed affectionately as "Uncle Henry."

Actually, Pinchot did not spend a great deal of time with this Commission. Although the members did some traveling and held some thirty hearings, the pressure of work kept Pinchot in Wash-ington. Not entirely satisfied with the Commission's work, he felt that the ideas of Wallace and Page and himself were being some-what thwarted by chairman Bailey. The Commission, he wrote Plunkett, "has made about 75 per cent of the use it might have made" of the opportunities it had.[29] Although he felt that "accepted plans have been thrown overboard without ceremony,"[30] he decided to make no protest and signed the report.

The report discussed steps which should be taken by government and by the farmers themselves to better their condition.[31] The needs were summarized by the President in his letter of transmission:

better means of communication, including good roads; more effective schools; and more effective cooperation among farmers. Although Roosevelt stressed that this Commission, like the others, had worked without an appropriation, he asked for $25,000 to enable it to complete its work. The Congress answered his request with the Tawney amendment which made the Country Life Commission one more casualty.

Despite Pinchot's reservations about the effectiveness of this particular Commission, he echoed and reechoed some of its main themes, such as the necessity for good rural roads, for a period of three decades.

CHAPTER 6

FAREWELL TO TR

As THE SEVEN YEARS of Roosevelt's Administration flew by, Gifford Pinchot came into greater and greater national prominence. Universities began to proffer honorary degrees. Princeton, not to be outdone by his alma mater which had made him a Master of Arts, presented him with a similar degree in 1904. To Pinchot the most impressive part of the Princeton ceremonies was his chance to have a few words with former President Cleveland and his opportunity to meet Woodrow Wilson.[1] Michigan Agricultural College, when it induced Roosevelt to deliver an address on the campus, gave honorary Doctor of Science degrees to both James Wilson, Secretary of Agriculture, and to Gifford Pinchot.

Pinchot was "very proud" that McGill University, in Montreal, granted him a Doctor of Laws degree, but when, at about the same time, the University of Wisconsin offered him the same honor he decided against accepting. Fully realizing that he had many bitter critics who were always ready to discredit him, he explained his fears to the president of the University who also was a staunch conservationist, ". . . there would undoubtedly not be wanting men in Congress next winter who would announce that conferring this degree was the result of a corrupt bargain; and there are always some people who believe slander of any kind."[2]

As any public man must, who takes strong stands on controversial economic questions, Pinchot always went to great pains to conduct his personal affairs in an irreproachable manner. He was especially careful in financial matters. It was one of his steadfast rules, for example, that, in view of his intense drives for conservation, he would not invest in corporations, such as mining or lumber companies, which might be affected in some way by governmental conservation policies. Believing that his critics would find it difficult to impugn his actions in public life as motivated by a desire for personal financial gain, he confided to his father that it was "a great thing to be beyond the need of money far enough to have it generally understood. Indeed it is almost an unfair advantage in a man's work."[3]

It is no criticism of Pinchot to say that although he had no need or desire for accumulating additional wealth, he was ambitious for a more eminent position than that of bureau chief. Although careful not to give the impression that he was hoping for promotion, there is no question that he had a strong desire for a cabinet post.

As early as 1904 his name was considered for the position of Assistant Secretary of Agriculture. Pinchot apparently had mixed feelings on the appointment. Reporting to his mother that Secretary Wilson would recommend him to Roosevelt if he consented, he almost decided to decline.[4] But within forty-eight hours Wilson made the recommendation with an understanding that, if appointed, Pinchot would remain in full charge of the Bureau of Forestry.[5] Roosevelt quickly dispatched a letter, marked "Personal," to "Dear Gifford," expressing surprise that Pinchot was interested in the position. The President directly asked if he wanted the job and if he thought his knowledge of agriculture was sufficient to qualify him for it. "If," wrote Roosevelt, "I had dreamed you would have accepted the position I would have at the outset settled the matter by your appointment."[6] After talking with the President about the matter, Pinchot came away convinced that he would not receive the appointment. He was cheered by the comment of Secretary Wilson, however, who, when he learned that Pinchot would not be the man, told him he was the "unanimous choice" of the whole Department for the position.[7] But Roosevelt, informed of the feeling of the farmers that Pinchot neither "represented them" nor was "in touch with them," appointed another man.[8] Pinchot understood the situation well enough to write the President that he was "thoroughly glad" he had not been appointed, since "It seems evident from what Secretary Wilson told me that you would have had trouble with the Grange."[9]

Only a few months later Pinchot happily recorded that while talking with Roosevelt, the President had told him he was "the best man he knew" for Secretary of the Interior, but it might not be possible to appoint him.[10] On more than one occasion TR gave him to understand that politics would preclude the placing of another New Yorker in the cabinet, and Pinchot at this time was a legal resident of the Empire State. Another two years rolled by before the Interior Department post became vacant in 1906. Several days before making the new appointment, Roosevelt informed Pinchot that James R. Garfield was in line for the position. According to Pinchot, however, Roosevelt told him that only geography prevented a different choice. "Fond as I am of Jim," Pinchot quoted the President as saying, "if you came from a Western State I would put you in as Secretary of the Interior. But I cannot put a New York man there."[11]

Pinchot, in talks with both Roosevelt and Garfield, urged the appointment of his classmate, George Woodruff, as Assistant Attorney General assigned to the Interior Department. He even suggested that he himself go to the Department on a temporary six-month basis, either as Commissioner of the General Land Office or as Assistant Secretary of Interior, for the purpose of helping "to clean up" the Department.[12]

Woodruff shortly became an Assistant Attorney General as suggested, but Pinchot stayed on as Forester. For one of the very few times during TR's Administration, Pinchot was nettled at the way things were going. Although keeping his complaints to himself, he stormed freely in his diary. He was not happy, for example, that George Cortelyou, "without financial experience," became Secretary of the Treasury. Nor did he approve of sending Victor Metcalf, "an admitted failure as an administrative officer," to the Navy Department. He sarcastically described the new Postmaster General, George Meyer, as a man "who looks like an ass." He expressed resentment that his friend Garfield had gone to the Department of Interior when he was, in fact, the "best possible man for Commerce and Labor."[13]

Pinchot's feathers were still further ruffled when he learned that Oscar Strauss, a New Yorker, had become Secretary of Commerce and Labor. Unable to understand "why a New York man had been put in the Cabinet after I had repeatedly been given that reason why I could not," he resolved to ask the President directly. Whether or not Roosevelt's explanation that "Strauss went in as a Jew and his locality indifferent"[14] was entirely satisfactory to Pinchot is questionable, but his grievances were not so deep that they affected for any length of time his loyalty and admiration for the President. For the most part he tried to hide his disappointments. One week after Garfield's appointment, for example, he replied to a letter from Senator Beveridge by saying, "I, too, am happy over Jim Garfield's promotion. . . . If, as you say, I come along later, that I shall be glad of too, but I am pretty happy just now where I am."[15]

During this same year of 1906 rumors floated around the country that Pinchot was about to succeed Wilson as Secretary of Agriculture. But these stories were quickly denied when brought to Pinchot's attention. "I am honestly glad to tell you," he wrote in a letter, "that Secretary Wilson is not going out. He is the best Secretary of Agriculture we have ever had."[16]

Wilson by now was an old man, however, and the rumors of his retirement persisted. After Taft won the presidential election of November 1908, the stories multiplied. When a friend wrote that many persons were glad to hear that he was to be in Taft's cabinet, Pinchot made no effort to deny the possibility, but confined his reply to a eulogy of Secretary Wilson, "I know of no one except the President himself who has rendered greater service to the American people."[17] But he wrote to Senator Beveridge that there was "nothing" in the rumor. Admitting he would "greatly like to be in Taft's cabinet for certain reasons," he nevertheless maintained that for other reasons "almost if not equally as strong," he preferred to remain in his present position.[18] He was already beginning to display an apprehensiveness, now insignificant but soon to develop into a sincere dread, that Taft would not thoroughly and unequivocally support forestry and the conservation movement.

Pinchot worked so steadily and at such breakneck speed in his crusade for forestry, for conservation, and for Roosevelt that at one period he showed signs of exhaustion. Senator Beveridge was worried enough to write Roosevelt suggesting that the latter urge Pinchot to take a relaxing canoe trip with the Senator.[19] But Pinchot was reluctant to ease his pace. A letter to his friend Newell was typical, "I am dictating this . . . at 7:50 in the morning, just because I cannot bear to lie in bed. Also just because I can hardly see over the accumulated papers."[20] Realizing, nevertheless, in the summer of 1906 that he needed a rest "in order to restore the snap and spring which I used to have,"[21] he obtained both change and relaxation by sailing with his mother to Europe on a vacation. Feeling refreshed after his return to the Forest Service at the end of the summer, there was nothing to indicate that he reduced his speed. Sir Horace Plunkett once said that Pinchot could safely do the work of two or three men, but that, for the sake of his health, he should not be allowed to do ten men's work.[22] Indeed, by the time 1908 arrived, if there was any change in his pace it was in the direction of increased acceleration. This was the year of the White House Conference on the Conservation of Natural Resources and of the establishment of the National Conservation Commission—both projects requiring a great deal of work by Pinchot.

Pinchot at the same time tried to crowd as much accomplishment as possible into the remaining months of Roosevelt's Administration. He was enough of a realist to know that the next President, no matter who he turned out to be, probably would not supply the same vigorous backing that Roosevelt had given. "Undoubtedly, my time will come in the end," he prophetically wrote to Plunkett, "but just now the President's prestige is keeping us on the top of the wave."[23] Aware that the days ahead might not be so bright as the present, he took advantage of every possible moment while the sun was still shining. A notation by Mrs. Pinchot in a letter to her husband indicates how intimately and tirelessly their son was working with the President; Gifford "could not get off this afternoon," she wrote, "as the President wanted him to ride to talk over some things—Every day of late he has had to be at the White House—and he is much pleased with what he has been able to accomplish."[24]

Less than three weeks before the end of Roosevelt's term of office there was held in Washington a kind of small replica of the earlier White House Conference on the Conservation of Natural Resources, called for the purpose of bringing conservation to the attention of a continent rather than just a nation. Roosevelt had sent Pinchot as his personal emissary to the Governor General of Canada and the President of Mexico to invite them to send delegates to a North American Conservation Conference in Washington. Ten delegates (including three members of Roosevelt's "tennis cabinet"—Garfield, Robert Bacon, and Pinchot) met for the better part of a week under the chairmanship of Pinchot. Although attending a smaller and far less spectacular meeting, the delegates received much the same treatment that had been given to the governors. Roosevelt spoke at their first assembly in the White House. Later meetings were held both in the State Department and in Pinchot's home.[25] The President, the Secretary of State, and Pinchot all entertained the delegates at various times. The "Declaration of Principles" which they approved at the end was in general similar to the resolutions adopted by the governors. In both cases the principles enumerated were those that Roosevelt and Pinchot and other leaders of the conservation movement had been incessantly preaching. The new twist to the statement was agreement that conservation was a problem broader than the boundaries of one nation, and that it required concerted action.[26]

In the closing paragraph of its Declaration, the Conference expressed its belief that conservation of natural resources should become world-wide in scope, and accordingly proposed that Roosevelt call a world conservation conference. Actually, some of the principal nations had already been approached to determine their reaction toward such a meeting. Late as it was in his term, the President complied with the suggestion by sending invitations to fifty-eight nations to attend a conference in Holland in September. After Roosevelt had left office and about half of the invited countries had accepted, however, the world meeting was called off. Pinchot, bitterly disappointed, never gave up hope of holding such a conference, especially since he later became firmly convinced that conservation of natural resources was a primary means of insuring a permanent peace.

The North American Conservation Conference was merely one factor in making the final month of Roosevelt's term a hectic one for Pinchot. Every minute of the day he was on duty, ready to answer any call from the President. His mother's entry in her diary for February 9, 1909, was illustrative, "G[ifford] out from 8:00 a.m. to 11:00 p.m. Says until March 4 all he has and is is for the Chief and his work."[27] In addition to his work, moreover, he attended a round of social events: one evening, for example, he dined with the Secretary of Agriculture; the next, with the British Ambassador.[28]

In the last days of the Roosevelt Administration the "tennis cabinet" assembled on two different occasions: at Garfield's home the President presented to each member a mock diploma; three days before leaving office, the President, entertaining the group at a luncheon, brought tears to the eyes of some by extolling their loyalty and helpfulness.[29] The record does not show whether Pinchot wept, but there is no question of the feeling of dejection and melancholy which took hold of him as his idol prepared to leave the capital.[30] When this small group decided to present TR with a bronze replica of a mountain animal—Henry L. Stimson called it a puma, and Pinchot described it as a lion[31]—it was Pinchot who collected ten dollars from each man and forwarded the $250 to Stimson, who made the purchase.

Roosevelt, as he prepared to leave, sent warm letters of appreciation to many persons who had helped to carry the burdens of his Administration, but he was especially generous in his praise of Garfield and Pinchot. As he admitted to Pinchot, "There has been a peculiar intimacy between you and Jim and me, because all three of us have worked for the same causes, have dreamed the same dreams, have felt a substantial identity of purpose as regards many of what we three deemed the most vital problems of today."[32]

When Pinchot and Garfield were planning to write a book on the Rooseveltian policies, the President penned a flattering foreword in which he maintained that "No two men have been as closely identified with so many of the policies for which this administration has stood." Pinchot, the President went on to say, "has been in a peculiar sense responsible for all that the administration has done in connection with the conservation of natural resources and the development of a healthy country life. His has been peculiarly the responsibility for what has been accomplished in working for the preservation of the forests, for National aid to irrigation, for striving to secure the utilization of our navigable waters, for the betterment of social conditions in the country."[33] Roosevelt, on second thought, believed the foreword was not suitable for this particular book, and therefore drafted a briefer and more restrained comment. But he sent the authors copies of the more effusive statement because he wanted them to know how he felt. The book, unfortunately, never was completed.[34]

The letter from Roosevelt that Pinchot prized above all others, however, was the one in which the President said he was a better man for having known Pinchot. Writing only two days before he left office, Roosevelt, briefly but impressively, extolled "Dear Gifford" in a series of superlatives. "I have written you about others; I have written you about many public matters; now, just a line about yourself. As long as I live I shall feel for you a mixture of respect and admiration and of affectionate regard. I am a better man for having known you. I feel that to have been with you will make my children better men and women in after life; and I cannot think of a man in the country whose loss would be a more real misfortune to the Nation than yours would be. For seven and a half years we have worked together, and now and then played together—and have been altogether better able to work because we have played; and I owe to you a peculiar debt of obligation for a very large part of the achievement of this administration."[35]

A decade later, only a few weeks after Roosevelt's death, Pinchot expressed a profound veneration for his old Chief. Speaking at a memorial service in Philadelphia, he told his audience that "In Roosevelt above all the men of his time, the promise of the Master was fulfilled—'I came that ye might have life, and that ye might have it more abundantly.' "[36] While a skeptic might assume such a tribute to be merely part of a high-sounding funeral oration, Pinchot in February 1909 might have uttered the same statement with genuine sincerity.

In his engagement book Pinchot had placed a notation that on March third at 10:30 a.m., the day before Taft's inauguration, he was to meet the outgoing President "at the White House to bid him adieu." But adieu was not goodbye, for the next day he spent the entire morning in Roosevelt's office. As noon approached, and Roosevelt left to join Taft in riding to the capitol for the inaugural ceremonies, Pinchot, and the President's secretary, William Loeb, followed in a landau immediately behind the carriage carrying the two Presidents. As soon as the ceremonies were completed, Pinchot and other members of the regular and "tennis cabinets" met on Delaware Avenue to escort Roosevelt to Union Station. It was symbolic that Pinchot, who had started conferring with Roosevelt in Washington even before the latter moved into the White House, was with the Chief until his last minutes in the capital.

The parting was indeed sad for Pinchot. He and Roosevelt had worked well together as a team. Pinchot had proved himself most valuable to the Administration as an innovator of ideas, or at least as a person to carry new ideas to TR. He kept supplying ideas, but they would have been useless without strong and enthusiastic support from a higher level. Roosevelt needed Pinchot, and Pinchot needed Roosevelt; each complemented the other.

The devoted Pinchot was aware of the strong influence which Roosevelt exercised on many facets of his life, but he could scarcely have realized the breadth of this influence and the lasting qualities of the spell which the magnetic Roosevelt had cast over him. It was far more than the use of words and phrases, such as "bully," which he learned from TR. It was more than the frequent and continuing allusions in his speeches to words or actions of the Chief. Time and again, especially while serving as Governor of Pennsylvania, when a particularly puzzling problem came before him for his decision, he asked himself what Roosevelt would have done.

Two of the most lasting and profound effects on Pinchot of his work with Roosevelt were ones which Pinchot himself would undoubtedly have denied at this time, but which, in retrospect, are unmistakable. The first, as has been suggested, was the result of the President's tendency to accept such a large proportion of Pinchot's advice and to support him so unwaveringly. As a kind of unofficial crown prince in the Roosevelt realm, Pinchot was almost spoiled for any future work under a superior who did not have full and implicit faith in his every move.

A second consequence of Pinchot's service under Roosevelt, although it cannot be proved by reference to any spoken or written word, was the planting of a seed in his mind, however tiny it may have been in 1909, that some day he himself might be President. After all, he had been about as close as a man could get to an incumbent of the office without actually living in the White House.

He had wrestled with many of the problems which a President must face, and many of his opinions and decisions on major matters had been accepted by the President as his own. In other words, Pinchot probably was rather well convinced that the presidency was a position not beyond a person with his capabilities. Even if such thoughts were not going through his mind by March 4, 1909, the basic ideas were being stored away, consciously or unconsciously, in the back of his mind, to be brought forth in the future at regular intervals when friends and admirers, even as early as 1910, began whispering in his ear that a forestry expert might be presidential timber.

CHAPTER 7

COLLISION WITH BALLINGER

WILLIAM HOWARD TAFT and Gifford Pinchot had for some years been cordial, although they were not intimate friends. The two men, as members of Roosevelt's Administration, sometimes were thrown in contact with each other, and their governmental and social relations had been pleasant. Pinchot had happy memories of his visit in 1902 with Governor-General Taft in the Philippines. Later, when Taft was back in Washington as Secretary of War, the cabinet member and the bureau chief were on each other's entertainment lists. Pinchot was, for example, one of the invited guests of Mr. and Mrs. Taft to ride in a private train to the Army-Navy football game in 1905.

The closer the time came for Roosevelt to leave the White House, however, the more fearful Pinchot became that the new President would fail to promote conservation policies with the same zeal as did Roosevelt. His concern was understandable. For several years he had devoted a large part of his abundant energy toward nurturing the conservation movement from infancy to young manhood. Although by the end of 1908 it was beginning to receive nationwide acceptance, it was perhaps insufficiently robust to withstand a strong onslaught from the still formidable opposition. It seemed essential to Pinchot, therefore, that it continue to have the most vigorous support from the presidency.

Pinchot reported that Roosevelt, experiencing some of the same sort of anxiety, summoned Taft and Pinchot to the White House one evening shortly after the election of November 1908, and received assurances from the President-to-be that he would vigorously support conservation.[1] But Pinchot's apprehensiveness made him especially alert to evidences of backsliding by Taft. He hoped for the best but feared the worst.

Only a month after the election an incident occurred that did nothing to allay Pinchot's suspicions. As chairman of the National Conservation Commission, Pinchot had persuaded Taft to act as chairman of the Joint Conservation Conference held in Washington. As soon as the Conference was called to order and an invocation pronounced, Pinchot spoke for a minute or two on the general subject of conservation and then introduced Taft who in turn was to introduce Roosevelt. "I have the honor," said Pinchot, "to present to you your chairman, the President-elect."

Taft, in an apparent spirit of fun, wished to make the point that technically he could not yet be referred to as President-elect since the members of the electoral college had not yet met. "Mr. President, ladies and gentlemen, there is one difficulty about the conservation of natural resources. It is that the imagination of those who are pressing it may outrun the practical facts. I have been introduced as the President-elect. I am not the President-elect, except in the imagination of Mr. Pinchot. But it gives me great pleasure, as an unofficial person, to present the President of the United States."[2]

To Pinchot this was no joke. It represented, instead, a kind of scorn for conservation, and was a portent of a dark future for the persons behind the movement. To add to Pinchot's consternation, Taft chose not to use the speech which Pinchot had helped to prepare. Pinchot had become accustomed to hearing his words and phrases included in innumerable speeches delivered by Roosevelt, but Taft was starting in a different manner. "I had some notes that I was going to read," he chuckled, "but the truth is they contained so many expert statements that I am afraid you might suspect their authorship, and so if you will excuse me . . . I shall content myself only with the statement of my deep sympathy with this movement and with my purpose . . . to do everything I can to carry on the work so admirably begun and so wonderfully shown forth by President Roosevelt."[3] Taft, upon the conclusion of his brief extemporaneous remarks, once more, with an obvious reference to Pinchot, brought in a light touch, "Ladies and gentlemen, if the real power behind the throne consents, I declare this meeting adjourned."

Taft's remarks were probably innocent enough. But they seemed to represent at least a different state of mind about conservation than had been demonstrated by Roosevelt, Pinchot, and other zealous fighters for the movement. To Pinchot, conservation was deadly serious business; joking about it was out of place. A neutral observer at the Conference might have come away with the mild impression that Taft, although a backer of conservation, was hardly as dedicated a supporter as was Roosevelt. But Pinchot was not a neutral. This demonstration by the next President was to him a matter for intense worry.

Although Pinchot had his suspicions, all was not black. For one thing, he himself was to continue under Taft as head of the Forest Service; and James Wilson, who as Secretary of Agriculture had allowed Pinchot wide freedom, also was slated to retain his post. Pinchot was highly pleased, moreover, that his trusted and true friend in conservation, James Garfield, was to remain in the key position of Secretary of the Interior. Or, so Pinchot believed. Roosevelt, indeed, had asked Taft to retain Garfield, and was under the impression he had Taft's assurance that this would be done. So certain was Garfield of continuing in office that a few months before the end of Roosevelt's term he renewed the lease on his Washington home. It came as a shock, therefore, to Roosevelt, Garfield, and Pinchot when late in January Taft informed Garfield that he would not be a member of the new cabinet.

No one knows exactly why Taft chose to drop Garfield, but many of the various explanations boil down to a general feeling on the part of Taft that Roosevelt's Secretary of the Interior was a bit overzealous in his support of conservation and was inclined to stretch the exact letter of the law on occasion in order to protect what Garfield felt was the public interest. Garfield, in other words, had the same conception as Roosevelt and Pinchot of the duty of an executive to take such steps to benefit society as were not prohibited by action of Congress. To Taft, this was unjustifiable. In addition, he was painfully sensitive to the opposition in the country, especially in the West, to the conservation movement. He was, moreover, subject to extensive pressure to increase the representation in his cabinet from areas outside the East.

Regardless of the precise reasons for Taft's decision to drop Garfield, Pinchot's suspicions were further heightened. Now it was clear that of the triumvirate of Roosevelt, Garfield, and Pinchot, who had seen alike on so many conservation matters, soon only Pinchot would remain to protect the conservation movement. At this point, according to Pinchot, "Taft's betrayal was a constant topic of conversation between TR and his intimate advisers."[4] With Garfield slated to leave the government on March 4, the "intimate advisers" began to take steps to batten down the hatches and to lash all movable objects to the deck in order to assure as little disturbance as possible when the anticipated storm broke.

The most important and the most spectacular action to protect conservation from assault was the "withdrawal from entry" of sites along rivers in the public domain which might some day be used for the development of electric power. Pinchot had become impressed with the danger that such sites might, as the result of trickery, pass from public into private hands. Under existing laws, private persons were unable to obtain possession of land in the national forests for the purpose of developing power, but they were permitted to buy land for mining or for quarrying stone. Unless something was done to protect the power sites, Pinchot feared they would wind up in the possession of power companies who then, when they were ready, could develop electricity free of the restrictions that the Forest Service placed on them when it leased land for fifty-year periods.

Pinchot met the problem by directing his men in the field to recommend for withdrawal—as "administrative sites" for ranger stations—one piece of land in each potential power site in the national forests. A ranger station was a tract of from 100 to 200 acres of land which was set aside for the headquarters of a forest ranger, where he could have a home and plenty of land for pasturing his horses. It was pure pretext that more than a very few of these withdrawals were to be used as ranger stations. Instead, it was hoped that each withdrawal, taken from the center of a potential power site, would give the government a key area by means of which it could maintain some control over the development of the site. The actual withdrawals were made by Secretary of the Interior Garfield. Both Secretary of Agriculture Wilson and President Roosevelt also knew what was being done, and gave their approval to the procedure.[5]

At the time these withdrawals were made, all parties concerned were aware that they might not hold. The Administration supposed, however, that this was the only procedure it could use to try to protect the sites. But further study by lawyers revealed two other possible justifications for withdrawals. The first was a law passed by Congress in 1902 authorizing the setting aside of water power sites for future use in connection with reclamation projects of the federal government. The second sprang from the Rooseveltian philosophy that an executive often was duty bound, if not specifically prohibited by the Constitution or by a law, to take positive steps for the public good. Thus Secretary Garfield reasoned that the President, and in turn the Secretary of the Interior, had a "stewardship duty" to protect the public resources. Citing an impressive list of court decisions, the Secretary maintained that under the "supervisory power of the executive" he could withdraw lands from entry to make certain they would not be acquired wrongfully, and to give Congress time to pass protective laws.[6]

During the last two or three months of the Roosevelt Administration, therefore, there was a mad scramble to place under protection as many power sites as a handful of dedicated government officials could process in the short time available. Pinchot later said that in the final two months he put in the hardest work of his whole life in an effort to leave no loose ends that could be untied by the incoming Administration. Since the available figures are inconsistent, no one knows exactly how many acres of potential power sites— both within and without the national forests—were withheld from disposal to private persons. In the helter-skelter of the closing weeks, it was of course impossible to lay out precise boundary lines for the withdrawn sites. In some instances, all of the land within about a mile of each side of a river was included in a site; the understanding was that the size of the withdrawn areas could be reduced by restorations to entry as soon as data for more accurate locations of boundaries became available. Between December 4, 1908 and inauguration day on March 4, 1909, upwards of 4 million acres containing immensely valuable water power sites were withdrawn under either the reclamation law or the supervisory power. Some of them were withdrawn as late as March 2, less than forty-eight hours before Taft took over. Once again it should be emphasized that these withdrawals were made by Garfield and Pinchot with the full knowledge and concurrence of President Roosevelt.

Some of the withdrawals occurred when Garfield and his friends still thought that Taft would retain him as Secretary of the Interior. Not until late in January, when it became known that Garfield would be dropped, did the speed of withdrawal change from a walk to a frantic race. Pinchot's conviction of the necessity for haste was further increased when it was announced that Richard A. Ballinger was Taft's choice to replace Garfield.

Ballinger had acquired a favorable reputation in the northwestern part of the country as a judge and especially as a reform mayor of the city of Seattle. Chairman of the delegates from the state of Washington to the Republican national convention of 1908, his name had often been associated with good government. When Garfield early in 1907 became Secretary of the Interior, he recommended Ballinger, whom he had known while they were students at Williams College, as commissioner of the General Land Office. Roosevelt made the appointment. Ballinger accepted with reluctance, partly because of the financial sacrifice he would have to make. Considered to be a good administrator, he ran his bureau with dispatch. After serving as commissioner from March 1907 to March 1908, he resigned to go back to his law practice in Seattle. Roosevelt wrote kind words to him about the way he ran his agency.[7]

Pinchot, as a bureau chief in another department, whose duties brought him in contact with the commissioner of the General Land Office, did not become an admirer of Ballinger. Almost immediately a difference of opinion developed between the two men over the proper method for the disposal of public coal lands. This matter came before the Public Lands Commission, composed of Pinchot and Newell under the chairmanship of the commissioner of the General Land Office. Newell and Pinchot favored leasing public coal lands to private developers whereas Ballinger preferred outright sale. Rather than issue a divided report, Newell and Pinchot regretfully concluded that the better strategy was to produce no report at all.

Another brush with Ballinger over the creation of a national forest in Alaska did not raise Pinchot's estimate of the sincerity of Ballinger's interest in conservation. When Pinchot prepared a suggested proclamation to be signed by the President for establishing the Chugach National Forest, Ballinger in a letter to Secretary Garfield protested the action.[8] Pinchot eventually got his forest, but he continued to entertain at least a mild resentment toward this man. Indeed, when Pinchot learned Taft was not keeping Garfield he told a friend he "could not work with" Ballinger as he had with Garfield. "Jim and I think alike concerning the matters in which the Forest Service and the Department of the Interior are closely related. Ballinger and I might clash."[9]

The truth of the matter was that Ballinger's ideas on conservation were poles apart from those of Pinchot. This is not to say that Ballinger could be classed as a clear opponent of conservation. Contrary to some of the rabid members of the opposition in the West, he could see the value of using natural resources carefully and without waste. On some occasions he supported some aspects of conservation in words that might have been used by Roosevelt, or even Pinchot. While Secretary of the Interior, for example, he called to Taft's attention the need for conservation of the petroleum resources of the public lands. Reporting that the "present rate of production of petroleum cannot be maintained beyond a very few years," he urged, and Taft approved, the temporary withdrawal of oil lands until needed legislation could be passed to assure conservation.[10] On another occasion, one of the extremists among the opponents of conservation went so far as to accuse Ballinger of embracing "Pinchotism."[11]

Ballinger was not one of the extremists, but neither could he justifiably be called a conservationist. Like a good many other citizens he was a little scornful of the conservation zealots, and remained closer to the old school of thought which was not yet ready to endorse the growing opinion that conservation was almost a matter of life and death to the nation. Although Pinchot was not aware of it at the time, Ballinger had given to Garfield as a reason for resigning from the General Land Office his lack of sympathy with the public land policies of the Interior Department.[12] As between the forces seeking to develop the West and those working for the preservation of natural resources, his heart was with the former.

Pinchot was far more skeptical of Ballinger than of Taft; for several months he continued to hope that Taft would hold the conservation line and act as a restraining force on the new Secretary of the Interior. Perhaps it was mere whistling in the dark, but a month before Taft took office Pinchot assured a friend that he was "very much pleased" with the election and that it meant "four years of prosperity and progress for forestry and conservation." Although disturbed by some of Ballinger's actions in his first weeks as Secretary, he continued to rely on Taft's help. His feelings were revealed in letters he wrote in April and May to Garfield who had returned to his law practice in Ohio. Keeping the former Secretary informed on developments in Washington, he spoke optimistically of an interview he had with Taft, "I think the corner has been turned, and that the conservation policy is going to be perfectly safe in Taft's hands whenever he himself gets action on it, although there are some disquieting things about [Attorney General] Wickersham's attitude."[13]

At the end of May his letters still reflected confidence in Taft. "I am sure," he wrote to a critic of the President, "that you do injustice to President Taft's sincerity and strength of purpose. His stand has been definitely taken for the defense of the interests of the country in the entire field of conservation, and his official acts have already shown very clearly that he is ready to maintain this stand vigorously. I hope that you will at least suspend judgment."[14] Pinchot at this time seemed to be taking his own advice; although his doubts continued to linger, he still welcomed reassuring signs. This comment to his mother in the middle of June was part confidence and part hope: "Taft is getting more and more committed to conservation. He will simply have to stick now."[15]

Pinchot never did believe that Taft himself was actively opposed to conservation, but he came to hold the opinion that the President was not the kind of person to stand up in its defense against the "villains" who sought to throttle it. And, more especially, he became thoroughly convinced that Ballinger was the foremost of the villains. The new Secretary of the Interior had been in office exactly eight months when, as will be seen, Pinchot told Taft that Ballinger was "the most effective opponent the conservation policies have yet had."[16]

What had Ballinger done to induce Pinchot to make so strong

a statement concerning a member of the President's top official family? First in order of time was the Secretary's action with respect to the water power sites which had been withdrawn in the waning moments of the Roosevelt Administration. Ballinger had scarcely entered the door of his new office when protests concerning these withdrawals began to reach him. Within about two weeks after the inauguration he was writing to Senator Heyburn, who had complained about withdrawals in Idaho, that he hoped to be able, with the help of the Attorney General, "in a short time to dispose of this question."[17] The "short time" was only ten days; March 30, 1909, Ballinger signed the first paper leading toward the restoration to entry of the withdrawn Idaho lands.[18] To Ballinger, the danger, at least in the near future, of a power monopoly was nonsense. Equally important was his belief that when Congress by law opened public lands to entry for any purpose, such as homesteading or mining, there existed no power in the President or the Secretary of the Interior to protect any part of this land by withdrawing it until Congress could act. The supervisory power, therefore, also was a form of nonsense.

By the middle of April, Ballinger had approved the restoration of most of the power sites that Garfield had withdrawn. On March 17 the Secretary told Arthur P. Davis, chief engineer of the Reclamation Service, that the withdrawals were illegal unless the sites were specifically needed for reclamation projects. Ballinger therefore issued what was tantamount to an order directing the Reclamation Service to recommend to him the restoration of a number of power sites.[19] Both Davis and the director of the Service, Pinchot's friend Newell, protested but to no avail. On paper, the restorations were made at the suggestion of the Reclamation Service, whereas in reality its officers were firmly opposed to this action.

Pinchot was so shocked by the overthrow of Garfield's handiwork that he rushed to the President and in two interviews, on April 19 and 20, protested as vigorously as he knew how. Taft, however, concurred in Ballinger's recommendation for the restorations.[20] The President, trained in the law, was literally unable to go along with the Rooseveltian opinion that the Chief Executive had the power to take action for the public welfare—provided it was not specifically prohibited by an act of Congress. Taft's conception of his office was rather that a President needed specific authority for any action which he might take.

Pinchot's representations, however, apparently brought some results. Within a few days Taft saw Ballinger, and on April 23 there began a reversal of policy under which the power sites were once more withdrawn. On this occasion, with more time to perform the operation than in the hectic days at the end of the Roosevelt Administration, and with more geographical information available, the boundary lines of the protected sites were more carefully prescribed, and less unneeded land was included within them. Although Ballinger some months later tried to give the impression that he had planned the rewithdrawals from the very beginning,[21] the evidence seems to indicate otherwise. As the sites were once again put into safekeeping, Ballinger found himself in the awkward position of taking the kind of action which he had been charging was illegal. Pinchot, naturally, was highly pleased with the turn of events, and, as has already been noted, gained renewed faith in Taft's good intentions. He was still troubled, however, by what seemed to him a kind of vacillation on Taft's part. Did the incident show that the President might tend to side with the person with whom he last talked?

Another point of dispute between Pinchot and Ballinger came to a head only a few weeks after the latter assumed his cabinet post— approval of withdrawals of land (both inside and immediately outside of national forests) to be used for ranger stations. Normally a routine procedure, it has already been seen that during the last days of the Roosevelt Administration a good many sites had been withdrawn ostensibly to be used for ranger stations, but in reality to protect power sites from falling into the hands of monopolists. It was still true, however, that the Forest Service now and then needed to create additional bona fide ranger stations. Shortly after Ballinger came to office, a routine request came across his desk from the Secretary of Agriculture asking for withdrawal of an area two miles square for the location of a station within a national forest. Refusing the withdrawal, he reasoned that such action would be contrary to the act of Congress which permitted mining entries in the national forests. He also disallowed other requests for stations just outside some of the national forests because, he felt, they would in effect increase the size of the national forests in states where Congress had specified that such forests were to grow no larger. Moreover, even in cases where the law might permit a legitimate withdrawal for a ranger site, Ballinger asked that the Secretary of Agriculture support his requests by a statement showing clearly why the location was needed. Ballinger intended to see that there were no more withdrawals by pretext. Pinchot was not accustomed to such frustrations.

Ballinger increased Pinchot's ire and distrust by still another reversal of procedures established under Roosevelt and Garfield. Once again there was room for a difference of opinion on the exact meaning of the law. A strong conservationist could with justification interpret it to permit certain activities; a cool or lukewarm conservationist could—also with justification—find a different meaning. This time the controversy involved a cooperative agreement that had been worked out in 1908 between the Secretaries of Agriculture and the Interior. By its terms trained experts of the Forest Service (in the Department of Agriculture) were used to care for the forests on Indian reservations administered by the Office of Indian Affairs (in the Department of the Interior). Pinchot was convinced that the arrangement assured better forest care and the avoidance of wasteful duplication. Over his protest, however, Ballinger, concluding that the plan was illegal, abrogated the agreement.

Pinchot had other complaints against Ballinger, only one of which will be mentioned here. Ballinger apparently lacked confidence in F. H. Newell, the director of the Reclamation Service; this organization, somewhat like the Forest Service, stood as one of the symbols of Roosevelt and the conservation movement. Its fundamental activity was to build dams and provide irrigation for the reclaiming of otherwise arid land. It was this same Newell who, back in 1901, went with Pinchot to talk conservation with Roosevelt even before the new President had moved into the White House. He and Pinchot had worked together on commissions, had planned together as government bureau directors, and had spent long and happy hours together in the woods. Pinchot, holding much the same warm affection for Newell that he had for Garfield, sincerely believed that Newell was "without exception the best Bureau Chief in Washington."[22] Even before Ballinger arrived in Washington to become Secretary, there were rumors he would get rid of Newell. In his dealings with the Reclamation Service, he sometimes ignored the director completely. The uncertainty of his position brought Newell to the verge of a nervous breakdown.[23] Word got around, for example, that a Seattle friend of Ballinger's was slated for the post.[24] Ballinger later denied he had decided on this move, but he apparently was giving it serious consideration.

Ballinger, furthermore, opposed a financial scheme which had been worked out for the Reclamation Service under Secretary Garfield. Under the law, the users of water supplied by the Service had to pay for the benefits in annual installments. Without specific authorization by Congress, the Interior Department had issued due bills, sometimes called "Garfield currency,"[25] to water users for work which they had performed on the reclamation projects; these certificates could be used by the customers in lieu of cash to pay their annual charges.[26] When Ballinger inquired of Attorney General Wickersham concerning the legality of this arrangement, he received an opinion that it was illegal. Pinchot, maintaining that no one had complained about this procedure, was unable to see why the question had to be raised—unless the Secretary was determined to do all he could to block conservation.

On the very day that the *Washington Post* carried the story of the likelihood of the dismissal of Newell, Pinchot went to President Taft to plead his friend's cause. He had many grievances against Ballinger. Just how forcefully Pinchot presented his point of view to the President it is impossible to say; but it was not his temperament to soft pedal a complaint. Taft apparently was cordial, but there are indications that he was becoming impatient with his zealous Forester. The President may have felt that Pinchot, who after all was subordinate to a cabinet officer, was making too many visits directly to the chief executive; Taft once complained that when he served as Secretary of War under Roosevelt, TR had been too much inclined to deal with underlings rather than to work through the chain of command.[27] The new President, moreover, was increasingly aware of a difference of opinion between himself and Pinchot concerning the powers of administrators. Had Pinchot seen the letter that Taft wrote around this time to his brother, Horace Taft, he might have had more reservations about the usefulness of his visits to the President, "I do regard Gifford as a good deal of a radical and a good deal of a crank, but I am glad to have him in the government."[28] Pinchot obviously was not getting the same sympathetic hearing from Taft that he had from TR. Pinchot also did what he could at this time to muster friends of the Service and of conservation to write Ballinger in support of the retention of his friend.

By the middle of July, Pinchot was troubled by the general situation. "Things do not look very good to me either," he confided to a friend. But he was not laying the blame at Taft's doorstep. "The difficulty seems to be not Taft himself, who responds beautifully whenever direct appeal is made to him for any of the policies you and I stand for, but more particularly with Ballinger and some of the others in the Cabinet, who seem not only opposed to them, but seem to be actively trying to do them up."[29] At the same time, as was characteristic, he managed to combine some optimism with pessimism, "Personally, I am feeling more hopeful as time goes on," he revealed to another friend. Although convinced that Ballinger was doing "his best" to "turn over the Government lands to the power trust," Pinchot tartly expressed his happiness that "so far, his success has been no greater than the mind which inspired the attack."[30]

Pinchot's feelings at this time were bared in a talk he had with George Otis Smith, director of the U.S. Geological Survey, a unit within the Department of the Interior. Although Smith had been recruited by Roosevelt on the recommendation of both Garfield and Pinchot, the strong loyalty he was showing to Ballinger was judged by Pinchot to be a repudiation of Garfield. Late in July, when Smith innocently went to the Forest Service on business, Pinchot called him into his private office and gave him an unmerciful tongue-lashing. Pinchot was not provoked to anger either easily or regularly. On infrequent occasions, however, especially when an irritation continued over a period of time, he would go into a fiery rage. Pinchot made it perfectly clear to Smith that he believed him a traitor to Garfield and to conservation.[31] In the midst of his anger he referred to Ballinger as a "yellow dog," an evaluation which was frequently quoted in later hearings by a congressional investigating committee. It was an expression that Pinchot used on several occasions to describe men of whom he was not fond; in his own mind it did not have the extremely harsh ring that it produced in the ears of the average person.

Pinchot once more turned part of his attention to the manipulation of public opinion. With Roosevelt and his energetic support gone from the scene, and the opposition, as Pinchot saw it, circling for the kill, he sensed a pressing need for the creation of an organization of public-spirited citizens to help wage a defensive war for conservation. Although the word "pressure group" had not yet been coined, Pinchot envisioned the kind of an organization to which that label came to apply. A few days before Taft came to the presidency Pinchot had written to Walter L. Fisher, an ardent conservationist (later appointed Secretary of the Interior to succeed Ballinger), describing his dream of an organization to serve in an educational capacity by putting conservation "before the people."[32] Although there already existed a loosely organized Conservation League of America (of which Taft was honorary vice-president), Pinchot saw the need for a stronger society. It should be able, he guessed, to attract 50,000 to 100,000 members.

Pinchot reached high to find a president for his new group which he called the National Conservation Association. Charles W. Eliot, outgoing president of Harvard University, a sincere sympathizer with the general movement, consented to serve as president. The executive committee included Garfield, and Henry L. Stimson (a future Secretary of State as well as of War) was on the board. Pinchot had a sense of accomplishment when his hand-picked executive board, including of course himself, held its first meeting late in July in Cambridge, Massachusetts. No one in the room would have guessed that within a few months president Eliot would move up to the post of honorary president to make room for Pinchot, then out of a job.

CHAPTER 8

THE GLAVIS STORY

GIFFORD PINCHOT'S bill of particulars against Ballinger was of sufficient length to leave no doubt in his mind that the Secretary of the
Interior was dragging his feet with respect to conservation. But on
July 16, 1909, began a chain of events which would convince Pinchot
that the Secretary and his Department of the Interior were even
willing to wink at fraud.

On that date, Louis R. Glavis, an obscure, young employee of the
General Land Office field service in the Far West, sent a wire and
a letter to the Forest Service in Washington, D.C., asking its assistance in obtaining a postponement of Land Office hearings scheduled
to begin on charges of an allegedly fraudulent attempt to seize government coal lands in Alaska. Since most of the disputed land, called
the Cunningham claims, was located in a national forest, Glavis, who
had been desperately trying to get his own Interior Department to
order the delay, felt justified in calling for help from the Forest Service. Explaining that the property involved was worth "millions,"
and that the Guggenheim and Morgan interests were trying to obtain
monopolistic control of the entire area, he urged that further time
was needed before the government could present its best case.[1]

A charge of this kind was more than enough to arouse the Forest
Service. For a number of years there had been marked jealousies
and disagreements between some members of the staff of the General
Land Office and of the Forest Service. The Forest Service group
was convinced that government land slipped too easily through the
fingers of the General Land Office. As a result of the mounting
bitterness between Ballinger and Pinchot, these feelings had intensified, and the country in general had become increasingly aware
of this fact. Newspaper headlines were referring to a quarrel. Only
a few days before the Glavis wire was sent, the Secretary of the
Interior had sputtered to a newspaperman that "The department
of the interior has charge of all public lands and does not intend

that the forestry bureau, a part of another department, shall run the department of the interior."[2]

A. C. Shaw, a legal officer in the Forest Service, quickly went into action after receipt of Glavis's request for help. After consulting with associate forester Price (Pinchot was out of the city) and the Portland, Oregon office of the Service, and going over the Cunningham files in the General Land Office, he recommended that Secretary of Agriculture Wilson request a delay of the hearing. This request had already been made and granted by the time Pinchot returned to Washington. If Shaw had any doubts concerning the wisdom of his request for the delay—and there is no evidence that he did—he must have felt vindicated when he received another wire from Glavis, "Have damaging and conclusive evidence showing official misconduct of parties."[3] When Shaw asked for names, Glavis replied that "Secretary [Ballinger] and Commissioner [Dennett] are parties referred to."[4]

Pinchot did not know Glavis well, although he had met him twice during the past half dozen years. But when he saw Glavis's correspondence, he became extremely excited. Perhaps there was something here, he thought, that could be used to show the Department of the Interior in its true light—pronounced lack of sympathy for conservation.

Both Pinchot and Ballinger were scheduled to speak before the National Irrigation Congress opening on August 9 in Spokane. Immediately before heading for the West, Pinchot conferred with Garfield at the latter's Ohio home. Although there is no record of their conversation, Pinchot was in an optimistic frame of mind. Confidently and almost jubilantly he wrote to his mother from Ohio, "It looks to me as though the time is not far distant when B. and I can't both stay in the Taft Administration. And as B. comes in the alphabet before P., and age before beauty, I think there is no reason why we should advertise 1615 [the street number of his home] for sale yet awhile. I am much pleased with the situation."[5]

The air was tense in Spokane on August 9, for the delegates were now aware of the Ballinger-Pinchot feud. Only a few hours after Pinchot arrived, Glavis called on him. Pinchot later asserted he had not expected the call, but he was "mighty glad" to find the young accuser in town.[6] During the Garfield administration of the Interior Department, Pinchot had heard casual references to the Cunningham claims, but Glavis's communications to the Forest Service had whetted his appetite for more information. Moreover, Pinchot had learned through his friend George Woodruff of a rumor that Ballinger was an attorney for the Cunningham interests. Glavis showed him the documents he had accumulated, and explained the inferences which he drew from them. Pinchot, impressed with what he saw, obtained the permission of Glavis to share the material with his friend George C. Pardee, former Governor of California, who was in Spokane to attend the convention. To Pinchot, and to Pardee too, the Glavis papers served to confirm their worst suspicions concerning Ballinger.

A further bit of disquieting and perhaps useful information reached Pinchot and Pardee through a newspaper reporter who confided that during the brief period between the time that Ballinger restored Garfield's power sites to entry and the time that he withdrew them again, 15,800 acres of valuable sites had been snatched up by private power interests.

Pinchot's speech the next day before the Irrigation Congress was limited to ten minutes. Although making no direct attack on Ballinger, his implications were clear. Without mentioning names, he criticized those who insisted on strict construction of the laws; such interpretation, he maintained, "necessarily favors the great interests as against the people. . . . The great oppressive trusts exist because of subservient lawmakers and adroit legal constructions." His key point came in a sentence over which he had labored with great precision and care, "An institution or a law is a means, not an end, a means to be used for the public good, to be modified for the public good, and to be interpreted for the public good." And, he added, "The people, not the law, should have the benefit of every doubt."[7]

This explosive speech could easily be considered an attack on Taft. But Pinchot did not mean it that way, and most people believed it to be directed toward Secretary Ballinger. To avoid any misunderstanding on this matter, Pinchot wired the *New York Times* that no reflection of any kind was intended on the President.[8] Some persons, including Woodruff, were disturbed by the specific words that

Pinchot used to expound his theme. Woodruff's philosophy concerning the law had helped to influence both Roosevelt and Pinchot to take the position that the executive is bound to do what he can for the general welfare in the absence of specific prohibitions. But he feared that Pinchot's remarks might be interpreted to mean that the law be ignored if it interfered with something an administrative officer believed was best. He therefore urged Pinchot in the future to stress his desire to keep within the law. The point to emphasize, advised Woodruff, was that sometimes there can be two reasonable constructions of a law, in which case the administrator should take the one which is best for the people.[9]

But if Woodruff and others had reservations concerning the speech, the audience at the National Irrigation Congress displayed none. A Spokane newspaper reported that the 2,000 delegates, when Pinchot had finished, stood up to cheer and wave their hats in enthusiasm.[10] The happy speaker was deeply impressed. "Never in my life have I had such a reception as the Irrigation Congress gave me," he wrote to his mother.[11]

Pinchot was fully aware that some people were predicting he would be forced out of the Taft Administration. This type of headline from the *New York Times* of August 12 was not uncommon, "Pinchot in Danger of Losing His Place." His continued references to the matter in letters to his mother showed he was not ignoring such a possibility—"Even if Taft were disposed to remove me, which I am satisfied he is not, I doubt if he could do so after that [Spokane] speech." But equally important was what seemed to be another effect of the speech, "Without fully intending to do so, I think I have probably forced Taft to take his stand openly for or against the Roosevelt policies in act as well as in word."[12]

When on the day following Pinchot's speech Ballinger rose to address the same group, the audience was hushed in anticipation of a dramatic scene. Ballinger, like Pinchot, however, did not choose to involve himself in a personal conflict. Reading a prepared speech he pledged to do everything possible within the law to protect the public domain. The melodrama did not begin until Ballinger had finished his address and left the hall. George C. Pardee, former Governor of California, who followed Ballinger, discarded his manuscript and instead launched into an attack on the Secretary for his conservation policies. Pinchot always stoutly insisted he had no part in planning or preparing Pardee's remarks, but the outburst was sweet music to his ears. A generation later he was still chuckling over what took place. "Did you give Ballinger what Paddy gave the drum?" he reminisced to Pardee in 1938. "I'll say you did! Them was the happy days!"[13]

The total effect of the National Irrigation Congress was to intensify further the struggle between the opposing forces. As one New York paper suggested, "The situation presents a tangle which apparently will require all Mr. Taft's skill as a peacemaker to straighten out."[14]

The Spokane conference, by the demonstrations of its delegates and the resolutions which it adopted (Pardee was chairman of the committee on resolutions), showed strong sympathy with Pinchot's point of view. But sizable opposition still remained. Only a few weeks before the meeting a major Oregon newspaper had editorialized that the Pinchot policies were "all wrong." Much of its reasoning followed a common pattern, "That there should be a radical difference of opinion between Mr. Pinchot and Secretary Ballinger is not surprising when the character of the two men is considered." Pinchot, the editor argued, was "a very wealthy man who has made a hobby of forest preservation," but with "little personal experience in the practical side" of the question. Ballinger, on the other hand, was "a poor man who has spent the greater part of his life on the frontier with other poor men who were endeavoring to wrest from nature the means of livelihood. To him the vast forests of the West, many of them having reached maturity and being ready to decay and thus become a total loss, represented cold hard cash that was needed" by the settlers. These settlers, the editorial continued, needed the land occupied by the forests in order to grow "apples, pears, potatoes and other products, vastly more useful and profitable than the growing of pine cones." This newspaper, in common with much of the opposition, relied basically on an appeal to regional loyalties. "The difference between Mr. Pinchot and Secretary Ballinger is the difference between the rich and finished East and the poor and struggling West."[15]

The highly involved story of suspicion and frustration which follows had been pieced together by Glavis and was presented by him to Pinchot on August 9 in Spokane, just before the meetings of the National Irrigation Congress. In essence, Glavis had become convinced that Ballinger, during his short term as head of the General Land Office under Garfield in the Roosevelt Administration and later as Secretary of the Interior under Taft, had taken steps to permit allegedly valuable coal lands in Alaska to go from government into private ownership without properly protecting the interests of the people of the United States.

Congress in 1904 had charted the steps by which private individuals could obtain public coal lands. A simplified description of the exceedingly intricate procedure will suffice. First, the prospective owner had to stake out a claim or make a location, and open up a mine. Within three years, he was required to apply for a patent and to make a payment to the government of $10 an acre. Assuming the law had been fully complied with, the purchaser, or entryman as he was called, would receive a certificate of entry after at least 60 days from the time of payment. He did not obtain full title to the land, however, until he received the patent. During the period prior to the issuance of the patent, the Department of the Interior, in case it detected fraud, might cancel the entry. If the claim was found to be valid, it was "clear listed" from one division to another division within the General Land Office, which finally issued the patent.

From the point of view of getting any coal mined in Alaska, the law was defective. By its terms an individual could not acquire more than 160 acres. While a piece of land of this size was adequate for a farm, it simply was not large enough for profitable development of a coal mine, especially in distant Alaska. In accordance with the spirit of the law, however, an entryman when he applied for a patent was required to swear that his entry was made in good faith "for my own benefit, and not directly or indirectly, in whole or in part, in behalf of any person or persons whomsoever." This regulation absolutely prohibited purchasers from entering into any agreement, prior to their formal application for patent, by which they could combine to operate a mine.

The best information obtainable at the time indicated that huge deposits of rich coal were available in Alaska. Since existing law made it most difficult if not impossible to develop the area commercially, it probably was to be expected that some entrymen would attempt to defeat the law. One of the most obvious possibilities for circumventing the regulations was a tacit understanding, among men who staked out adjoining claims, that after patents were issued they would work the claims together for the benefit of all. If such an agreement was made before patents, it was illegal; if after patents, it was permissible. Clearly, it was a difficult provision to enforce.

Glavis's principal concern was with a group of 33 locations called the Cunningham claims, which had been staked out together at the headwaters of the Bering River. Clarence Cunningham, an Idaho prospector and miner, had located all of the 160-acre parcels, one for himself and one for each of 32 other individuals. It was perfectly legal for one man to lay out the claims for all. Most of the members of the Cunningham group lived in the states of Washington and Oregon. Three were residents of Ballinger's home town of Seattle. Several were men of considerable influence, including Miles C. Moore, a former Governor of Washington.

By the end of 1906, when Roosevelt withdrew Alaskan coal lands from further entry, some 900 claims had been staked out. When Ballinger took charge of the General Land Office in March 1907, not a single claim had been carried to the point where a certificate of entry was issued. At about this time, however, the members of the Cunningham group paid the fee of $10 an acre for their parcels. In due course the Juneau, Alaska, branch of the General Land Office issued certificates of entry for all thirty-three claims. All that remained before the Cunningham group obtained full possession of the land was the clear listing and issuance of the patents.

Meanwhile, fragments of information were coming to the General Land Office in Washington, D.C., indicating possible fraudulent practices in obtaining Alaskan coal lands. In June, Fred Dennett, Ballinger's assistant, consequently directed special agent Horace T. Jones to make a "thorough, complete, and energetic investigation" of the validity of Alaskan coal claims.[16] Jones proceeded as instructed, but when he saw Ballinger in Seattle his mission was narrowed. Ballinger, explaining that he proposed to go before a congressional committee to urge amendment of the Alaskan coal laws, directed Jones to confine his investigation to a few sample cases in each group of claims. By speeding up the process, Ballinger asserted, he hoped to have supporting information available in time for use before the committee; he also assigned another special agent, H. K. Love, to join Jones in the investigation.

Since the scope of the inquiry was reduced, Jones was able to make a limited report in August. Statements which he and Love had obtained from some claimants, he felt, created more than a little suspicion that the law had been flaunted. He recommended, therefore, that "a strict investigation be further made" of each and every locator's connection with other locators.[17] In a second letter to Ballinger, Jones reported rumors about monopoly, "From the talk of attorneys and individuals interested in the Alaskan coal lands, I feel that the disposal of the lands all tends toward one direction, and that is the Guggenheim Companies." And once again he reiterated his recommendation that "these entries be carefully investigated by an experienced and fearless agent."[18]

Love, the second investigator, had looked into the Cunningham claims prior to this new investigation and had recommended that certificates of entry be issued to the members. He now reported how Cunningham had told him that "it had always been the hope" of the members of the group that arrangements might be made "after entry" for the joint working of the lands. It was Love's opinion that the "hope" for a company, prior to the application for patent, did not constitute an invalid agreement. But he "deem[ed] it proper" to lay the information before Ballinger.[19]

The rumors reported by Jones that the Alaskan coal lands were on their way to the Guggenheims were based on some substance. Only a year or two before, the firm of J. P. Morgan and Co. and the Guggenheims had formed the Alaska Syndicate. Gradually, by highly intricate financial arrangements, this partnership extended its holdings in Alaska until by 1910 it controlled copper mines, a steamship company, and a salmon-packing concern. The syndicate also owned a railroad company which was building a line to its copper mines and was considering the construction of a branch line to the coal fields in the vicinity of the Cunningham claims.

At the time Jones was making his investigations in 1907, it was common knowledge that the Morgan-Guggenheim group was heavily involved in Alaskan ventures. He had no way of knowing, however, that only a few days prior to his reports to Washington, representatives of the syndicate and of the Cunningham group had met in Salt Lake City. There the Cunningham representatives signed a proposed option agreement by which the Morgan-Guggenheim group could obtain for $250,000 a half interest in a coal-mining corporation to be organized by the Cunningham claimants. The syndicate was given a period of time to decide whether to accept the proposal. The agreement, obviously, would have been completely meaningless if the Cunningham group did not receive final patents to their claims.

Glavis, the young informer who came to Pinchot in 1909, first entered the story in the summer of 1907. As a special agent of the General Land Office in the Portland area, he was deeply troubled by what Jones told him and by common gossip in the district. Increasingly he became convinced that further inquiry was an absolute necessity. Upon his promotion in October 1907, to the position of chief of the field division in Portland, he felt a growing responsibility for seeing that the laws were faithfully executed. Some interpreters of his actions during the ensuing two years have suggested that he was inspired by a desire for personal advancement and gain. Glavis may have had a little too much of the bloodhound in him, but it is difficult for an objective person, after carefully analyzing the course which he pursued, to conclude other than that he was primarily motivated by a sincere and profound desire to see the public interest protected.

Fearful that government lands were in danger of passing illegally into private hands, Glavis on November 5 wrote to Commissioner Ballinger in Washington, asking that he be authorized to investigate "the Alaska coal-land cases."[20] In support of his request he enclosed a letter from Jones to Ballinger which once more urged the need for further inquiry. Impatient at receiving no reply to his letter, Glavis on November 22 wrote a personal letter to his immediate superior and friend, H. H. Schwartz (later United States senator from Wyoming), chief of the field service in the General Land Office, asking permission to travel to Washington, D.C. Called almost immediately to Washington by telegram, Glavis discussed the Alaskan coal situation with both Schwartz and Commissioner Ballinger. Ballinger without hesitation directed Glavis to conduct an inquiry.

Four days before Glavis arrived at Washington headquarters, Daniel Guggenheim wired Clarence Cunningham formally accepting the option proposal. Having sent an engineer to Alaska to study the land included in the Cunningham claims, the syndicate members had decided it was a good investment. In acknowledging receipt of the telegram, Cunningham undoubtedly expressed the sincere hopes of both parties to the agreement, "I trust that our patents will soon arrive, so we may take up active development."[21]

Shortly after Glavis left Washington, ex-Governor Moore of Washington, one of the Cunningham group, called on Ballinger to try to hurry the patents. In the presence of Moore, Ballinger called in the chief of the field division, Schwartz, to advise on the status of the claims. Schwartz showed Ballinger only the favorable report made by Love. Although he failed to produce any of the correspondence from Jones, Ballinger had knowledge of the contents of the Jones letters.[22] Ballinger and Schwartz, after briefly discussing the Love report, agreed that the claimants were entitled to the land. Ballinger thereupon directed that the claims be clear listed, or in other words passed on to the division that issued the final patents. The date was December 26. Later, when men like Glavis and Pinchot learned of the order, they could see it as nothing other than an unjustified giveaway of valuable public land which, although perhaps in line with the prevailing Christmas spirit, was ordered almost casually and without the careful investigation that it deserved.

Glavis was in the process of making the inquiry ordered by Ballinger. Not until January 7 did the General Land Office get around to informing him that the Cunningham claims were clear listed. Glavis, being away from home, did not receive the letter for two weeks, but, as soon as he read it, quickly sprang into action. "Coal entries mentioned in your letter," he telegraphed, ". . . should not be clear listed."[23] Confirming the wire by a letter, he explained that in view of Love's political aspirations and because of the conclusion reached by Jones, he was recommending that the clear-listing order be revoked pending his own investigation. He hoped, he added, to be able to submit a report on the matter "within a few months."[24] The home office, in accordance with Glavis's request, immediately revoked the clear-listing order. But Dennett, the assistant commissioner, notified Glavis that the vague deadline of "a few months" for the report was "not sufficient." Pointing out that the Cunningham claims had already been considerably delayed, he asked Glavis to complete his investigation promptly.[25]

Meanwhile, Ballinger was preparing to leave the government service and return to his law practice in Seattle. The day before his departure, March 3, 1908, he appeared before a congressional committee to advocate the enactment of a bill drafted by the General Land Office which, among other things, would have removed all question of the validity of the Cunningham claims. Partly because of the opposition of Garfield, the bill failed to pass.

Ballinger's successor as Commissioner of the General Land Office was Fred Dennett, his former assistant, who was a close personal and political friend of Ballinger's. A fellow resident of Seattle, he continued to keep Ballinger informed. In the year which elapsed between Ballinger's resignation from the Land Office and his elevation to Secretary of the Department of the Interior, he kept in touch with Dennett by mail and not infrequently queried or prodded him on matters which some of his friends or clients had pending with the Department of the Interior.

On March 31, 1908, Ballinger, informing Dennett that a representative of the Cunningham group had called on him in Seattle, clarified his position on their claims. "I think that it will be a mistake," he advised, "to continue to hold up the entries in this [Cunningham] field against which no reasonable protest exists, and that it would be good policy to speedily clear up the situation."[26]

The impatience of the Cunningham group to get final title to their land was understandable. A number of months had elapsed since they paid their $52,800 ($10 an acre for the 33 claims of 160 acres each). More than three months had gone by since Mr. Guggenheim had agreed to the terms of the option. They were most eager to proceed without further delay. There followed a long series of efforts by the home office of the General Land Office to get a final report or recommendation from Glavis. Since Dennett received complaints with regularity from the Cunningham purchasers, he pressed Glavis hard. When ex-Governor Moore on March 17 grumbled about the "tedious technicalities" that were holding up their claims, Dennett telegraphed Glavis to "wire quick" the nature of his report and when it would be ready.[27]

Glavis, insisting on March 30 that he could not complete his investigation before May, nevertheless stated that he expected to recommend cancellation of the claims. The basis of this prediction was the discovery, earlier that month, of a journal kept by Mr. Cunningham. Glavis, accompanied by Jones, had called at Cunningham's home in Seattle. Although the two investigators explained they were making inquiry concerning the Cunningham claims, Cunningham had jumped to the conclusion they were there to learn the truth or falsity of a current rumor that the Cunningham group had from the beginning merely served as dummies for the purpose of illegally acquiring coal land for the Guggenheims. Since this rumor had no justification, Cunningham was eager and ready to disprove it. When he produced some of his old records, however, Glavis noticed on the first page of a journal a memorandum of an agreement entered into in 1903 by the Cunningham claimants, which seemed to indicate that the group had drawn the agreement before the time of entry, and therefore in violation of the existing law.[28]

Glavis, on the pretext that he wanted to compare the books with some papers in his hotel room, received Cunningham's permission to take the journal with him. Before seeing Cunningham again that same afternoon, Glavis, without telling Cunningham, had a copy of the journal made. Additional evidence damaging to the claimants was Cunningham's affidavit, taken that same day by Glavis and Jones, in which he strongly denied that his group had served as dummies for the Guggenheims or any other corporation. But at the same time he unwittingly admitted that the members had "always proceeded with [the] end in view" of forming a company to develop the coal fields—which strongly suggested a procedure not in accordance with the law.[29]

As Glavis was further pressed to speed the investigation, he began to wonder why things needed to be done so quickly. A meticulous inquirer, who believed in turning over every possible piece of evidence before being satisfied that his work was done, he was unable to see how one could hurry a thorough investigation. Was there some ulterior motive behind the request for haste? Was it possible that Ballinger and Dennett had some direct or indirect interest in the claims? Or were they merely careless guardians of the public domain? Nor was his troubled mind eased by an order from Dennett on May 2 to drop the Alaska investigation. Glavis protested vigorously, but the home office pleaded a shortage of funds, a position which in retrospect seems to have been justified. Be that as it may, Glavis felt better some five months later when he was directed to resume the inquiry.

Ballinger, meantime, had a number of talks in Seattle with various members of the Cunningham group. It is difficult to determine whether these contacts were merely between friends, or between lawyer and clients. Although ex-Governor Moore, at least, thought of Ballinger at this time as counsel for the Cunningham claimants,[30] Ballinger always insisted he was not actually their lawyer.

On one occasion, however, he clearly served as legal consultant when he helped Cunningham draft another affidavit. Cunningham, seriously embarrassed by his journal and by what he had admitted in the statement given to Glavis and Jones, attempted in the new affidavit to deny that any illegal understanding or agreement had existed. It was later charged that Ballinger acted contrary to the law in serving as counsel for a client who was pressing a claim against his old agency. Although technically not a violation, he did use poor judgment in helping a client to try to obtain a clear-listing order which he [Ballinger] as a government official had recently cancelled. It was as if a lawyer in a controversy should quit the service of one client and enter the service of the opposition.[31] Whatever additional advice or service Ballinger may have supplied to the Cunningham group, he gave on a friendship basis without fee; for the work in drafting the affidavit, however, he accepted $200 or $250. Although this payment may have been, as he maintained, more in the nature of expense money than remuneration for services rendered, it had the earmarks of a modest fee. Ballinger, since he was going East anyway, agreed to deliver personally to Secretary Garfield, in Mentor, Ohio, a copy of the affidavit.

Garfield was not sufficiently impressed with the affidavit to believe that it overbalanced the previous evidence against the Cunningham group. Even Schwartz, the chief of the field service, described it as "ingenious, but not convincing."[32] Although officials of the General Land Office were divided on its validity, the new affidavit was not allowed to prevail. The truth of the matter was, as later events showed, that the doubters were justified in questioning the veracity of Cunningham's statements. In his first affidavit, for example, he swore that "The Guggenheim syndicate . . . is not directly or indirectly interested in the [Cunningham] coal lands and they have never been interested";[33] whereas, as has been seen, Cunningham himself only eight months before had been one of the signers of the Guggenheim option agreement.

Although Glavis received permission in October, 1908, to continue the Alaska investigations, the matter lay idle for several months. He had decided that the next step in the inquiry should be a trip to Alaska to corroborate evidence already accumulated, but such a journey seemed out of the question during the winter.

During this lull in activities, President-elect Taft chose Ballinger as Secretary of the Interior. Only six days after Taft and Ballinger took office, the Secretary's protégé, Dennett, still Commissioner of the General Land Office, wired Glavis, at Ballinger's instructions, directing him to submit immediately a complete report on the status of all his investigations of Alaska coal lands.[34] In the ensuing weeks several communications went to Glavis explaining the desire of Ballinger to settle the claims quickly. The most insistent was a wire of April 20 directing that "Alaska coal investigations must be completed within sixty days. What number additional agents do you require?" Glavis, protesting that snow would prevent any field examinations until July, estimated that to complete the cases in two months he would need five agents. The Washington office gave him two.[35]

Ballinger, about the middle of May, received personal calls from representatives of both sides of the controversy, ex-Governor Moore and Glavis. Moore had been confident that with Ballinger as Secretary of the Interior the Cunningham group would soon be able to procure their coal lands. His interview with Ballinger, however, was frustrating. The Secretary, because of his association with some of the Cunningham group during the preceding year, took the position that he should divest himself of handling their claims, and delegated such matters to Frank Pierce, Assistant Secretary. It can be argued that Ballinger's subordinates, since they were fully aware of his feeling that the Cunningham claims should be granted, were likely to act accordingly. But Ballinger appears to have made an honest effort to keep his hands off the subject. Moore, in a letter to the Secretary "not intended for your official files," complained that Pierce was a disappointment and that further delays in getting their patents seemed likely. Begging Ballinger to reconsider his decision to remain aloof, he stressed the "feeling of disappointment felt by myself and many of your former friends."[36] But Ballinger, generally speaking, did not interfere.[37]

Glavis's mid-May trip to Washington only served to arouse his suspicions further. He sought, among other things, to learn how the Hepburn Act, which Congress had passed the previous year, would be construed. This act, aimed at easing the restrictions in the previous law, allowed consolidation of Alaskan coal entries to the amount of 2,560 acres if the claims had been made in good faith. If the new law were going to be interpreted to validate claims like those of the Cunningham group, there obviously was no point in his continuing the investigation. In conferring with Ballinger and officials of the General Land Office, he found divided opinion concerning the effect of the law. Ballinger took no position. It was agreed, therefore, that Attorney General Wickersham should be asked for an opinion on the meaning of the act.

Although the request for information was addressed to the Attorney General, the letter never reached him. Two lawyers in the law office of the Department of the Interior took it on themselves to answer the query. According to their interpretation of the act it allowed the patenting of claims like those of the Cunningham group, regardless of agreements that might have been made at the time the claims were staked out.[38] When Glavis learned that the letter to the Attorney General, which he had helped draft, had never reached its destination, he understandably became further distrustful of Ballinger and other officials in the Interior Department. Although the preponderance of later testimony showed that Ballinger had had nothing to do with detouring the letter, it could easily be implied at this time that the Secretary was involved.

Glavis now was convinced that his superiors were erecting a road block in his path. If the ruling by the law office of the Interior Department were allowed to stand, he saw "100,000 acres of Alaskan coal lands . . . slipping from the United States with no hope of recovery." Without consulting his superiors, therefore, he went directly to Attorney General Wickersham. Eventually it was arranged that Wickersham would render a formal opinion on the matter. The Attorney General accordingly held that the act did not validate agreements between coal land claimants which had been illegal under prior law. Some attempt was made later to show that the Wickersham opinion did not actually overrule the holding by the law office of the Interior Department, but to take such a position requires an undue emphasis on technicalities. For all practical effects, the Attorney General's opinion was a reversal of the first one.[39]

After the Wickersham decision of June 12, Glavis returned to his job on the west coast. Schwartz, the chief of the field service, who had been Glavis's best friend in the Washington office, was by now thoroughly disgusted with the delays. Just as Glavis believed that his superiors were not endeavoring in good faith to protect the public interest in the Cunningham claims, so Schwartz was certain that Glavis was dawdling unnecessarily. On June 29 he wired Glavis that the hearing, to determine whether the Cunningham lands should go to patent, was to be held immediately. "Be prepared with your evidence," he ordered.[40] Glavis vigorously protested again that he needed more time and that a field examination was necessary before the hearings began. Several wires followed in a telegraphic tug of war between Schwartz and Glavis. Finally, on July 17, Schwartz wired that he was sending a young attorney in the Interior Department, James M. Sheridan, to take "complete charge" of the Cunningham case. Glavis was directed to assist him. Complained Schwartz,

"Case already consumed more time and expense of men than any other case pending. Investigation cannot proceed indefinitely."[41]

Schwartz, contrary to his superiors, still agreed with Glavis that the Cunningham claims might be fraudulent. But he believed that Glavis's suspicions concerning Ballinger and Dennett were unfounded. The young investigator, he held, "is suffering from a case of self-poisoning . . . [he] has been patted on the back by Pinchot and Shaw and led astray by the Lincoln Steffens brand of muck-rakers."[42] Schwartz was in favor of starting the hearing; additional evidence that might be uncovered during the proceedings could be included in the record. Sheridan, after looking into the situation, decided that Glavis had been right. On his recommendation to Schwartz, therefore, the hearings were postponed until after a field investigation in Alaska could be made.

It was on July 16, the day before Schwartz's wire replacing Glavis, that the latter, in a mood of desperation, appealed to the Forest Service for help. On August 9 he presented his account of the foregoing story to Pinchot in Spokane.

Pinchot listened to Glavis's recital of his investigation and discussed the situation with ex-Governor Pardee; he became positive that here was a matter of gravest consequence, and that Ballinger must go. Glavis was inclined to publish his findings in the hope of forestalling the government's loss of valuable lands. But Pinchot advised otherwise. The only proper place to take this evidence, he maintained, was to the very top—to President Taft himself. Offering to send his man Shaw from the Forest Service to help with the preparation of a report to the President, he also promised a letter of introduction to Taft.

Glavis and Shaw worked for three days in Chicago on a report of about fifty pages addressed to President Taft. Glavis then proceeded to Taft's summer home at Beverly, Massachusetts, armed with two letters from Pinchot. The first, a brief letter of introduction, expressed Pinchot's belief that the statements and documents collected by Glavis should be in Taft's hands "with the least possible delay. The issues involved are large, and can be handled by no one but yourself."[43] In this note Pinchot, in referring to Glavis, stated that "I have known him for several years." Later, on the witness stand before the congressional investigating committee, Pinchot contradicted this declaration when he inadvertently testified he was not certain whether he had known Glavis prior to 1909.[44] The misstatement was inflated by the opposition lawyer out of all proportion to its importance. The fact was that Pinchot had met Glavis some half dozen years before in the West, but was not really acquainted with him.

Pinchot's other letter to the President, which was sealed, contained a warning. Since parts of Glavis's story were "so much known," cautioned Pinchot, it would be impossible to prevent its becoming public "in part at least, and before very long." He also called to Taft's attention the information, received in Spokane, that when Ballinger briefly restored some of the government land to entry, private persons had been able to take over a number of valuable water power sites. Ex-Governor Pardee had made this same charge in his speech before the National Irrigation Congress in Spokane. Both men were guilty, however, of using information insufficiently verified. To their embarrassment it was soon learned that someone had mixed the decimals—that only 158.68 acres (none of them including power sites) rather than 15,868 acres of such land had gone into private hands.[45]

Pinchot closed his second letter by stating that his "function" ended with seeing that the Glavis information reached the President. And for a few weeks he acted accordingly. Following his Spokane address, he traveled in the Far West delivering speeches in support of conservation, and incidentally inspecting field stations of the Forest Service. Although careful in his public appearances not to make personal attacks on anyone, he left no doubt in the minds of his audiences that he was opposed to any "watered-down," Ballinger version of conservation. Since his point of view had become increasingly popular in the West, the crowds that met him and listened to his speeches were large and friendly. He could not resist telling his mother proudly that "Really, I seem to be getting to be a person . . . strength with the people generally seems to grow by leaps and bounds, so I don't think I am the one to walk the floor."[46]

While traveling, Pinchot of course was aware of events in the

East. He knew that Glavis on August 18 personally presented his charges to Taft. Taking an attitude of watchful waiting he was not, at the moment, interested in enlisting help from the press. Approvingly he wired Price, his associate forester, from Seattle to "Continue careful reticence."[47] From San Francisco, he enlarged this theme by declaring that "The strength of the Service's position in this whole controversy rests very largely, indeed, on extreme caution and the avoidance of all newspaper controversy."[48]

Pinchot was certain it was too late for any sort of reconciliation between the opposing forces. When Charles L. Pack, a friend of forestry, wired urging that Pinchot and Ballinger have a heart-to-heart talk, he replied confidentially that "there can be no question of an agreement between us except on the basis of whole hearted support by him of the Conservation policies."[49] The differences, he insisted, were on basic matters of policy; Ballinger's ideas were not in the interest of the public welfare.

Pinchot at this time was in regular consultation with his old friend and hunting companion, Henry L. Stimson, and he was inclined to treat Stimson's advice with respect. Not only was his friend an able lawyer but he had his ear close to the political ground. Seeming to fear that Pinchot might go too far in promoting his case for conservation, he cautioned him in a letter marked personal and confidential, that unless he had clear and overwhelming proof of bad faith on the part of Ballinger or others in the Interior Department, he should try to avoid a fight. Stimson was not as certain as was Pinchot that Ballinger really was a traitor to conservation. A battle would, he felt, result in a division of friends of conservation because not all of them would be on Pinchot's side. It was also significant, in view of later events, that Stimson reported Attorney General Wickersham as confident of Ballinger's honesty and ability, and as skeptical of the legality of some of the activities pursued by the Roosevelt Administration in the name of reclamation.[50]

Following his exhausting series of speeches in the West, Pinchot insulated himself from mail and newspapers by going to an island off the coast of southern California to fish and relax. On his way back to Los Angeles after the vacation he received a letter from the President. Enclosed was a copy of a long letter from Taft to

Ballinger authorizing the Secretary to dismiss Glavis from the government service "for filing a disingenuous statement, unjustly impeaching the official integrity of his superior officers." Although admitting that Glavis was "honestly convinced of the illegal character" of the Cunningham claims, Taft contended, after examining "the whole record most carefully," that Glavis's case "embraces only shreds of suspicions." Approximately half of the letter to Ballinger was devoted to a point by point refutation of various "unfair" charges in the press that the Secretary was unsympathetic to conservation. Insisting that Ballinger was "fully in sympathy" with "the attitude of this administration in favor of the conservation of natural resources," the President stated his sincere belief that the best friend of the policy of conservation is he "who insists that every step taken in that direction should be within the law and buttressed by legal authority."[51]

Taft's letter to "My Dear Gifford" was really a plea to him to refrain from exploding—the President begged that Pinchot keep his peace. Sensing the serious damage that could befall his Administration if the controversy continued to rage, he emphasized that he had made no reference to Pinchot in the letter to Ballinger. He had instructed officials of the Interior Department, moreover, to leave Pinchot's name out of any letters or references which might later have to be submitted to a congressional committee. Reminding Pinchot that he had no way of knowing some of the answers to Glavis's charges, he urged "that you do not make Glavis's cause yours." Declaring that it would be "fatal to proper discipline" to allow Glavis to remain in the government, he assured Pinchot he would do everything possible to maintain conservation policies. Although Taft was apprehensive of an extended newspaper discussion of the controversy, he perhaps dreaded still more the political consequences of a resignation by Pinchot. "I should consider it one of the greatest losses that my administration could sustain if you were to leave it, and I sincerely hope that you will not think my action . . . is reason for your taking a step of this character."[52]

In a further effort to pacify Pinchot, the President, on a trip to the West, arranged for a talk with him in Salt Lake City. For over an hour, extending past midnight on September 24, and also again the next day the bureau chief and the chief executive conferred. Although it was by no means a new experience for Pinchot to be closeted with a President, this first meeting seemed to him of such major importance that a few minutes after they parted he set down on paper his best recollection of what was said.

The interview was hardly reassuring to Taft. True, Pinchot did say he was not going to resign. And, according to Pinchot's notes, Taft "said he was greatly relieved, and said it with emphasis." The Forester made it clear, however, that he "might find it necessary to attack Ballinger. . . . I explained fully that I have no confidence in Ballinger." Taft, noted Pinchot, "said my zeal was so great I tended to think any man who differed as to method was corrupt." Pinchot maintained, however, that he "had not accused Ballinger of being corrupt."

The most serious storm warning of the interview, however, was the assertion by Pinchot that he "would not make trouble" if he "could avoid it, but might be forced to"; and then came the direst threat of all—Taft "might be forced to fire" him.[53]

Part of the purpose of the conference between Taft and Pinchot, at least from Pinchot's point of view, was to counteract the assumption by the press and the public that Taft's letter to Ballinger was a direct slap at Pinchot. Both men, accordingly, agreed to issue conciliatory statements to the press. Each had a chance to see the other's comment before it was handed to reporters. Taft's statement was an assurance that his letter to Ballinger was "not intended in any way" to reflect on Pinchot. The President let it be known he had written Pinchot and conferred with him, and that he was most eager to have him remain in office. Once again he proclaimed his support of conservation.[54] Pinchot, in turn, after quoting some of the laudatory remarks in Taft's letter to him, pointed with approval to Taft's assurances of his championship of conservation. He also made a direct promise, "I shall not resign, but shall remain in the government service."[55]

Ballinger, on September 20, referred to the dispute as "the controversy just closed by the President's letter [of September 13 to Ballinger]."[56] He could not have been farther from the truth. Both Taft and Pinchot knew that the end was not in sight.

When he conferred with the President in Salt Lake City, Pinchot promised to prepare a letter presenting a bill of particulars of Ballinger's alleged opposition to conservation. Much care and thought went into the drafting of this letter. In an effort to hit with a one-two punch, Garfield and Pinchot agreed that each of them would send a letter to the President. The two friends spent several days at Pinchot's home in Milford putting their complaints on paper. Finally on November 4 Pinchot sent his letter in the form of a reply to Taft's "most appreciative letter" of September 13. Maintaining that the President had been misinformed concerning certain "relations of the Interior Department to conservation," he presented illustrations of Ballinger's "unfriendly attitude" toward the movement. Following detailed accounts of the Secretary's actions, he concluded that Ballinger "has shown himself actively hostile to the conservation policies." Careful to avoid the word corruption, or anything resembling it, Pinchot believed that hostility to conservation was just as serious and just as censurable as actual corruption. Indeed, he went a step further. A Secretary of the Interior, he argued, was more directly responsible for conserving natural resources than any other government officer. "Unless he is vigorously friendly to the conservation policies and prompt to defend our natural resources against the unending aggression of private interests, the public interest must suffer." Therefore, he reasoned, mere indifference may be as wrong as open hostility. "Both because of his attitude and of what he [Ballinger] did, I am forced to regard him as the most effective opponent the conservation policies have yet had."[57]

Two days later Garfield sent his letter to Taft. Inasmuch as Taft's letter to Ballinger had indirectly criticized some of Garfield's actions as Secretary of the Interior, Garfield's letter was largely a detailed defense of those activities.[58]

Taft thereupon submitted both Pinchot's and Garfield's letters to Ballinger for comment. The Secretary went to great lengths, in a "personal" letter to Taft dated November 15, to present his side of the story. Admitting that there was an "irreconcilable difference" between his own and Garfield's views of the power of administrative officers, he showed particular sensitivity to the criticism that he had endangered the public interest by restoring to entry the water power sites which Garfield had withdrawn. This peremptory action had, in fact, reflected on the sincerity of Ballinger's professed support of conservation principles. In his letter to Taft he offered an explanation. "The only error I made in the whole affair," he pleaded, "was in not having the restorations and rewithdrawals made concurrently, which I would have done had I been as conversant with the facts then as I am now."[59] This statement does not appear to be justified, however, on the basis of all the available information. The evidence indicates, rather, that when Ballinger restored the sites to entry he had no intention of withdrawing them again. Indeed, he believed such action illegal. Only after it was clear that the restoring action engendered stiff protest was the decision made once more to set the land aside. Pinchot pointed up Ballinger's lack of logic in the matter by offering an apt illustration, "The obvious thing which would have been done if proper care had been taken for the public interests was to restore only the lands which were not wanted for power sites. . . . If a lot of chickens had gotten into my chicken yard that belonged to my neighbor, my plan to restore those chickens to my neighbor would not be to drive the whole flock out into the road and then take the chance of driving my own chickens [back] into the yard. I would go into the yard and pick out my neighbor's chickens and throw them back over the fence."[60]

Taft enclosed Ballinger's statement in a letter sent to Pinchot on November 24. Although renewing "his earnest desire" that Pinchot remain in office, the tone of the letter was noticeably stiffer than the one written in September. Previously it had been "My Dear Gifford"; now it was "My dear Mr. Pinchot." Obviously the President hoped the controversy would evaporate. "I do not think," he wrote, that a continuance of the controversy "is in the interest of the public service."

The President was unwavering in his support of Ballinger, "[You] have not by anything that you have suggested in your letter shaken in the slightest my confidence in Secretary Ballinger's good faith, and in his earnest and hearty cooperation in carrying out the policy of the conservation of our resources." But he was unable to see why Pinchot and Ballinger could not live together in the same government.[61]

Pinchot, believing for some weeks that the Taft Administration was not big enough to hold both the Secretary and himself, had entertained at least a modest hope that in the end Ballinger would be the one to go. Now that Taft made clear his unqualified support of the Secretary, Pinchot increasingly saw the possibility of his own dismissal. He continued to talk, however, as if his position were secure. "Personally, I do not believe there is any danger of my being fired," he wrote to the secretary of Yale University.[62]

He was, nevertheless, in an awkward situation. In spite of Taft's appeal for peace, Pinchot thought it hopeless to try to work with Ballinger. As he testified a few months later, "cooperation between the Forest Service and the Interior Department, which must be of the closest character if the government work is to prosper, was obviously impossible."[63] If Pinchot resigned, he could be charged with deserting his post. He had given his word to Taft, moreover, that he would remain in the service. If, on the other hand, he did not continue to protest as vigorously as he knew how, he might be accused of countenancing actions which he and other ardent conservationists believed were seriously injurious to the nation.

Although most careful not to disclose it, Pinchot at about this time apparently swung around to the conclusion that both he and the conservation movement had little to lose if the President chose to dismiss him. It is perhaps too strong a statement to say that he courted dismissal; but it is clear that he was willing to be dismissed. No other course seemed open to him. He firmly believed that the controversy to date had done conservation more good than harm. "When I think of the situation as to conservation three or four months ago and what it is now," he wrote Pardee, "I cannot avoid being exceedingly thankful. As you remember, Jim Garfield and I were going to write a book about the Roosevelt policies in order to help to keep conservation on the surface of the public mind . . . but the trouble that has come up this summer has done a thousand times more than we could possibly have hoped to do."[64] In line with this reasoning, a discharge of the nationally prominent Forester might go far to elevate conservation to the position of the number one national issue.

All through the heat of this battle Pinchot thought of himself as acting defensively rather than offensively; his attacks on Ballinger were protective attacks. This attitude was revealed, among other places, in a statement he made at the end of 1911, some months after the fight had ended. In reply to a query from his friend, Senator Beveridge, who wanted to know in one paragraph the exact central point of disagreement between Pinchot and Ballinger, Pinchot summarized his position as follows, "The essential reason of the trouble between Ballinger and me was this—that Ballinger had attacked the Conservation policies, especially as to water power and the proper care of forests on Indian Reservations, in addition to his efforts to give away the fraudulent Cunningham claims. I was never able to get people to understand that my fight was a defensive one— to preserve policies already in effect—and not an attack on Ballinger out of a clear sky, but that is the fact nevertheless."[65]

The act that did more than any other to bring the controversy to a head and to bring about a congressional investigation was the publication of Glavis's story in *Collier's Weekly* of November 13. Pinchot, who saw very little of his Washington office in the fall of 1909, had no direct hand in the preparation or printing of the article, but two officials of the Forest Service, Price and Shaw, were deeply involved. These two had decided after Glavis's dismissal that an appeal to the people was necessary if the Cunningham coal lands were to be saved. With their knowledge and approval, Glavis wrote an open letter on September 20 to the President asserting it was his duty to his country to publish the "facts" he had collected.[66] Both Price and Shaw had opportunities to see the manuscript of the magazine article which Glavis was preparing.

Collier's in 1909 had a circulation of 500,000 a week and was growing steadily. Of a crusading bent, it was assuming leadership among magazines of its type.[67] Glavis's decision to send his manuscript to this publication tended to refute the conclusion presented by Attorney General Wickersham to Taft that "Glavis's actions appear to have been founded upon a wholly exaggerated sense of his own importance, and a desire for personal advancement rather than on any genuine desire to protect the interests of the Government."[68] Rejecting a $3,000 offer from another magazine, he accepted no remuneration from *Collier's*.

Collier's for some weeks had been criticizing Ballinger. Since the Glavis article fit in well with their editorial policy, they featured it prominently. Glavis did not write in sensational style—in rather simple fashion he presented the story of his efforts and frustrations in trying to protect the Cunningham coal lands for the people. *Collier's* chose, however, to dramatize it highly. An editorial in the November 6 issue whetted the appetites of its readers for Glavis's revelations the following week by referring to "the reckless immorality with which the head of a great department is willing to work against the interests of the people."[69]

The issue in which the article appeared sported a sensational cover posing the question, "Are the Guggenheims in Charge of the Department of the Interior?" A huge, red question mark at the end of the sentence included a picture of Secretary Ballinger in its loop. Prominent in the background was a large black hand reaching out to grasp the natural resources of a mountainous terrain. Glavis carefully avoided making specific charges, "I made no [charge of criminality], nor do I make it now." Although he insisted that his basic purpose was to save the Alaskan coal lands for the people, the magazine, by its choice of a title for the article, "The Whitewashing of Ballinger," and by its subheadings—"The Alaska Frauds," "The President Whitewashes Ballinger," "Wickersham Overrules Ballinger," etc.—shifted the emphasis to implications of wrongdoing by Ballinger. A reader who depended entirely on this article for his information would have been convinced that "something rotten" existed in the Interior Department.[70]

As the controversy continued to grow warmer, Pinchot was cheerful. At least, the conservation movement was gaining wide attention. His far-flung speeches in support of the movement, furthermore, were meeting with considerable success. Henry C. Wallace, for example, wrote to congratulate Pinchot on his fight and to assure him that sentiment in the Midwest was with him. Pinchot elatedly reported to a friend, "Maybe my head is coming off, but if it does I shall try to be like the gentleman in the Arabian Nights, whose most important remarks were made after his decapitation."[71] To Judge Woodruff in Honolulu he wrote that "so far as I can tell there is no prospect of any serious trouble in the near future."[72] Moreover, the drama of the whole affair was not unappealing to Pinchot. When a "Mr. Davis," who said he was connected with *Collier's*, came to his office to get a story, Pinchot grew suspicious and refused to talk. A letter to his brother Amos, asking that the publisher be checked, brought the response that the magazine did not employ a Davis and that the inquirer probably was a detective.[73]

The ramifications of the controversy were by now so complicated that Pinchot frequently felt the need to consult a lawyer. His brother Amos was especially helpful with advice, and Henry L. Stimson, who had taken a sincere interest in the case, also lent a hand. Stimson late in October had a long talk on water power matters with Senator Elihu Root, former Secretary of War and of State, who had once been Stimson's law partner. Inasmuch as Root was to take a prominent place in the coming congressional investigation, it is interesting to note that Stimson found him firmly believing in Pinchot's water power ideas, but at the same time aware of legal difficulties with this policy. Stimson, writing to Pinchot concerning his interview, urged that nothing drastic be done until he had a chance to talk with Root again.[74] Pinchot obligingly replied on October 25 that "you may be sure that I shall do nothing you would not approve of until after I see you, and not then if I have luck."[75] When Pinchot forwarded to Stimson a copy of his lengthy letter of November 4 to the President, Stimson complimented him on it and on the spirit in which it was written. He expressed the hope, however, that Pinchot had carefully checked all his facts.[76]

Both Stimson and Pinchot considered Root a key man in the battle. Stimson, a few days after he had seen Pinchot's letter to Taft, advised Root to urge the President to look into the facts himself rather than rely on any member of the Cabinet.[77] Whether this advice ever reached Taft is only a matter of conjecture. In any case, Taft either would not or could not take the time which a thorough personal investigation would have required.

Pinchot considered it a "great piece of good luck" that he accidentally saw Root on the street in Washington and later talked with him for ten minutes just before Root had an appointment with the

President. "Since then I have heard nothing," Pinchot told Stimson, but added optimistically that "I judge things will go pretty well so far as my end of it is concerned."[78] But Stimson reported ten days later that Root was upset over the entire controversy, and saw serious danger ahead for both the nation and the Republican party.[79]

CHAPTER 9

FIRED

WHEN Congress convened for its new session early in December 1909, it was a foregone conclusion it would authorize an investigation of the Ballinger-Pinchot dispute. When this happened, both Glavis and Pinchot would need lawyers. It was reported, moreover, that Ballinger was proposing to sue *Collier's* magazine for $1 million for libel. To plan the strategy for meeting these problems, a half dozen of the persons directly involved gathered at Henry L. Stimson's home in New York.[1] *Collier's* was represented by Robert Collier and its editor, muckraking Norman Hapgood. Pinchot and his brother Amos were of course present, as was Garfield.

A newcomer to the group was George Wharton Pepper, against whom seventeen years later Pinchot was to run in a bitter campaign for United States senator from Pennsylvania. Pinchot had hoped to have Stimson as his attorney in the coming inquiry, but his friend begged to be excused because he was occupied with another government case. Stimson, indeed, had gone so far as to mail a letter to Pinchot agreeing to serve, but with a change of heart, had sent Felix Frankfurter, then a clerk in his office, to the post office to retrieve the letter.[2] It is possible, although not verifiable, that Stimson, who ran for Governor of New York in 1910, was shying away from an unpredictable client who might prove to be embarrassing. Pinchot believed that Root persuaded him to forego the case.[3] Pinchot's brother, Amos, was under the impression that Stimson felt he could not handle the case because he was a former law partner of Root who was a member of the investigating committee.[4] Stimson, at any rate, highly recommended Pepper to take his place. Pepper, with some hesitation, accepted. The group also agreed on Louis D. Brandeis as counsel for *Collier's* and for Glavis.

The joint resolution calling for the investigation of both the Department of the Interior and the Forest Service immediately became embroiled in the attack which the Republican Insurgents were making against the leadership of the House of Representatives. In a dramatic skirmish the Insurgents and the Democrats, aided by a small handful of regular Republicans friendly to Pinchot, pushed through an amendment providing that the six members of the investigating committee from the House should be chosen by election in the House rather than by Speaker Cannon.[5] Since Cannon had no sympathy for Pinchot, conservationists had feared that appointments which he made would be heavily weighted with standpatters. As a result of the amendment, however, three Republicans, two Democrats, and one Insurgent composed the House group. In the Senate, the Vice-President appointed four Republicans and two Democrats. Time and again throughout the hearings, when votes were taken on matters of procedure, the seven Republicans lined up on one side in opposition to the solid Democratic-Insurgent bloc of five.

Among the distinguished group of persons involved in the case were three future members of the United States Supreme Court—Taft, Senator George Sutherland of the investigating committee, and counsel Brandeis.

Ballinger announced that he welcomed an investigation into his Department, but insisted that the Forest Service be included in the inquiry. In support of this demand, he complained that "the pernicious activity of certain [of the Forest Service's] officers" had inspired the charges against his Department.[6] Pinchot thereupon, in order to answer the Secretary's allegation, formally requested Price and Shaw to report to him what they had done to bring about the charges.[7]

Pinchot must have known in general what had been taking place in his bureau. Although away from Washington during much of the period from August through November, it is inconceivable that during his brief trips to the office his subordinates failed to inform him of their involvement in efforts to expose the Department of the Interior. He was pleased with what he did know about the way the office had been run. Returning to Washington at the beginning of October, he wrote that he found things "in excellent shape (Price has been handling things beautifully in my absence)—I can find no loop-holes left unguarded, nothing that indicates any chance for anyone to attack the Forest Service."[8]

On the surface, relations between Taft and Pinchot were still cordial. On New Year's Day, Pinchot and his mother were invited to a reception at the White House and he noted in his diary, "Taft spoke to me pleasantly. Wished me a Happy New Year, and I him."[9] The President's half-brother, Charles, had suggested firing Pinchot, but Taft thought perhaps that was exactly what Pinchot wanted. If Pinchot was given enough rope, thought Taft, he might hang himself.[10]

The joint reply from Price and Shaw to Pinchot was a frank account of their activities. They described how one or both of them had helped Glavis prepare his report to the President, how they had given to newspapers and magazines material on the Cunningham claims and other matters (obtained not only from their own files but from those of the General Land Office), how they had in confidence shown three newspaper men a copy of Glavis's report before it had been acted upon by the President, and how they had examined the manuscript of Glavis's article for *Collier's*. "We are of course aware," they admitted, "that, from the point of view of comity between the departments, our conduct has been irregular." Confessing that their release of material to the press, which they said they made without Pinchot's knowledge, was contrary to the spirit of his instructions regarding the importance of avoiding all unnecessary publicity, they insisted that everything they did was for the purpose of protecting the property of the people against fraudulent claims.[11]

Price, in his eagerness to spare Pinchot and the Forest Service undue embarrassment, had gone to Pinchot's boss, Secretary of Agriculture Wilson, with an offer to resign. Wilson immediately wrote Pinchot expressing astonishment at Price's revelations and asking for Pinchot's recommendations.[12] In drafting a reply, Pinchot sought help from Stimson and Pepper. The two lawyers, who were both in Washington the first few days in January, carefully edited a letter which it was understood would be a major instrument for bringing Pinchot's case before the country.

Having approved the draft of the letter, the lawyers apparently were nervous lest their client decide to strike out on his own and undo their careful work. Stimson, who had a warm personal liking for Pinchot, wrote him on the fifth of the month strongly urging him to make no changes whatsoever in the letter without conferring with Pepper. Stating frankly that he was not impressed by some of Pinchot's closest supporters and advisers, he warned him not to place reliance on the judgment of either his brother Amos or Price.[13]

Stimson and Pepper were "dismayed" when, on the same day that Stimson sent his warning, Pinchot revised the letter and sent it instead to Senator J. P. Dolliver, the chairman of the Senate Committee on Agriculture and Forestry. Pepper made no written complaint at the time, but in later years stated that Pinchot had changed the letter "both in substance and form."[14] Stimson, wiring for a copy of the revised letter, received Pinchot's explanation that he "was obliged to modify [the letter] in certain respects because of information which reached me after you left, and which I could not get your opinion upon before it was necessary to act upon it. You will, I think, find the report as to all essentials in the shape you left it."[15] At the same time he half apologized to Pepper for the "considerably modified" letter, but pleaded that he and his brother Amos had tried to get in touch with Pepper after the changes were made.[16]

Dolliver read the letter, which Pinchot said was written at the Senator's request, on the floor of the Senate. It was neatly timed to help counteract the effects of an imminent report from the President to Congress on the Glavis case. In vigorously defending Price and Shaw, Pinchot did not allow niceties to reduce the forcefulness of his advocacy. Leaning on one of his favorite themes, he stated that "A public officer is bound first to obey the law and keep within it. But he is also bound, at any personal risk, to do everything the law will let him do for the public good." When Price and Shaw helped publicize the Cunningham claims, "they broke no law and at worst were guilty only of the violation of official propriety." In view of the "purity of their motives" and the "results which they accomplished, their breach of propriety sinks well-nigh to insignificance." Pinning on them this medal of honor, Pinchot nevertheless informed Senator Dolliver—and the country—that their action "deserved a reprimand, and has received one." He recommended that no further disciplinary action be taken.[17]

A few weeks later when members of the congressional investigating committee asked Pinchot about the nature of the reprimand, he affirmed that it was verbally given and that he used the word "reprimand." Beyond that he could not remember the exact words.[18] It is reasonable to assume that Price and Shaw did not experience extended suffering from their punishment.

Pinchot's letter seemed calculated to force Taft to move against him. He referred to Glavis's dismissal as resulting from "a mistaken impression of the facts" and voiced the opinion that Price and Shaw in reaching their conclusion that a national danger existed in Alaska had the benefit of "many considerations . . . which had not been brought home to the President's mind."

Although Pepper and Stimson were not aware of Pinchot's intention to write Senator Dolliver, he had planned it when the two lawyers were in Washington. On January 3, while discussing business matters with Secretary Wilson, Pinchot informed him that Senator Dolliver had asked for a letter.[19] There followed a discussion between the two men, the nature of which remains a matter of controversy. Pinchot came away from the conversation convinced that he had obtained the Secretary's permission to write the letter. Such permission was necessary in view of a presidential order that no bureau chief should respond to any request for information from a member of Congress unless authorized by the head of the department.

Wilson, however, while admitting that he may have given approval to some kind of letter, was hazy on the whole matter. Unquestionably he was shocked as well as highly embarrassed, when he saw the text and tone of the letter that was sent. When he tried later to explain the situation to the investigating congressmen, he seemed to be mildly incoherent and confused.[20] By this time, in addition, he was thoroughly angry at Pinchot for what he had done. It is probable that both men were partly at fault. Pinchot may have played down the importance of the letter and tended to generalize too much concerning its nature. Wilson, in view of the widespread knowledge that this controversy was becoming a crucial battle, may have been careless in not asking more questions concerning what was proposed. Both men, however, were acting in their customary pattern—Wilson never had used more than a light check rein on his bureau chief. Pinchot could recall no single instance when Wilson had asked to see a letter before it was sent.

Pinchot, who had always spoken highly of Wilson, was reluctant to make an issue of their disagreement concerning what had transpired between them. Certain in his own mind that Wilson's memory had failed him, Pinchot was inclined to excuse it because of the Secretary's advanced age of seventy-four. "I have seldom had anything more painful to do," he told Henry C. Wallace, "than . . . to hear him in his old age tempering with his own reputation."[21] At first he stated this position only to a few friends. In a confidential letter he insisted that he "could not do otherwise than believe that I had [Wilson's] consent to write to Senator Dolliver."[22] But the investigation inevitably brought the difference to public attention.

Whether or not Pinchot had properly cleared his letter through the Secretary, however, the reluctant President was now maneuvered into a position where he had to act. Taft knew that Pinchot's supporters were legion. He also knew that a dismissal of Pinchot would reinforce the suspicions of Rooseveltians that he was gradually undermining the policies and dismissing the personnel of his predecessor. He could almost hear the anticipated howl of protest by the former President from distant Africa.

January 7, 1910 was a miserable day for the President of the United States. Archie Butt, the White House confidant of both Roosevelt and Taft, reported that Taft looked "haggard and careworn . . . like a man almost ill." Foregoing his customary exercise, the President groaned that he had to "wrestle with Pinchot."[23] On two occasions during the day he convened the Cabinet. Even Senator Root, who, like Taft, had tried to avoid drastic action, assured the President that the sending of the Dolliver letter had made dismissal mandatory. Pinchot himself later testified that he believed there was "about an even chance" he would be fired.[24]

Taft finally hammered out a letter charging Pinchot, in effect, with disrespect to the President and official insubordination. "By your own conduct you have destroyed your usefulness as a helpful subordinate to the Government, and it therefore now becomes my duty to direct the Secretary of Agriculture to remove you from your office as the Forester."[25]

That same evening Pinchot's mother was having guests for dinner. "In the midst," she noted, "came in John Callan (O')Laughlin and G[ifford]. He with President's letter in hand—saying 'Fired.' " But the dismissal was not a cause for gloom. Mrs. Pinchot recorded only five additional words to describe the scene, but they significantly revealed that she and her son scarcely considered his martyrdom as a catastrophe, "Great rejoicing. Lots of reporters."[26]

The Pinchot home at 1615 Rhode Island Avenue was, for the next ten weeks, a whirlpool of activity. For several days following the firing, a steady stream of people came and went. Letters and telegrams of congratulation and encouragement poured in; by noon of the day after Taft's letter of dismissal, the number had reached 150.[27]

A signed petition, for example, expressed the "deep regret" of the students of the University of Wisconsin at the dismissal. William Allen White in an editorial on the firing praised Pinchot and called him "a thoroughbred. . . . He has made it impossible for the unwilling not to see the facts."[28] The *Chicago Tribune* found some thirty editors who believed Pinchot should run for President if Roosevelt did not.[29]

The acclaim was intoxicating to both mother and son. Mrs. Pinchot, now seventy-two, was bursting with pride. When she went to a lecture, she "got a most cordial reception from lots of women." When she attended church, "Lots of people congratulated" her. When she listened to Gifford speak before the Civic Federation, she noted that he was "greatly applauded."[30]

Although Pinchot denied before the investigators that he had been guilty of "official insubordination,"[31] years later he acknowledged that "from the official and technical point of view my dismissal was entirely justified."[32]

The day after Pinchot was fired he went to his office to bid a dramatic "good-bye" to his friends and fellow workers in the Forest Service. First, to a group of about a dozen officials, and then, before all the employees of the Service who were in Washington, he extolled them as the finest body of men in the government and urged them to "stand by the ship." They were engaged, he assured them, in an outstanding public service. Following brief eulogies to both

Price and Shaw, who had also been dismissed, he thanked one and all for their loyalty.[33] To many of those in the audience he was an idolized hero. When he finished his remarks, the applause was thundering.

Pinchot's entrance in the ranks of the unemployed did not bring him any moments of idleness. For one thing, the congressional investigation, which was to begin soon, necessitated a great deal of careful preparation. Moreover, by the end of January his mail was in such "bad shape" that he had 2,000 letters of congratulations to answer.[34] More immediately pressing was the need for issuing a statement to the press. Reluctant at first to make any official comment concerning his dismissal, he sought advice and assistance from a friend who was a journalist. Finally on January 13 he gave a release to the newspapers which, after expressing his "profound regret" at leaving the Forest Service, stated his determination to remain in the fight for conservation. The tone of this statement, as well as of the speeches he had been delivering in recent weeks, might have provoked a guess that in the near future he would be mounting the political hustings, either for himself or for Roosevelt. With the ring of a politician's campaign speech, he declared himself "ready to support the Administration" when it became interested in the welfare of the "plain people," and insisted that the great issue of the moment was whether the nation "shall be managed by men for human welfare, or by money for profit."[35]

Pinchot clearly revealed his keen disappointment in the Taft Administration in a long letter which he wrote to Roosevelt on the last day of 1909. When Pinchot and Garfield had been in Milford together in October, they had begun preparing for the former President (who was still hunting in Africa) a detailed report on the first seven or eight months of Taft's presidency. The two friends had drafted a seventeen-page memorandum which they proposed to sign jointly. Outlining the details of the Ballinger-Glavis feud, they bemoaned the encirclement of Taft by men who were not on the Pinchot-Garfield-Roosevelt side. The first sentence of the proposed letter indicated its general tone, "Not until now have we felt like interfering with your hunting of African beasts by telling you anything about the beasts in this country who have been coming again into the open since you left."[36] Although the letter was sufficiently completed to be read to Pinchot's mother, it was, for some unknown reason, never signed and mailed. When Pinchot himself wrote to TR on December 31, he began by saying that he had set out several times to do so, but had thought Roosevelt would be glad to be free "from the echoes of trouble."

Now, however, as the old year rolled out, Pinchot bared to "Dear Theodore" his grief over the turn that the government had taken. Although his letter was somewhat more moderate than the Garfield-Pinchot draft, he complained that "The tendency of the Administration thus far, taken as a whole, has been directly away from the Roosevelt policies." Enumerating sixteen reasons for thinking that Taft had "gone far toward a complete abandonment" of the policies, he cited alleged evidence of the President's alignment with persons in Congress and the Cabinet who were opponents of Roosevelt. Only one of his complaints referred to Ballinger, "By the appointment of Secretary Ballinger he [Taft] brought about the most dangerous attack yet made upon the Conservation policies— an attack now happily checked, at least for the time."

"We have," summarized Pinchot, "fallen back down the hill you led us up." Sharp as was his criticism, however, he was careful to explain that he did not attribute the conditions to "deliberate bad faith" on Taft's part. He blamed them, rather, on "a most surprising weakness and indecision," and the President's failure to serve positively as "the advocate and active guardian of the general welfare." He insisted, moreover, that he had not yet lost all hope. Writing, it will be remembered, only seven days before his dismissal, Pinchot proclaimed his attitude toward the President, "I have supported Mr. Taft and I shall continue to support him up to the point where my loyalty to the people of this country requires me to break with the Administration."[37]

Not many months later it was apparent that Pinchot avidly hoped Roosevelt would run for President in 1912. The closing sentences of this December 1909 letter, while carefully refraining from any specific suggestion, unmistakably represent a call from Pinchot to his idol to start thinking of 1912: "Just a final word. The hold of your policies on the plain people is stronger than ever. Many of your former enemies are now your friends. The line between the friends of special privilege and the friends of an equal chance is daily growing sharper."

Before Roosevelt received Pinchot's letter, a special runner brought him the news that his friend had been fired. Poorly informed as he was of the events that had been occurring in Washington, the former President was shocked at the news. "I cannot believe it," he wrote to Pinchot. "I do not know any man in public life who has rendered quite the service you have rendered; and it seems to me absolutely impossible that there can be any truth in this statement. But of course it makes me very uneasy." He pleaded that Pinchot write him "just what the real situation is."[38]

As the climax to the Ballinger-Pinchot feud approached, Stimson proffered frequent advice. On the very day that Pinchot was dismissed, Stimson sent him a handwritten note of general suggestions. Having recently seen the letter that Pinchot sent to Roosevelt, he admonished him not, under any circumstances, to make the letter public. He further counseled that if the President decided to remove him he should keep absolutely silent and not say a word without first obtaining the approval of Pepper. It was Stimson's judgment that Pinchot should say nothing publicly until the investigation was completed.[39] Stimson firmly believed that Pinchot needed to concentrate exclusively on preparing for his appearance on the witness stand before the investigating committee. Like an athlete, he would have to train for the ordeal both physically and mentally. He reminded him that the whole country would be watching to see whether he was precisely accurate in his statements or was merely engaging in enthusiastic generalizations.[40]

In his early associations with his counsel, George Wharton Pepper, Pinchot was highly pleased. At the end of December, for example, in asking Price to get in touch with Pepper, Pinchot wrote, "He is a first class man, with great wisdom and steadiness, and I think you will like him as much as I do."[41] Although Pinchot did not follow his lawyer's advice in writing the letter to Senator Dolliver, he sent a gracious note to Pepper, "I should like to tell you if I could how deeply we have all here appreciated your interest, your sympathy, and your most valuable direction and help. I feel as if I had made a new friend."[42] This early admiration, however, was gradually modified as the differing points of view of Pinchot and his lawyer became increasingly apparent.

Ballinger, himself a lawyer, entered the investigation without counsel. It soon became apparent, however, under the procedure being followed, that he needed legal help. Although always insisting that the use of attorneys in the investigation was a mistake, he reluctantly agreed that John J. Vertrees, a friend of President Taft's from Tennessee, should act as his counsel. Neither as suave nor witty as Pepper, nor as sharp of mind as either Pepper or Louis Brandeis (counsel for Glavis and *Collier's*), Vertrees was a reasonably able attorney. He fought his case, however, more according to rural Tennessee rules than those of Washington. Tall and gaunt, dressed in an old-fashioned frock coat, a former military fighter who was an expert shot with a revolver, he was bitter and vitriolic in pounding away at the opposition. He was inclined to scoff at much of the conservation movement. Partly because of his general attitude, he was somewhat ineffective in this case. Some of the opposition took delight in referring to him privately as "Pervertrees."

Two tables were set up in the investigating committee's hearing room in the Senate Office Building. At the head of the larger table, facing the audience, sat the chairman, Senator Knute Nelson; flanking him on both sides were the other members of the committee. At the opposite end of the table was a raised chair reserved for the witness. The opposing counsel lined the table—to his right and to his left. The second table, off to the side, was provided for the press.[43]

The committee members thought of themselves as judges who sat back and allowed the lawyers for both sides to bring out the facts by means of examination and cross-examination of the witnesses. Although they sometimes posed their own questions, the bulk of the proceedings had the atmosphere of a courtroom trial where the lawyers held the center of the stage. However, the committee members frequently became impatient with the involved and lengthy examinations which counsel for both sides sometimes pursued—in spite of their original adoption of judicial attitudes.

The first witness, called on January 26, was young Glavis who, along with Pinchot, was a principal accuser. On and off for a period of about three weeks, he was bombarded by questions—first, from Brandeis, and then, from the committee and Vertrees. Holding firmly to the allegations he had enumerated in his report to President Taft, he never directly charged misconduct by Ballinger.

On most days throughout the investigation the hearing room was filled with spectators sympathetic to both sides. Well behaved for the most part, one group or the other on rare occasions burst into applause or even hissing when a witness made a particularly dramatic or effective point. Among the frequent visitors was Pinchot's seventy-two-year-old mother, who was regularly ushered to a seat near the front of the spectators. Glavis's testimony impressed her as "admirably given," and in her opinion he stood up "wonderfully well" under cross-examination by Vertrees.[44] Biased as she was, other observers agreed with her. The Glavis memory, encyclopaedic and precise, made him a competent and impressive witness.

If a completely disinterested spectator had listened to every word spoken during the interrogation of Glavis, however, or had read the 770 pages of the recorded transcript,[45] he would have been justified in guessing that the majority of the committee was likely to support Ballinger at the end of the investigation. Committee members from both political parties were naturally very much aware of the possible effect of the investigation on their organizations. The regular Republicans were painfully conscious of the potential damage that could be inflicted on their party if the committee were to censure a high administrative official supported by the President. The Democrats saw a real opportunity to embarrass the party in power. The questions asked Glavis revealed that members on both sides were quick to seize any possible political advantage. As the hearings progressed, the predilections of various members became increasingly apparent. Chairman Nelson, for example, was quick to step in to help Ballinger and other pro-Administration witnesses when they ran into difficulties.

If one man on the distinguished committee stood out above the others in striving to conduct an impartial hearing and to arrive at an objective decision, it was Judge E. H. Madison, an Insurgent

Republican member of the House from Kansas, whose appointment to the committee had been sponsored by Representative (later Senator) George Norris of Nebraska.

By the time Pinchot was called to the stand at the end of February, it was manifest that he and Pepper had different viewpoints on the way the case should be handled. Pepper was primarily interested in presenting the most persuasive arguments possible to the committee members in an effort to win their verdict. Not at all favorable to a grandstand performance in the "trial," he built his case on cold logic, sprinkled appropriately with polished and well-turned phrases and even wit. His brief was a model of well-reasoned arguments, certain to impress a lawyer and to carry weight with a judge in a court. Stimson, having gone over with Pepper his plans for the examination of Pinchot on the witness stand, told Pinchot he fully agreed with them.[46]

Pinchot, on the other hand, was not basically interested in trying to win the committee's support, and was even willing to concede that he stood little chance of gaining their approval. The jury he sought to convince was not the committee but the public. In his mind, any statement in the hearing that carried weight with the persons seated at the press table was more important than one aimed toward the committee itself. Amos Pinchot, who from the first had not been keen about the choice of Pepper as counsel,[47] was fully in accord with his brother's ideas of strategy. At Amos's urging, Gifford agreed to call in his brother's friend, Nathan A. Smyth, to help with the case.

When Pinchot sent the letter to Senator Dolliver, Pepper had considered resigning, but finally decided against it. He now continued, although with misgivings, as Pinchot's principal counsel and did almost all the examining and arguing before the committee. Outwardly, Pinchot and Pepper were cordial. But the whole business was distasteful to the Philadelphia lawyer. "Of all the difficult and disagreeable duties that I have ever performed," he wrote in later years, "this was the most arduous and nerve-racking." Dismayed that the hearing was "not in the least degree a legal situation but wholly political," he recorded that while he was trying to win before the committee, "Pinchot's associates and his corps of journalistic friends were busy trying the case in the newspapers and incidentally making statements for which I often could find no adequate supporting evidence."[48]

During the three-week period when Glavis was testifying, Pepper strongly advised against issuing a press release proposed by Pinchot. Pointing out that at the moment the Pinchot-Glavis group had the best of the situation, he warned that a press release might be construed as a form of discourtesy toward the committee before which he would soon testify.[49]

In this instance Pinchot acquiesced to the advice of his counsel. In friendly fashion, however, he wrote what both men knew, that "Your point of view and mine necessarily differ a good deal because our principal objects differ also, yours being and quite rightly, to win before the Committee; mine being, and quite rightly, to win before the country. "I think," he concluded optimistically, "we shall do both."[50]

Pinchot, in a later account of the investigation, was highly critical of Pepper's work as counsel. The evidence shows, however, that although he was not entirely satisfied with his counsel during the investigation in 1910, he realized that Pepper provided valuable help in the case. It may be that Pinchot's posthumous criticism of Pepper was intensified as a result of their political battles in Pennsylvania in the 1920's.

Pinchot appeared before the committee as a witness on four different days between February 26 and March 5. At the start of his testimony, with the consent of the committee, he read a brief statement outlining the points that he proposed to make. Copies of the statement were released to the press before he entered the hearing room. "I shall show you," he began, "that Secretary Ballinger entered his office with the clear determination to make short work of" the Roosevelt policy of protecting water power sites from monopolistic control. Proclaiming his belief that Glavis was telling the truth, he stated his conviction that the facts proved Ballinger's unfaithfulness "to his trust as a servant of the people."[51]

Nowhere in his testimony did Pinchot specifically accuse Ballinger of actual corruption. But he did make a serious allegation of misconduct when he charged that Ballinger had misrepresented a number of facts in explaining his actions to the President. As a result, reasoned Pinchot, Ballinger was "disloyal" to the President.

Pinchot completed his statement with a dramatic paragraph which whetted the appetite of the public for spectacular revelations: "When this story has been told, and the witnesses whom I shall ask you to call have been heard, you will realize that the interests of the people are not safe in Mr. Ballinger's hands, and that the country will demand of this committee a verdict in harmony with the general conviction that the Secretary of the Interior has been unfaithful both to the public, whose property he has endangered, and to the President, whom he has deceived."[52]

Although not formally charging corruption, Pinchot gave at least some of his friends the impression that he considered the Secretary dishonest. Theodore Roosevelt, after the hearing was completed, revealed Stimson's evaluation of Pinchot's charges. "Stimson told me," wrote Roosevelt, "that he became convinced that Glavis was an honest man, and that Ballinger was not fit for the position of Secretary of the Interior, but that he thought Pinchot entirely wrong in his belief that Ballinger was a crook, and felt that Pinchot had made a serious mistake in saying that he would show Ballinger was guilty of a number of things of which as a matter of fact he was not guilty. Of course I don't wish you to tell this to Pinchot."[53]

The preponderance of the testimony presented to the investigating committee amply sustained, however, the opinion that Secretary Ballinger was far from an enthusiastic conservationist. It was not difficult to show in the hearings that he bore contempt for the ardent conservationists of the Roosevelt-Pinchot-Garfield type. He was satisfied to have the Department of the Interior do things as they had in the past, and primarily follow a policy of assisting in the development of the frontiers. A negative attitude, in itself, was to Pinchot a sufficient reason for declaring Ballinger unqualified for the position of Secretary. "It is not enough that a man who is charged with the responsibilities of the Secretary of the Interior toward Conservation can not be proved to be actually hostile. Unless it can be proved that he is actively friendly it goes without saying that he is unfit for the place."[54]

Pinchot was able to make a case that Ballinger had indeed made some misstatements to the President in defending himself against the accusations of Glavis and Pinchot. Officials of the Reclamation Service, for example, reported that, contrary to the information Ballinger gave Taft, they had not recommended that various withdrawn lands should be restored to sale.[55] The Secretary further had shown a lack of candidness when he informed the President that it was not as a result of Glavis's protest that he had revoked the order clear listing the Cunningham coal land claims.[56] Ballinger was able to show, however, that some of his statements, which Pinchot labeled untruthful, could have resulted from honest differences of opinion concerning the facts.

Although Pinchot gave examples of some coloration of the facts by Ballinger, it was not so clear that the final effect of these instances of "misrepresentation" was of real importance. Pinchot implied that Ballinger's misstatements were a significant factor in persuading Taft to endorse the Secretary in the face of the Glavis charges.[57] It is highly questionable, however, whether a complete elimination of the "color" would in any way have modified the President's support of Ballinger.

In contrast to Pepper, who was the essence of courtesy in dealing with all the participants in the hearing, Vertrees, and Brandeis too, tended to handle the opposition witnesses somewhat roughly. Pinchot, while on the stand, ran the risk on several occasions of being goaded into losing his temper, but managed to keep his decorum. Once when Pinchot started to protest a question by Vertrees, the lawyer facetiously countered, "I was going to help you out." To which Pinchot snapped, "I do not need your help, thank you."[58] But he did remain calm.

Several minutes later, however, Vertrees threw a loaded question at the witness, "when did you form the purpose to assault and attack Mr. Ballinger?" Leaping to Pinchot's aid, Representative Graham protested that this was an improper question. Almost as quickly, Chairman Nelson, whose sympathies were on the opposite side, expressed his opinion that Graham misunderstood the question. After other members of the committee had had their say on the matter, the questioning continued until Vertrees asked, "When did you first conclude that the defense of those [conservation] policies required that some sort of a movement should be made to remove Mr. Ballinger?"

"That," complained Pinchot to the chairman, "is another of those questions."

Representative Madison thereupon offered legal advice to Pinchot, "The best way to answer that, a question of that kind, is 'I do not know,' and then explain."[59]

Vertrees, in an effort to shift from the defense to the offense, tried to prove that Pinchot engaged in a conspiracy against Ballinger, but such an exaggerated charge was torn to shreds by Pepper. Ballinger's lawyer also displayed a lack of astuteness in sizing up the situation when he informed the committee that he was going to show Pinchot was not prompted by "patriotic purposes," but by the "disappointment and resentment which comes in the bosom of a discharged public servant."[60]

In his final argument before the committee, Vertrees chose to ridicule the Pinchot type of conservationist, "men who have gone to seed on that subject . . . the thirty-third degree conservationists— who have run off with this as a fad." "You would imagine," he scoffed, "from the way Mr. Pinchot talks about conservation that he has as many children as Jacob of old, and that his solicitude lest they should freeze is making him shiver now." Vertrees was frank in adding that a "great deal of this cry about conservation comes from the East. It may be a good thing, but I am against it."[61]

Vertrees seemed to be confining his appeal to the committee and ignoring the effect on the general public. As he began his final argument, indeed, he made a point of saying that he was addressing his remarks to the committee table and not to the press table. He even went out of his way to antagonize the newspapermen present by declaring that the press had reported the inquiry "in a way that has not pleased me at all," and by asserting that newspapermen "habitually" did injustice to persons "who may be assaulted and impugned." Obviously nettled by the degree to which the nation's press had taken the Pinchot side in the controversy, he issued a devastating statement on the press (despite its confusion of the Lord's Prayer with the Ten Commandments): "There is but one part of the Lord's Commandments which they seem solicitious to observe, and that is, 'Give us this day our daily bread.' They write that which they believe will sell their papers in order that they may obtain money wherewith to buy their bread."[62] No strategy that the "defense" attorney might have used could have been better calculated to drive the press into the eager and open arms of the Pinchot opposition.

Although the resolution authorizing the congressional investigation listed both the Department of the Interior and the Forest Service as objects of inquiry, no specific charges were made against the latter. At one point lawyer Vertrees sought to cast reflection on witness Pinchot by asking about "your forestry students."[63] The reference was to a plan whereby the Forest Service under Pinchot had sought to improve the training of some of its rangers by sending them to attend short courses on the campuses of four western universities. Under the plan, the expenses (including tuition) and salaries of the rangers were to be paid by the Forest Service while they were attending school. A few days following Pinchot's dismissal, however, a departmental attorney by the name of McCabe, temporarily acting as chief of the bureau, had informed Secretary Wilson that he believed the scheme was illegal. Wilson, asking the Comptroller of the Treasury for his opinion, had gone to pains to state that the plan had just come to his attention for the first time, and that he shared the attorney's grave doubts concerning its legality.[64] Only one day after he wrote the letter, Wilson had received the Comptroller's opinion that he was not authorized to pay the salaries of the rangers while attending classes, nor to reimburse them for traveling expenses to and from the colleges.[65]

With the aid of friendly questioners on the committee, however, Pinchot was able to bring out that Secretary Wilson in the past had approved somewhat similar training programs conducted at Forest Service camps, and that the college plan was in reality a less expensive method of performing the job.

Vertrees was no more successful in embarrassing Pinchot when he asked a series of questions on the publicity tactics of the Forest Service.[66] And at the end of Pinchot's testimony, when members of the committee themselves plied him with a limited number of questions on the administration of his bureau, he was able to assume the role of a proud proclaimer of his Service's accomplishments rather than that of a cornered defender.[67] Counsel Pepper, therefore, in his summary remarks at the end of the hearing, was justified in proceeding "upon the assumption that there is a general recognition of the failure of any attempt to make a case against the Forestry Service."[68]

Pinchot, as has been said, was trying to present his case primarily to the public rather than to the investigating committee. His charges that Ballinger was not sympathetic to conservation and that he had deceived the President did not, however, have the effect of drawing a strong wave of public opinion to Pinchot's side. The evidence in support of the accusations did not have the dramatic quality necessary to make them catch fire with the average citizen. Newspaper readers, who had been led by Pinchot's opening statement to expect more spectacular revelations, found the evidence anticlimactic. The Glavis-Pinchot forces were already foredoomed to lose their case before the committee. When Pinchot finished his testimony on March 5 it was by no means certain that his side stood much of a chance to win before the bar of public opinion.

As soon as the testimony of two or three friends of Pinchot, including Garfield, was added to the record, Pepper strongly advised his client to disassociate himself as much as possible from the rest of the case. Carefully refraining from any direct criticism of the other counsel, he urged Pinchot to avoid becoming implicated with the type of injurious evidence which Brandeis, as attorney for *Collier's*, was planning to produce against Ballinger, and which, incidentally, was certain to embarrass the White House. The best strategy for Pinchot, advised his lawyer, was to steer clear of it.[69]

Pinchot's polite reply signified agreement, "Your idea of the policy to be pursued is exactly my own."[70] Only four days later he completely removed himself from the immediate scene by sailing for Europe.

A few weeks previously, however, Pinchot had in fact become involved in the preparations for bringing the more startling evidence into the hearing.

CHAPTER 10

VICTORY IN DEFEAT

MUCH of the new evidence presented to the congressional investigating committee proved to be damaging to the Ballinger side of the case. This might have been avoided if the Administration forces had been more astute. Taft himself was not blameless for the poor showing that his Administration made in the remainder of the hearings. The President's ineptness in the whole matter induced Henry C. Wallace to say, as reported by Pinchot, that "if you put Taft and a trap on a section of land in the night, and wanted to find him you would simply need to go to that part of the square mile where the trap was located, and you would find him in it."[1]

The chain of events which put the Administration, including Ballinger, in such a bad light stemmed from Brandeis's careful study of the documents in the case. One of the most interesting and pertinent questions concerning the controversy was what precisely had been the basis for Taft's decision to write his letter of September 13, 1909, exonerating Ballinger and dismissing Glavis. On January 6, 1910, in response to a Senate resolution, Taft submitted to the upper house all documents "upon which he acted in reaching his conclusions"[2] on the Glavis charges. Included in the papers were Glavis's documented allegations together with detailed replies to the President from Ballinger and other members of the Department of the Interior—a veritable mountain of material which, when printed, came to 717 pages. Added to these documents was an 87-page report and summary of the volume, dated September 11, prepared for Taft's use by Attorney General Wickersham. The general tone of the entire summary was demonstrated by its final sentence on the Glavis charges—they are "so unjust and unfounded as to merit his immediate separation from the service."[3]

Brandeis, however, in reflecting on Wickersham's summary, detected what he thought might be a flaw. When he saw that Ballinger had not submitted his various documents to the President until September 6, and that the Attorney General, while preparing the summary, was burdened with many other official duties, Brandeis could not believe it had been humanly possible within five or six days to conduct the research necessary to write the detailed report. Working on this hunch, he painstakingly studied the report until he discovered a reference by the Attorney General to an event that had not happened until two months after September 11, the date of the report. Although Brandeis bided his time, preferring not to make a public disclosure until thoroughly sure of himself, he was reasonably certain that at the time Taft dismissed Glavis he did not have available the Wickersham report.

While the hearings were in progress, and at the time Brandeis was working on his date puzzle, Frederick M. Kerby, a young stenographer from Ballinger's office, brought an astonishing bit of information to his former employer, ex-Secretary Garfield. At a subsequent meeting in Pinchot's home, Kerby told Pinchot and Brandeis (and Garfield again) of a pertinent memorandum that the President had not submitted to Congress.[4] Kerby's story, later supplemented by a letter from Taft and by testimony at the hearing, disclosed that Ballinger, when he went to Taft's summer home at Beverly in September to deliver his written defense against the Glavis charges, took with him the Assistant Attorney General assigned to the Interior Department, Oscar Lawler. At the direction of the President, Lawler returned a few days later with a suggested draft of a letter for Taft to send to Ballinger fully supporting him against the charges. Kerby, who had worked on typing the letter, revealed how, after it had been submitted to Ballinger and other persons in the Interior Department for corrections, copies of the rough drafts were carefully burned in a fireplace. The omission of this relevant letter from the documents submitted by Taft to the investigating committee was bound to cast serious suspicion on the Administration.

By the time that Pinchot, using an assumed name, quietly sailed out of New York harbor for Europe, he could lie back in his deck chair content with the way the hearings were going. While willing to admit that he had not performed as ably on the witness stand as had Glavis, he had, with the help of Pepper, brought home some points against Ballinger and made no serious blunders. He knew, too, that in a short while the press and other interested persons would have a printed pamphlet, prepared from the Pinchot point of view, surveying the results of the first two months of the hearings.[5] Now, Brandeis, who was in effect taking over the leadership of the Glavis-Pinchot side of the case, was armed with two spears that likely would prove exceedingly damaging to the Administration forces—an apparently misdated letter, and a missing Lawler memorandum.

Shortly before he sailed, Pinchot received a letter from Africa written by Roosevelt on March first. The former President, acknowledging receipt of Pinchot's December 31 letter of complaint concerning the Taft Administration, and affirming that he now had the definite news of Pinchot's dismissal, was eager to learn the details. "I do wish I could see you. Is there any chance of your meeting me in Europe? . . . I wish to see you before I in even the smallest degree commit myself."[6] In a letter written the same day to Senator Henry Cabot Lodge, Roosevelt lauded Pinchot as "one of our most valuable public servants [who] loved to spend his whole strength, with lavish indifference to any effect on himself, in battling for a high ideal." But, he observed, "not to keep him thus employed rendered it possible that his great energy would expend itself in fighting the men who seemed to him not to be going far enough forward."[7]

When Pinchot reached Europe and the home of his sister at the British embassy in Denmark, Roosevelt was in Rome. The former President wired him suggesting they meet in Porto Maurizio, Italy, on April 11.[8]

There is no question that this meeting created widespread anxiety among Republicans. Administration stalwarts, as well as others primarily interested in party unity, feared the political consequences of having current events presented to Roosevelt from Pinchot's point of view. One of his friends believed the investigating committee would have taken steps to keep him from leaving the country if they had known he was going.[9] Senator Lodge even suggested to the former President that he should not see Pinchot, but Roosevelt disagreed. "The only man I invited to see me was Root," Roosevelt somewhat inaccurately informed the Senator, "and Root said he could not come; but when Pinchot said he wanted to see me I said I should be more than delighted."[10] Explaining he would listen to all that Pinchot had to say, the ex-President promised not to commit himself until he received additional information.

When the former President and his loyal colleague had their reunion on April 11, the Chief was starved for news. Only a few driblets of information had come to him concerning Pinchot's dismissal; and he had not yet been able to form final judgments on the Taft Administration. Lodge, a regular correspondent, had taken the position that Pinchot "was all wrong" in writing the letter to Senator Dolliver,[11] and Roosevelt had concurred. But beyond this, the former President was noncommittal.[12]

Pinchot's diary throws no light on what the two friends said to each other, but he was pleased, "One of the best & most satisfactory talks with T.R. I ever had. Lasted nearly all day, and till about 10:30 P.M."[13] As he contentedly wrote to Garfield, "I found everything just exactly as you and I had foreseen. There was nothing changed, nothing unexpected."[14] Even though the exact comments were not recorded, the general tone of Pinchot's remarks can be inferred from the testimony he gave before the congressional investigating committee, and from the criticisms of the Taft Administration which he had poured out to Roosevelt in his December letter. To fortify his own opinions he had brought with him other critical letters written by such Roosevelt friends as Senator Beveridge, Senator Dolliver, and William Allen White.[15]

Making the most of his persuasive way with the Chief, Pinchot probably contributed materially to the gradual formation in Roosevelt's mind of a high disregard for Taft's performance as President. The effect of Pinchot's visit was perhaps shown in Roosevelt's opinion, written that very day to Lodge, that the Taft Administration had "completely twisted round the policies I advocated and acted upon."[16]

Although the main purpose of his trip to Europe was completed, Pinchot was in no hurry to return home. His brother Amos at least twice advised him to stay away.[17] Several other friends gave him the same advice and so did his mother.[18] His absence, according to Amos, was helping to increase the anxiety and discomfiture of the other side. Both Amos and Overton Price wrote optimistic letters on the progress of the hearings.[19]

Pinchot, therefore, chose to remain on the other side of the Atlantic and forego a front-row view of the drama which he felt certain was about to unfold. While Ballinger squirmed in the witness chair, Pinchot renewed old European acquaintanceships and reveled in a delightful Irish spring with Sir Horace Plunkett. One of his happier interludes was a lunch in Paris with Mrs. Roosevelt.[20]

Meanwhile, Brandeis, with monotonous regularity, kept asking in the hearings for additional documents, in the hope of uncovering the Lawler memorandum without having to request stenographer Kerby to testify.[21] And just as persistently he was met by denials that any such document existed. When, in addition, he called on the investigating committee to procure copies of both the final and earlier drafts of Attorney General Wickersham's summary of the Glavis-Ballinger material, his request was rejected by a vote which followed the customary seven-to-five division along political lines.[22] Two days later, in an effort to obtain a reversal, he explained to the committee his suspicions concerning the misdating of the Wickersham report. The committee, after going into executive sessions, refused to budge from its seven-to-five verdict.[23]

Brandeis, however, by the time Ballinger came up for cross-examination, was sure of his facts. As he once admitted to Pinchot, it was fortunate for the Glavis-Pinchot forces that Ballinger's testimony had not occurred early in the hearings before they could have detected his evasions and misstatements. Only after a series of searching questions was Brandeis able to get the reluctant Ballinger to admit that Lawler had "made up" and taken to Taft "a sort of résumé of the facts."[24] Now that it was openly conceded that Lawler had prepared some kind of document, Brandeis asked explicitly for "the so-called memorandum prepared by Mr. Lawler at the request of the President." An embarrassed Attorney General then sent to the committee a copy of the memorandum which, he explained, "seems to have been overlooked in collecting papers in answer to your previous communications."[25]

The timing of Attorney General Wickersham's letter revealing his discovery of the memorandum cast the worst kind of suspicion on the Administration. To the general public it seemed more than coincidental that on the same Saturday the memorandum was un-covered, May 14, there appeared in a chain of newspapers a signed statement by the Interior Department's stenographer, Kerby.

Kerby had made his own decision to tell publicly what he knew. Brandeis had been careful not to place undue pressure on him to do so. But when the young man learned that the committee and the Department were thwarting the lawyer's efforts to obtain papers, and, equally important, when assured by a newspaperman that he could have a reporting job if the Department of the Interior fired him, he agreed to tell his story. Accusing Ballinger of attempting, by his silence on the stand, to "smother truth which the whole country has a right to know," he told in minute detail how Lawler, in Ballinger's private office, had dictated to Kerby part of the memorandum for Taft. He recounted, moreover, how Ballinger and various officials in the Department of the Interior had been given a chance to make corrections in the original Lawler version, and how Lawler and others had systematically burned the earlier drafts of the memo-randum.[26]

Kerby did, however, overstep the bounds of accuracy when he exaggerated the extent to which Taft had leaned on Lawler in writ-ing the letter exonerating Ballinger, "The general arrangement of facts—the order in which they come—in the president's letter is practically identical with the arrangement of facts in the final Lawler . . . memorandum."[27] The President, in reality, while he did use some of the Lawler ideas, wrote a letter vastly different from the one proposed by Lawler. Especially noticeable was Taft's effort to soften Lawler's thrusts at Pinchot.

Kerby's newspaper statement, added to Brandeis's insinuation that the Wickersham report had been misdated, threw the Administration into a state of confusion. Taft, placed on the defensive, did not wait until Monday to act, but addressed a Sunday letter to the chairman of the investigating committee. Carefully explaining the exact amount of attention he had been able to give to studying the answers to the Glavis charges, he related how Ballinger on September 6 sent to the summer White House at Beverly the various reports of members of the Interior Department together with the voluminous record of exhibits. After a conference with Ballinger on the evening of the sixth, following which the President sat up until three a.m. going over the documents, he saw the Secretary again on the evening of the seventh. By the time of the second conference, he said, he had made up his mind that "there was nothing in the charges upon which Mr. Ballinger or the others accused could be found guilty of either incompetency, inefficiency, disloyalty to the interests of the Government, or dishonesty."[28]

Without in any way impugning the motives of the President, it may be pointed out that Ballinger in the role of the accused had a chance to present his case orally as well as by documentation. Glavis, however, when he was presented with charges serious enough to bring about his dismissal, had no opportunity to defend himself with oral argument. Charles W. Eliot, president emeritus of Harvard University, was only one of the people who expressed surprise that a decision of guilty was pronounced against Glavis without his being heard.[29]

Taft's letter went on to explain how he had asked Lawler, who was present at the second of the Taft-Ballinger discussions, to write a detailed statement supporting the decision which the President had already reached. When Taft saw the Lawler memorandum on the twelfth, he found some "useful" references in it; but it "did not state the case in the way in which [he] wished it stated."

The President on September 12 also conferred with Wickersham. On his way from New York to Beverly, the Attorney General, who previously had seen the Glavis charges, read as many of the answers by Ballinger and others as he could. After a morning conference with Taft, Wickersham withdrew and spent the day going over the entire record, taking notes, and tabulating his own conclusions. Returning in the evening to the summer White House, where the President had drafted a tentative opinion, he helped round the letter into final form. "The conclusions which I reached," explained Taft, "were based upon my reading of the record and were fortified by the oral analysis of the evidence and the conclusions which the Attorney-General gave me, using the notes which he had made during his reading of the record." Taft concluded by revealing that, as Brandeis had surmised, the President had then directed Wickersham to embody in a written statement his own analysis and conclusion and to "date it prior to the date of my opinion, so as to show that my decision was fortified by his summary of the evidence and his conclusions therefrom."[30] Other evidence indicated that this pre-dated statement was not actually completed until between two and three months after the date of September 11 which it bore.

Taft's frank letter came too late to allay criticism of his Administration. Actually, the two main admissions in his statement when objectively analyzed did not reveal clearly censurable practices. It is often necessary, for example, for a busy executive to delegate to some subordinate the authority to draft for his signature a letter or statement, however important the subject matter. If someone in the Administration had sped the Lawler memorandum to the investigating committee before—or at least as soon as—Brandeis began asking for additional papers, it could have produced no great amount of criticism. It was the misguided secrecy that caused the trouble for the Administration.

In much the same way, the misdating incident which did the Taft forces so much harm was largely avoidable. Taft's decision to fire Glavis and vindicate Ballinger had in fact been supported by the Attorney General. Some of Wickersham's notes were of assistance to the President in writing his opinion. The mere fact that the Attorney General's analysis and conclusions were not, at the time Taft acted, set down in a formal written document, did not actually make a great deal of difference. Certainly this was not the first or the last time that a government official, without violating any code of ethics, advanced the date on a document—especially one for which all the material had been available before it took final form. The determination of the Administration sympathizers on the committee to kill any attempt to produce evidence on the matter, however, gave the public the impression that they were in reality trying to hide something of great importance.

Perhaps the principal criticism that could be directed at Taft was his failure to give the problem as much careful attention as it deserved. Brandeis forcefully maintained that "the President's engagements were such that he could not possibly have given to this question the attention which was necessary for its proper consideration."[31]

Lawyer Vertrees, darkly referring to "a conspiracy to injure or destroy," charged that Brandeis's statements before the committee "plainly revealed" that the Kerby statement was given to the public "for the sole purpose of injuring the President."[32] Such an accusation is not supportable by the evidence. Brandeis, rather, was intent on proving that his client, Glavis, was dismissed on insufficient grounds, and in a somewhat haphazard manner. If he could show that the President had based his decision on only a part of the facts, or on an extremely partisan statement, it was certainly pertinent to his client's case. He was not one to hold his fire simply because persons in high places might be embarrassed.

No one knew better than Brandeis that up to the middle of May the Pinchot-Glavis side had not yet won its appeal to the public mind. But on the day that Wickersham finally produced the Lawler memorandum, the case took a new turn. Brandeis must have realized that, regardless of the final vote of the committee, the Pinchot-Glavis forces were now destined to gain the public's favor. It is not surprising that both Brandeis and Amos Pinchot were "in great glee" when they dined with Pinchot's mother that evening after the memorandum was made public.[33] Brandeis was always ready to admit that the Administration bungled themselves into defeat. As he told Pinchot in later years, "the Lawler memo would not have been very damaging except that it was lied about and concealed."[34] In much the same way, he admitted elsewhere that the Administration could have saved themselves, "It was the lying that did it. If they had brazenly admitted everything, and justified it on the ground that Ballinger was at least doing what he thought best, we should not have had a chance."[35]

Pinchot, still abroad, wrote Roosevelt, who was also in Europe, that "The latest developments in the Ballinger-Pinchot controversy seem to establish my case more completely than ever." Writing only two days after the disclosure of the Lawler paper, and therefore obviously relying merely on telegraphic reports, he discussed the case in terms which did not fully square with the facts. Mistakenly asserting to Roosevelt that the Taft letter exonerating Ballinger had been prepared in Ballinger's office, he also caustically described the whole affair as "a spectacle to make every decent American squirm in his skin when the Attorney General of the United States falsifies an essential public document, and the President transmits the falsification to Congress."[36]

Judging by this letter, Roosevelt hardly received from Pinchot an objective analysis of what occurred in the Pinchot-Ballinger fight. This was undoubtedly counterbalanced, however, when Roosevelt had an opportunity in London to talk with a key Administration supporter from the investigating committee, Elihu Root.[37]

When the hearings of the investigating committee finally drew to a close on May 27 and 28 with the oral arguments of Vertrees, Pepper, and Brandeis, Pinchot was on the high seas returning home. Arriving in New York on the thirtieth, he found much to make his pulse run faster. After a week's sounding of opinion, he happily painted for Sir Horace Plunkett, his recent host in Ireland, a picture of what he had found in America. "I feel," he wrote, "that the sentiment in favor of conservation and against Ballinger is at least twice as vigorous as when I left, while Taft seems to have lost even what shreds of respect for his effectiveness he still retained at that time. Everybody is sorry for him; everybody recognizes that he moves with absolute accuracy from one blunder by the shortest route to the next." Conceding that "the anticipated [committee] majority whitewash will doubtless be applied," he maintained that "it makes absolutely no difference what the majority may say, the country has made up its mind."[38]

Pinchot's congratulatory notes to Brandeis and to Kerby (who had been dismissed by Ballinger) showed his appreciation for what these two men had done to bring the "victory." Complimenting Kerby on his "very fine" stand, which was taken with "courage, restraint, frankness, and ability," he hoped the young reporter would "do me the honor to count me among your friends."[39] To Brandeis he wrote with sincere feeling, "The way you brought the investigation to an end seemed to me simply beyond all praise, if you will allow me to say so."[40]

The members of the investigating committee submitted three different reports to Congress.[41] The seven orthodox Republicans, who had voted together consistently throughout the hearings, found nothing to criticize in Ballinger. "Neither any fact proved nor all the facts put together exhibit Mr. Ballinger as being anything but a competent and honorable gentleman, honestly and faithfully performing the duties of his high office with an eye single to the public interest." Elihu Root was partly responsible for holding the criticism of Glavis and Pinchot to a minimum.[42] Although the unqualified support of Ballinger was in itself a severe rap at Pinchot, the unsympathetic majority refrained from singling him out for much censure. They did charge that logging operations of the Forest Service on an Indian reservation had been "wasteful and extravagant," and that Pinchot "had not always been considerate in his dealings with other public officials . . . [he] could at times assume a threatening attitude." The more indirect criticism, such as that implied in the reference to "excessive" withdrawals of the public domain, was of course equally applicable to Garfield and to Roosevelt.

The final paragraph of this report, however, represented a triumph for Roosevelt's and Pinchot's views. The majority stated, in accordance with what Pinchot had been preaching, that "it would be the height of unwisdom to permit these great coal fields to be monopolized, or gathered into the private ownership of a few for speculative purposes." Proposing legislation under which the government would retain ownership of the coal lands in the public domain and lease them for limited periods of time to private enterprise, they recommended that, pending such legislation, the existing withdrawal of the lands from entry be continued.[43]

The four Democrats on the committee, who during the hearings had shown themselves to be as consistently opposed to Ballinger and the Administration as the Republicans had been favorable, presented a lengthy bill of particulars against the Secretary. In summary form they announced their finding that "Mr. Ballinger has not been true to the trust reposed in him as Secretary of the Interior; that he is not deserving of public confidence, and that he should be requested by the proper authority to resign his office as Secretary of the Interior."

The Democrats could scarcely say enough in praise of Pinchot. "We believe," they stated, "the evidence shows Mr. Pinchot to be a man of high character, of fine honor, of stainless integrity, and of patriotic purpose." They eulogized him in a manner seldom offered to the living. The minority saw him as a witness who was "prompt, frank and fair." His desire was "to faithfully serve the American people to the best of his ability. . . . Not an act that he committed is fraught with the slightest suspicion. . . . He was a faithful public official . . . he was a just officer . . . he was a viligant [sic] and courageous defender of the public property; he was an enemy and implacable foe to the land grabber and grafter." Indirectly reproaching Taft for Pinchot's dismissal, they offered their opinion that Pinchot "dared to be insubordinate, if such he was, in the interest of his country. It was that character of insubordination which inspired the men of other days who laid the foundations in this country for an enduring people."[44]

It would be difficult for an objective person to read the records of the hearings without becoming impressed with the judiciousness of the twelfth member of the committee, Representative (Judge) Madison. Voting more often than not with the minority, he showed, more than any other member on the committee, a desire to fathom through the extraneous material and get at the pertinent facts. Criticisms that he sometimes made of witnesses and lawyers were directed at both sides. His decision to sign neither of the two main reports, but to write his own, revealed his independence. Although more restrained in his comments, his basic conclusion paralleled that of the minority report. Ballinger, he maintained, "has not shown himself to be that character of friend to the policy of conservation of our natural resources that the man should be who occupies the important post of Secretary of the Interior in our Government, and he should not be retained in that office." In reaching this conclusion, Madison made clear that he was sustaining the general charges of both Glavis and Pinchot.[45]

The total vote, therefore, was five against Ballinger and seven in his favor. But Pinchot, as has been seen, never thought of the investigation as anything other than a victory. And well he might. Although a substantial amount of the testimony tended to show Ballinger, however misguided, as not essentially dishonest, the Attorney General's misdating and the revelation of the Lawler memorandum influenced a sizable number of citizens to believe the worst about the Secretary. What the senators and congressmen said in their reports did not matter much. Any person who condemned

185

Ballinger by giving much weight to the Wickersham and Lawler episodes, however, was hardly judging the case on its merits. It is significant that Madison in his report gave no consideration whatever to either of these events.

Ballinger, although remaining a center of controversy, continued to serve as Secretary of the Interior for several months. He had, of course, his supporters. Perhaps he obtained a measure of satisfaction from letters sent to him by Pinchot's enemies who expressed their contempt by the use of such epithets as "coward," "arbitrary," "lawless," "unfair," "a leech on the government," and "scoundrel." But the encouragement which Ballinger received from these sources was not sufficient to overbalance the mounting criticism. During the hearings, he had complained to Secretary of Agriculture Wilson that some of the field men in the Forest Service were calling him such unsavory names as grafter.[46] Now, he was humiliated by the increased demands for his resignation.[47]

Ballinger could hardly have been enthusiastic over Taft's choice of a successor to Pinchot. The Secretary once confided to a friend that he believed the next Forester should be an expert in legal matters in order to cure the "evils" of the past.[48] The President, however, with the enthusiastic approval of Pinchot and other conservationists, picked Pinchot's intimate Yale friend and forestry associate, Henry S. Graves. Pinchot claimed that he and a friend, by means of a series of telegrams, were responsible for getting Graves's name before Yaleman Taft.[49] Pinchot showed his pleasure by remarking that "Graves is following out the lines I laid down in the Forest Service with great courage and ability. He is the best man in this country for the work."[50]

Amid the clamor for Ballinger's resignation, one might have guessed that Pinchot would have been in the front rank of those striving to unseat him. Curiously, however, he began to believe that the fight had had some effect in changing the color of Ballinger's spots. Reinforcing this belief was a letter from Roosevelt quoting a member of the Forest Service as saying that the Secretary of the Interior had become interested in protecting power sites. "That quotation . . . does me lots of good," replied Pinchot. "I believe we have sterilized the Secretary of the Interior pretty effectually, and the cure appears to be fairly permanent. That is one of the reasons I am not anxious to see him leave the public service."[51]

Pinchot, of course, was not saying that he would go into mourning if Ballinger resigned. When, indeed, he heard early in March that the Secretary had left his post, he admitted that he was "Feeling cheerful."[52] He was nettled, however, by Taft's unrestrained letter to Ballinger which described the Secretary as a victim of "one of the most unscrupulous conspiracies for the defamation of character that History can show."[53] Pinchot, although keen to answer this "furious" letter,[54] decided it would not be wise, especially since once again Taft appointed a man highly acceptable to Pinchot. The President, showing clearly that he was not bent on crippling conservation, chose Walter L. Fisher as the new Secretary of the Interior. A staunch supporter of the conservation movement, Fisher at the time of his appointment was vice-president of the National Conservation Association, of which Pinchot was president. Pinchot, in a statement to the press, was restrained in his comment on the retiring Secretary, "Ballinger's resignation was inevitable, and will be received with general satisfaction." The appointment of Fisher, he added, "is admirable . . . we have been working together for years."[55]

Simultaneously with the hearings of the congressional committee, the General Land Office of the Department of the Interior was conducting its own inquiry into the validity of the Cunningham claims. Pinchot and his brother Amos, determined that the coal lands should remain the property of the government, wrote President Taft in November 1910 requesting that in case the Interior Department should recommend patenting the claims, "you will allow us to submit for your consideration a brief before making a decision as to whether or not you will permit your signature to be affixed to the patents."[56] When the printed brief was ready on January 1, 1911, the Interior Department had not yet made a recommendation, but the Pinchot brothers sent a copy to the President. Prepared by Amos, and by Nathan A. Smyth, who had assisted Pepper in the congressional hearings, the pamphlet found the claims clearly illegal.

Not until late in June was the final decision on the Cunningham claims announced. On the recommendation of Ballinger's man Dennett, still the Commissioner of the General Land Office, and concurred in by Secretary Fisher, the claims were cancelled. "So that job is done," Pinchot triumphantly noted in his diary.[57] Within a few days he received warm congratulations from Roosevelt, "What a superb vindication it is!"[58] Pinchot, glowing inwardly, in turn offered his congratulations to Brandeis. "What luck it was," he continued, "that Ballinger should have announced, as he did yesterday, that he would have patented the claims anyhow. If anything further was needed to justify our fight that was certainly it."[59] In like manner he felicitated Glavis for his "splendid victory." "It is a good thing for every young man in the country to know that such things can be done."[60]

When the Cunningham claims were officially invalidated, Senator Joseph Bristow of Kansas proposed that Taft should reinstate both Pinchot and Glavis to their old positions. Pinchot, thanking the Senator, made his position clear by maintaining that "Of course . . . I could not go back holding the opinion of Mr. Taft that I do."[61] Pinchot was never one who could quickly forgive and forget. In his crusading zeal, he was likely to keep hammering away at the obstacle when he ran into opposition. His attitude toward the majority on the congressional committee remained one of resentment. Subsequently, for example, he went to Detroit in an effort to help defeat committee member Edwin Denby for re-election to Congress.[62]

Perhaps his strongest indignation was reserved for Senator Root. "Since he joined in the majority report of the Ballinger case," he told a friend, "parts of which he knew to be false, he is clear out of my reach, and I have nothing to do with him."[63] Pinchot's resentment lingered on. One day on a station platform, as he turned away from talking to General Leonard Wood, the General's companion put out his hand. "I shook hands," said Pinchot, "before I recognized who he was." It was Root, who "was smiling in an embarrassed way." Pinchot then records, "when I did [recognize him] I dropped his hand and walked away, and on the train debated whether I would go and tell him I had shaken hands by mistake. Decided against it."[64]

One biographer of Roosevelt has called the Ballinger-Pinchot controversy historically unimportant because Roosevelt's eventual indignation toward Taft would have been the same if it had never occurred.[65] Be that as it may, it is clear that the fight did positive harm to Taft and Ballinger and the orthodox Republican party in general. The Taft Administration admittedly suffered other serious injuries—the President's support of the Payne-Aldrich tariff, for example. But just as it is difficult to determine which one of several wounds is most responsible for the death of an injured soldier, so it is not easy to dismiss the Ballinger-Pinchot fight as unimportant in the election of 1910 when the Republicans lost their majority in the House of Representatives, and in 1912 when Taft trailed Wilson and Roosevelt in the election for President.

When Pinchot returned to the United States from Europe on Memorial Day, 1910, one thing was certain—he would soon be deeply immersed in some activity. A man of his seemingly limitless drive and energy could never be happy on the sidelines. Would he, as some persons were beginning to suspect, direct an increasing proportion of his fervor toward political activities?

CHAPTER II

POLITICS BECKONS

GIFFORD PINCHOT was literally flooded with letters of good wishes after his dismissal by President Taft. In many of his replies to these letters he included a sentence which had the sound of a clarion call to political wars, "Now that the lines are being clearly drawn between the special interests and the rest of us in the fight for conservation and the square deal, we shall win, for the people are on our side."[1]

Upon returning from Europe in May 1910, he unquestionably commanded wide popularity. Invitations from all over the country begged him to deliver speeches. Thousands of American citizens, of course, considered him a misguided zealot; but to countless others he was a white knight. Scattered among the flattering letters were references to a political future for Pinchot. An esteemed Pennsylvania forester, for example, predicted that first Roosevelt and then Pinchot would succeed Taft in the presidency.[2] At a dinner meeting of the Roosevelt Club of St. Paul, there was loud applause at mention of a third party with Roosevelt, Garfield, and Pinchot as its leaders.[3]

It was perhaps natural that at this time of national prominence, Pinchot's fancy turned toward politics. For the past couple of decades he had shown some susceptibility to the political virus. Back in 1897 he had written his mother from South Dakota that he hated being away from home and missing the election campaign.[4] After a long talk with Roosevelt in 1904 he had noted his great pleasure when the Chief "said I didn't show at all a lack of political training in dealing with men."[5] There had never been any question concerning which of the two major parties he would follow. In view of his upbringing it was almost a matter of course that he should support and contribute to Republican candidates.

As has already been seen, Pinchot did a little stump speaking for Roosevelt in the campaign of 1904. When the campaign was ended and Pinchot wrote to congratulate Albert Beveridge on winning a seat in the United States Senate, he acknowledged an inner craving for the political arena, "Now that I have gotten a little taste of matters political, I want to talk a lot of things over with you when you get back. . . . I foresee such opportunities to do things that I can hardly wait to get at them."[6] Beveridge had encouraged Pinchot by saying that men of his kind were needed in politics, but the tug-of-war which was taking place in Pinchot's mind was apparent from his note to the Senator a year later, "Every now and then I, too, wish I was in politics; and then again I don't. My own fight looms so large."[7] About this time he threw additional light on his feelings, however, by expressing a hope, "The time is not long past when it was not considered respectable to go into politics. I hope the time is not far distant when it will not be respectable not to go into politics."[8]

Pinchot's name was mentioned in some quarters as a candidate for Governor of Pennsylvania in the 1910 election, but any steps in this direction were quickly halted when it became known that he could not meet the constitutional requirement of seven years' residence in the state. Although he was maintaining homes in New York City, Washington, and Milford, Pennsylvania, his voting residence had always been New York. But the "half-baked boom" for governor[9] was enticing enough to induce him to prepare for the future by wiring a Milford lawyer at the end of the year, "Please have my name entered on tax list as resident. Immediate action desirable if practicable."[10]

When Pinchot returned to the United States and sized up the situation, he could scarcely wait to see Roosevelt, who was scheduled to arrive in New York on June 18. Less than a week after Roosevelt's homecoming, Pinchot was at Oyster Bay for a talk. His early access to the former President, indeed, was a source of uneasiness to Taft, who fretted that both Garfield and Pinchot, because they stayed over night and played tennis with TR, must have been formally invited to Oyster Bay.[11]

Although there is no record of what was said between the former President and Pinchot, it is apparent that at this time the two were not seeing eye to eye. Pinchot was disappointed because Roosevelt was in a cautious and compromising mood, two characteristics for which Pinchot was not noted. Roosevelt, aware of the rift that had been growing in the Republican party, was eager to keep the con-

191

servative and the progressive wings pulling together. In his efforts to maintain party unity, it was unavoidable that he should do some straddling. Pinchot, on the other hand, although having always attached himself to the G.O.P. as a matter of course, was not inseparably bound to the party. Much more so than Roosevelt, he was intent on reaching progressive goals regardless of the vehicle used. By his very nature, moreover, he preferred to strike out directly for his objectives unhampered by the necessity of making compromises and adjustments to other peoples' wishes. It was inevitable that Pinchot, who was continually tugging at Roosevelt's left arm, should on occasion prove embarrassing to the former President.

Roosevelt was not ready to accept Pinchot's estimate of Taft. Reminding Pinchot that it would probably be necessary to nominate Taft for President again in 1912, he urged that he take no position that would make his support impossible. In fatherly fashion he cautioned Pinchot "to speak with the utmost caution, and not to say anything that can even be twisted into something in the nature of a factional attack." TR also reminded him that his "enemies are hoping and praying for anything in the nature of an indiscretion on your part, and I want you to disappoint them."[12] Only a few days later, William Loeb appeared at the summer White House in Beverly with the story that Roosevelt had given Pinchot "an awful dressing down" and had insisted on his supporting Taft in the next nomination and election.[13]

Roosevelt, torn between the two factions of his party, pleased first one and then the other. On a western tour during August and September, he tended to satisfy the liberals; but when he spoke in the East, the conservatives were happier. Perhaps the most radical speech on the tour was delivered at Osawatomie, Kansas, in September 1910. Advocating the "New Nationalism," he proposed a master state wherein the national government would possess wide authority to direct the economic power of the nation.[14] Pinchot reported that he had "never seen a crowd that affected me as much as that one did. They listened to TR for nearly an hour in perfect silence . . . and then they listened to Jim and me with precisely the same attention and silence. I have never seen anything like it."[15]

Pinchot, however, was scarcely a disinterested listener, for it was he who had written the speech. Roosevelt, before delivering it, had notified him of his general approval of the draft, "I took the Osawatomie speech substantially as you left it, with one or two additions, and two or three changes."[16] Roosevelt's performance at Osawatomie was encouraging to Pinchot. Hopefully he wrote his mother, "You have seen how his own Progressiveness has grown steadily stronger."[17]

Although "delighted" that Roosevelt accepted the speech, he was less pleased by TR's warning in his letter that "extreme men on the Insurgent side" were as harmful to the Republican party as were the ultraconservatives, and that for a political leader to go beyond what the people wanted was "considerably worse than useless."[18] Roosevelt, then in the midst of a fierce struggle for control of the Republican party in New York state, spoke of the difficulties he was encountering in keeping the party united. Pinchot took the opportunity to deliver a polite lecture to the former President on holding the progressive line. Admitting the uselessness of "going ahead faster than public opinion will warrant," he argued that there was "at least equal danger of going ahead slower than public opinion demands." Conceding that the Republican party in New York might be defeated in the coming election for governor, he insisted that "you can afford to be beaten after making a fight for Progressive issues, but you can not afford not to make the fight."[19]

The week after the Osawatomie speech, Taft and Roosevelt both delivered addresses before the National Conservation Congress in St. Paul. Pinchot had obtained Roosevelt's agreement to speak at these meetings when they met in Italy in April. Again Pinchot wrote the first draft of Roosevelt's speech, and again it followed the New Nationalism by advocating national instead of state control for the conservation of natural resources. Such a program was bound to meet with substantial opposition, but the ovations given to Roosevelt and Pinchot left no doubt of the preferences of a majority of the delegates. Pinchot, called to the platform at one time during the meetings as the result of applause that followed the mention of his name, was obviously moved. "There are but few moments in a man's life like this. It is magnificent to hear the principles

193

of conservation of natural resources acclaimed as you have done. I have fought many years for conservation, and conservation has won. I thank you."[20]

Differences between the two old associates, however, continued to appear. Roosevelt, unlike many of the Insurgents, was working for the election of a Republican Congress in 1910. His general policy was to endorse Republican candidates, regardless of their political complexion.[21] Pinchot, on the other hand, confined his energies to the election of a selected list of old friends and other pillars of the liberal wing of the Republican party. Concentrating during the primaries in the districts where the Taft Administration was strenuously battling to block the progressive surge, his itinerary in July, August, and September took him to such states as California, Colorado, Kansas, Wisconsin, Minnesota, Tennessee, and Indiana. In California, he campaigned for Congressman William Kent, in Indiana, for Senator Beveridge, and in Wisconsin, for Robert M. La Follette. Having entered the Wisconsin campaign in response to a telegraphic request from La Follette, he put his best into it and was especially happy over the outcome. "Your splendid victory," he wired the Senator, "will help every man who stands for right things throughout the United States."[22]

Pinchot also made it clear to Roosevelt that he did not like the turn that political events took in New York. Roosevelt, who was instrumental in bringing about the nomination of Henry L. Stimson for governor, was piqued at the lukewarm attitude taken by Pinchot. "The wild-eyed ultraradicals," he wrote his son, "do not support us because they think we have not gone far enough. I am really sorry to say that good Gifford Pinchot has practically taken his place among the latter. He did not like the New York plank on the tariff (and neither did I), and because of this, and because he thought the platform praised Taft too much, he has been really offensive in his criticism to and of me."[23] Roosevelt, only two days later, admitted to Elihu Root that he was "bitterly disappointed with Taft."[24] But, still playing the game on the Republican team, he resented the stronger aspersions that Pinchot was casting at the President. "Gifford Pinchot," he complained, "objected . . . because

I used the word 'upright' in describing Taft, but personally I think it absurd to say that Taft is not upright."[25]

Stimson, a few weeks before he was nominated, had also mildly tried to restrain Pinchot. In a very cordial letter he expressed the hope that rumors that Pinchot was intent on founding a new third party were untrue, and gave his opinion that the wiser course was to revolutionize the Republican party. After the nomination, Pinchot wrote Stimson of his "strong desire to see you elected Governor," and offered to campaign for him.[26] But Pinchot wanted so free a hand in his campaigning that, as Roosevelt put it, "it was impossible to accept" the offer.[27] For the sake of old friendship, however, Pinchot sent Stimson a contribution of $500.

Following his electioneering tour in the West, Pinchot in a statement to the press criticized the New York platform. "Insurgency permeates both parties. I see it in every state. It is growing with tremendous speed," he announced. The New York statement of principles, he held, was lagging "too far behind the progressive West to fight shoulder to shoulder with the pioneer progressive States." Nevertheless, with a bow to Roosevelt he maintained that TR was fighting to close the gap.[28] Roosevelt unquestionably was still Pinchot's hero—if he would just stand firm against inroads on progressivism.

The November election in New York was a solid defeat for Roosevelt. Deserted by a number of the old guard Republicans who in this way asserted their control of the party, Stimson lost to the Democratic candidate by over 50,000 votes. As the dust of the battle cleared away, TR showed how thoroughly irritated he was by Pinchot's recent performances. "Gifford has in him great possibilities of usefulness," he told Stimson, "but if he travels much farther along the road on which he has been recently traveling, he will relegate himself to the company of single taxers, prohibitionists and the like."[29] The former President could hardly have guessed how accurate a prediction he was making on the prohibition matter.

Shortly after the election a rumor spread that Roosevelt and Pinchot had had a quarrel. "I hope this is true," recorded Archie Butt, "for be it so, a great obstacle is removed from the path of reconciliation [between Taft and Roosevelt]."[30] But "quarrel" was too strong a word to describe Roosevelt's irritation. Pinchot, noting reference to the rumor in a newspaper, confidently wrote to the Chief, "I see there is an idiotic story in today's *Tribune* that you and I have had a quarrel . . . it seems to me this fabrication needs no answer."[31]

Once again Pinchot was approaching the point of physical exhaustion. The Ballinger-Pinchot controversy had of course been a tremendous strain. His trip to Europe during the hearings had provided a respite but not a thorough rest. No sooner had he returned home than he rushed pell-mell into preparing for a vigorous summer and fall of speech-making and campaigning. Whereas his normal weight at this time of life ran between 165 and 170 pounds, after the election his six-foot one-inch frame tipped the scales at only 145. To get back on his feet he retreated to his beloved home in Milford. "Resting up is what I am," he reported, ". . . 10 hours in bed every night and most of the rest of the time out-doors, with simple grub and a quiet mind."[32] His own diagnosis of himself was probably accurate, "What was the matter with me was nothing but pure brain fag." Whatever the correct name for it, it could be cured by rest. Only a few weeks later he was boasting to his brother that he weighed 161.[33]

As Pinchot relaxed at his Pennsylvania estate, he had time to think of his future. Now a middle-aged man of forty-five, he had a good many productive years before him. It was by no means clear, however, in what direction his great energy and obvious talents would be directed. To a close friend he divulged that he intended to pursue two avocations, "I am proposing to spend my spare time on two things. First, a careful study of the methods of popular government, like direct primaries and the recall, and second, the writing up of the history of the Conservation movement."[34] Pinchot did, in fact, devote many hours of a long life to both of these subjects. He could hardly have conceived in 1910 of the months and months of labor which, intermittently over a period of thirty-six years, he would contribute to the writing of his autobiographical history.

These avocations reflected what had now become his two primary interests—politics and conservation. Although conservation had occupied the center of the Pinchot stage until about 1910, politics,

Gifford Pinchot, Chairman of the National
Conservation Commission

At his desk around 1900

On the stump

With TR on the Mississippi River, 1907

Governor reviewing National Guard troops
at Mt. Gretna, 1932

Riding to second inauguration as Governor, 1931
(with retiring Governor Fisher)

contrary to the belief of some of his critics, had remained secondary in his mind. From 1910 until the early 1920's, as president of the National Conservation Association, he served vigilantly to protect the country's natural resources and to alert the nation to any proposed attacks on conservation. At the same time, however, his craving for politics increasingly asserted itself. When he was elected Governor of Pennsylvania in 1922, conservation tended to move to the rear of the stage. All his life he maintained a strong interest in forestry and conservation, but in his last quarter century his interest in politics overshadowed his concern for conservation.

Characteristically, as he began to regain his energy in 1911, Pinchot became restless. "I am having a fine rest," he wrote, "and a great good time, but I confess to a certain anxiety to be back in the fight again."[35]

CHAPTER 12

GUARDIAN OF NATURAL RESOURCES

ONE MAIN OUTLET for Pinchot's energy in 1911 was the National Conservation Association which he had been instrumental in organizing in 1909. Established, it will be recalled, as a pressure group to assist in the "fight" for conservation, it was a prototype of what one man could accomplish in attempting to guide public opinion. The National Conservation Association was really a one-man organization, even though people of national prominence—former president Eliot of Harvard and Henry L. Stimson—sat on its board of directors. Many of its officers and members were sincere advocates of conservation, but Pinchot was the energizing force without which this organization could never have existed. It was he who handpicked the board and induced them to serve.

Among the officers were men who had long been his close associates. Thomas R. Shipp was the first secretary; he was a newspaperman and publicity specialist who for several years adroitly helped to keep the conservation movement and the Pinchot name before the public. After serving as a private secretary to Senator Beveridge, he had gone to Pinchot's U.S. Forest Service in 1907 as an "editor." Pinchot had thereafter leaned heavily on him for public relations work, placing him, for example, in the posts of executive secretary of the Inland Waterways Commission, and general secretary of the 1908 White House Conference on the Conservation of Natural Resources.

Shipp was followed as secretary of the Association by Harry Slattery, who through the years developed a peculiarly intimate relationship with Pinchot. Hired in his early twenties as a private secretary to Pinchot, he was shifted to the National Conservation Association in 1912. Remaining in this position almost until the demise of the organization in 1923, he developed into a kind of super lobbyist for conservation legislation. Senator La Follette considered him "a veritable watchdog of the Nation's resources."[1] A great deal of mutual admiration existed between Pinchot and Slattery. As the end of the Association approached, Pinchot highly recommended his protégé for other positions. Slattery chose to set up a law office in Washington, however, where he continued his unceasing support of conservation legislation. Pinchot continued to call on him frequently for help. Especially in the early 1930's, when Pinchot, now Governor of Pennsylvania, was paying him a retainer of as much as $7,500 a year, Slattery served as a useful pipeline for conducting inside information from Washington to the state capital at Harrisburg.

Slattery and Pinchot had much in common in their views on electric power. Slattery, whom Roosevelt once allegedly had called the "Irish rebel from the South," was pictured as a "relentless crusader against corruption in Government and deadly enemy of the Power Trust."[2] When Harold L. Ickes was about to assume his duties as Secretary of the Interior in 1933, Pinchot recommended Slattery to him in the most laudatory terms. "Whatever I have been able to do in conservation matters," he modestly proclaimed, "has been very largely due to him." Asserting that if he were Interior Secretary "the very first man I would have gone after would have been Harry," he portrayed him as "an animated guide book to public life in Washington." Stressing that Slattery had a "photographic memory and an eye entirely single to the public interest," he added that "he knows the newspaper men and the news field in Washington as few men do."[3] The recommendation must have sounded convincing to Ickes, for within three months Slattery was sworn in as special assistant to the Secretary. Eventually he progressed to administrator of the Rural Electrification Administration.

The treasurer of the National Conservation Association was Overton Price, formerly associate forester under Pinchot in the U.S. Forest Service. After his untimely death in 1914, he was succeeded by the closest of all of Pinchot's friends—classmate George Woodruff. Completing the circle of Pinchot intimates was the counsel, Philip Wells, another classmate from Yale, who had served as a law officer in the Forest Service. Some time later, both Garfield and Amos Pinchot were added to the Association's legal staff.

Additional proof of the Association's reliance on the enthusiasm of one man was furnished in 1923 when, as a result of Pinchot's inability to give it much attention after he became governor, it disappeared from the scene.

The National Conservation Association would not have survived as long as it did without Pinchot's financial help. The income from membership dues was disappointing. Although Pinchot had dreamed of a total of 50,000 to 100,000 members, there were only 2,160 subscribers to the magazine, *American Conservation*, which was published for six issues and then discontinued. The Association's budget for 1916 listed only $2,500 as the expected income from dues. One year, the board of directors, to help meet a deficit, decided that each director and officer would raise $150 within a three-month period.[4] At another time the board voted to assess each person $250, although the records show that Gifford and Amos Pinchot and one other person were the only members present at the meeting.[5] Time after time, when the treasury was pinched, Pinchot was the financial angel who sent a check to the secretary—for $250 or even $1,000. When Slattery wrote in 1920 saying that the Association's balance was down to $168.97, and that it would take about $2,250 to finish out the year, Pinchot sent $2,500 with the comment that "If we raise enough a little later, you can consider it a loan."[6] The narrowness of the support on which they could depend was strikingly illustrated by an audit for the year ending January 31, 1922: Pinchot had made a contribution of $20,000 and the entire budget for 1921 was $18,000.[7] Slattery was frank in telling Pinchot that one of the greatest handicaps to raising money on the outside was the exaggerated idea of his personal wealth; he also warned that too many news releases concerning Pinchot were coming out of the millionaires' haven of Newport.[8]

Regardless of the limited range of its membership and support, the organization was reasonably effective. It would be neither fair nor accurate to label the Association, as some of Pinchot's enemies were inclined to do, an organization primarily motivated by a desire to advance the personal political fortunes of Gifford Pinchot. True, there were political overtones to some of its activities, but basically it was devoted to protecting the nation's heritage of natural resources from abuse. One might disagree with the wisdom of some of Pinchot's decisions, but could scarcely question the sincerity behind his shepherding of the Association's drive for conservation.

When a seemingly important piece of legislation concerning conservation was introduced in Congress, it was customary for either Slattery or Wells, in the headquarters office in Washington, to prepare a memorandum on its contents. In the earlier days of the Association, printed analyses of pending legislation were distributed to members, signed "National Conservation Association, By Gifford Pinchot, its President." Only a month after Pinchot's dismissal from the Forest Service, for example, a seven-page printed folder reported on nine bills in Congress: three were good bills; two were both good and bad; one was predominantly bad; and three were "thoroughly unfortunate and should be rewritten entirely."[9]

With considerable regularity, Pinchot sent personalized letters to newspaper editors throughout the country, sometimes as many as four to five thousand at a time. Making no reference to the Association and typed on green-tinted paper across the top of which "Gifford Pinchot, Milford Pike Co Pa" appeared, these letters were individually addressed and customarily signed by a secretary in the Association office who had learned to imitate Pinchot's signature. Such communications to the press usually were appeals for or against specific bills. Pinchot's hope, frequently fulfilled, was that newspaper editors would either print his letters in full, or pull out of them bits of information to use on their editorial pages. When informed that a particular editor had taken a stand in line with his appeals, he was meticulously careful to convey his thanks.

Pinchot was extremely resourceful in seeking support in every possible corner. When he wanted to stir up opposition to a particularly obnoxious bill, he induced Harold L. Ickes to supply a long list of names of "influential Progressives" in the West to whom he could address his appeals.[10] When worried about a possible transfer of national forests to the states, he sent a statement on the subject to the editor of the *Saturday Evening Post* "with the very strong hope" that he would treat it editorially.[11] Or when the Ways and Means Committee of the House was about to decide on a recommendation for chairman of the Committee on Public Lands, Pinchot tried to enlist help for his preference from the Democratic leader, William Jennings Bryan.[12] Nor was he hesitant about asking all kinds of organizations and associations to pass resolutions favoring conservation.

Pinchot received much personal satisfaction from his efforts to sway opinion. With unconcealed enthusiasm he recorded in his diary the main events of a happy day, more than a year after his dismissal, when he went to the Forest Service Offices "about 10:30." Reading the office copy of the *Congressional Record*, he learned of the passage of a "Heyburn amendment" that would reduce the size of some of the government forests. "Sent for Shipp and Price. Dol came in. We four prepared statements for the press. Price arranged for me to address Lumber Dealers then in session and I did about 12:30." By two o'clock a "strong resolution" backing the Forest Service was passed and was delivered to the President that same afternoon with a letter asking him to veto the bill. "It was effective, and great fun. Like old times. Also we wired all over West, and protests began reaching Warren [the acting chairman of the Agriculture Committee] at once." Triumphantly Pinchot added at the end of the day's notes, "Heyburn Amendment went out in conference this P.M."[13]

The Association kept constant watch on senators and representatives, and bombarded them with information. By means of letters and personal appearances before congressional committees, Pinchot and other officers of the group argued their case. When an influential member of Congress took the "right" stand on legislation he was likely to receive a word of encouragement from Pinchot. To Scott Ferris, chairman of the House Public Lands Committee, for example, Pinchot addressed a letter complimenting him for standing "vigorously and effectively for the public welfare" in the "fight against the waterpower grabbers."[14] In like manner he wrote to assure Senator La Follette of the "high appreciation" felt for his blocking of a coal and oil bill.[15]

Pinchot and his organization, in other words, for over a decade stood constant guard over the nation's natural resources. Poised ready to strike against any threat of unwarranted depletion of this wealth, his activities took him into a wide variety of fields. In the year 1914, for example, impressed by the "priceless" nature of radium in fighting cancer, he used all his skill to warn the country of the danger of "exploitation by private interests" of the remaining radium lands then government-owned.[16]

Although the Association interested itself in many conservation problems, it concentrated most consistently on two main objects: fighting a movement to turn over the national forests to the western states; working for legislation to control the development of water power on federal government property.

Legislation to transfer the national forests, which was repeatedly introduced in Congress, received strong support from persons favoring as little government control as possible. The more powerful and effective the U.S. Forest Service had become, the more persistent were the appeals for placing the forests under the generally less efficient management of the states. Pinchot's experience, both in the Forest Service and the Association, convinced him that the "states rights" issue too often was used by those opposed to effective government regulation. Nor did his later involvement in state government administration alter this point of view. He kept hammering home that the states, having mismanaged their forests in the past, should not now be entrusted with additional wooded areas. The sentiment for the transfer was not strong enough to carry legislation through Congress. On the contrary the conservationists, strongly supported by the Association, were successful in obtaining enactment in 1911 of the Weeks law which permitted federal purchase of additional forest lands on the headwaters of navigable streams.

The second major purpose of the organization—water power legislation—was aimed at winning congressional approval of laws which would place the entire public domain under the same sort of regulations for control of power development that the Forest Service had established for government forest lands under its jurisdiction. Woodruff and Wells, who had done so much under Pinchot to formulate this policy, now joined him in battling for its broader adoption. Basic to the plan, it will be remembered, was the provision that no water power site owned by the government should be sold or leased in perpetuity and that the government should exercise tight enough control over the development of such power to protect the public interest and prevent excessive or unwarranted profits by private enterprise.

The Federal Water Power Act, finally enacted in 1920, was the culmination of a long struggle to obtain the kind of legislation that Pinchot had been seeking. Although the new law was in some respects a compromise, much of it, including a fifty-year term for government leases of water power, harked back to the early regulations of the Forest Service. No sooner had Congress passed the legislation than Pinchot wrote to Wells, "I feel like congratulating you on the end of a great piece of work."[17]

Although another organization, the National Conservation Congress, paralleled to a considerable extent the activities of the National Conservation Association, Pinchot did not fully believe in the sincerity of its purpose. Early in the life of his organization, he had considered, in view of the difficulty of raising money, a merger of the two groups,[18] but in the end thought better of it. Convinced that the Congress, which held its first annual meeting (or congress) in Seattle in August 1909, was started "largely by men hostile to the policy of Conservation,"[19] he was satisfied that friends of conservation were successful at this inaugural meeting in gaining control of the organization. For the next few years he made concerted drives, sometimes more and sometimes less successfully, to keep the Congress under the influence of the Pinchot philosophy. It was largely as a result of his objections, for example, that the original list of proposed speakers for the second meeting of the Congress in St. Paul was enlarged to include persons, including Roosevelt, more friendly to the cause.

Pinchot was especially jubilant over the victory he won at the meeting of the Congress in Washington in 1913. Unhappy at the report of its committee on water power, which he labelled favorable to the power interests, he and Henry L. Stimson and Joseph N. Teal issued a printed nine-page minority report in which they complained that "Ten groups of power interests control 65 per cent of all the developed waterpower in the United States." There were, they insisted, three essentials of a sound water power policy: "1. Prompt development. 2. Prevention of unregulated monopoly. 3. Good service and fair charges to the consumer."[20] Pinchot had written such phrases in the report of the Inland Waterways Commission back in 1908; they were to be enunciated incessantly during much of his service as Governor of Pennsylvania.

The minority report served as the basis for a proposal by Pinchot to amend the committee's report. Following a stormy session on the convention floor, during which the opposition attempted to block the amendment by motions to adjourn and other parliamentary devices, Pinchot's resolution passed by 317 to 96. Garfield and Stimson, Pinchot wrote his brother, "did splendid work."[21]

It is usually difficult to gauge accurately the amount of influence that a pressure group exerts on public opinion. Certainly it would be a mistake to assume that the wide public support in America for forestry and conservation were largely the result of shrewd publicity campaigns, such as those by the Forest Service and the National Conservation Association. Much of the basic support for these two interrelated programs would have existed with or without the attempts at manipulation. Pinchot, himself, like a good many leaders of such organizations, tended to exaggerate the role of the Association in obtaining or blocking legislation; he boasted, for example, that it was "mainly responsible" for the passage of a number of laws including the water power act of 1920.[22] Similarly, after the House decisively defeated a bill considered undesirable, he noted in his diary, "Raker Bill killed this P.M. 128 to 10!!! Great credit due Price and Slattery."[23] When in 1923 the Association closed its doors, Pinchot's final words were delivered in the most glowing terms, "no other organization in Washington has ever begun to approach its record of constructive service to the people of America."[24]

Pinchot may have engaged in overstatements to a degree, but his influence and that of the Association can as easily be underestimated as overestimated. There is abundant evidence to show that the Association was at least moderately effective. Had there been no Pinchot, some of the laws passed by Congress would undoubtedly have had a somewhat different complexion.

Although Pinchot had sprung back to good physical shape in the spring of 1911, he decided to take a quiet, restful, two-month cruise around the Mediterranean with his mother. Out of the country until the middle of May, he returned full of vim, and eager to resume an active life.

Almost immediately he became intrigued with new rumors that pointed to possible scandal in the Taft Administration. While Pinchot was away the *Philadelphia North American* had dramatically featured in a headline that "Taft Secretly Gives Control of Alaska Coal to Guggenheims."[25] The similarity between this statement and the language used by *Collier's* magazine in 1909 to publicize the Glavis charges was striking. The new article referred to an order issued by Taft in October 1910, withdrawing 12,800 acres of land from the Chugach National Forest in Alaska and making it available for sale. Situated on Controller Bay, the land was to be used to encourage private capital to build a railroad and terminal facilities to serve the coal areas, including the former Cunningham claims, in the vicinity of the Bering River. The implication of the *North American* article was that the Guggenheim's Alaska Syndicate, which already had a terminus at Cordova, was acquiring a monopoly of coal transportation. Actually, Taft had issued his order with the understanding that the law prohibited such monopoly, and that a new railroad would not come under the control of the Syndicate.[26]

Although the Senate approved a resolution asking Secretary of the Interior Fisher to send it full information on the subject, the matter at first failed to attract much attention. But in June 1911, Miss M. F. Abbott, an independent writer, published in several newspapers a syndicated article charging that the Alaska Syndicate, working through a dummy, had in fact conspired to seize control of the newly proposed railway and terminal facilities. Miss Abbott based her conclusions on notes she took after receiving Secretary Fisher's permission to look through some of the Interior Department's files.

The part of the article which did most to convince Pinchot that duplicity had occurred was a postscript allegedly taken from a letter written on July 13, 1910, by Richard S. Ryan to Secretary Richard A. Ballinger. Ryan, whom Miss Abbott charged with being the key man in the supposed deal by the Syndicate, was quoted as writing: "Dear Dick: I went to see the President the other day about this Controller Bay affair. The President asked me who it was I represented. I told him, according to our agreement, that I represented myself. But this didn't seem to satisfy him. So I sent for Charlie Taft and asked him to tell his brother, the President, who it was I really represented. The President made no further objection to my claim. Yours, Dick."[27]

Once more President Taft was thrown on the defensive. Roosevelt, writing in the *Outlook*, was highly critical.[28] Again the word "investigation" was in the air. Miles Poindexter, progressive Senator from Washington, obtained Senate approval of a resolution asking the President for a full report. Exactly one month later Taft submitted his explanatory message. Flatly denying that the disposal of government land around Controller Bay was in any way contributing to monopoly, he lashed out at the "wanton recklessness" of some of the critics. The "Dick-to-Dick" letter he branded as a "wicked fabrication" which was not in the files and never had been.[29]

Pinchot and some of his friends remained suspicious. But his friends were also cautious. The editor of *Collier's*, Norman Hapgood, after talking with Secretary Fisher, had declined to publish Miss Abbott's accusations. Louis Brandeis had agreed to help with a proposed investigation by a House committee, but made no public statement pending a thorough investigation. Pinchot, however, unsatisfied by the President's explanation, characteristically jumped in with both feet. Visioning a deadly parallel between the missing "Dick-to-Dick" letter and the Lawler letter in the Ballinger-Pinchot inquiry, he immediately went to work to write a reply. Meanwhile he and his brother Amos visited Secretary Fisher to warn that "documents had been denied to exist" in the former investigation and afterward produced.[30]

Pinchot was pleased that "nearly all N.Y. and other papers" carried his reply in full. Ignoring the controversial letter which Taft said did not exist, he hit hard at the President for not holding the lands around Controller Bay under government ownership. "The President's defense of his course," mocked Pinchot, "shows how hard it is to make a good excuse for a bad mistake." Holding it "Unfortunate" that the friends of conservation had to "expend their strength" against government officials who ought to be protecting natural resources in Alaska, he declared that it looked like unnecessary duplication of work "when we must first fight the police-man before we can get a chance to stop the looting."[31]

Secretary Fisher, interested in obtaining first-hand information as a basis for recommendations on the future of Alaska, set out in August to make a tour of the area. John E. Lathrop, correspondent for a newspaper in Portland, Oregon, who was anathema to a good many Alaskans, followed the Fisher party.[32] Disturbed by what he thought were some of the effects of the tour, he urgently wired Pinchot on August 19 to hurry to Alaska, "The other side has a horde of men up here . . . I am the only one on our side . . . we need you here."[33]

Although there was little justification for the implication that Secretary Fisher was on the other side of the fence from Pinchot—at least in basic beliefs—no time was wasted in arranging a trip. After all, he had never seen the land about which he had talked so much in the past two years. As a kind of self-appointed godfather to Alaska, it was only right that he should take a good look at his godson. At the same time, he might be able to pick up "some val-uable material" to assist Brandeis in the projected investigation.[34]

Sailing from the west coast on September 1 with Senator Poin-dexter, his reception in Alaska was decidedly mixed. Pinchot had of course been aware that a substantial number of Alaskans, be-lieving that conservation meant an arrestment of development, re-sented the whole movement. Whether or not, as some conservation-ists maintained, this critical attitude was partly encouraged by busi-ness interests intent on opening up the area, there was no question of its existence. In the midst of the Ballinger-Pinchot controversy, for example, the delegate from Alaska to the United States Con-gress wired Ballinger that both the people and newspapers of Alaska were behind him.[35] Only four months before Pinchot's trip to Alaska, rampaging inhabitants in two towns demonstrated their impatience with the slow development of coal mining in the area. In imitation of the Boston Tea Party, residents of Cordova staged a Cordova Coal Party in which they dumped imported Canadian coal in the bay and burned Pinchot in effigy. The next day, people in nearby Katalla burned another Pinchot effigy. After he had spent a few days in Alaska, however, he wrote home from Seward, "Never in my life have I had more courteous treatment than since reaching Alaska."[36]

Some of Pinchot's other correspondence indicates that this description of his reception was an overstatement. On several occasions he ran into open hostility. A score of years later, he gleefully recalled the time when Jack Dalton "came down to the dock with two guns on to prevent certain citizens of Cordova from carrying out their doubtless laudable purpose of keeping me from landing from the steamer."[37] Now and then he faced placards denouncing both conservation and himself. A banner displayed with the following message was at Seward the day Secretary Fisher arrived: "Conservation Prices . . . British Columbia coal, $17 per ton . . . Wood, $7 a cord . . . But you must not mine your own coal, nor cut your own wood . . . All reserved for future generations . . . Signed . . . G. Pinchot . . . 'Pinhead.' "[38]

Pinchot kept telling the Alaskans, however, that land frauds rather than conservation were responsible for the bottling up of Alaska's resources.[39] His activity in the Ballinger-Pinchot dispute, he argued, was "an effort to prevent the men who were trying to plunder and monopolize Alaska from carrying out their plan."[40] Full of confidence in his ability to convert the inhabitants to his point of view, he related to his mother how, after the Chamber of Commerce of Cordova had refused to call a meeting to hear Senator Poindexter and himself, "the citizens took it up . . . and held what I understand was at least a third larger meeting than Fisher had when he was here . . . I really believe that by now Poindexter and I have a substantial majority of the citizens of the town feeling friendly toward us."[41] In Valdez it was the same story, "I think I did pretty well in Valdez as to changing public opinion."[42] As Pinchot prepared to return to Seattle after a six weeks' tour he wrote, "I am coming back with no reason whatever to change the essential position I have already taken about Controller Bay or any other matter of real importance."[43]

By now so anti-Taft that he had difficulty in crediting any member of the Administration with good intentions, he was even losing confidence in Secretary Fisher—whose appointment he had praised highly. "Fisher," he wrote Roosevelt, "saw very little coal, because where he went there was very little coal to be seen."[44]

Pinchot came back to Washington prepared for a battle with Taft, but he never had the opportunity to start one. Brandeis's research into the whole matter pointed to the conclusion that the Administration had acted unwisely but not improperly. Miss Abbott later was discredited, and there never was any conclusive evidence that the "Dick-to-Dick" letter was anything other than a hoax.[45] Secretary Fisher, moreover, shortly after he returned from Alaska, proposed a program for the area which included lease rather than sale of coal lands to private operators, and construction by the government of a railway into some of the coal fields. Such a measure plainly was in line with the philosophy of both Roosevelt and Pinchot.

One sequel to the controversy over Alaska and the Cunningham claims occurred early in 1917 when Daniel Guggenheim met at length with Pinchot to urge him to correct his "unjust" holding that the Morgan-Guggenheim interests through their Alaska Syndicate had attempted to obtain a monopoly in Alaska. Pinchot took no exception to the facts presented by Guggenheim, "I am very far from disputing your statement." But, whether or not the Syndicate had aimed at a monopoly, Pinchot refused to accept any blame for an injustice. "[The] Natural and inevitable result of what was actually done in your name," he wrote Guggenheim, "was to produce the impression that an effort was under way to monopolize the resources of Alaska. Hence I find it impossible to agree with you that the fault lay with myself and the others who so believed rather than with you, whose acts, directly or indirectly, caused that belief." Any charge of injustice, reasoned Pinchot, should be applied to Guggenheim rather than Pinchot or the public.[46] The key to several of Pinchot's actions throughout his long life are found in this letter to Guggenheim—as well as to the feeling of some of his opponents that he did not always fight fairly. In other words, on some occasions Pinchot felt justified in attacking when only the impression of improper behavior was given.

PART TWO

Politics in the Ascendancy

CHAPTER 13

LA FOLLETTE IS DROPPED

GIFFORD PINCHOT wrote to his friend and colleague Overton Price in 1913 in these words, "I am not satisfied that my activity in Conservation has been anything like it ought to have been for the past couple of years."[1] A less energetic person might have felt that the number of hours Pinchot devoted to conservation and the National Conservation Association was all that could be expected from one man. But the former Forester was no ordinary man measured in terms of vigor.

If he was dissatisfied with the amount of consideration he gave to conservation, what was diverting his attention? The answer, as has already been suggested, was politics. The 1910 primaries and elections had given him his first real taste of practical political campaigning; he enjoyed the experience. The pull of his new interest even kept him away from the National Conservation Congress in September 1912; telegraphing his regrets, he explained that he was too busy campaigning and "working to make this continent a better home for a better race."[2] To some people, especially his enemies, the thought of Pinchot active in politics was more than a little awesome. Charles J. Bonaparte, a member of Roosevelt's cabinet, reflected such qualms when he portrayed Pinchot as "a combination of an enthusiast and a politician" who could be a "useful agency under firm and tactful control but a dangerous compound under other circumstances."[3]

Pinchot was one of the group of about twenty-five members of Congress, half a dozen governors, and other friends of insurgency, who formally organized the National Progressive Republican League on January 21, 1911, at Senator La Follette's home. Officially, the purpose of the new organization was to promote popular government and progressive legislation. The name Republican was retained, according to La Follette, because some of the members were skittish about becoming identified with a third party movement.[4] Pinchot, however, had made up his mind that the primary objective for all good Republicans in the election of 1912 was to unite behind a progressive candidate who could defeat Taft for renomination, and, in the event this was unsuccessful, to launch a third party. From the first he was impatient with the League's progress. Pleased that he himself was chosen to be on the executive committee, and that Representative George W. Norris was elected first vice-president, he was not happy over the choice of Senator Jonathan Bourne of Oregon as president. "A good meeting," he noted, "although I wish we had some one else than Bourne as Pres. I don't trust him much."[5] Further discouraged by the League's February meeting in Washington, which was attended by about fifteen persons, he told Brandeis "It was the most melancholy attempt at a meeting of a great movement I have happened to see. . . . The whole thing was desultory, ineffective, and pretty well useless."[6] With an eye on publicity, he proposed a June convention, which was opposed by Bourne and voted down. "Amos and I thoroughly disgusted. The League can't do much if this is a sample."[7]

Roosevelt, trying to prevent a split in the Republican party, was disturbed. As he confessed a few years later, he believed that both Root and Pinchot veered too far from the middle of the road. Admitting that he perhaps owed more to them than to any others for their help during his presidency, he lamented that "As soon as I left office both obeyed the centrifugal tendencies of the time and flew in opposite directions—Root in the direction of sacrificing idealism to an excessive taste and desire to be severely practical, and Gifford in the direction of sacrificing practical achievement to an excessive, and sometimes, twisted idealism."[8]

During much of 1911, while Roosevelt was still willing to support Taft for renomination, he was especially annoyed by Pinchot's animosity toward the President and his flirtations with the idea of a third party. At the opening of the year he complained that Pinchot was joining "some of the extremists" in Congress "with the expectation of trying to form a third party if Taft is nominated." The former President, moreover, showed that he was still nursing a grudge because Pinchot and other liberals had given him "much less help than I was entitled to" in the recent New York election.[9]

Two weeks before Pinchot left for his Mediterranean cruise in the spring of 1911, he and Norman Hapgood lunched with Roosevelt. In answer to a question from Hapgood, TR stated he could not support a third party, and would have to back Taft if he was nominated. Pinchot, maintaining that it was "foolishness," since the Chief did not want Taft, to sit still and let him be nominated, directly asked if Roosevelt would support La Follette as a candidate for nomination. "He said not publicly," reported Pinchot, "but at my suggestion wrote a . . . letter to La Follette and gave it to me for him, asking him to come to NY or Oyster Bay on Mar 5 or 7 (so I could be there too) for a conference, and bring whom he would." Strongly as Roosevelt was disclaiming any interest in the nomination for himself, Pinchot came away from the meeting with a different notion. "Was impressed," he wrote, "that Roosevelt is looking to run himself in 1912 as compromise candidate, although I told him I thought he ought not to run."[10] Why Pinchot advised against running can only be guessed; perhaps he was merely raising a trial balloon to discover Roosevelt's reaction. It is also possible that at this time he sincerely believed Senator La Follette to be the most acceptable candidate with strong chances of winning.

Roosevelt and La Follette did not have high admiration for each other. Pinchot delivered TR's longhand letter, but was unsuccessful in getting the two men together—he tried on several occasions, but La Follette resisted.[11] The Senator, however, got the impression from talking to Pinchot that Roosevelt was encouraging him and would support him, quietly at first, and then openly.[12] Pinchot later insisted that no such assumption had been warranted.

Upon Pinchot's return from vacation in the middle of May, he tried to size up the political situation anew. A brief talk with Roosevelt on May 16 assured him that TR "Is evidently feeling decidedly more progressive."[13] The next day, after seeing La Follette and various other Progressives, he learned that a few evenings before it had been decided at a meeting at the Senator's home to announce La Follette's candidacy as soon as $100,000 could be raised. The group at this meeting, moreover, seemed to have agreed that Pinchot would be the best man to run on the ticket as candidate for vice-president.[14]

Pinchot's evaluation of the situation scarcely filled him with wild enthusiasm. "Politically the Progressives have made little advance," he wrote to his mother in Europe, "but La Follette's candidacy is likely to become public in the near future, and I think we will be able to go ahead vigorously from now on."[15] Ten days later he declared that his "personal regard" for La Follette was growing "steadily greater."[16]

Whatever his inner opinion of Roosevelt's intentions, Pinchot steadfastly maintained a public position that the Chief would not run. "Frank Kellogg came in to find out if T.R. will run," he noted. "Told him emphatically No." The same day, June 12, Pinchot and a few others in conference with La Follette decided that the time for action had come. "Decision to go ahead," he wrote in the diary, "get out men to spread the La Follette gospel, and proceed. I am to see Amos and get some money at once."[17] Gifford agreed to help financially, and within a few months had contributed $10,000.[18]

A few days later La Follette formally announced his candidacy on the Republican ticket.

During the ensuing weeks, before he sailed for Alaska in September, Pinchot continued to make plain what he thought of Taft. When Henry L. Stimson, newly chosen as Secretary of War, dined with the Pinchots, the host explained "quite frankly" that his attitude toward Taft "was settled once for all when he went back on TR after his election."[19] An article that Pinchot wrote for the *Saturday Evening Post* in October 1911 was so vehement in its criticism of the President that Price, Shipp, brother Amos and sister Nettie— none of whom was noted for caution—urged him not to print it; but, with the approval of Brandeis and La Follette, he went ahead.[20]

Nor did he mince any words when talking to Roosevelt. While sitting one day in the outer offices of the *Outlook*, which Roosevelt now edited, Pinchot spied in the current issue of the magazine an editorial on Controller Bay. Because it took a moderate tone in discussing the subject, Pinchot was incensed. "It certifies to Taft's good intentions," he noted in his diary, "in a needless way. I told TR so vigorously." He further recorded how he insisted to Roosevelt that in order to avoid "four extra years of fighting" for conservation, the "thing to do is to beat Taft for nomination."[21]

Believing the worst about Taft's actions, Pinchot told Roosevelt that "Controller Bay would prevent Taft's nomination," and that the Chief "might be nominated by acclamation." TR's response, according to Pinchot, was that "we'd handle that when we came to it." Whereupon Pinchot told him "for the nth time" of his opinion that "Taft is dishonest." Roosevelt protested "as usual . . . but couldn't make it stick."[22] Although Pinchot was not the only ardent critic of Taft, Roosevelt remained unconvinced. Comments by Congressman Kent evoked a mild letter of reproach from TR, "Come, come! You and Gifford are altogether crazy about Taft . . . you use language about him that is not justified."[23]

Roosevelt's belief that Taft was honest did not mean that in the summer of 1911 the former President was pleased with his successor. In an August letter to his son, for example, he maintained that Taft would be nominated, but stated frankly that he thought "less of him as time goes on," and called him a "flubdub with a streak of the second-rate." He believed, moreover, that Taft's strength was actually increasing, for which he blamed the Insurgents who had played into his hands by their lack of coherence and tendency to go to extremes. "Gifford Pinchot is a dear," he wrote, "but he is a fanatic, with an element of hardness and narrowness in his temperament, and an extremist."[24]

When Pinchot left for Alaska at the end of August, he apparently was on the La Follette bandwagon. Upon departing he wrote a check for $5,000 "on the general chance that it will be needed for campaign expenses while I am gone."[25] On his way to the Pacific coast he stopped in St. Paul to deliver a speech praising La Follette.[26] The very day he returned to Seattle from Alaska he openly declared for the Senator as a presidential candidate, knowing that only twenty-four hours earlier a few hundred Progressives from thirty states, meeting in Chicago, had voted a similar endorsement.

Back in Washington, the political news was disquieting. Several Progressives were of the opinion that Roosevelt was the only one of their group who could be nominated. Senator Beveridge believed that neither Taft nor La Follette stood a chance.[27] Garfield, noting a rapid growth of Roosevelt sentiment, took the view that La Follette could not win Ohio.[28] Moreover, some of Roosevelt's friends, who had given up hope of his running in October, were a trifle more optimistic in November.[29]

Pinchot, who had committed himself rather deeply to the La Follette cause, began, almost imperceptibly at first, to withdraw. Despite recent differences with Roosevelt, he still retained much of his old worship for the Chief. He was determined, moreover, that Taft must be beaten. Never certain that La Follette could accomplish this task, his apprehension began to grow. By the end of November, furthermore, he doubted that TR would refuse to run. Although his allegiance to the Senator began to waver, he continued to support La Follette publicly. Speaking before the Insurgents' Club in New York City on November 27 he brought prolonged applause by his statement that "whoever the Republican National Convention does nominate will be a man satisfactory to the progressive wing of the party. And in my judgment before very long we shall all understand that that man is going to be 'Bob' La Follette."[30] Steadfastly he asserted in speeches that Roosevelt would not be a candidate; "I am in a position to know," he would say.[31]

Although La Follette was a little skeptical of the sincerity of Pinchot and some other supporters, he did not have much concrete cause for worry until early December. One of the first signs of trouble was a passage which appeared first in Pinchot's December 7 address before the Chicago Press Club, and was later repeated in both Boston and New York. Pinchot explained that the Wisconsin Senator was chosen primarily to serve as a "rallying point" to hold the Progressive movement together rather than as a candidate who was expected to win the nomination. "[The] most we hoped to accomplish," he announced, "was to prevent the nomination of any reactionary . . . I know of my own knowledge that when Senator La Follette allowed his name to be used as a candidate, he did not expect to win the nomination, and that is one reason why I know that he is fighting for a cause and not for a man."[32] Noble as this passage sounded, however, it did not accurately portray La Follette's current feelings about his campaign, for by now he was a thoroughly serious contender. Although Pinchot claimed later that La Follette had read and approved the statement before it was used, the Senator could not have been happy about its tone. Certainly, he had good cause to wonder how long he could keep Pinchot in his camp. Mean-while, his position became increasingly awkward as rumors grew that Roosevelt would run.

The men acting as La Follette's campaign committee met with him for a two-day conference at Pinchot's home on December 11 and 12. The Senator here proposed that he write a letter to Roosevelt asking him to state his intentions. Both Pinchot and William Kent later asserted that La Follette offered to withdraw and throw his support to Roosevelt if the former President desired to be nominated.[33] On the first day of the meeting La Follette asked others besides himself to prepare suggested drafts of a letter. The next day, however, after prolonged discussion, no agreement could be reached on its text. La Follette now refused to pledge his support to Roosevelt if he ran.[34] According to Pinchot's account of the meeting, "It was decided by Bob to write no letter and instead to send a committee. Then, at last, about 1:30, to send no one." At lunch and after, Pinchot repeatedly pleaded for harmony among the Progressives, al-though harmony apparently meant to him that La Follette would, if necessary, make way for Roosevelt.

Two of the guests, Medill McCormick and Gilson Gardner, both newspapermen, stayed after lunch for a talk with Pinchot. About ten o'clock that evening, Pinchot called on the Senator and issued the ominous warning that if he broke with Roosevelt, the three could not continue as his supporters. Pinchot felt that he obtained "more or less formal assent to my demand for harmony," but he neverthe-less had a feeling of "much uneasiness."[35]

It was Pinchot who arranged for a luncheon conference December 17 between "TR and La Follette men." Present were Roosevelt, McCormick, Gardner, Kent, Congressman Lenroot, and Pinchot. According to Gardner, La Follette refused to allow his manager, Houser, to attend. "We had," said Pinchot, "a very frank and straight talk." Roosevelt was still adhering to his watchful waiting. The emphasis of the meeting was on harmony; as Pinchot put it, the La Follette men were to "keep in close touch with" Roosevelt, and "some solution [was] to be reached to prevent crossing of wires."[36]

At a dinner at Medill McCormick's on the day after Christmas Pinchot learned his host had reached the conclusion that La Follette should retire as a candidate in favor of Roosevelt. According to Pinchot and other leaders, even Walter Houser, La Follette's campaign manager, agreed that this was the only way to prevent Taft's nomination.[37] The group was of one mind, however, that they should wait and see what happened at the Ohio State Conference of Progressives, scheduled to meet in Columbus on New Year's Day, 1912.[38]

Some of La Follette's supporters planned to have the Ohio Conference unanimously approve a resolution endorsing his candidacy.[39] Prior to the Columbus meeting, Pinchot, in fulfillment of a promise, made two Ohio speeches for La Follette. At the convention, however, he joined forces with Garfield and one or two others in leading a move to block a blanket endorsement.[40] As finally approved, 52-32, the resolution voiced support for the nomination of La Follette, or Roosevelt, "or any other Progressive Republican." La Follette interpreted this move as a bitter betrayal. Pinchot and others, however, explained it as desirable strategy for keeping Roosevelt's followers in line; he continued to forecast the eventual nomination of La Follette by the Republicans.[41]

Pinchot at this time was working in the dark in guessing Roosevelt's intentions. He could surmise and he could hope that TR would run, but could not be certain. In an interview shortly after the Ohio Conference, he denied rumors that he had said Roosevelt would not accept the nomination if it were tendered. "I know nothing of Mr. Roosevelt's affairs," he could still say honestly, "either as to whether he would accept the nomination, or whether he believes he could be elected."[42]

By the middle of January, however, it became more obvious that Roosevelt, however reluctantly, was a candidate, in fact if not in name. At the same time, Pinchot's readiness to switch horses was increasingly apparent. To ease the difficulty of accomplishing this, he tried to convince La Follette and other Progressives of the advantage of placing on the ballot as delegates to the Republican national convention candidates who might vote for the nomination of either La Follette or Roosevelt. When the La Follettes had Sunday dinner with the Pinchots on January 14, however, the host decided the

Senator "evidently was against" the plan. Pinchot reported, on the other hand, that Houser "fully" approved.[43]

After sounding out a few other persons, Pinchot called another meeting, this time at La Follette's Washington headquarters. Try as he would, however, he could not get this group to endorse his ballot scheme. Even his brother Amos voted against him. Gifford, nevertheless, openly objecting to La Follette's playing a "lone hand," told the Senator, in the presence of the others assembled, that he "could not recognize [the] right of one man to dictate policy." He promised, however, to follow the majority.[44]

The next day, January 20, Pinchot addressed a Progressive Republican meeting in Worcester, Massachusetts. Publicly, he was still the champion of the Wisconsin Senator, "While I understand this meeting is held in the interest of no candidate, I can not refrain from saying that the Progressive Republican whose nomination I advocate is that soldier of the common good—Robert M. La Follette."[45] But that very afternoon, in the offices of the *Outlook*, Roosevelt and others had drafted a letter to be signed by a half dozen state governors asking the former President to run again. Pinchot had sat with the group at the beginning, but, at the suggestion of Roosevelt, withdrew before the important business was transacted.[46] How many of the details of Roosevelt's budding campaign were known to Pinchot at this time is uncertain; but he was now confident that TR would enter the race.

Pinchot's problem of the moment, therefore, was how best to drop La Follette. Wrestling with his conscience, he discussed with Roosevelt and others a proposed statement for the press, but decided to delay action until the "middle or end of February."[47] Although Pinchot was later accused of contributing money to the Roosevelt movement as early as the middle of January, there appears to be no evidence that he did so at this time. Indeed, as late as January 8 the La Follette campaign committee received from him a gift of $4,000.[48]

The evening of January 22 provided what must have been an embarrassing experience for Pinchot. La Follette, billed for a speech at Carnegie Hall in New York City, drew such a crowd that several thousand were turned away. After addressing an overflow meeting outside the hall, he came to the stage to be introduced by Pinchot. Although the audience could hardly have detected any lukewarm quality about Pinchot's remarks concerning the Senator, he scarcely spoke with the unrestrained enthusiasm expected at such a rally. He lauded La Follette the man, but not La Follette the presidential candidate. An entry in his diary for that day plainly revealed what was uppermost in his mind, "Must find a way to let Bob down easy."[49]

Within two weeks, he had found his way to leave La Follette's camp, but the method was anything but "easy" on the Senator. Impatient of further delay, Pinchot was instrumental in calling one more conference in La Follette's Washington headquarters on January 29. For the first few hours of the meeting, before the Senator joined the group, the participants voiced their frank opinions on the proper policy for La Follette to follow. Brandeis was opposed to the group's allying with any one candidate. Kent rather thought La Follette should drop out. The Senator's manager, Houser, expressed the fear that his candidate might reach the Republican convention with no delegates whatever except those from Wisconsin. La Follette, before he entered the meeting, was presented with two written alternatives drafted by Pinchot and others of the pro-Roosevelt group. Both of them demanded his withdrawal from the campaign. Under the first option, he would step aside "in favor of Roosevelt, with reservations as to differences of opinion, and continue to stump." Under the second alternative, he would not withdraw in favor of anybody, but would "continue to stump, leaving the individuals of the group to take what course they choose."[50]

Joining the conference, La Follette announced his flat refusal to withdraw under any conditions. Pinchot then frankly informed the Senator that he was glad the situation was now "cleared up enabling me to decide what I would do." Promising that he would not come out for any other candidate unless the group so decided, he "refused to yield to dictation," and reminded the Senator of his prior warning "to count me out if he came to fight TR."

The accounts by La Follette and Pinchot of what happened do not exactly square. The Senator recorded that both Pinchots, Gardner, and McCormick withdrew their support, but that "all of the others" assured him of their continued backing.[51] Pinchot admitted that "several" decided to stick with La Follette, but that a show-down made it clear that "a strong majority believed his position wrong." Pinchot further wrote that some of the participants, including Brandeis, were "much shaken."[52]

Pinchot discovered an escape hatch in Philadelphia on February 2, when La Follette delivered his famous and disastrous speech before a publishers' dinner. The Senator, physically run down, began reading a thirty-five-minute speech at about 11:00 p.m. following a brilliant address by Governor Woodrow Wilson. From the beginning he was off on the wrong foot as a result of his explanation, especially inept before a gathering of editors and publishers, that he would read his remarks because "there may be some here who will not report what I say correctly."[53] Sensing, before long, that he was not holding his audience, he discarded his manuscript and stumbled on, seemingly endlessly, for about two hours. Uncharacteristically swaying from point to point, sometimes repetitiously, his determination to finish his remarks was intensified by the biting comments which came through to him from the rear of the room. His observations on the press were considered so insulting that, after he finished, the toastmaster apologized for the speaker's "attack."[54] If Pinchot had had no prior desire to desert La Follette, this performance before an influential segment of the nation's press probably would have made him wary of continuing his support. As it was, the unfortunate event provided a plausible justification for casting the Senator aside.

Rumors and newspaper reports of a collapse by La Follette now caused many of his supporters to hesitate. While they waited for further word, there appeared in the press on February 12 a copy of a telegram which Pinchot had sent to an officer of the Progressive Republican League in Minnesota, "In my judgment La Follette's condition makes further serious candidacy impossible."[55] Actually, rest was what the Senator needed, as proved by his return to active duty following a vacation. Pinchot's wire, however, since it came from a supposedly close affiliate of La Follette was accepted by many persons as proof that the Senator had suffered a breakdown. La Follette's sister believed that this telegram "probably contributed more than any other single factor to the belief that Bob had been seriously incapacitated." Bob himself considered it a blow "below the belt."[56] Pinchot's letter a few days later to the recipient of the wire sounded a little lame, "Your making public my telegram was a surprise, for I had not intended it for publication. . . . Except for its effect on Senator La Follette himself, I do not believe any serious harm has been done."[57]

Pinchot was encouraged to take a more positive stand on Roosevelt as a result of a conference with the former President, three days after La Follette's Philadelphia disaster, when TR finally told him "he would 'stay through if he did not get a single vote in the Convention.' "[58] Determined to ask the Senator formally for a release, Pinchot telephoned La Follette's secretary for an appointment on February 15. "[If] he will not give it to me," he told George Woodruff, ". . . I will take it anyway . . . there is nothing whatever to do except work for TR."[59] Although he hardly could have expected a warm reception to his request for an interview with La Follette, he was incensed when the Senator's secretary sent a brief note saying that, in view of Pinchot's actions and because of the misconceptions which might be drawn from a meeting between one candidate and the supporter of another, La Follette would be unable to communicate with Pinchot during the rest of the campaign.[60]

Pinchot responded with a ten-page "personal and confidential" letter which was not designed to spare La Follette's feelings. Almost half the space was used to develop Pinchot's thesis that La Follette's name had been placed in the field as a candidate "without serious hope" that he could win. In the balance of the letter Pinchot charged, in effect, that La Follette had become so badly stung with the presidential bee that he was ignoring the general good of the Progressive movement. Insisting that Roosevelt was the only Progressive who could be nominated, he urged La Follette in the name of patriotism to withdraw. Striking directly at the Senator's health, he charged that "the change in your outlook brought about by overwork and over-strain, [has] made it difficult for you to face the facts."

With a pontifical tone he reached the climax of the letter, "Whatever part I have taken in politics has been based directly and openly on the proposition that when a man can not follow both his leader and his conscience, he must stick to his principles and let the leader go." In view of La Follette's action, asserted Pinchot, he must now "advocate the nomination of Colonel Roosevelt."[61] In an elaborate defense of his switch, he made not the slightest offer of an apology. Copies of the letter went to Roosevelt, to Hiram Johnson in California, and to his sister in England.

Price and Gardner advised Pinchot to publish the letter, but he "decided not to, as being too hard a slam at a sick man."[62] Forty-eight hours later, however, in formally announcing his new position to the press, he repeated some of the less crushing portions of his letter. "I have notified [La Follette]," he declared, "that since in my judgment his candidacy no longer will advance the Progressive cause, I shall hereafter advocate the nomination of Colonel Roosevelt."[63] Before the month was out, Roosevelt officially tossed his hat in the ring.

La Follette's state campaign manager in Massachusetts, Elizabeth G. Evans, saw Pinchot's letter before the Senator read it. Irate, she first called on Pinchot and then wrote him. "She came down," wrote Pinchot, "and explained my letter was a very mean one because it laid all the blame on him. I said I had to treat Miss Dunn's [the secretary's] letter as an insult from La Follette or explain it by his condition."[64] Accusing Pinchot of trying to protect his own reputation by knifing the Senator in the back, the Massachusetts manager begged him to send a softer letter for La Follette to read.[65] Receiving her written request while out of town, Pinchot wired, "Can make certain changes following your suggestion."[66] Returning to Washington, however, he learned that La Follette had already read the original.

Pinchot had now broken seriously with the two men in the Republican party who seemed the most likely possibilities for blocking Roosevelt's bid for the nomination. Although agreeing far more with the political philosophy of La Follette than of Taft, he was not inclined to forebear in his criticism of the Senator.

A half dozen years later when Pinchot traveled to Wisconsin to campaign for a state candidate not endorsed by the Senator, he declared he was "having lots of fun going after La Follette."[67]

La Follette, for his part, forever believed, and not entirely without foundation, that Pinchot had betrayed him. To the end of their respectively useful lives, neither of these two men lost a feeling of animosity toward the other.

CHAPTER 14

BOLT FROM THE REPUBLICAN PARTY

GIFFORD PINCHOT the campaigner traveled extensively and almost continuously during the presidential election year of 1912. "I have been on the stump," he wrote in March 1913, "for fourteen months."[1] During the first half of the year, when delegates were being chosen to the Republican nominating convention, he carried the Roosevelt message to both the East and the West. La Follette, despite his crumbling support, was still a candidate. Pinchot concentrated partly on such La Follette strongholds as North Dakota, and, at the request of Roosevelt, on areas such as California, where the Senator was speaking.

One of the most satisfying meetings was held at Pittsburgh in Pinchot's newly adopted state of residence. With an eye to his political future, he was especially eager to become better acquainted with Pennsylvania and known to its voters. Roosevelt, reaching the city in the early morning, drove to a hotel where he met Pinchot. Retiring to Pinchot's suite of rooms, the two friends came down to breakfast together. Throughout the day and also at his evening speech, Roosevelt won a tremendous ovation. Pinchot, who spoke after him, also was well received; singling out for attack the most politically powerful man in the state, he called Senator Boies Penrose a disgrace to Pennsylvania, and predicted that two years hence he would be defeated for re-election.[2] He might have hoped, but could not have prophesied, that he himself would be the candidate trying to remove the long-time boss.

Pinchot had a chance in Pittsburgh to further his rather recent acquaintance with William Flinn, state chairman of the Roosevelt organization in Pennsylvania, with whom he was destined to have a close political relationship during the next few years. Flinn, a former partner in the old Matthew Quay Republican machine, had a limited interest in progressivism, but was a bitter opponent of Penrose.

Four days after the Pittsburgh rally, Pinchot was in the other end of the state, at Milford, casting his vote in the primary. The results of the election were most reassuring to a Progressive contemplating a political future in the Keystone State. So successful was the Flinn faction that of the 76 delegates chosen for the Republican national convention, at least 64 were pledged to Roosevelt.

Although Pinchot was considered as a possible delegate from Pennsylvania to the national convention, the Republican leaders, fearing his defeat, did not place his name on the ticket.[3] In an unofficial capacity, however, he attended some of the sessions and was in Chicago both before and during the entire period of the convention from June 18 to 22. Much in evidence around Roosevelt's headquarters in the Auditorium Hotel, he conferred with the candidate at least twice. As one of the orators at the headquarters who participated in a marathon of speechmaking from a platform on the second floor of the hotel, he talked to crowded and enthusiastic audiences.[4]

The details of the explosive convention need not be repeated here. Over a quarter of the seats were contested between the Roosevelt and Taft forces. The court for deciding such disputes in the first instance and for compiling the temporary roll was the Republican national committee. Dominated by Taft men, it awarded 235 of the disputed seats to Taft and 19 to Roosevelt. When a disgruntled alternate delegate circulated a petition denouncing the national committee and threatening the organization of a new third party, dozens of Progressive delegates signed. The first signature was that of Governor Hiram Johnson of California; lower down on the list, although he was not a delegate, was that of Gifford Pinchot.[5]

After a majority of the delegates approved the final report of the credentials committee, Roosevelt appealed to his supporters to decline from participating further in the convention.[6] Only two names, therefore, were placed in nomination, and the first ballot gave Taft his required majority.

The same evening, June 22, the Roosevelt delegates and five to six thousand other ardent admirers, including Pinchot, met in Orchestra Hall, less than a mile from the site of the Republican convention, to participate in the birth of a new party. Brought to a high pitch of excitement by Hiram Johnson's fighting speech, the audience listened with great enthusiasm to an address by Roosevelt.

Invoking the commandment, "Thou Shalt Not Steal," he castigated the convention which had selected Taft, and announced his own willingness to accept nomination by a Progressive convention which could be called later in the year. He was, informally at least, nominated that very night, as the *New York Times* acknowledged in its headline the next morning, "Roosevelt Named as Candidate by Bolters."[7]

Pinchot undoubtedly was pleased that his Chief had taken the plunge. But his exact thoughts during this hectic week will never be known. Too busy to write letters, he found time for only one simple entry in his diary, "Birth of the New Party this day."[8] Within three weeks, however, after the Democratic party had nominated Woodrow Wilson, Pinchot's letter to a relative in Europe revealed his optimism concerning Roosevelt's chances, "At first, I was inclined to think that the only thing Roosevelt's candidacy would do would be to lay the foundation for victory four years from now, and absolutely insure Taft's defeat. Now I am satisfied he is going to have a good chance of winning himself this fall."[9]

The formal Progressive convention met in Orchestra Hall on August 5 to 7. Pinchot, in high spirits, arrived in the city a few days early. "The situation here in Chicago," he wrote Henry C. Wallace, "seems almost too good to be true. Everyone I meet is happy, cheerful, and confident."[10] The crusading spirit and appearance of the 2,000 Bull Moose delegates marked this gathering apart from the average convention. Contrary to custom, a number of them were women. Relatively few were ward heelers or career politicians. Many sincerely believed they were fighting for a cause. With an unusual kind of fervor they heartily sang "Onward Christian Soldiers" and other hymns. Pinchot was in his element. "The mooses are mooing in plenty these days," he told a friend, "with loud and attractive sounds."[11]

With Roosevelt's nomination certain, the most contentious matter to be considered by the convention was the party platform. The chairman of the resolutions committee was William Draper Lewis, dean of the University of Pennsylvania Law School and a future running mate of Pinchot's in a Pennsylvania election. A subcommittee of this committee, including both Lewis and Pinchot, was appointed a few weeks before the convention to prepare a tentative draft of a platform. "I hope," said Pinchot, "[it] will be by all odds the most radical yet adopted by any party in the United States except the Socialists, and much more sensible than theirs."[12]

When Pinchot arrived in Chicago on August 2, he devoted most of his time to refining his draft of the platform and comparing it with those of other members of the committee. The day before the convention met, he worked all day and through the evening until 1:30 in the morning.[13] The platform was finally hammered into shape between sessions of the convention, in rooms in the Blackstone Hotel. Included in the small drafting group, which sometimes met in Roosevelt's room, was Pinchot who spoke for the more radical wing of the Progressive movement, and George W. Perkins—far removed from him on the political spectrum—who represented big business. While others in the group represented divergent points of view, these two, as well as any, symbolized the important wings of the Roosevelt following which the former President was trying desperately to weld together.

Perkins, a former partner of J. P. Morgan and a policy maker in the U.S. Steel and International Harvester corporations, was an outstandingly able self-made man. One of Roosevelt's principal financial backers, he contributed over a quarter of a million dollars to TR's campaign in 1912.[14] Some of the more fervently liberal Progressives considered Perkins an interloper, who they feared might bring Roosevelt under his spell.[15]

Pinchot from the beginning had not trusted Perkins's motives. "George Perkins has been most cordial to me of late," he told Mrs. Garfield in January 1911, "asking me to come and see him and so on, but I am not yet altogether relieved from suspicion in the matter, and have not been to his house."[16] Perkins nevertheless received the backing of Roosevelt to such an extent that, despite the vigorous opposition of a minority including the two Pinchots, he was elected as chairman of the executive committee of the Progressive national committee.[17]

It was inevitable that Perkins and Pinchot should collide over the wording of some of the planks in the platform. Pinchot described how Perkins "said that if a certain not important plank, something about State constitutions" stayed in, he would leave the Progressive movement. "I said," continued Pinchot, "You don't mean to say you would leave for such a reason. That's childish. Then he started to leave the room complaining. . . . He acted like a small spoiled child. Then TR came and went to work to mollify him."[18]

One of Roosevelt's more difficult jobs in Chicago was to get agreement between these two strong-willed men. William Allen White chronicled how he saw the former President, somewhat amused by his predicament, shuttling across the hotel hallway between Perkins's and Pinchot's rooms, trying to work out agreements on some of the planks.[19] Dean Lewis, referring to the same incident, added that the two delegates "were temporarily on less than speaking terms."[20] Both writers agreed that the differences in wording often were less than vital.

There were real disagreements over the antitrust plank, however, which seriously divided not only Perkins and Pinchot but the entire resolutions committee. Pinchot and the liberal group favored a plank for strengthening the Sherman antitrust law and spelling out specific business practices as illegal. Perkins and his sympathizers wanted a plank endorsing a more general law.

After a prolonged deadlock the resolutions committee recommended a platform to the convention delegates. But the exact wording of the antitrust plank was muddied by a notorious controversy. When Chairman Lewis read the finished product to the convention he included a compromise plank on trusts which was more in line with Pinchot's preference than with Perkins's.[21] Perkins, insisting that this plank had been deleted the night before in a meeting with Roosevelt, left the convention floor. The next day, when the platform appeared in the nation's press, the portion endorsing the Sherman act and listing the malpractices of business had disappeared. William Allen White spoke for other Progressives when he wrote that the antitrust-plank incident was a "disturbing disillusion."[22] Some members of the party never believed otherwise than that Perkins was guilty of surreptitious manipulation. Roosevelt completely disagreed with this judgment.[23] No final verdict can be made with absolute certainty.

Regardless of the antitrust plank, the Progressive platform was indeed, as Pinchot had hoped it would be, a relatively radical document. Among its provisions were proposals for social and economic reforms—such as unemployment insurance, minimum wages for women, and prohibition of child labor—which were closely associated with the other Roosevelt's New Deal two decades later.

The Bull Moose delegates, both before and after formally nominating Roosevelt, greeted him with wild and emotional cheering, hand clapping, and hymn singing. As soon as TR gave the nod to Governor Hiram Johnson of California as his running mate, the convention unanimously chose him for Vice-President. As early as May, Pinchot had written to Johnson sounding him out on his attitude toward this nomination.[24] Learning that the Californian was willing, he climbed aboard the Johnson wagon and, on the convention floor, made one of the nominating speeches for the Governor.

Pinchot realized full well that the Bull Moose party had no easy task in trying to win the election. Confident that Taft could be beaten, he was not so sure about Wilson. "I wish the Democrats had nominated Champ Clark instead of Wilson," he ventured, "for then TR's fight would have been less difficult."[25] With all the vigor and enthusiasm at his command, he earnestly entered the campaign to do his part. Although Pinchot resented the influence of Perkins in the movement, he was, like a good many other crusading Progressives, deeply sincere in his belief that his party could improve the lot of mankind. "Of all great political movements since the world began," he declared to a Washington rally, "none has ever been based so sincerely, so wisely, and so broadly upon the welfare of all the people as this of ours."[26]

Despite some differences with Roosevelt, he still idolized the Chief. Hearing that Roosevelt had been wounded by an assassin in Milwaukee, he refused at first to believe the story. But when the news came through of the Chief's dramatic insistence on delivering a speech in spite of the wound, he wrote TR a sentimental letter, "It may seem like a queer thing to say, but your being shot has been one of the finest things that has ever come into my life on account of the way you have handled the whole situation."[27] Roosevelt was deeply touched by the letter.[28]

In addition to his campaigning in the East, Pinchot spent much of his time during September and October speaking to large audiences in the Midwest. Up to October 21, on which date he stopped keeping a tabulation, he had delivered 64 major campaign addresses.[29] Traversing the country, he tried to keep Roosevelt informed of the political situation. In August he was cautious, "I don't want to be over-enthusiastic, but certainly things look well."[30] At the end of October, however, he was highly optimistic, "On the basis of what I have seen across the continent, I am satisfied you are going to win."[31] This same optimism shone in an analysis he sent to Horace Plunkett in England, although he did admit there was some uncertainty; predicting that Taft would carry no more than four small states (he actually carried two), Pinchot concluded happily that "In any event, the Republican Party is done for."[32]

Although the Bull Moose did not win, a respectable showing was made in the election for President. Roosevelt polled 4,126,000 votes to Taft's 3,484,000. Wilson, although far ahead in the electoral count, mustered only 45 per cent of the total popular vote. Pinchot was of course disappointed, but not by any means completely downcast. Admitting to his aunt that he was wrong in his election prediction, he bragged that the Progressives secured "for Bill Taft the magnificent sum of eight votes out of 533 in the electoral college. That is something to be proud and happy about."[33] Also heartening to a man with a political eye cast toward Pennsylvania was Roosevelt's spectacular success in that state—Taft polled 273,000 votes; Wilson, 396,000; and the Chief, 445,000. Moreover, in characteristically optimistic fashion he expressed the hope "that Wilson will split the Democratic Party, and that all the Progressives will get together."[34]

Pinchot had had no real affection for the Republican party since the Ballinger-Pinchot affair. Before knowing that Roosevelt would run, he perhaps flirted a little with the idea of joining the Democrats. When in Rome in early 1911, it was significant that he bothered to jot down in his little-used diary that his sister asked him why he didn't "turn Democratic and run for President."[35] Moreover, as late as October of that year his mother was not yet certain whether he would assist "on the Progressive side or the Democratic" in the 1912 campaign.[36] The candidacy of Roosevelt, of course, had assured his alignment with whichever party nominated the former President.

Now that TR stood defeated, Pinchot was determined to help keep the Progressive party flame burning, and to resist either the party's or his own return to the Republicans. At a Lincoln Day banquet in Philadelphia he picturesquely described the Republican party as "paralyzed from the waist up" and unable "to offer serious opposition to any organization with a living heart and a thinking head."[37] And he told Ray Stannard Baker that he was "through with the Republican Party for good and all . . . we came out from among the Republicans to get clean."[38] Pinchot, indeed, was one of the last passengers to leave the sinking Progressive ship. Not until the election of 1916 had shown the utter hopelessness of the party's future, did he finally relent and once more cast his lot with the Republicans.

Less than a week after the election of 1912, Pinchot's mother visited with the Roosevelts at Sagamore Hill. There, apparently for the first time, TR revealed that if elected, he would have chosen her son as Secretary of State.[39] The next day he began a letter to Pinchot using the salutation, "O Mr. Secretary of State that-was-to-have-been!"[40] It is tempting, however fruitless, to speculate on the possible effects on history of having Roosevelt in the White House and Pinchot in the State Department during World War I. Pinchot himself once confided his belief that if Roosevelt had won, "the chances were that we would have had no World War at all. Kaiser Wilhelm held him in the highest esteem and, I think, awe."[41] The marked warmth of this post-election cordiality was short lived. Almost immediately relations between the radical Pinchot and the more middle-of-the-road Roosevelt again became strained.

One of the lessons to be learned from the election, according to Pinchot, was the need for deflating the influence of the chairman of the party's executive committee, George W. Perkins. In spite of the fact, which must have been evident to Pinchot, that the views of Roosevelt and Perkins on the subject of big business and trusts were really not very far apart, Pinchot believed in the one and distrusted the other.

Only four days after the election, in a polite letter to Roosevelt, he listed his suggestions for strengthening the party. After expressing the opinion that Roosevelt had waged a "most remarkably successful" fight, he urged that Perkins "be kept in the background from now on." Although graciously acknowledging the valuable contributions of work and money that Perkins had made to the party, he described him as "the heaviest single load the Progressive cause has had to carry in this campaign." Insisting that he did not mean to reflect on Perkins's sincerity or "devotion to the Progressive cause," he maintained that the presence of Perkins in the party's high command had been used by TR's enemies to awaken doubts in the minds of a good many people concerning Roosevelt's own sincerity. To help lessen Perkins's dominance, Pinchot suggested, among other things, that the party headquarters be moved from New York to Washington.[42]

Roosevelt, knowing Pinchot was leaving for Texas, first sent merely a brief but cordial acknowledgement assuring that he was "in entire sympathy" with the proposals, but adding a reservation about Perkins, "Like . . . myself he has been partly a burden and partly an asset. But frankly I don't think we could have carried on the fight at all without him."[43] In this way there began a long and sometimes acrimonious battle over Perkins which on occasion threatened to tear the remains of the Progressive party asunder. In the forefront of the opposition forces were the two Pinchot brothers. Amos was more adamantly resentful of Perkins's prominence than was Gifford. But Gifford finally was sufficiently aroused to write the harshest words he ever used against the Chief.

Roosevelt in another letter to Pinchot analyzed the reasons for his strong support for Perkins. Seriously doubting whether any other man in the campaign did as much as Perkins, he professed his own leaning toward the type of "*sane* radicalism" which Perkins stood for. What the party principally needed, he argued, was a first-class organization; and Perkins was an excellent organizer. "I know of no one who can take Perkins' place." But most of all the letter was a plea for peace within the party. "I trust there will be no fight? Not a voice should be raised against Perkins continuing as chairman of the Executive Committee. If there is, I trust it will be behind closed doors."[44] The agreement was general that the controversy should not be brought into the open. But both Pinchots were determined that Perkins's place in the party should be discussed by the Progressives themselves. Since Senator Joseph M. Dixon, chairman of the national committee, had called a Progressive conference to be held in Chicago during the second week of December, Amos and Gifford looked forward to "thrashing over" the problem at that time.[45]

Late in November the two brothers "had a long talk with T.R. about Perkins," after which Amos decided to record some of their thoughts in a letter to Roosevelt. By way of assistance, Gifford wrote Amos that one of the points for his letter "might well be based on the fact that both the Harvester Trust and the Steel Trust exclude union men from their works. This, I think, has had a good deal of bearing on the attitude of the unions during the past campaign." Far more than most politicians of his day, Pinchot was sensitive to the labor vote. As a kind of afterthought, moreover, he added a significant sentence at the bottom of his letter, "Unless we as a party are radical enough to be clearly separate from both the old parties we can hold few people indeed. That is a strong argument our way."[46]

The same day that Amos sent his letter, Roosevelt, growing a little weary and irritated at trying to halt the continuing battle, complained to his son Kermit that "The good Pinchots and their kind, the advanced radicals, want to fight Perkins and others, who as a matter of fact have been even more useful than the Pinchots in helping us in this fight."[47]

The Pinchot brothers traveled together to the Progressive conference in Chicago, where they worked long hours, in company with a few others including Miss Jane Addams, drafting a report and trying to drum up support for the clipping of Perkins's wings. Among those listed by Gifford as agreeing "about the Perkins domination" were Francis J. Heney, Professor Charles E. Merriam, and Franklin Roosevelt's future Secretary of the Interior, Harold L. Ickes.[48] Only a minority, however, were convinced. The two brothers sat up one evening until 1:30 a.m. arguing with Senator Beveridge on his contention that Perkins was not a load on the party. "Talk got very sharp at times," Gifford recorded.[49] The national committee, moreover, with the powerful support of Roosevelt, voted 32-12 to leave the party's headquarters in New York, although they did provide for a branch office in Washington. Pinchot seemed to enjoy his rebel role at the conference. No sign of regret appeared in his notation of an "Evident feeling among a lot of men that Amos and I are trouble makers."[50]

Despite his defeat on the Perkins question, Pinchot was delighted over several events of the convention. Roosevelt's speech to the 1,500 delegates he called "excellent," particularly because of the special emphasis on there being "no use talking about" joining the Republican party. Equally gratifying was chairman Dixon's announcement—Pinchot said that Amos "forced" him to make it—that the missing plank on the Sherman antitrust law "is a part of our platform." Pinchot was highly flattered, moreover, when, twice in one day, he "was called for by the crowd" to make brief speeches.[51]

Back in New York, Pinchot read a long letter that Roosevelt had mailed to Amos the week before. TR, obviously riled by some of Amos's complaints concerning Perkins and the party, was emphatic in stating that Perkins should remain as chairman of the executive committee. In utter frankness he told Amos of his conviction that the Progressives had lost a million or two votes because of the suspicion that the party was "overradical" and was "jeopardizing property and business." Bluntly asserting that anyone who provoked an assault on Perkins was "doing everything he can to wreck the Progressive cause," he ended with a word of fatherly advice to the two brothers. Reminding them that they tried to work with both Taft and La Follette, only to break with them—although he admitted that in both cases it was "absolutely justifiable"—he stressed the bad impression they would give if they were unable to cooperate with the Progressive party. "You know how fond I am of Gifford and of you," he pleaded. "I believe I am advising you for your own good when I say that you impair your power of future usefulness if you give the impression that you never can work with any people for an achievable end."[52]

Gifford was incensed at what he read. "A rotten letter," he called it, ". . . he assumes that Amos wants Perkins thrown out of the party, which is utterly baseless and without excuse."[53] Mingled with his resentment undoubtedly was some feeling of hurt. Only a day or two earlier in Chicago he had heard of Roosevelt's telling Jane Addams that he was disappointed in Gifford and considered him too radical. Perhaps never before had the Chief given him the frank kind of lecture that was contained in the letter to Amos. Indeed, prior to this time he may not have realized how much Roosevelt's patience with him had been tried, nor how much the former President seemed to be swinging into the arms of men like Perkins.

Determined to answer the letter to Amos, he discussed his reply with such persons as Hapgood and Brandeis.[54] The finished product was an eight-page conciliatory letter which started a fruitless debate over whether the Pinchots meant that Perkins should be dropped from the party or merely from his chairmanship. "I do object," protested Pinchot, "to having it reported that I have taken a stand which would mean the elimination of all men of means from the Progressive Party." He requested a letter from Roosevelt, therefore, which would correct the "wrong impression." Revealing more moderation than his brother, he professed that "For myself, I have not the slightest reason to think that Perkins is anything but sincere in his work for the Progressive Party." Standing his ground about the need for Perkins's withdrawal from high party office, he was eager at the same time to remain friendly with Roosevelt. "Whatever differences of judgment I may have with you," he reminded the ex-President, "they will not dim my affection for you, nor cloud the recollection of the good work we have done together."[55]

On the same day he wrote Roosevelt, Pinchot further expressed his faith in the Progressives by promising to contribute to the party $1,000 for each of the next four years. With Perkins in mind, however, he wanted it "clearly understood" that he was "emphatically and definitely opposed to the Progressive Party being supported by large subscriptions."[56]

Roosevelt was in no mood to "correct" his impressions of the attitude of the Pinchots toward Perkins. Instead, he reiterated in a letter to Gifford that he failed to see how any other interpretation could be put on Amos's letter than that it was a call for ruling Perkins out of the party. In an indirect rap at Gifford, who admired and worked closely with Boss Flinn in Pennsylvania, Roosevelt suggested that if Flinn had been in Perkins's place in the party there would have been "a much more virulent assault" made on Flinn than there had on Perkins.[57] Pinchot was not happy over TR's reply. "You may not know," he wrote to Hiram Johnson, "that Amos and I have been getting ourselves cordially disliked for carrying on the fight against the domination of Perkins."[58] Refusing to avoid frankness for the sake of friendship, he wrote the Chief on New Year's Day, "I was keenly disappointed by your letter of December 21. Like your former letters to Amos and to me, it leaves altogether unanswered our actual proposal, but in its place sets up and then attacks a proposition which we never made." But he was willing to call a halt to the controversy, "[S]ince it does not appear likely that anything will be gained by merely discussing further your interpretation of our statements, I suppose we may as well let the discussion stop. A Happy New Year and many of them."[59]

Roosevelt, however, was not willing to let the matter drop. In a reply to Gifford he referred to the many complaints about all sorts of people having too much influence in the party. Indeed, he bitingly maintained, there were more protests about the management of the party in Pennsylvania than in any other state.[60] TR clearly remained irked, and Pinchot knew it. If he was not positive of the Chief's sentiments, a talk with Sir Horace Plunkett set him straight. "Plunkett said," noted Pinchot, "I had better keep away from T.R. He [T.R.] was sore."[61]

It was with some relief, therefore, that Pinchot wrote in his diary several weeks later, after seeing Roosevelt in Michigan, "[he] was most cordial."[62] Perhaps encouraged by this friendliness, he finally, on May 6, answered the Chief's letter of January 3. Explaining that he delayed because it seemed "wiser to interrupt the correspondence for awhile," he politely reaffirmed his belief that Perkins "is constantly doing damage" to the party, and that the Bull Moose could not win the next election under his chairmanship.[63]

A few months later, Pinchot was toastmaster at a New York dinner of more than 2,000 Progressives arranged to pay farewell to Roosevelt before he left for South America. Lashing out at "magnates" and the privileges that they enjoyed, he dramatically and pungently illustrated his point by comparing the situation to what he knew best, a forest tree. "The tree of privilege," he orated, "has grown great through half a century during which the vast bulk of what is now the wealth of this Nation has passed from the public hands into a few private hands. Much time, many hands, and various tools will be needed to cut it down. It has shaded many, and its fall will make some suffer. But we can not stop, and we will not stop, until the wood of it has been divided and built into the homes of all the people, and until its very root is dug out and split into fragments to keep the people warm."[64] Was Pinchot in this somewhat ambiguous metaphor advocating an extreme share-the-wealth plan? Roosevelt, who had been regarding him as too radical, was scarcely led to modify his opinion by what he heard.

TR, by going to South America for more than seven months, stepped out of the Perkins controversy. But before he returned, the problem became acute again. Pinchot by early 1914, however, had a different outlook on the situation. In February of that year, as will be seen, he was slated by the Progressives to run for United States senator from Pennsylvania. Inevitably, therefore, he was increasingly concerned with keeping the party strong. Informed that Amos was considering a further attack on Perkins, he now was "most anxious" that his brother "should not ruin the party by such a break just before election."[65] As he explained to Amos in a letter, "I would rather see the Progressive party win with Mr. Perkins still a member of it." He assured his brother, however, that he was still for getting "rid of" Perkins "most surely and most completely." And, contrary to what he had told Roosevelt a year before, he declared that he wanted "to put Mr. Perkins clean outside the party before the fight is over."[66] Overton Price remarked, after a walk with Pinchot one afternoon, that Pinchot was under a great deal of strain as a result of his brother's plan to open fire in the near future.[67]

The attack came in May in a long letter from Amos to the members of the Progressive national committee. Maintaining that Perkins was using his position to further the interests of monopolies, and was opposed to labor unions, Amos insisted that his resignation was necessary.[68] Although, according to Gifford, Amos did not intend to publish the letter in the press, it probably was inevitable that portions of it leaked. Once this occurred, Amos released it in full and the country was treated to the details of the intraparty strife.

Although Gifford had counseled against precipitate action, he stood firmly by his brother. "My Brother is right," he proclaimed. "I am in hearty agreement with his desire that the Progressive Party should be free from the burden of Perkins' chairmanship. Perkins has had, and will have nothing whatever to do with my fight against Penrose in Pennsylvania."[69] The Pinchots were not the only party leaders who were restless under Perkins's leadership. Others gave both warm and lukewarm support to the drive to overthrow him. In the face of the continued vigorous backing of Perkins by Roosevelt, however, the rebellion was never successful. Perkins remained in power more than long enough to witness the party's gradual demise.[70]

During the heat of the feud over Perkins there occurred an incident seeming to show that Roosevelt was in no mood to confer on Pinchot the kind of flattery he had offered when they were together in the government. While working on his autobiography early in 1913, Roosevelt asked Pinchot to prepare a statement to be used as the basis for the chapter on conservation. Pinchot was gratified at being asked to do this job. For two months, intermittently, he worked hard on the project and visited Oyster Bay to go over the material with the Chief. The retracing of the history of the prior decade brought back fond memories and proved to be a delightful task. Following the conference with Roosevelt, he was happy to label it a "most cordial visit—almost exuberant."[71]

Roosevelt, upon completing a draft of the chapter, sent it to Pinchot, who read it aloud one evening to his mother. Both the proud mother and her son were more than a little disappointed, however, at the brief reference to Gifford. "Mamee," Pinchot wrote, ". . . was indignant at the scant mention of me." And, he added, "So was I, a little, especially in view of his declarations that he would give me much credit, several times repeated."[72]

Although Pinchot was hurt, there was nothing he could do about it. Mamee, however, was not content to let the matter rest. A letter to Roosevelt, in which she frankly expressed her disappointment, brought results. A few days later, at a Progressive lunch in New York City, Roosevelt took Pinchot aside to tell him that "he had intended to treat me as he did himself (in his autobiography) by merely reciting facts." Without mentioning Mamee, TR went on to say that he had now decided to include a statement on Gifford. Pinchot was puzzled by the explanation, "He had previously told me both in New York and on way to Marquette that he would give me full credit for what I had done during his Administration."[73] But Pinchot admitted that Roosevelt was "doing his best to be nice."[74]

The former President, accordingly, inserted in his conservation chapter a glowing tribute to Pinchot, fully reminiscent of some of the statements he had made a half decade earlier. Pinchot was ever-lastingly proud of the eulogy, especially of the concluding thought that "among the many, many public officials who under my adminis-tration rendered literally invaluable service to the people of the United States, he [Pinchot], on the whole, stood first."[75] Repeatedly Pinchot used the quotation in his later election campaigns.

The proud mother gratefully wrote to the "Dear Colonel: You told me I would be satisfied with your article on Conservation in the autobiography, and so I am. I thank you for your admirable and well deserved tribute to Gifford."[76]

Meanwhile, Pinchot had been concentrating much of his attention on the state of Pennsylvania. His activity in this new field of opera-tions, together with major changes in his family, combined to make 1914 one of the most momentous years of his life.

CHAPTER 15

FIRST CAMPAIGN FOR THE SENATE

IN 1914, for the first time in his career, Gifford Pinchot became an avowed candidate for elective political office. The decision to run was not an easy one to make. Possessing a craving for politics, he was aware that an active political life could play havoc with his chosen career of forestry. Moreover, it was highly doubtful whether he could, in an elective office, promote national conservation as effectively as he was able to do in his present role of president of the National Conservation Association.

Approaching fifty years of age, Pinchot had taken enough stands on social questions to convince all but the most doubting observers that he was a genuine supporter of the "little man." In a message to a meeting of the Progressive party in Illinois, he showed his dissatisfaction with the division of wealth, "No man is so foolish as to propose the confiscation and division of property. Nevertheless, we must recognize that the work we are engaged upon is a class war . . . a war of the unprivileged classes against the privileged classes." Arguing the injustice of having, as a result of privilege, "such an undue proportion of the total wealth . . . in so few hands," he maintained that Progressives were fighting "not so much to take it away from them now as to make it certain that the concentration of riches and opportunity which curses the Nation today shall not curse the Nation of the future."[1]

These were strong words, which showed that Pinchot was at the peak of his radicalism in 1913 and 1914. In January 1914, he showed his interest in socialist theory by expressing an opinion in a personal letter that he "look[ed] forward to the time when we shall have Government ownership of railroads in this country, and when certain of the great resources, like coal, iron, copper, lead, timber, and water power, will all be held and administered by the public, as will the public utilities of our cities."[2] Pinchot, however, receded from this extreme position—except for timber and water power—

and in later years usually advocated government regulation rather than government ownership.

The most plausible explanation of Pinchot's swing to the left of his normal position was his close association at this time with his brother Amos. Gifford was by no means a great compromiser, but on occasion he was willing to give a little to win at least part of a point from his opponents. Amos, however, was more inflexible. Indeed, Amos was to Gifford as Gifford was to Roosevelt—one who kept trying to pull his companion to a more liberal, or radical, position.

Beyond these strongly progressive stands, however, Pinchot was embracing other causes which would bring him political support in future years. Earlier than most Pennsylvania politicians, for example, he appeared at suffragette meetings and praised the women for their work. Moreover, ever since the days of Roosevelt's 1908 Country Life Commission, he had been cultivating the friendship of farmers. Illustrative of the breadth of his concern for the rural population was a curious agreement he made in 1909 with Reverend Charles O. Gill. Pinchot promised to finance a study by Gill of country churches in two counties, one in Vermont and the other in New York; their names appeared as co-authors of the book which reported the findings.[3] "The object of this book," wrote Pinchot, "is to help in getting the country church back into the position it ought to occupy as a great power working effectively for the improvement of country life."[4] Pinchot's initial contribution to the work was $3,000, which grew considerably as additional money was needed not only for this first book, but for a second broader study of 6,000 country churches in Ohio.[5]

Pinchot's interest in country churches brought him to the attention of the Federal Council of the Churches of Christ in America, which asked him to head its Commission on Church and Country Life. With Pinchot as chairman and Reverend Gill as secretary, the Commission, with a budget of $5,000 a year—supplied mainly by Pinchot—had letterheads and an office in Columbus, Ohio, but no listing in the telephone book.[6] In spite of limited means, however, it sponsored in December 1915 a country church conference in Columbus. Attended by over 600 delegates from 31 states, its main attraction, arranged by Pinchot through Colonel House of the White House staff, was an address by President Woodrow Wilson.

As Pinchot became more deeply interested in practical politics, he began preaching the need for farmers to organize. "The farmers have not had justice," he told a meeting of agriculturists in Washington. "For the last half century they have been content to sit in the background and hold their peace. They have not had justice because they were not organized to get it."[7] From this view it was but a short step to his advocacy of a merger of the political forces of organized agriculture and organized labor. Although by 1914 he had not yet proposed such a union, he did so only a few years later. In 1917, for example, he maintained before a convention of the American Federation of Labor that "there is nothing the organized farmers and the organized wage-earners of America can not do if they set out to do it together."[8] One of the results of these activities among farmers was Secretary of Agriculture Henry C. Wallace's assertion in 1922 that only a few men in the country had served agriculture so loyally and so effectively as Pinchot.[9]

Pinchot attracted some church people to him by his concern for the country church, and still others were attracted by his stand on the prohibition of alcoholic beverages. Although some of his critics in later years considered his support of prohibition as mere political opportunism, the evidence shows that he took a stand for prohibition prior to its emergence as a possible political asset.

Pinchot was not the kind of prohibitionist, if any such there were, who had never let alcohol touch his lips. While living in England at the age of fifteen his tutor informed his father that he had paid a bill for Gifford for beer at one of the pubs. "He has given that up now by your wish," reported the teacher, but added that "if you will allow me to suggest it I think a little beer would do him good."[10] In Munich in his middle twenties, he drank his mug of beer, but obviously without much relish. "As they only give mugs of about 1 quart each the same was a labor of time and perseverance,"[11] he noted. What he saw of beer in Germany, indeed, disgusted him more than it pleased. On one occasion he tartly reported to his father from Germany that "The incredible fact that I have never been drunk has led to my being considered as a sort of grossly inferior being entirely devoid of moral sense. . . . The Germans seem to be still in that retrograde condition where a man's chief duty to society lies in the willingness to drink all he can get."[12]

As head of the Forest Service, Pinchot had been faced with making decisions on the sale of alcoholic beverages in the national forests. In reply to an inquiry from the White House in 1908, he told Roosevelt that he had always refused to license "any saloons," but admitted that the Service had issued permits to "hotels and road houses" with the knowledge that they would operate bars. He now hoped, he said, to prohibit absolutely the sale of liquor in any national forest. "The fight will be a difficult one. . . . But . . . the wave of prohibition which is now sweeping the country will justify our action."[13]

Pinchot had no qualms at this time about serving an alcoholic punch to guests at his home. Ardent drys who supported him in the nineteen-twenties might have raised their eyebrows at the ten cases of champagne that he ordered in the winter of 1907 for a reception for 500 persons. He was, however, merely following Washington custom. When prohibition became a part of American law, he scrupulously avoided serving alcohol of any type.

Pinchot for some years prior to 1914 had behaved as an ambitious politician should, delivering a host of speeches and enlarging his circle of acquaintances in different walks of life. Although campaigning for the Progressives in 1912 in many parts of the nation, he was especially eager to become better acquainted with his newly adopted state. Offering himself as a stump speaker in Pennsylvania, he came to the attention of an increasing number of voters. Nor did his barnstorming cease with the close of the campaign. At the end of the year he told a Progressive leader that he had refused an invitation to deliver an address elsewhere on Washington's Birthday on the grounds he was going to speak that day in Pennsylvania. "Will you," he pleaded, "make my word good by giving me the chance?"[14] He was busy, moreover, building up the volume and breadth of his personal correspondence. With a touch of pride he told how in the first twenty-three days of 1913 he wrote almost 700 letters.[15]

Since the Progressives, or Washington party as they were listed in Pennsylvania, were so spectacularly successful in winning the state in 1912, it was small wonder that some Pennsylvania Progressives were looking ahead to the 1914 elections for governor and United States senator with anticipation and optimism. But the greatest obstacle in the path of any group which hoped to win Pennsylvania was Boies Penrose, that physical and political giant who was just completing his third term as United States senator and his thirtieth year as a state or national legislator. As acknowledged boss of the Republican party in Pennsylvania, he was certain to run for a fourth term in 1914.

Pinchot apparently received some assurances by William Flinn and other party leaders that he could have the Washington party nomination for senator. By the middle of December 1913, he was asking advice from some of his closest friends on whether to run. Explaining that "practically everyone" he consulted, including his family, felt he "should accept the nomination," he confided to Horace Plunkett that "The decision I must make on this question involves the general direction of my work for the rest of my life, . . . there would be . . . no other excuse for refusing this call than a determination to stay out of politics for good, and give myself up on non-political lines to the Country Life and Conservation work."[16] A year before, incidentally, Plunkett had advised him to quit "active connection with politics."[17] Pinchot admitted to former Governor Pardee of California that he was "pretty hungry" to get into the fight with Penrose, but that his "one objection" was he "might lose what little chance I have to be effective in Conservation if I were badly beaten."[18] But he became convinced that serious defeat was unlikely; "I have been to Philadelphia," he wrote his sister, "talking with the leaders there, and find that apparently there is a fair chance to win."[19]

The advice from his friends was mixed. Senator Beveridge, for example, thought he should run.[20] Henry L. Stimson and Henry C. Wallace felt it would be a mistake to do so.[21] Although Pinchot's inclination was to make the race, and he may have been hoping for advice which would support this feeling, he seems to have gone through a long, painful struggle in an effort to reach the final decision.

Because his bond of friendship with Roosevelt was somewhat

strained, Pinchot wondered whether he could expect any aid from the former President. But the word, received through a party leader in Pennsylvania, that Roosevelt was willing to come into the state in support of the Washington party ticket, helped to tip the scales in favor of Pinchot's entering the campaign. Joyfully he wrote to the Chief that this was "One of the strongest arguments in favor of going in. . . . If I do go in, I shall of course bank on your support."[22]

When the leaders of the Washington party met to choose a slate to run in the primary they quickly and unanimously endorsed Pinchot for senator. At about the same time, the Democratic party announced as its candidate Congressman A. Mitchell Palmer, future Attorney General under Woodrow Wilson. The last aspirant to make formal announcement of his candidacy was Boies Penrose on the Republican ticket.

The opening blast in Pinchot's campaign was fired in a letter to the state chairman of the Washington party, who had formally notified Pinchot of his selection. The "first great task now before the citizens of Pennsylvania," intoned the candidate, "is to drive out of power and destroy the bi-partisan political machine which has so long dominated and exploited the State in the interest of the privileged few and private monopoly."[23] Pinchot's assertion that Penrose's powerful political machine was bipartisan was no exaggeration. Democratic party members were at this time woefully few in the state; in the years before Woodrow Wilson captured the presidency, the Democrats had to some extent been a kept party in Pennsylvania, existing with the help of crumbs of patronage and other favors which Republican bosses were willing to toss their way.[24] Pinchot's letter of acceptance ended with several characteristic phrases which were to become familiar to Pennsylvanians as standard weapons used by him in future political battles. "Private monopoly [of natural resources] is the backbone of all our troubles . . . the public good comes before private profit . . . the object of government is not great riches for the magnates, but human welfare and justice between man and man."

In a personal letter to E. W. Scripps, Pinchot demonstrated once more that his opinions concerning "magnates" were not merely catch phrases used as political slogans, but sprang from sincere feeling. He believed, he wrote, that "there can be by no possibility any great amount of wealth held by one man, without that man's power to accumulate and hold the wealth having rested on special privilege." Then he added, in his own handwriting as an afterthought, an interesting reservation, "with exception, perhaps, of a man who earns it as Henry Ford has done. I am not clear about his case." Before closing his letter he admitted to getting "some consolation out of the fact that I am already being called a demagogue with assorted trimmings by the newspaper representatives of the boiled-shirt class in this State."[25]

In his campaign, Pinchot gave an enlarged meaning to conservation by calling for conservation not only of natural resources but also of human rights, human welfare, and citizenship.

On primary day in May, the machine candidates were victorious on all three major tickets. Penrose, against only weak opposition, polled a vote of 220,000. Pinchot was high man on his ticket, but polled only 47,000 votes; the total vote of the Washington party was forebodingly light.

Pinchot was able to coast along in his unopposed primary, but in May, with the November race against Penrose in mind, he began campaigning in deadly earnest and with unbounded vigor. The tall, wiry bachelor of forty-nine years, handsome in a rugged way, made a striking appearance. The core of his campaign was a series of trips over bumpy roads throughout the state in a Ford touring car, usually with the top down. Most of the driving was done by his mother's chauffeur. Pinchot's graying, bushy moustache often fluttered in the breeze. Partly because he wore a proper black bow tie set on a stiff-winged collar, a kind of dignity and impressiveness pervaded the automobile and its occupant. Some months later, after his marriage, his bride persuaded him to give up the bow tie by chiding him for looking like an undertaker. Driving with the top lowered, which became one of Pinchot's distinguishing traits, was a symbol of the virility of which he was so proud. The citizens of Pennsylvania through the years came to recognize him readily as he sped across the state in his open car—even in the bitter cold of midwinter.

Much of the planning of the 1914 campaign was the work of

Stephen Stahlnecker, who began a long and intimate association with Pinchot back in 1909. Hired first as a personal secretary, he developed into Pinchot's chief political adviser. Although other persons usually carried the formal title of campaign manager for Pinchot, Stahlnecker supplied the guiding hand for five of his six major campaigns for office. Pinchot, as Governor, named him secretary to the chief executive, where he also handled the heavy responsibilities of distributing patronage. The two men formed an excellent political team. Pinchot, an idealist, did not mix easily with the rough and tumble ward leaders and other professional politicians that formed an important part of any party organization in Pennsylvania. Stahlnecker, a shrewd, down-to-earth party worker, served as a useful link between idealism and the practicable. "Steve," as Pinchot called him, was not a crusader, but was devoted to his boss; not even a political rupture between the two men in the late nineteen-thirties could shatter Stahlnecker's respect and admiration for his long-time employer. At the end of his first term as Governor of Pennsylvania, Pinchot was sincere in labeling Steve as "the best Governor's Secretary that ever sifted the wheat from the chaff at Harrisburg."[26]

Although Pinchot had hoped to cover the entire state in his "machine," he was unable to meet his goal, partly because of the serious illness of his mother. Early in the year he and the other members of the family had become concerned about Mamee's health, and he had made frequent trips to Washington to see her. On the last page of her diary she recorded how her beloved Gifford visited her on a Sunday in May, and drove with her through the park and "sat under trees, having a delightful talk."[27] In June, they moved her from the heat of Washington to her brother's home in Saugutuck, Connecticut. In July, Pinchot wrote that there was no hope for her recovery, but that she was comfortable and cheerful.[28] A month later, on August 25, she died.

Mrs. Pinchot's death inevitably left a void in Pinchot's life and in the home at 1615 Rhode Island Avenue. But the emptiness was at least partially filled by a new Mrs. Pinchot. Pinchot and Cornelia Bryce, sixteen years his junior, had known each other for a few years. Daughter of a distinguished magazine publisher and one-time

United States minister to the Netherlands, and great-granddaughter of Peter Cooper, she was one of the few persons whose whirlwind energy matched Pinchot's. Wealthy and beautiful, possessing a sparkling humor and brilliant red hair, "Leila" was not noted for her retiring nature. She had received some prominence, at least around New York State, as a champion of the working girl, and more than once had marched in parades advocating woman's suffrage. The new Mrs. Pinchot was equally at home on a picket line with striking workers or as a lovely and gracious hostess at a formal reception. Pinchot proudly claimed that Roosevelt had said she knew more about politics than any other woman among his friends.

Judging by Pinchot's diary, he first became interested in Miss Bryce, in more than a casual way, in 1913. One of his earlier letters about her, to an officer of the Progressive national committee, seemed to indicate that he was thinking of the party above self. "Yesterday afternoon," he wrote, "I had a talk with Miss Cornelia Bryce . . . about taking part in the Progressive movement. Miss Bryce has a great deal of money, is greatly interested in the Progressive movement, as well as in modern advance of all kinds, and I think could be gotten to take a vivid and productive interest in the work of the Progressive Service."[29] But it soon became apparent that his intentions were beyond mere politics. Ten weeks later the two were fishing together at Grey Towers, and Pinchot was fascinated by her blouse and rubber boots.[30]

By the time Pinchot entered the 1914 campaign, he had made up his mind to bring to a close his forty-nine years of bachelorhood. Although no exact time had been set for the wedding, the couple decided that, in accordance with the ailing Mamee's wishes, the event should take place while Mrs. Pinchot was still able to know of her son's happiness. Ten days before Mrs. Pinchot's death, on August 15, they were quietly and unpretentiously married, in the presence of the family and a few close friends (including Theodore Roosevelt), at Roslyn, Long Island, the bride's home. Amos Pinchot served as best man. Immediately after the wedding, the couple crossed Long Island Sound by boat to be at Mamee's bedside.

Pinchot was as deeply in love as a man half his age might have been. The next spring, for probably the first time in his life, he actually confessed that he hated to think of a coming fishing trip because it would keep him apart from his wife.[31] His deep affection for Leila, moreover, was enduring; "21 years ago today," he wrote in 1935, "we were married. Praise the Lord!"[32]

Pinchot lost about a month of campaigning as a result of his mother's illness. But when he returned to the race, he had his new wife as a helper. Sometimes, for example, while he spoke to a group of workers, she would pass literature through the crowd. "Leila is helping me immensely," he told Amos.[33] Continuing up and down the state proclaiming Penrose unfit to represent Pennsylvania in the Senate, Pinchot spoke with conviction. Penrose was, after all, the kind of man who, when he chose to get drunk, might do so in public. His nomination for mayor of Philadelphia had been thwarted once by the publication of a picture allegedly showing him leaving a celebrated brothel at dawn.[34] Pinchot abhorred the moral standards that he believed Penrose stood for, and opposed him as much on spiritual as on political grounds. That the feeling was mutual was evidenced by Penrose's sneering remarks concerning the virtuous and angelic Pin-*shot*.[35]

As a challenger of the champion, Pinchot drew support throughout the nation from his liberal-minded friends, who could not forget that Penrose had helped engineer the nomination of Taft over Roosevelt in 1912. Moreover, as chairman of the Senate Finance Committee he was in a strategic spot to favor big business. The breadth of Pinchot's support was indicated by the thirty-two-page campaign booklet, "What Gifford Pinchot Stands For," which reproduced favorable quotations not only from Roosevelt, but from such persons as Judge Ben B. Lindsey, Henry L. Stimson, Jane Addams, and Senator Moses Clapp of Minnesota. Other names listed as belonging in Pinchot's column were Albert Beveridge, Hiram Johnson, George Wharton Pepper, and Booker T. Washington. For a state election, the list of supporters was strikingly dominated by non-Pennsylvanians who, of course, were unable to help the candidate with their votes.

Accustomed to a generally good press, Pinchot was keenly disappointed in the publicity side of his campaign. With the exception of the *Philadelphia North American*, a Progressive organ, Penrose had most of the press in Pennsylvania solidly behind him. The *Philadelphia Public Ledger*, for example, repeatedly called Pinchot a carpetbagger, a "rank outsider . . . [who] aspires to be United States Senator on the High Moral Ticket."[36] Two days after the primary, the *Ledger*, although admitting that Pinchot was a "gentleman of high ideals and pure character," branded him as "one-ideaed, a whimsical, erratic, misguided enthusiast, entirely unfitted for legislative functions."[37] The *Philadelphia Inquirer* was similarly unimpressed, "Mr. Pinchot can mend a sick tree, but there has never been the slightest suspicion that he could tell a tariff schedule if he should happen to see one from a hole in the wall."[38]

Pinchot unquestionably was relying heavily on Roosevelt's help. The former President returned from his South American trip on the very day of the Pennsylvania primary. Within twenty-four hours, Pinchot was at his Oyster Bay home asking for assistance. Finding the Chief thin and still weakened from a fever contracted in the Brazilian jungle, he nevertheless came away with a promise that Roosevelt would take an active part in the Pennsylvania fight. Enthusiastically Pinchot noted in his diary, "TR just like his old self. . . . Like old times."[39]

Pinchot was not the only Progressive candidate seeking assistance from the former President. Pressing appeals came from candidates in a number of states including New York, Kansas, Illinois, and Ohio. Far from physically fit, and despite his apparent realization of the futility of the Progressive cause,[40] Roosevelt played the game for his old friends by scheduling more speeches than his condition warranted. In Pennsylvania he had an extra incentive to help— Pinchot was trying to topple one of his prime political enemies.

TR's first appearance in the campaign was in company with Pinchot at a Progressive rally in Pittsburgh, where he attacked Penrose and the Wilson Administration with equal vigor. Later he spoke, among other places, in Philadelphia. He also agreed to sandwich in during the last week of the campaign, between speeches in West Virginia and New York, a flying tour across the state of Pennsylvania in a private train. When, however, he saw the list of appearances that were scheduled for this whirlwind tour—amounting each day to about twenty stops, including brief appearances on the train's platform and two or three longer addresses—he sent wires of protest to Pinchot and other Progressive leaders. In reply to the Chief's request that the load be lightened, Pinchot wired plaintively, "I have never asked you for anything personal before. I ask you now to keep this schedule."[41] Roosevelt went through with the tour as planned, but with a feeling bordering on resentment at the burden that was loaded on his weary body.[42]

The prestige of the Roosevelt name was further marshaled in support of Pinchot when over one million cards were mailed from Oyster Bay containing a facsimile of Roosevelt's handwriting and signed "Theodore Roosevelt." "I am writing," it began, "to ask you personally for your support of Gifford Pinchot against Boies Penrose. . . . They are fighting this year for the same things for which we fought in 1912."

Like any good politician, Pinchot publicly predicted his own victory. Honestly believing he had a chance to dethrone Penrose, he wrote his intimate friend Slattery a few days before the election, "things look very well in the campaign, and I believe we are going to win."[43] But the crusading Pinchot had failed to capture the public fancy in the campaign. Some voters, indeed, showed more interest in the European war headlines than in the election. Pennsylvania, which had veered from its accustomed Republican path in 1912, swung back to familiar ground and to Boies Penrose in 1914. Penrose amassed 520,000 votes, which was almost as many as the total of both Democratic Palmer (266,000) and Pinchot (269,000). Palmer captured Pinchot's home county. Pinchot carried only 14 rural counties of the total of 67.

The fate of the Progressives was not unique in Pennsylvania. Every prominent candidate of the party except Governor Hiram Johnson went down to defeat. In the country as a whole, as well as in Pennsylvania, the Progressives as a party had collapsed. The defeat, then, was a rout. But it is probably safe to say that without the political experience and the acquaintances gained in the 1914 campaign, Pinchot would not have been able to wage a successful race for governor eight years later.

By nature an optimist in politics, Pinchot was not willing to concede the Progressive party's demise. The election, he insisted, was the result of a "frightened vote, blindly hoping to secure prosperity." And he made it clear that one defeat was not enough to discourage him from further participation in the great game of politics. "I am going ahead with the fight for political and economic freedom in Pennsylvania," he wrote his supporters. "I propose to keep on, and I count on your help."[44] Politics was now in his blood.

Early in January, however, leaving Stahlnecker in charge of political and personal affairs, Pinchot and his wife sailed to Europe. Eager to play an active role in alleviating some of the suffering of the current war, Pinchot, who spoke French fluently, was gratified to receive an appointment as a special agent of the State Department at a salary of ten dollars a month, for the distribution of food to hungry French civilians inside the German lines. "No political significance whatever," he cabled Stahlnecker, "solely to facilitate work."[45] But he was highly disappointed when the Germans at the last moment objected to his going into the part of France under their control, on the ground, said Pinchot, that "my sister had married an Englishman."[46]

With a feeling of frustration, he sought work with the Commission for Relief in Belgium, of which Herbert Hoover was chairman. Hoover was "good and angry about the German action, and very nice,"[47] but once again the possibility of a position evaporated. "The Governments," explained Pinchot, "decided to transfer the population elsewhere, so now I am out of a job, and coming home to find one."[48]

Returning for a quiet summer at Grey Towers in Milford, Pinchot showed signs of restlessness over his uncommon inactivity. As colder weather approached, they moved again to Washington. Three days before Christmas, Gifford Bryce Pinchot was born. The elder Pinchot, now fifty, was as boastful as any average father. "It looks," he wrote a friend when the boy was four weeks old, "as if this youngster of mine was going to weigh 27 pounds by the time he is 27 weeks old, if this chart curve keeps up. I judge, however, that that won't happen, for if sustained it would make him 52 pounds at the end of a year, and that is a little too much."[49]

Pinchot directed most of his political efforts in 1915 toward trying to prevent the complete disintegration of the Progressive party. "The one essential thing," he told Hiram Johnson, "is to hold our organization, and be ready to act in 1916."[50] To emphasize the point he composed a letter, individually addressed to a large number of Pennsylvanians, urging that "there is no place for Progressives in either of the old Parties, and there is nothing to gain and everything to lose by going back." For himself, he stated categorically, "I intend to remain a Progressive, and to vote as a Progressive. . . . I am not a Republican, and I am not a Progressive-Republican. . . . I am a Progressive straight."[51]

Pinchot had his differences with Roosevelt, but he never lost faith in the former President's sincere interest in bettering the lot of the "little man." Despite some evidence that TR was swinging to the right, Pinchot still considered him the ablest and most fit candidate for 1916. As the election year opened, Pinchot hoped above all else that the Progressive party could be kept together, and that both they and the Republicans would nominate Roosevelt. Optimistic over the possibilities, he told former Senator Dixon in March that "the prospects for the Colonel's nomination were very bright."[52] A few weeks before the nominating conventions, in a letter to several thousand newspapers, he assumed without question that the Progressives would designate the Chief as their candidate, and also maintained that Roosevelt's nomination by the Republicans "may be regarded as settled."[53]

As a delegate to the Progressive national convention in Chicago, he arrived a few days before its formal opening in early June. The Republican convention was meeting at the same time and in the same city. Pinchot drafted a handwritten letter to Roosevelt assuring him that the Progressives would nominate him at "the first possible moment" if he was willing. But, he advised TR, "we ought not to nominate you unless you are fully prepared to make the race." He declared, "I do not see how you can avoid taking [Charles Evans] Hughes, if he comes through with a declaration along your lines." But, he added, "I don't see how you can accept him unless he does." It is not certain that Pinchot ever sent this note to the Chief; but, whether or not he did, it represented his feelings at the opening of the convention.[54]

The details of the pulling and hauling that occurred in the Progressive convention have been related elsewhere.[55] Pinchot was not stationed at the nerve center of this assembly as he had been in the 1912 convention. He was not a member of the committee that tried to arrive at an agreement with the Republicans on a candidate that both parties would support. Nor was he, as George Perkins was, in constant communication with Roosevelt over a private wire to Oyster Bay.

Pinchot, however, aligned himself with the faction that planned to nominate Roosevelt as soon as possible, perhaps Thursday, and then adjourn. Hoping thereby to force the Republicans to follow suit, they were ready to form a fusion by accepting the Republican nominee for Vice-President. Perkins and others favored waiting to see what the Republicans would do. In the end, Perkins had his way. Not until the Republicans were selecting Hughes on Saturday noon did the Progressives by acclamation choose Roosevelt. The wild cheering for TR was reminiscent of the 1912 nomination. As the demonstration continued, Pinchot stood in the crowd waving an American flag. Not until it had subsided and the convention had nominated John M. Parker for Vice-President did Roosevelt shock the delegates by his message that he could not accept the nomination "at this time." "I shall never forget," said Pinchot in later years, "that horrible sense of defeat and futility which followed."[56]

Although Pinchot described himself as "heartbroken," he did not show extreme bitterness. Perhaps he was not really surprised at what Roosevelt had done under the circumstances—or perhaps he was incapable of extreme wrath toward the Chief. "Of course, we are going to do the best we can," he philosophized, "and I suppose that means backing Hughes. It is tough though, and no mistake."[57] Resentful, however, of the method Roosevelt used to decline the nomination, he told his sister he had never seen anything "more cruel and unnecessary . . . you never saw a madder lot of men in your life than the Progressives when his message reached them."[58]

Although Pinchot was not quite the last to leave the Progressive ship, he clung longer than most. Now that Roosevelt had pulled away, however, he was ready to face realities. "I suppose," he wrote to Harold L. Ickes, "on the whole the endorsement of Hughes was the right thing." But he was not yet ready to go the whole way and call himself a Republican. His personal strategy for the time being was to make no public announcement of his position in the campaign for President. In this way, he reasoned, he could work more effectively to defeat anticonservation legislation then pending in Congress. But, he assured Ickes, "Later on I shall, of course (this is confidential for the moment) come out for Hughes."[59]

Pinchot wanted Woodrow Wilson to lose the election more than he wanted Hughes to win. His attitude toward Wilson had gone through a marked transition. Back in 1911, while Wilson was Governor of New Jersey, the two men had had a talk on conservation. Pinchot at that time registered approval of the future President's position on the need for the federal government's retention of forests and water power.[60] Later, when he read Wilson's *New Freedom* he labeled it "Very admirable."[61]

In the first days of the Wilson Administration, Pinchot had acted as if he were on a honeymoon with the Democrats. "Gifford," his mother wrote, "is very well content with the powers that be."[62] Eager to keep his lines of communication open to some of the key policy makers in the field of conservation, he began, on the day after the President's inauguration, a series of calls on several of the new cabinet members. He was "much delighted" with the appointment of Secretary of the Interior Lane.[63] He considered his talk with Secretary of Agriculture Houston "Very satisfactory indeed." And he liked Attorney General McReynolds "immensely." "It seems," he declared, "to be an excellent cabinet."[64] He even had tried, although unsuccessfully, to obtain from the White House an appointment for himself, the exact nature of which is not clear.[65]

It did not take Pinchot many months to swing around to an opposite viewpoint. He had no sympathy with Wilson's policing action in 1914 at the Mexican border. Referring to "the thoroughly unjust character of the war against Mexico," he called it "so needless, so completely the result of inexcusable blundering."[66] One cannot help feeling that his attitude toward Wilson was shaped partly by TR's opinion of the President. When Roosevelt wrote him in mid-1915 that Wilson was the worst President since Buchanan,[67] Pinchot was in no mood to contradict. Nor was he now pleased with the Secretary of the Interior. Lane, he said, "has put over the idea that he stands for Conservation when as a matter of fact he does nothing of the kind."[68] As the involvement of the United States in the European war became more imminent, Pinchot, perhaps thinking how he would have handled matters if he had been Secretary of State, grew increasingly critical of Wilson's foreign policy and alleged neglect of preparedness.

As part of his drive to prevent the reelection of the President in 1916, Pinchot in September sent several thousand copies of two letters to the nation's newspaper editors. One of them, dealing with conservation, related how Wilson "talked well, began to act well, and then, yielding to the political pressure of the special interests, went back on Conservation."[69] The other letter discussed Pinchot's reasons, as a Progressive, for deciding to support Hughes against Wilson. "I can not vote for Wilson," he concluded, "because I can not trust him. He does not do what he says. Hughes does."[70] The text of this second letter was issued by the Republican national committee as a campaign folder under the heading, "Gifford Pinchot for Hughes."

But Hughes needed more votes, Progressives or otherwise, than he got, and Wilson was reelected. "If TR had been nominated," Pinchot told his sister with assurance, "he would have been elected with a whoop."[71]

Now for the first time, Pinchot was fully convinced of the futility of his remaining outside a major party. Some of the liberals whom he admired, like Brandeis and Dean Lewis, joined with the Democrats. But during almost all of his life something pulled him away from the Democrats and toward the Republicans. A large part of the Republican magnetism undoubtedly stemmed from his upbringing. He had been raised in a Republican family, and in a climate which was predominantly one party. The G.O.P., moreover, was the party of Roosevelt; and what was suitable for the Chief was suitable for him. Pinchot was able to rationalize his avoidance of the Democratic party, moreover, on two grounds. The party, he argued, was and would be "controlled by the solid South. The solid South is Reactionary." Rightly or wrongly, and in spite of the presence of reactionaries in the Republican party, he believed that the true Progressives had more of a chance to make their weight felt in the party of Lincoln than in the party of Wilson. His second complaint against the Democrats was their "fundamental principle of States Rights," which seemed to him "utterly wrong and supremely dangerous."[72] As has been seen, Pinchot firmly believed that many states righters were principally interested in having relatively ineffective government in control. It is probably more than coincidental that in later years when, although remaining a Republican, he sometimes lent aid to the Democrats, the latter party had veered away from its traditional stand on states rights.

To a leader of the Progressives in Pennsylvania Pinchot wrote that "to take possession of the Republican Party offers us our only practicable method of getting action on our principles." His faith in the "rank and file" of that party probably was much too optimistic; they were, he maintained, "progressive and overwhelmingly so." Moreover, he was confident that they were ready to buck "the bosses" out of the saddle; "I propose to put a burr under the said saddle to aid in the bucking process."[73]

CHAPTER 16

YEARS OF FRUSTRATION, 1917-1920

GIFFORD PINCHOT found it painfully difficult to accept the re-election of Wilson. The President's policies of caution and neutrality in the European war seemed to him incredible; he could scarcely contain himself when Wilson sent a peace note to the belligerent powers. Privately, in strong language, he accused Wilson of taking the part of the "Lusitania murderers" when they were on the "verge of punishment." "As for me," he vowed, "I shall stand with the people who fight against this man, and shall keep on standing with them until he is driven from public life. . . . I can't stand for Wilson."[1] Publicly, he pleaded with the nation to support the Allied cause because it was "right," and because "our security will be promoted by their coming victory." He charged that Wilson by his note had "slapped in the face the men who are fighting for the principles of human liberty."[2] From the early days of the war, Pinchot had been convinced that the struggle was primarily the result of "German militarism," and had said that if he thought there was any danger of a German victory, he would favor "immediate participation" by the United States.[3]

As our entry into the war became more likely, Pinchot continued to lash at Wilson with abandon. "He may not be the father of lies," he told a friend, "but he certainly is high up in the family."[4] Four days before the declaration of war on Germany, he wrote a belligerent letter to Senator Henry Cabot Lodge, "War is not the worst of evils. Self respect is a jewel beyond price, and righteousness and justice are the only foundations of enduring peace." Asserting his approval of universal military training, he accused the Germans of practicing "murder as a habit" and urged that the United States fight them at once. "We should have done so long ago."[5]

When war came, Pinchot was already on record at the White House as a volunteer. Two months earlier he had addressed a note to the President, "In the event of war, I have the honor to place myself at the disposal of the Government, to serve in whatever capacity I may be of greatest use."[6] It is hardly surprising, in view of some of his comments on Wilson, that the White House did not rush to enlist him in its war organization.

In the interest of national unity, Pinchot during the war kept his criticisms of Wilson private. Especially disturbed that the President would not permit Roosevelt to take a volunteer force to Europe, he told TR, "I believe you would be worth a dozen army corps if you were in Russia right now."[7] Had Roosevelt received the necessary permission, he would have made Pinchot a lieutenant colonel on his staff.[8] When official notice of the refusal came through, Pinchot resorted to uncustomary profanity in expressing his feelings to the Chief. "It is a damned shame," he wrote to Roosevelt, "but by no means a surprise," and went on to explain that he had hopes himself of raising and taking to France "a regiment of foresters."[9] When news of this project was rumored in the papers, however, Pinchot wrote to Harold L. Ickes, in an apparently embarrassed manner, that he had decided not to go.[10]

Having no official position with the government, Pinchot took it on himself to try to aid the war effort by urging the growing of more food. Late in April he addressed a letter to more than 5,000 editors in which he suggested that the nation had a duty to guarantee fair prices to farmers,[11] and followed up this letter by a "talking campaign" in the South.[12] Hopeful of obtaining a position with Herbert Hoover's Food Administration, he made his first approach by writing the future President in March. Pinchot's first impression was that Hoover was shying away from using him,[13] but he was delighted when, after a "thoroughly satisfactory" talk with Hoover, he was given the "real job" of trying to "increase the head of livestock in this country."[14]

In less than three months, however, Hoover had Pinchot's resignation. At the outset of his job, Pinchot had concluded that the way to persuade farmers to produce more pork was to have the meat packers guarantee sufficiently high prices for all hogs raised. When the packers objected to this system, Hoover, taking a position which reminded Pinchot of Taft, insisted that his organization did not have the authority to impose such a scheme. Pinchot, impatient with such hesitation, reminded Hoover that he "had spent many years making the same kind of people do things they declared they would not do." If the Food Administration made a vigorous effort to compel the packers to agree, he argued, they would have no choice but to comply; in case of refusal, the government actually had the power "under the law, in addition to the moral weight of the War situation," to take over the packing houses.[15] But Hoover believed in neither the legality nor the wisdom of such drastic action.

As tension between the two men grew, Hoover suggested that Pinchot, with his ability to speak French, should give up his live-stock work and take charge of the distribution of farm tractors in France. Given but a day to consider the proposition, Pinchot sur-mised, with justification, that it was "merely a way to dispose of me." Returning to Hoover's office, therefore, he submitted his writ-ten resignation. "Because," it read, "of the continued failure of the Food Administration to take effective action for increasing the pro-duction of meats, which failure is certain to result in higher prices to our people and a shortage in the food supplies needed to win the War, I hereby resign."[16]

Pinchot's account of his ensuing discussion with Hoover showed how far apart the two men were in their philosophies concerning the proper role of the Food Administration. Hoover, in the course of their talk, revealed he had been warned "on all sides" that Pinchot would not be loyal to him. Whereupon Pinchot listed the occasions on which he felt Hoover had not been loyal to him, and complained that Hoover had offered nothing but objections to his proposals.[17] Pinchot's resignation was announced only briefly in the press. To his credit, he refrained from continuing the debate in public. "I have neither the desire nor the intention of doing anything that would hamper the Food Administration."[18] From Henry C. Wallace, fu-ture Secretary of Agriculture under President Harding, he received both advice and hearty approval for his actions. Hoover, although profoundly pained by the resignation, and especially by the way it was worded, agreed that, in view of the national emergency, it warranted no controversy.[19]

One of Pinchot's weaknesses, when engaged in a conflict, was a tendency to ascribe to his opponent every possible shortcoming.

Too often a man in Pinchot's eyes was all black or all white; there was no grey. It had been this way with Ballinger and Taft, then with Woodrow Wilson, and now with Hoover. Pinchot granted in his private correspondence that Hoover was an able mining engineer, and had capably handled Belgian relief. But relief work, he reasoned, consisted merely "in the purchase and delivery of supplies already produced. . . . The Belgian people took what was given them and were thankful." Managing a Food Administration agency in a democracy, maintained Pinchot, was "a wholly different matter." Hoover had "no knowledge of how to deal with masses of people" under such circumstances. "His knowledge of democratic institutions appears to be elementary. Indeed I understand that he has never voted." Complaining that the Food Administration was largely in the hands of men representing "the packers and other great special interests," he asserted that Hoover began his services as head of the agency "with a contempt for public opinion." Describing Hoover as "actively hostile" to the farmers, he reported to Colonel House that "So far as I can recall, in every interview I have had with him since early in September, Mr. Hoover has taken occasion to berate the farmers, and to accuse them of greed, lack of patriotism, and other shortcomings."[20] In view of various statements of this nature, it is understandable that Pinchot faced some embarrassment in explaining his support of Hoover for President in 1928.

Once more a free lance, Pinchot experienced a feeling of frustration at having no official role in the war effort.[21] Eager to return to Europe, he pulled wires in an effort to get there. First, as a member of the executive committee of the National Board of Farm Organizations, he got himself designated as their representative to study in Europe the proposed plans of Allied and neutral nations for post-war agricultural reconstruction. But he struck a snag when the State Department refused his application for passports for himself and his secretary, Stahlnecker. The State Department, relying on a statement by Secretary of Agriculture Houston, held that Pinchot's trip was not of urgent necessity. Pinchot was incensed. Appealing directly to Secretary of State Lansing, he maintained that the denial of this right to the farmers "would be in line not with American democratic ideals, but rather with the policy and practice of autocratic governments."[22] The State Department, however, refused to budge.

The second job opportunity that Pinchot pursued was with the Army. At Pinchot's request, Roosevelt wrote General Peyton March describing Pinchot's eagerness to get to the front and suggesting that he might be used for intelligence work.[23] The letter brought action—within two weeks the Director of Military Intelligence in the War Department wrote Pinchot of the possibilities of using him in a civilian status, ostensibly on a mission connected with forestry, in Switzerland or some Scandinavian country. Once more Pinchot's hopes rose, only to be dashed again; two weeks before the armistice, he received a letter from the War Department explaining that efforts to obtain a passport for him "have been unsuccessful."[24]

Stopped twice in his efforts to do some war work, Pinchot could not help believing that the Wilson Administration was singling him out for punishment. His bitterness toward Wilson, although not publicly expressed, continued unabated. The results of the November elections, which gave the Republicans a majority in Congress, therefore, brought deep satisfaction. "My warmest and heartiest congratulations," he wrote to Republican chairman Will H. Hays, "on the magnificent victory under your leadership. . . . There can be no German peace now."[25] When the armistice was signed, he once more confided to Roosevelt, "What a pitiful spectacle at Washington. Unready for war, unready for peace, without a plan or a policy."[26]

His lack of respect for Wilson was contagious in at least part of his family. Sister Antoinette, writing from Paris in January 1919, described to Gifford her meeting with the President the night before. Wilson told her, she said, that there was nothing personal in the denial of a passport for her brother, but she refused to believe it. In a triumphant tone she wrote how she had informed Wilson of her opinion that there were no great men in the world at that time. In a battle of parlor wits, he had countered quickly with the observation that Colonel House was a great man, whereupon she acidly admitted that there were two—House and her brother Gifford.[27]

As has been seen, Pinchot thought of his inherited money as advance wages which he hoped to work out over the years. When the people of Pennsylvania, in the election of 1914, declined to accept his services in the United States Senate, he had continued to pour both time and money into the National Conservation Association and other conservation work. During the war, he had tried desperately to do his patriotic bit. It became increasingly apparent, however, that he preferred to earn his wages as an elected public official.

His wife, too, had an active interest in politics, shown partly by her three campaigns for a seat in the United States House of Representatives. Perhaps even more than most wives of politicians she was acutely ambitious for her husband's political success. Early in 1915, for example, she asked Roosevelt if he did not think Pinchot was making a mistake by staying out of the country too long. Roosevelt's reply was not encouraging, for he said frankly that he believed her husband had no future in politics since the people as a whole were not sympathetic with his views. The former President hastened to add that the same was true of his own future, and he hoped that Pinchot's situation was only temporary.[28]

Whether or not he knew of Roosevelt's letter, Pinchot was undaunted. With cold calculation he set out to build a following in Pennsylvania. Joining the Grange in his local area, he continued his vigorous championing of the farmer—soon he was state chairman of the committee on conservation. His growing attachment to the prohibition movement certainly did him no harm in numerous sections of Pennsylvania, including the so-called "Bible belt" which spread through a considerable portion of the rural areas. In 1915 he presided at a meeting of a national convention of the Anti-Saloon League of America; during the war he became an earnest advocate of preventing the brewers and distillers "from using the grain that is needed for food."[29]

Early in 1917 Pinchot began concentrating his attention on the 1920 election for a seat in the United States Senate. Although an election for Governor of Pennsylvania was scheduled for 1918, he probably preferred the Senate. The Washington atmosphere was more attractive to him than that of the small state capital of Harrisburg. After all, he had enjoyed national prominence there, and still had his home on Rhode Island Avenue. Fond of his inherited estate in Milford, he also relished living in his Washington home and participating in the possibly more exciting politics of the nation's capital.

He needed reassurance, however, that he was wise in placing his future firmly in Pennsylvania politics. It still was not too late to return to the field of conservation or forestry. Following a talk with Roosevelt on both national and Pennsylvania politics, he had an interview with Edwin A. Van Valkenburg, editor of the *Philadelphia North American*, which helped persuade him to continue his political fence building. Pinchot happily reported to Roosevelt that Van Valkenburg promised to "throw the whole power" of his paper "behind me" in the primary race for the Senate. "He believes," continued Pinchot, "that it was not only wisest but my duty to stay with the work in Pennsylvania." The more he thought about it, he explained to Roosevelt, the more he agreed that the "effort" was "worth making."[30]

Despite his apparent preference for a seat in the Senate, Pinchot quietly entertained some hope that the anti-Penrose Republicans in the state might call on him in 1918 to defeat Senator Penrose's candidate for governor. Their selection of another man served as a lesson to Pinchot. The controlling reason for passing him over, he surmised, was that he had "been too much absent" from the state during the previous two or three years. "It seems a shame," he ruefully admitted, "that I should have allowed such a chance to get by from plain failure to take advantage of the situation. It is a lesson which I shall not forget."[31]

After the war when Pinchot began to concentrate on the 1920 Senate race in Pennsylvania, he earnestly tried to overcome his earlier mistakes. The 1918 defeat of the anti-Penrose forces in no way deterred him. He played his cards carefully. When the chairman of the Republican state committee asked him to attend a meeting of the group he shied away, hoping, it would seem, to avoid being marked with the label of the regular Republican organization.[32] He and his wife, moreover, took the unusual step of living in Philadelphia during the winter of 1918-1919. In the

spring and much of the summer of 1919, he toured the state, talking in churches, before Rotary clubs, and at Grange picnics. Pounding home to farmers his now familiar theme that they should organize and get into politics, he was highly pleased when representatives of both the Grange and the Pennsylvania Federation
of Labor approved a platform he drafted emphasizing the common interests of workers and farmers. He offered to pay the expenses of sending copies to all Pennsylvania newspapers.[33] Similarly
satisfying was a letter sent by the president of the Federation to
all local unions, in which he referred to Pinchot as one "whose
friendship for organized labor is well known."[34]

It will be recalled that when Pinchot lived with his mother in
Washington, she was a constant as well as a gracious hostess. Hardly
a luncheon or dinner went by when guests were not present at 1615
Rhode Island Avenue—many of them prominent government officials and foreign diplomats. Cornelia Bryce Pinchot, in her entertaining, carried on in the Mary Eno Pinchot tradition. The new
Mrs. Pinchot, indeed, younger and more energetic than her mother-
in-law had been, entertained even more frequently—both their
Washington and Milford homes were a veritable beehive of activity.
The *Saturday Evening Post* described her home as a "sort of political boarding house."[35] Droves of politicians—national, state, and
local—delighted in Pinchot hospitality. Sometimes invitation was
by formal card—4:30 p.m., March 6, 1917, 1615 Rhode Island
Avenue. At this party two United States senators spoke on "certain
phases of education among the cowboys, ranchmen, and miners of
the northern rocky mountains." At the other extreme, the invitation
might be an advertisement in a newspaper announcing that on September 13, 1919 the Pinchots would entertain all soldiers from
Pike County at Grey Towers, from 2:00 to 6:00 p.m.—rain or
shine, refreshments and speeches.[36] Much of the Pinchot entertaining of course had no political implications, but some of it obviously
benefited an eager candidate.

To dramatize his contempt for Penrose, Pinchot, more than a year
before the 1920 primaries, sent a bristling open letter to the Senator.
Asserting that he wanted to see the Democrats beaten in 1920, he
suggested that one of the main obstacles to a Republican victory was

the knowledge that as a result of seniority it would place Penrose in the chairmanship of the Senate Committee on Finance. Choosing his words carefully, he stressed the importance to the Republicans of the vote in the Middle West, but stated frankly that "The middle West knows you mainly as the most perfect living representative of the worst type of politics in America," and Pinchot added that he thoroughly agreed with their opinion. "You are a liability," he charged. "If you are not a good enough Republican, are you a good enough American to withdraw your name" for consideration as chairman?[37]

Penrose's answer was brief and contemptuous. "Mr. Pinchot seems to me about as important as a cheap side show outside the fence of a county fair, like the tatooed man or the cigarette fiend."[38]

In view of his drive against Penrose, it came as a distinct shock to Pinchot that Penrose candidates for local offices showed "unexpected strength" in the primaries in September 1919. He feared that the results in the state's two large cities, Philadelphia and Pittsburgh, "greatly advanced" Penrose's prestige and made it improbable that Pinchot or any one else could defeat him for the Senate in 1920.[39] "[It] may be," he wrote in despair, "that the chance to get effectively into Pennsylvania politics for some years to come will vanish away . . . I feel like fighting, but there is no use butting your head against a stone wall."[40] Pinchot chose to bide his time and to train his sights on some more distant goal, perhaps the next election for governor in 1922.

In the midst of his determined efforts to win a political following in Pennsylvania, Gifford Pinchot lost the friend who, with the possible exception of his mother, did the most to influence his life. On January 6, 1919, Theodore Roosevelt died. Despite Roosevelt's latter-day impatience (some of it not fully revealed to Pinchot) with his radicalism, Pinchot had continued to hold the Chief in high esteem. Although some of TR's former admirers saw him in his later years as pulling away from true liberalism, Pinchot's confidence in Roosevelt's fundamental humanitarianism was never seriously shaken. Senator La Follette once reported a remark by Amos Pinchot that Roosevelt was always able to pull the wool over Gifford's eyes.[41]

Be that as it may, there can be no question that Gifford's long and close association with Roosevelt convinced him of the genuineness of Roosevelt's concern for the common man. Roosevelt's death was a great personal loss to Pinchot. He was certain that it also represented a serious loss to the nation. It "may result in such control by the reactionaries," he wrote his brother, "as to put the policies you and I are interested in back many years."[42]

As a member of the Roosevelt Memorial Association, Pinchot became chairman of its Committee on the Perpetuation of Roosevelt's Ideals. Working hard to establish a fitting memorial, he agreed with most of his colleagues that it was proper to erect a great monument in Washington and to make Sagamore Hill into a modern Mount Vernon, but he believed something else was needed. His proposal to the Memorial Association that it sponsor a foundation "for carrying on Roosevelt's Conservation policies,"[43] however, failed to gain much support. Disgusted, he wrote to Harry Slattery, "The effort to keep Roosevelt out of the Roosevelt Memorial Association has made more progress than I thought."[44] Pinchot also was one of the handful of Roosevelt admirers who helped organize an annual pilgrimage to Oyster Bay on the anniversary of his death. Indicative of his continued loyalty to the memory of his idol was his presence, at the age of seventy-one, at the seventeenth pilgrimage in 1937; with fifty other men and women, he braved the January cold to stand by the grave of his old Chief.

Pinchot's active concentration on Pennsylvania politics did not in any sense diminish his profound interest in the national political scene. Even before the war ended, he repeatedly informed the Republican national chairman, Will H. Hays, of his belief that the best way to ensure a Republican victory in 1920 was to demonstrate to the farmers that the party understood their problems and was prepared to act. Feeling that labor had become an "adjunct of the Wilson Administration" (although not in Pennsylvania), he thought the farmers could be weaned away from the Democrats, but only if the Republicans avoided a reactionary viewpoint. "I feel very strongly," he wrote, "the pressing and immediate danger that the Democratic Party may succeed in becoming the progressive party in the United States, and thereby may secure for itself some such lease of power as the Republican Party secured after the Civil War."[45] The danger, as it turned out, was more imminent a dozen years later than it was in 1918. To strengthen the party's appeal to the rural voters still further, Pinchot advocated that the vice-presidential candidate should be a farmer.[46]

Announcing that he would submit his name as a delegate to the Republican national convention the next year, Pinchot pledged his opposition to the nomination for President of "a reactionary" like Senator Warren Harding or Senator James Watson.[47] On the list of possible candidates in his mind he probably included his own name, but was realistic enough to know that his chances were small. Some careful notes he made of an interview with a man in Philadelphia indicate that he was ready to take himself seriously. Asked if he would consider running on a third ticket in 1920 and 1924, he cautiously answered, "I would consider any proposition made at the right time and in the right way."[48]

Pinchot had some difficulty in choosing the man he would support for the nomination. Finally he had a talk with General Leonard Wood who stated that "he knew of no policy in which he was not in entire agreement with Colonel Roosevelt."[49] That was enough for Pinchot. In speeches in the East and even as far away as South Dakota, he began lauding Wood.

As the time for the Republican convention approached, Pinchot was gratified that chairman Will Hays placed him on an advisory board of 159 persons to work on the policies and platform for the party. Working diligently on this assignment, he was "well pleased" with the "farmer plank" and the "conservation plank" that finally were adopted.[50]

Watching the situation develop, however, he became increasingly fearful that the progressive Republicans would be left "absolutely out in the cold."[51] Although he sneered at Harry M. Daugherty's famous prediction that out of a smoke-filled room at the convention would come the nomination of Harding, he had confided to a friend that "the probability is that some Reactionary like Harding is likely to be the Republican candidate rather than Wood."[52] Harding, he told some University of Pennsylvania students, "would make a fine President to look at, but that is about all you can say of him."[53] He wrote to the *Philadelphia North American* that "Harding is utterly unfit to be President."[54] Further discouraging to Pinchot was the report that he had no chance of being chosen as a delegate-at-large to the Republican convention; Senator Penrose, it was explained, was against it.[55] In the end, Pinchot went to the convention, but not as a delegate.

After the convention decisively defeated the Progressives and nominated Harding, Pinchot privately expressed his misgivings that "Penrose and his crowd" had managed to put over their choice.[56] But he was in no mood to create a fuss. For some months, indeed, he had indicated that he was more ready than in the past to go along with the decisions of the majority in the Republican party. For one thing, he was determined that Wilsonianism must be beaten. Although striving to infiltrate the Republican party with as much progressivism as possible, he promised that "We are not going to do anything that will cause or look toward causing a split" in the party.[57] It is probably true, moreover, that his political ambitions were restraining him from appearing to be a maverick. In his 1914 election campaign he had toyed with socialism and had been called a radical. Now he seemed to be trying to redeem himself in the eyes of the conservatives whom he had frightened away. Perhaps almost unconsciously he had come to realize that if he hoped to win an election in Pennsylvania, he must forego some of his more liberal ideas. He had, for example, wired to Governor Calvin Coolidge of Massachusetts his congratulations for "your services to the whole nation" in breaking the Boston police strike.[58]

No sooner had Harding been nominated, therefore, than Pinchot fell in line. "Much as Harding's nomination leaves to be desired, Cox is a great deal worse," he told a Pennsylvania Progressive. And he asked to be excused from signing with other former Progressives a letter asking Harding to disavow some of the strong criticism he had directed at Roosevelt in 1912.[59] Late in August, Pinchot made a trip to Marion, Ohio, to see the candidate and to judge for himself. In personal interviews of this kind, Pinchot sometimes tended to be swayed unduly by what was said in the course of the discussion. Harding, in this instance, did not completely captivate his interrogator, but did remove a number of Pinchot's doubts. He was delighted that the candidate "has come through superbly on forestry," and "referred to our friends the grabbers as *hogs*, and said he would tell them so if it were not for its being campaign time."[60] Part of this enthusiasm stemmed from Pinchot's belief that Harding "liked me and wanted me in the picture."[61] Immediately after the interview, the news wires reported to the nation that Pinchot endorsed Harding.

Pinchot's support of Harding was considerably more than passive acquiescence. He supplied material for the candidate's speeches. He offered his services to the national chairman as a stump speaker. And early in October he proclaimed, in a letter to Republican papers all over the country, that, as a follower of Roosevelt "alive or dead," he had found Harding "by no means the Reactionary I thought him."[62]

In the midst of the country's drive "back to normalcy," which represented a retreat from the things Progressives stood for, Pinchot still was able to speak hopefully. With characteristic, though unwarranted, optimism, he assured Harold L. Ickes that the former Progressives were getting their point of view "far more widely accepted in the platform and in the speeches of the candidates than I had any idea would be possible. . . . I still have the feeling that our day is not over."[63]

Pinchot's hopes were raised for some sort of job with the newly elected Harding Administration when Henry C. Wallace wrote that he was urging his name for Secretary of Agriculture. Wallace himself, however, stepped into that post. Pinchot admired Wallace, but was sadly disappointed in most of the other members of the new cabinet, including Herbert Hoover. It might have been possible, he wrote, to pick a worse man than Albert Fall for Secretary of the Interior, "but not altogether easy."[64] Ten days after Harding took office, Pinchot ruefully admitted to his sister that while Harding was "extremely cordial" there was no prospect of a position in the Administration.[65] A quarter of a century later he conceded that he had made a mistake, "I voted for Harding and I've been sorry ever since."[66]

CHAPTER 17

POLITICAL SUCCESS

WILLIAM C. SPROUL, the successful candidate for chief executive of Pennsylvania in 1918, was one of the state's better governors. Able and honest, he was a businessman who had served a long term in the state senate. Because he was backed by Penrose, Pinchot had supported his opponent in the primary. In the November election, however, Pinchot remained regular, and sent Sproul a letter wishing him a successful Administration, "I for one shall be delighted to do anything I can to make it so."[1]

Upon learning that a local political leader had suggested his appointment as state Forestry Commissioner, Pinchot hastened to inform Governor Sproul that if this cabinet post were offered, he would be unable to accept it permanently. He indicated his willingness, however, to spend two or three months in getting "organization and policy" of the Forestry Department straightened out. He knew that Pennsylvania had got off to a better start than most states in forest conservation. But Dr. J. T. Rothrock, the acknowledged father of forestry in the state, had resigned as Commissioner in 1904. Since that time the Department had been under the direction of Robert S. Conklin. Governor Sproul, aware of the desirability of having a man of Pinchot's ability in the Department, prevailed on him to serve on the Pennsylvania Forest Commission (consisting of five members, with Conklin as chairman), which shared with the Commissioner the direction of the Department. Rothrock also was a member of the Commission.

The closer Pinchot was to the Department, the more he became convinced that Conklin had to go. Although the Commissioner had many supporters, both professional and political, Pinchot, unimpressed, believed implicitly that the head of a Forestry Department should be a trained forester, which Conklin was not. He maintained, furthermore, that Conklin was not the aggressive and fearless kind of administrator that was needed. "[One] of Conklin's main troubles," he complained, "is that the path ahead is always full of lions."[2]

273

Pinchot induced another member of the Forest Commission (not Rothrock) to join him in signing a severe sixteen-page indictment of Commissioner Conklin. Addressing their complaints to the Governor, they charged that the state forests were badly mismanaged and that the organization of the Department reflected the incompetence of the Commissioner. "The essential fact," concluded the two dissenters, "is that the present Commissioner not only appears to have no desire to do better, but does not know how."[3]

In the face of this attack, Governor Sproul saw that action was necessary. But when he suggested calling in two or three experts from outside the state to pass upon the dispute, Pinchot countered, with supreme assurance, that he "did not recognize that anyone in America had a right to pass upon [his] opinion as a Forester."[4] Governor Sproul, according to Pinchot, "entirely agreed" and promised to find another position for Conklin.

The man whom Sproul wanted for Commissioner was Pinchot. Forewarned of the Governor's wishes, Pinchot had been doubtful about accepting. But when the formal invitation reached him in early March while speaking in South Dakota for General Wood for President, he wired the Governor he would "accept gladly the important and responsible post."[5] Most Pennsylvanians would have agreed with the editorial comment of the *Philadelphia Evening Public Ledger* that Sproul "has done well."[6]

Pinchot began his new job with evident relish. He had not, after all, had a formal administrative position since President Taft fired him almost a decade before. Convinced that one of the Department's primary weaknesses had been the neglect of publicity for itself, he set out to dramatize the work of the agency. In speeches, pamphlets, and the press, he drove home his belief that wasteful lumbering and forest fires were costing Pennsylvanians twice as much as the outlay for running the entire state government, and were bringing about a "Pennsylvania Desert."[7] Everything the Department did seemed to find its way into the newspapers. To assist in building public sentiment favorable to increased state money for forests, he sponsored a "Committee on the Restoration of Pennsylvania's Timber Production."

Pinchot was, in a sense, re-enacting some of his earlier activities with the United States Forest Service, but this time in a smaller pond. Yale classmate George Woodruff came in to direct one of the bureaus. At a state foresters' conference in Harrisburg, Pinchot even harked back to the old days by staging a "smoker" and sentimentally serving baked apples and ginger bread.

Soon after becoming Commissioner he announced that twenty-four-hour service would be kept in the state capitol to receive reports of forest fires. When a bureau director questioned the value of such a vigil in view of the lack of night telephone service in many rural areas, Pinchot accepted a dare by agreeing to stay in the Department office all night during the first week and take turns with the director in manning the telephone. This extra service may not have done much to reduce the devastation by fire, but it helped to dramatize the need of more money for fire fighting. "It has been like trying to put out a burning building with water in a spoon," he reported to the Governor.[8]

In a state government saturated with political favoritism, Pinchot made strong friends as well as bitter enemies by refusing to consider politics in making appointments or promotions in his Department. Attempts at political interference irritated him. Because, in the typical Pennsylvania county, patronage appointments cleared through the Republican county chairman, that official often wielded a large measure of political power. But Pinchot was no respecter of county chairmen. Once, for example, upon receiving the copy of a protest addressed to a county chairman against Pinchot's retaining two women on the roll of the Forestry Department, he did not wait to hear from the chairman, but wrote him first instead. Pointing out that the charges against the women were made "wholly upon partisan political grounds," he brusquely displayed his contempt for the patronage system, "I know nothing and care nothing about the politics . . . of either of these ladies. I do know that they . . . are competent, faithful, and satisfactory servants of the State." He concluded with a warning that "If, while continuing to give satisfactory service, they are removed for political reasons, I will go out with them."[9] Truly, something new was happening in Pennsylvania.

Pinchot's salary as Commissioner was $5,000. Its low level made no real difference to him personally, but it had the effect of placing the Department in a salary strait-jacket, since the salaries of his subordinates had to be scaled below his figure. Appealing to the Governor for relief, he learned of a constitutional barrier which apparently precluded any increase in his remuneration during his term of office. In a Rooseveltian move, however, after an agreement with the Governor, he resigned one day and the next day was re-appointed at a salary of $8,000. Critics accused him of meddling with the constitution for the purpose of a personal salary grab, and his action became a major point of controversy in ensuing elections. Much of the criticism was mollified, however, when Dr. Rothrock and the deputy Commissioner affirmed, what only they and a few of Pinchot's closest associates knew, that he had sought the higher salary merely to permit better pay for some of his subordinates; and, in addition, that he regularly spent considerably more than his salary to bring experts into the Department at salaries higher than those permitted by law.[10]

At about this time, the newspapers were featuring stories of the efforts of the Eno family to contest the will of the wealthy bachelor, Amos F. Eno, Pinchot's Uncle "Mo." Mr. Eno, who inherited $3 million from his father, increased it to $10 million by the time he died in 1916. In his last will he designated specific amounts for various organizations and for his relatives, but bequeathed the resid-ual part of his estate, estimated at the time of his death to be $4 million, to Columbia University. Gifford Pinchot was slated for $250,000. The Eno family, including nephews Amos and Gifford Pinchot, charging that Mr. Eno had no interest in Columbia and questioning his sanity at the time the will was written, sued to break it. In litigation which dragged on for a half dozen years, two differ-ent juries found Mr. Eno incompetent to make the will, but in both instances their verdicts were overruled by judges. Finally in 1922, by a settlement arranged out of court, Columbia University obtained the residual part which it felt rightfully belonged to it.[11]

This and other publicity at various times in his life helped to give the public an exaggerated conception of Pinchot's wealth. He was by no means a poor man. From his parents and various Eno relatives he inherited a fortune. But he was not the affluent multi-millionaire that some persons pictured. He could have been wealthier if he had chosen to live within his income rather than use some of his capital. At the end of 1915, for example, he admitted that because of the large outlay of funds for his senatorial campaign of the year before, his "expenses for this year as well as last are still far more than my income."[12] A decade and a half later, still using his principal for electioneering, he asserted that he was "more than a hundred thousand dollars in debt" from his campaign for governor in 1930.[13] In addition, his investments were not well managed; he himself rarely gave them the attention they needed.

In the boom year of 1928, for example, Pinchot reported to the Internal Revenue Service a total income, before deductions, of approximately $65,000, of which about $47,000 came from rents. As the depression came on, and some of his New York City real estate operated in the red, he found it necessary to live on capital. To all sorts of persons who asked for help, he explained that two-thirds of his income had disappeared. In the midst of the depression he wrote Harry Slattery, reluctantly acknowledging that he could not continue to carry him on his payroll as a pipeline to Washington, "Everything I get substantially has to go to pay taxes and interest and, as you know, nothing comes at all from my Mother's estate."[14] Mrs. Gifford Pinchot's personal wealth unquestionably helped to finance their extensive personal and political expenses.

The political opportunity that Pinchot had been waiting for came on New Year's Eve in 1921—with the death of Boies Penrose. When the Senator was alive, his machine was practically unbeatable. But there was no heir to his throne who could hold the state in an iron grip the way Penrose had. The passing of the Republican boss brought about a wild struggle for power and offices within the party.

High in the leadership of the various factions of the Republican party were names which then or later were of national prominence. The Mellons in Pittsburgh, including President Harding's Secretary of the Treasury, Andrew W. Mellon, made their weight felt in state circles and especially in the smoothly running Pittsburgh machine. The Vare brothers, sometimes called the dukes of South Philadelphia, who usually had been at odds with Penrose, held the

Philadelphia ballot boxes in the palms of their hands; they could in most instances deliver the city vote to the highest bidder—even Penrose in spite of his state power had to make deals with them on some occasions. Both the Philadelphia and Pittsburgh machines were notorious for crooked voting. In the city of brotherly love, for example, fake names on registration lists and the casting of fraudulent ballots were common occurrences. Representatives of the Vare organization actually marked many ballots under the pretense of assisting the voters. So effective was the vote stealing in some instances that the election returns would reveal "zero districts," those in which 100 per cent of the votes were recorded for one candidate.[15]

Two other leading contenders for power in the party were W. W. Atterbury, the president of the influential Pennsylvania Railroad, and Joseph R. Grundy, the president of the Pennsylvania Manufacturers' Association. Through the years, Grundy in particular left a deep imprint on Pennsylvania politics, not to mention national. Once called the "uncrowned King of Lobbyists in the U.S.,"[16] he was also a masterful money raiser for the party. A strong supporter of Penrose, he fought persistently for high tariffs and against any government action which he believed might harm his manufacturers. Unfailingly he opposed old-age pensions and much labor legislation because of the burden they would place upon business. In 1921 he helped to engineer a spectacular fight in the Pennsylvania legislature against the establishment of a Department of Welfare in the state government. Much of the power of Grundy's organization in the state could be explained by its quiet financing of the campaigns of a number of legislators. Moreover, the managers of the district offices of the Pennsylvania Manufacturers' Association Casualty Insurance Company, an affiliate of the parent organization, were the basis for a state-wide political organization which, at least in some counties, wielded sizable power. Grundy and the Vares, incidentally, wasted no friendship on each other.

The Mellons, the Vares, Atterbury, and Grundy—all, Pinchot believed, stood for the things he had been denouncing for two decades. All were powerful men, but no one of them or their henchmen was powerful enough to step into Penrose's shoes.

Pinchot and his secretary-manager, Stahlnecker, were quick to see the possibilities of improving their own position while the various factions struggled for leadership. Within four days after Penrose's death, Stahlnecker, not yet ready to show his hand, was quietly taking steps to obtain lists of Pennsylvania voters. While Pinchot had not yet made up his mind what office to seek, it became increasingly apparent that his name would be listed somewhere on the ballot. When in a moment of harmony the leaders united in supporting George Wharton Pepper for United States senator, Pinchot determined to concentrate on the governorship.

Under the constitution of the state, Governor Sproul was ineligible to succeed himself. A raft of aspirants consequently had entered the race. By early March the state League of Women Voters considered Pinchot enough of a candidate to invite him to appear before their convention with other announced candidates. More than any of the others, he was attuned to the stirrings among the Republican women. Despite their rather newly won right of suffrage, they had not been accepted in the inner circles of the state Republican party. Since this was their first state-wide primary, they were hungry for recognition. Pinchot gave it to them in the form of a neat little talk, using material from an article he had published in the *Ladies Home Journal*, maintaining that women were especially trained to secure two of the great needs of Pennsylvania government—economy and efficiency. He was the hit of the convention and drew the longest applause of any of the candidates.[17]

Two days later Pinchot formally announced his candidacy and brought to at least five the number of serious contenders for the Republican nomination for governor. At this point in his career he was fond of referring to himself as a neophyte in politics. "[What] I know about practical politics," he wrote to Sir Horace Plunkett "is next to nothing."[18] But his campaign was marked by some very shrewd moves. Many of them were unorthodox enough in boss-ridden Pennsylvania to carry strong appeal to the "average" voter. No sooner had he asked for a leave of absence without pay from his position of Forestry Commissioner than he befuddled the politicians by writing to all employees in his Department that "you must not use your official positions to advance my candidacy," and that they were "wholly free as individuals to support any candidate" they pleased.[19]

Equally extraordinary was an open letter addressed to nine leaders of the Republican organization, including Grundy and one of the Vares. Because of illness, a second seat in the United States Senate was becoming vacant. Referring to rumors that the party leaders were about to meet for the purpose of trying to agree on one candidate for this position and another for the governorship, Pinchot in cocksure manner warned against such action. Appealing for a "genuine open primary," he asserted that "deals and set-ups" were at the moment "about as popular as an inkspot on a clean collar. . . . Let me warn you in advance that no candidate who has the slightest taint of a deal can win this year."[20] When one of the leaders countered with the suggestion that all gubernatorial candidates sit down in conference and agree on one candidate, Pinchot reminded him that the selection of the candidate should be made "by the Republican voters, and not by any little group of men, there is danger in that."[21] Such tactics were bound to incense the leaders, but they also evoked a good deal of approval throughout the state.

The rumored meeting took place in Philadelphia, however, in spite of Pinchot. Most of those present agreed to ditch the active candidates for governor and support a harmony candidate, George E. Alter, Governor Sproul's Attorney General, who accepted the assignment with some reluctance. A great deal of his campaign was to center on the theme that he was a "real" Republican as opposed to the synthetic Pinchot type.

As soon as the decision of the leaders was announced, three of the candidates for governor dutifully withdrew. Pinchot remained in the race and so did Grundy's man, John S. Fisher, state Commissioner of Banking. Grundy was angry; he had fought hard for Fisher against Alter. Determined to defeat the organization leaders who had outvoted him, he saw the futility of trying to win against their machine with two candidates. In due course, therefore, Fisher withdrew and threw his support to Pinchot. Grundy himself said little, but it was apparent he was more interested in beating the organization than in winning for Pinchot.

Not many of the professional politicians at the beginning of the campaign gave Pinchot much of a chance of winning. Forced to start from scratch against an established Republican organization in each county, he set out, with Stahlnecker's expert guidance, to create his own rival organization in each of the 67 districts. Furthermore, Mrs. Pinchot was invaluable in lining up support from women and from labor unions, at Philadelphia headquarters and throughout the state. Mrs. Pinchot's activities among the workers of the state were not well accepted by some of the more conservative Republicans; they viewed her with the same jaundiced eyes that were cast on Eleanor Roosevelt a dozen years later. Typical of some of the comment was an anonymous letter to Pinchot with a newspaper picture of his wife attached to it. "Dear Pinchot," it said, "Keep this off the stump if you have the interests of the Republican Party at heart," and was signed "A Regular Republican."

The "greatest fear" of the machine leaders, reported a commentator in the *New York Times*, was not of the nominee but of "his wife's proved political generalship."[22] Pinchot never had any doubt that she attracted many more votes to him than she scared away. "Cornelia and I are having great fun in this campaign," he wrote his sister, "to the success of which she is contributing fully as much as I am."[23]

As was customary in the slugging Pennsylvania politics of the day, Pinchot was subjected to some smear attacks by the regular Republican campaign committee. In exaggerated estimates of his wealth, he was portrayed as a "multi-millionaire with socialistic ideas."[24] A twenty-page bulletin, widely circulated, estimated that he had inherited $18,000,000 from his father alone. An alleged picture of Grey Towers (which in reality was the wrong house) was described as the place frequented by "the ultra-exclusive society set of New York who are backing the Pinchot campaign." Also pictured was his Washington "Palace" where he employed "25 servants." Dubbed during the campaign as a "tree surgeon" who knew nothing about Pennsylvania, he had to face a variety of charges ranging from the execution of a salary grab while serving as Forestry Commissioner to being a Christian Scientist and therefore unsympathetic to physicians. The latter charge, incidentally, led the Pinchots to inquire whether they should exhibit their appendectomy scars to the registered voters.[25] Another campaign sheet emanating from Republican headquarters referred to the "socialistic and communistic" conservation doctrines favored by Pinchot, and decried his attempts to "sovietize" the United States. "Will he also," pleaded the sheet, "tell the people whether he is not a believer in 'birth-control'?" His assured statements of 1912 and 1914 that the Republican party was "through forever" also came back to haunt him.

One of the most striking features of this campaign was Pinchot's determination to play the role of a safe and sane candidate. In 1914 he had frightened away some conservative support by such tactics as his damning of monopoly and his advocacy of government regulation of the anthracite coal industry. This time, however, he concentrated on improvement in the efficiency of the state government itself rather than on government regulations or controls.

The state government in Pennsylvania at this time was anything but a model of efficiency. Not only was it poorly organized, with many overlapping duties between agencies, but it was burdened with a good many drones who had been appointed mainly on the basis of political patronage rather than merit. The governor, although theoretically the chief executive, had only limited control over many of the executive agencies supposedly under him. The administration of state finances was so bad that no one really knew how much money was either received or spent; a "scrambled eggs and hash system," someone called it.[26] Like a good many other states, Pennsylvania had no budget system by which expenditures could be kept under control by the governor.

Having seen the government in action from the inside, Pinchot spoke often of the "mess in Harrisburg." Charging absenteeism, inefficiency, and financial mismanagement, he clamored for a thorough reorganization of the government and the establishment of an executive budget. By the middle of April, indeed, he resigned as Commissioner of Forestry because, as he explained to Governor Sproul, he could not "remain a member of your administration" and say "what must be said."[27] Other members of the Administration were obviously annoyed by what they regarded as a breach of political ethics in publicly criticizing the organization to which he belonged; he was, to their way of thinking, one of the "messmates."[28] But Pinchot persistently continued to find fault. "My opponents," he said in a speech in Scranton, "are protesting against washing the State's dirty linen in public. It seems to me far better to wash than to wear it."[29]

Pinchot was not a single voice crying in the wilderness for governmental reform in Pennsylvania. He had raised an issue that had wide appeal. The state legislature itself had recognized this need by creating a commission to study proposals for reorganization. The state Chamber of Commerce, following the provision in 1921 of a budget system in the federal government, was also recommending strongly that the same action be taken in Pennsylvania.

An unusual combination of forces lined up behind Pinchot as the campaign progressed. A number of progressives supported him, but they were not strong enough to win an election. He had the support of two strange bedfellows—Mr. Grundy's Pennsylvania Manufacturers' Association and a good many labor unions. The various women's organizations could be counted among his strongest backers. Added to these were the voters attracted by his promise to enforce the prohibition laws more rigidly than heretofore. The farmers, whom he had been courting for a number of years, were particularly lured by his pronouncements for economy; some of them had been more than a little restless at the overcentralization and "extravagance" in both the education and highway departments.[30]

By Pinchot's own estimate, he had two-thirds of the newspapers of the state against him.[31] His situation was considerably better, however, than it had been in 1914. Then he had had the support of only one Philadelphia paper. Now all the morning papers in Philadelphia backed his candidacy, including the alleged mouthpiece of Grundy—the *Inquirer*.

Two outside events during the campaign were of decided help to Pinchot. The first, President Harding's announced decision to remain neutral in the primary, was a disappointment to the "regular" Republicans who had counted on his help.[32] The second was the publication, only ten days before the primary, of the report of a special audit conducted by the state's Auditor General of the books of the Treasury from 1917 to 1921, which seemed to vindicate

Pinchot's charges of lax administration. Although the former Treasurer denied all the charges, and candidate Alter, as Attorney General, quickly appointed an investigator to study the situation, the revelations served to jolt the party's old guard.[33]

Although Pinchot was encouraged both by the extent of his support and the good fortune which seemed to be pointing his way, Alter still seemed likely to win. But Pinchot, completely disassociated from the candidates for all other offices, carried his campaign directly to the people with the greatest of vigor. Stumping every county but one, he incessantly referred to all opposing political machines as "the gang," a designation which he used regularly for the rest of his life. Promising to install "a new clean order with the people on top as against the old corrupt order with the politicians in the saddle,"[34] he talked with such force and persistence that he twice lost his voice.

On primary day, May 16, Pinchot and his wife voted in Milford. Returning to Philadelphia late in the day, they arrived in time to see the Vare forces celebrating Alter's victory. At precisely the same time, the regular organization in Pittsburgh was similarly announcing Pinchot's defeat. The early returns from the two big cities, however, were misleading. Although both metropolises gave resounding pluralities to Alter, they were not enough to overbalance the swelling totals for Pinchot from the smaller cities and rural areas.

By the next morning Pinchot had built up a lead of 50,000 votes, only to have it dwindle as the corrections and final figures drifted in. For a good many nervous hours he watched the figure drop to 25,000, then 15,000, then 10,000. It finally remained at 9,000 and Pinchot had his victory.

It was always Pinchot's contention that the overconfidence of his opposition brought their downfall. If they had delayed submitting their returns from Philadelphia and Pittsburgh until they saw how the rest of the state was going, he was certain that the "gangs" would have stolen enough additional votes to beat him. Be that as it may, his victory was a striking upset.

In Allegheny County, which includes Pittsburgh, Alter polled 101,000 votes to Pinchot's 50,000. In Philadelphia, where the Vares predicted a 150,000 lead for Alter, he gained 207,000 to Pinchot's

120,000. The broad base of Pinchot's strength was demonstrated by his victory in 61 of the remaining 65 counties.

The financial reports on the primary showed that Pinchot was what politicians like to call "a fat cat," because he personally paid a large proportion of the cost of his campaign. Of the total receipts of $118,000 by the Pinchot for Governor Committee, Pinchot contributed $82,000 and Mrs. Pinchot, $30,000. In addition, Pinchot paid over $11,000 for lists of state voters. A few days later, Senator Pat Harrison of Mississippi criticized the size of the expenditures on the floor of the United States Senate.[35]

Pinchot was the first to admit that his nomination was a "most remarkable combination of circumstances—one that could not be repeated . . . in a thousand years."[36] Some of his success could be attributed to luck, but it was the kind of luck which the candidate certainly helped to manufacture. As the editor of the *Saturday Evening Post* told him, the result was in large measure due to his excellent campaign.[37] Pinchot insisted on giving high credit to the women. "It was due to [Mrs. Pinchot]," he wrote, "and the women who she organized, far more than to any other single factor, that we won."[38] He was less eager to list another factor of equally major import— the professional backing of Joseph Grundy.

Within a few weeks more than 6,000 letters and telegrams of congratulation poured in on Pinchot. He noted with satisfaction that many of them mentioned Theodore Roosevelt in some way. Even more pleasing was their wide geographical origin. Although the majority came from Pennsylvania, he was flattered by the comments from admirers all over the nation. Once more he was receiving the national attention which he relished.

CHAPTER 18

HIS EXCELLENCY, THE GOVERNOR

THE REPUBLICAN STATE COMMITTEE of Pennsylvania was scheduled to meet in Philadelphia less than a month after the primary to pick a state chairman. The acting chairman during the campaign, a man named Baker, who had openly supported Alter, was a candidate to succeed himself. Privately, Pinchot referred to him as "Penrose's Eminence in Grey."[1] On June 7, 1922, a few days before the committee met, Pinchot addressed an open letter to the members contending that by precedent the nominee for governor was entitled to designate the chairman; he urged the election of a candidate other than Baker.[2]

At the meeting in Philadelphia, Gifford Pinchot and his candidate were soundly trounced by a vote of 81 to 32. One of the 32 voting for Pinchot's candidate was Mrs. Pinchot who represented the Milford area; another was Grundy, still at odds with the organization, who was hooted and jeered for more than a minute when he rose to cast his vote against Baker.[3] Both nominees for United States senator, Pepper and David A. Reed, favored Baker.

Although beaten, Pinchot took the occasion to threaten to run independently unless the committee abandoned its lucrative custom of assessing state employees for campaign contributions. This practice had been in existence so long that most employees paid their tribute, amounting on the average to about 3 per cent of their annual salary, as a matter of course. But Pinchot, in the role of crusader for clean politics, held assessments to be unethical. In the end the committee, with great reluctance, agreed to give up the practice, and Pinchot joined the team.

A further concession to Pinchot's wishes was that he would not disband the Pinchot organizations in the various counties. In view of the opposition to Pinchot by some of the regular Republican leaders, the preservation of his own organization was good insurance that his candidacy would not be treated apathetically.

There never was any question about Pinchot's winning the November election. In contests for state-wide offices, Pennsylvania still was, in effect, a one-party state. The Democrats had nominated a highly respectable candidate for governor, John McSparran, the head of the state Grange. He and Pinchot had worked together and had a sincere admiration for each other. In this election, therefore, the mud slinging which customarily occurred in Pennsylvania elections was not the order of the day (although in the heat of the campaign each candidate was somewhat annoyed by the other's "slurs"). Neither of the two Republican candidates for senator considered it necessary to make much more than a token campaign; Pinchot, however, in an effort to poll a vote large enough to impress the legislature, campaigned as if he and his Democratic opponent were running neck and neck. Appearing at county fairs, Granges, and labor meetings, he made an automobile tour which took him, usually in company with the nominee for lieutenant-governor, to 66 counties in 40 working days.

During the campaign Pinchot sought advice from his ally, Grundy, whose experience in Pennsylvania politics was far wider than his own. After outlining some of his plans to Grundy, he asked for counsel, "If you have any suggestions which you can let me have as to how the whole thing can best be handled, I shall appreciate them greatly."[4] In addition the candidate sought advice on how much independence he should show, how much he should contribute to the state committee, etc. Grundy's handwritten replies, although not very specific, were perhaps somewhat helpful.

At the beginning of the campaign, Pinchot decided to make no promises of appointments until after the November election and to delay all except the most indispensable ones until the close of his first session of the legislature. Astute politicians before him had followed a similar procedure, but the second of his major decisions on strategy was unique: he decided to talk personally with all the Republican candidates for the legislature and to obtain, so far as possible, pledges of support from them for his program. Then, when he campaigned in a particular county he would call the roll of candidates in that area and, while they listened, inform the public of the exact stand which each had taken. In this way he not only hoped to bring pressure to bear on reluctant candidates, but also to make it more difficult for them to change their minds in later months. Some of the candidates were furious at the treatment, but it was effective.

The Republican party in Pennsylvania at this time did not bother to write a state platform. Pinchot, however, used the one he had prepared for the primary. On the stump as well as in campaign letters he emphasized three main issues which he said would be the principal policies of his Administration—"the financial reconstruction of the State, the reorganization of the State Government, and the elimination of the saloon."[5] Because his victory was certain anyway, some members of the party organization urged him to play down his references to prohibition and "the mess" in Harrisburg, but such requests had little influence. Indeed, he apparently took delight in attacking saloons while speaking in an obviously wet district. Since his opponent, McSparran, was fully as "dry" as Pinchot, however, the question of prohibition played little importance in the campaign.

Pinchot served as an honorary pall bearer at the funeral of Edwin H. Vare three weeks before the election. One more political boss was gone, although his brother William remained to exercise control over the Philadelphia machine. Ten days later it was announced in dramatic fashion in a newspaper headline, "Vare's Dying Wish to Back Pinchot Delivered to G.O.P." The assembled party workers who heard this announcement were reported as "electrified" by the declaration.[6] Whatever their reaction, the announcement did the trick. In Philadelphia Pinchot polled the handsome total of 245,000 votes to only 65,000 for McSparran. In the state as a whole, Pinchot won by 250,000. He was popular with the farmers, but not as much so as McSparran, who won 31 counties, mostly in the rural areas where his Grange was a dominant political factor.

Without doubt a considerable number of Pennsylvanians sincerely believed that a bright new day was dawning in state politics. Comments in the *Pittsburgh Christian Outlook* illustrated some of the more fervent optimism—"Let Us Be Thankful—In Pittsburgh" it headlined on its cover, and then continued, "It was Almighty God and he only who could bring together the elements which resulted in his election."[7]

Once again the name of Gifford Pinchot was mentioned as a possible presidential candidate.

One of McSparran's strongest talking points during the campaign was his assertion that Pinchot, with all his good intentions, would if elected be helplessly bound by the old guard of the Republican party. Pinchot, surprised at the friendliness of some of the members of the machine who fought him so bitterly in the primary, was nevertheless suspicious of their sincerity. Following a reception for him in Harrisburg in the middle of the campaign, he wrote his friend Pardee that he "could just see them saying back of their eyes, 'Damn him, we didn't want him. Now we've got him. How can we keep him from doing to us what we would be so blankety blank glad to do to him?' "[8]

Once the election was over, Pinchot was "amazed" at the cooperation and cordiality of the machine. "It is beginning to look as if the Old Guard is really convinced that bouquets will get them more than brickbats." Their attitude, he reported to Pardee, is "mention what you want and it is yours."[9] Pardee at this point, drawing on his own experience as Governor of California, warned Pinchot to beware, but the latter assured him he was on guard against being trapped. "Of course," wrote Pinchot, "they don't love me and, of course, they are going to cut a hole in my diaphragm at the very earliest possible moment."[10]

Pinchot came to believe that the political bosses were endeavoring to absorb him into their organization and make a regular Republican out of him. He liked to call it the "amoeba treatment." Remarkably free of political obligations, he was determined to keep himself disassociated from any segment of the old machine. After his election one of his first lessons in the realities of Pennsylvania politics took place on a yacht trip down the Delaware River. Grundy, who was also one of the guests of the publisher of the *Philadelphia Inquirer*, approached Pinchot with the suggestion that John Fisher, who had stepped aside for Pinchot in the primary, receive an appointment as Attorney General with full control over patronage matters including the choice of the other members of the Governor's cabinet.[11] The host himself was reported by an eye-witness to have been startled by the brashness of the proposal. At any rate,

Grundy misjudged his man; he found Pinchot resolved to control his own patronage.

William Vare, who had served in Congress for a number of years, left that body at the end of 1922 to succeed his deceased brother in the Pennsylvania Senate. In the middle of December, in a spirit of harmony, he entertained the Republican aristocracy of Pennsylvania at a lavish dinner at the Shoreham Hotel in Washington. Pinchot, as guest of honor, sat between Vare and Andrew Mellon, Secretary of the Treasury. Outwardly, at least, oil and water mixed, although skepticism undoubtedly lurked on both sides.

Pinchot took great care at this time to avoid identification with or obligation to the more conservative old guard; he took similar pains to disassociate himself from radicalism. Writing to his brother Amos, who was gaining a reputation as the more extreme thinker of the two, Gifford asked that he "be very careful to make it clear in anything that may appear in the papers as to which one of us is speaking." It was especially important at this time, Pinchot explained, that the public not credit Gifford with some of his brother's statements since this might have an unfortunate effect on Gifford's getting his program through the Pennsylvania legislature.[12]

Before Pinchot took over the reins of government he received some sharp words of advice from H. J. Allen, the outgoing Governor of Kansas. Allen had often seen Pinchot in action during the old Progressive days, and knew his friend intimately. Calling Pinchot, like himself, an impatient man with a tendency to become angry too easily, he urged him, above all else, to show patience toward his real friends and to listen to their advice—even though he did not take it—without any trace of resentment.[13] Allen undoubtedly touched a soft spot in the new Governor's personality. One of Pinchot's strong admirers once remarked that he had the faculty of "antagonizing his friends" as well as "alienating his enemies."[14] Certainly some of his many breaks with friends could have been avoided, or at least eased, if he had acted less impetuously and been able to follow Allen's advice more precisely. His awareness of this "weakness" was shown by his reply to Allen, "You are exactly right about my tendency," he admitted. "While I am happy to get advice, I am apt to forget the amenities which should follow getting it and not taking it." Confessing to hurting the feelings of some of his friends by taking "a bull headed course" and openly disregarding their wishes, and conceding that he sometimes became impatient and "somewhat domineering," he acknowledged that he could have accomplished the same results by being more diplomatic.[15]

To help prepare himself for tackling some of the major problems in the state government, Pinchot, shortly after the primary, appointed a committee on the finances of Pennsylvania. For chairman he selected Dr. Clyde L. King, a teacher of public finance at the Wharton School of the University of Pennsylvania. Pinchot had taken a fancy to King while working with him for the Food Administration during the war. King was a Kansan with a very keen mind and a tireless capacity for work. Pinchot, as Governor, leaned on him heavily and placed almost unlimited faith in his judgment. For more than a decade, until a break came, King was to show the very highest admiration and respect for Pinchot.

Other members of the committee represented a wide variety of interests, including business, labor, and agriculture. All served without pay. King himself raised $30,000 ($4,000 of it from Pinchot) to cover the expenses of the committee. With the purpose in mind, as Pinchot described it, of helping to "put the finances of the State on a sound modern business basis,"[16] the committee looked into the work, the expenditures, and the methods of the various government departments, and dug out the material for the first state budget which Pinchot was to present to the legislature.

Pinchot was determined that his inauguration should take place with little pomp and circumstance. Although the two prior inaugurations had cost the state $55,000 and $28,000, he insisted on such simplicity that the bill for 1923 was only $3,015. There was no inaugural ball. Contrary to custom, the new Governor wore neither a stiff collar nor a silk hat. To cover his head in the freezing temperature, he fell back on an old slouch hat which during the campaign had become a symbol associated with the candidate. On the broad front steps of the lavish capitol building that Theodore Roosevelt had dedicated in 1906, Pinchot watched a parade for fifty minutes and then began his inaugural address. Reiterating, for the most part, his campaign pledges, he described the movement that resulted in his election as "the direct descendant of the Roosevelt Progressive movement of 1912." Asserting that the people of Pennsylvania had "declared for a new order" in their government, he proclaimed that the state needed "a new birth of political righteousness."[17]

Looking forward to his four-year term of office he was hopeful that the legislature and governor could work in harmony. But he was realistic enough to know that as soon as he pressed for some of the goals he had set for his Administration, a measure of discord was inevitable.

Pinchot admitted to a friend that the task of picking a cabinet was an "infernal job for a man who does not know the personnel of the State better than I do."[18] When he announced the appointments, the people of Pennsylvania had the first concrete indication that he differed from the typical Pennsylvania Governor of the past. Although asking six cabinet members from the previous Administration to continue in office, he did not, with two exceptions, choose as department heads persons who could wield much influence in either political or legislative circles. The principal required qualification for such posts was Pinchot's belief that a man was outstandingly able and had the same "point of view" as the Governor. When he wrote confidential letters to several prominent professional people asking for the names of qualified persons to direct the Department of Health and the Department of Welfare, he explained that they did not necessarily have to be either Pennsylvanians or Republicans.[19]

In one key post, that of Secretary of the Commonwealth, he placed his favorite, Dr. Clyde King, who was highly able but soon was thoroughly disliked by the legislature. George Woodruff, who had been in Pinchot's shadow for a large part of the past quarter century, was appointed Attorney General; Woodruff had not been prominent in law practice or politics in the state. During his campaign Pinchot had promised at least one cabinet office to a woman and to redeem this pledge he chose Dr. Ellen C. Potter as his Secretary of Welfare; she had more professional training than political backing.

No Pennsylvania Governor ever began his Administration with

more public confidence behind him: the liberals were naturally drawn to him by his past record; the conservatives were attracted by his emphasis during the campaign on economy and businesslike methods in government. On the day of his inaugural a double-page spread in the *Philadelphia North American*, carrying pictures of Pinchot, the Lieutenant Governor, and Senators Pepper and Reed, expressed greetings and congratulations to all four; signed by some fifteen persons, including a number of business and corporation leaders, the advertisement stated that Pennsylvania was "Fortunate . . . at this time in having such broad-gauged men as you."[20] Addressing a personal letter to each signer, Pinchot promised to do his best.

Sometimes working sixteen hours a day, Pinchot pitched into his new work with unlimited energy. Always full of new ideas, he made himself accessible to the public by establishing an "open door" policy at his office in the capitol. Instead of remaining secluded at his desk, he set aside two hours on three days each week when he moved to the huge reception room outside his office. A sign on the door was an invitation to "Walk Right In." There he conferred with all sorts of citizens in full view of the people waiting for conferences. "It works fine," Pinchot said, ". . . I am seeing at least three times as many people as I could the other way. Nobody gets sore waiting if they can see the reason why."[21] The stunt made news and the people liked it. Members of the legislature were given priority in the waiting lines.

In explaining his "open door" policy it is significant that Pinchot recalled how "T.R. did almost the same thing in Washington." Repeatedly during his years as Governor, he compared situations he faced with those faced by Roosevelt and speculated on how the former President would have handled them. Indeed, he emulated Roosevelt to such a degree, sometimes consciously and sometimes unconsciously, that his Administration might appropriately be called a "little square deal." As a fitting symbol, Roosevelt's picture rested above the Governor's desk at all times.

The first item of business on Pinchot's agenda was finances. In the fall, even before the election, King and his citizens' committee had requested estimates from Governor Sproul's department heads of the amount of money their units would need in the coming two years. When the totals were tabulated, however, they proved to be largely useless since they amounted to more than twice the state's anticipated income. Pinchot called them "wild wishes."[22]

Only a week after taking office, he presented to the General Assembly the first budget in the state's history. In 140 printed pages it contained King's best estimates of income for two years as well as detailed proposals for the amounts of money that the legislature should appropriate to the various government agencies.

Determined to get the state on a "pay as you go" basis, Pinchot held the proposed expenditures to a total less than that of the previous biennium. In this way he planned not only to balance the budget but also to start paying off an inherited debt of some $30 million. "The process will not be pleasant," he told the legislature, but "Neither is having a tooth pulled pleasant";[23] both were necessary, he added, to avoid even greater pain in the future. The General Assembly, in the end, appropriated to the various departments substantially the amounts proposed by Pinchot.

As part of his drive for economy, Pinchot fought hard to combat the somewhat casual atmosphere that had developed around the capital toward the spending of the taxpayers' money. To try to reduce "joy riding" in the state's automobiles, he ordered them painted grey with the state seal displayed on the outside. At the same time he insisted that the Commonwealth purchase more open model cars rather than expensive closed models.[24] A memorandum to all department heads reminded them of the "considerable saving" that could be effected if all office lights were turned out when not actually needed.[25] Believing that telephone costs were unjustifiably high, he directed that any employee making a toll call would be required to pay for any excess over five minutes unless he had specific approval from his department head for a longer call.[26] As part of his personal contribution to economy during the first two years, he accepted an annual salary of only $10,000, although the legislature had increased it, before he came into office, to $18,000.

Such concentration on economy and budget balancing, of course, precluded much extension of governmental programs. Citizens who favored low government spending and restricted activities—and there were many in Pennsylvania—were delighted with this phase of the Governor's program. His determination to hold spending to a minimum, indeed, went a long way to quiet the anxiety of those who feared that Pennsylvania had placed in the governor's chair a "radical" or a "socialist."

While a number of able men sat in the Pennsylvania legislature at this time, the General Assembly as a whole was not held in notably high repute. Although overwhelmingly of one party, it was not a well-knit body with a definite program. Reflecting the deep divisions within the Republican party in the state, it had no natural leaders acceptable to all factions: there were Grundy men, Vare men from Philadelphia, and adherents of the Pittsburgh machine. There were Pinchot men too, but this plainly was not a Pinchot legislature. The *Philadelphia Inquirer* had been so disgusted with the previous (1921) legislature's performance that it editorialized at the end of the session, "Pennsylvania's Legislature has departed from Harrisburg. Good riddance! A more boss-ridden and intimidated body of men never sat at the Commonwealth capitol."[27]

The 1923 legislature, which convened a few days before Pinchot's inaugural, was crying for leadership, and the new Governor was ready and eager to supply it. In the best Theodore Roosevelt tradition, Pinchot saw himself as a strong governor who was not only the chief executive but also the chief legislator. With a positive program, he set out to have it enacted into law.

In this honeymoon period of 1923 few persons were prepared to fight Pinchot. Both Grundy and Vare were willing to go along on most matters. Although a good many legislators and political leaders had inner reservations about the Governor, they had to admit, if they were honest with themselves, that much of the Pinchot program was popular with the voters and was actually in the best interests of the Commonwealth. Another factor explaining the support behind Pinchot, not to be dismissed lightly, was his decision, already noted, to refuse to consider the legislators' suggestions for appointments until the General Assembly adjourned.

Sensing the situation, Pinchot was optimistic in a letter he wrote to his sister in England six weeks before his inauguration. "[The] prospect for a harmonious session is growing steadily brighter," he reported. Speculating that the "old line leaders" were becoming convinced that it was better to work with him than fight him, he predicted that they were "getting ready to hand me everything I want (except, of course, the elimination of the saloon) on a silver platter."[28]

Boastful as this letter sounded, Pinchot did in fact obtain from the 1923 General Assembly most of the things he asked for. When he announced his preference for a particular man—Jay Goodnough, independent—for speaker of the House, that body, in accordance with custom, ratified the choice. Although the Senate chose an organization man for its president pro tem (T. L. Eyre), he gave Pinchot strong and helpful support throughout the session.

Probably the most important piece of legislation enacted in 1923 was the administrative code, a reorganization law aimed at cleaning up what Pinchot had described as the "mess" in Harrisburg. Designed principally by King, it provided, basically, for a more businesslike structure of the government. Despite some amendments by the legislature, it went a long way toward giving the governor the tools to remedy defects in the executive branch. Providing for the new budget system, it also centered in the governor the authority for bringing about a badly needed standardization of state salaries. These and a lengthy additional list of provisions in the code meant that the governor, more than before, could be a chief executive in fact.

But there was some substantial and sincere opposition to any strengthening of the position of governor. Additional hostility came from persons objecting less as a matter of principle than from reluctance to see the increased power go to Pinchot. When the Administration finally prevailed in the General Assembly, the battle was not over. Because the State Treasurer and the Auditor General, both elected by the Republican organization, held up the payment of some of the salaries under the new code, the constitutionality of the law had to be tested in the courts. This blocking tactic by the Treasurer (Charles A. Snyder) was just one episode in a running fight between him and the Governor; Pinchot, for example, by the use of his veto power, slashed $128,800 from the legislature's appropriation to the Treasury Department on the grounds that the Treasurer's employees were not working the hours required by law.

While the court case dragged on, Pinchot won the gratitude of a number of the state's employees by using his personal credit to borrow enough money in $10,000 lots from a bank to pay their salaries on a loan basis. When the state Supreme Court, early in 1924, sustained the code, Pinchot happily wrote, "Now that we have scraped the barnacles off the sides, the Ship of State will go ahead unhampered."[29]

But shoals lay ahead.

Gifford Pinchot's two main objectives as Governor of Pennsylvania—beyond economy and state government reorganization—were the regulation of electric power and the enforcement of prohibition. Roughly fifteen years earlier, it will be recalled, Pinchot had worked closely with Theodore Roosevelt to forestall electric power companies from obtaining public water power sites in perpetuity and at no cost. After Roosevelt left the Washington scene, Pinchot was a key figure in the long and grim battle to obtain the restraining legislation finally incorporated in the Federal Water Power Act of 1920. Governor Pinchot now asked and obtained the General Assembly's approval for a law coordinating state practices with those of the federal government. Since 90 per cent of all electricity in Pennsylvania was generated from coal rather than from water power, the Governor saw the need for further inquiry into the whole electric power question.

Pinchot's experiences with electric utility companies had not been pleasant. Many of them had fiercely opposed the controls that he exercised over them as head of the U.S. Forest Service. Moreover, their sustained antagonism to the enactment of the Federal Water Power Act persuaded him that they cared little for the public interest. Like Senator Norris, whom he once called the "most useful man" who sat in either house of Congress during a forty-year period,[30] he tended to consider the power people as public enemy number one. While he often admitted some exceptions to the general rule, he used many variations of colorful phrases, such as "greedy unreasoning selfishness," to describe their attitude. The utilities, in turn, both hated and feared Pinchot.

Pinchot saw from the first and more clearly than many of his contemporaries the dizzy speed with which electricity was to leap into importance in the everyday life of American citizens. Realizing that this industry, because it was not suited to competition, had to be a monopoly, he deeply and sincerely feared the consequences to society of an uncontrolled national monopoly. He had collected information and figures which convinced him that an alarmingly high proportion of electric energy in the United States was coming under the ownership or domination of a very few men or corporations.[31]

When he took over as Governor he believed that electric utilities in Pennsylvania could be criticized on at least two main counts—their rates were too high and they had unjustifiably refrained from extending their lines into many of the less lucrative rural areas of the state.

Even before his inauguration, Pinchot had a long discussion on power with a Philadelphia engineer, Morris L. Cooke. The two men, who had not met before, took to each other readily; both were fighting liberals and conservation minded.[32] At the insistence of Pinchot, Cooke agreed to work on a study of the best ways to secure an abundant and cheap supply of electricity in Pennsylvania. The Governor then obtained from the legislature $35,000 (he asked for $50,000) to create a Giant Power Survey Board to make such a study. Pinchot was chairman, and Cooke was selected by the new Board as its director. Among the other members of the Board were the two who had worked so diligently with Pinchot on power matters in the U.S. Forest Service—Attorney General of Pennsylvania, George Woodruff, and a new deputy Attorney General, Philip Wells.

The Board's final report of 480 pages was provocative and widely circulated. Pinchot's introduction to the report was called an "outstanding essay on power."[33] Requests for copies came from all over the country in such quantities that the 20,000 printed were soon distributed.[34] The report did not advocate government ownership of power, but proposed tight public control over the industry. The term "super-power" was used to describe the electric monopoly if it were not controlled or checked in the public interest. "Giant power," on the other hand, referred to the monopoly if it were aided and guided by the government for the common welfare.

To achieve giant power the report suggested that the state, after encouraging power companies to produce huge quantities of electricity at the major sources of supply (the coal fields), should require the pooling of all power systems in the state. The greater the area and population served by the interconnected systems, it was argued, the cheaper the current. Giant transmission lines would carry the current generated in the giant power plants to all electric companies in the state for distribution. Extension of electric service into the rural areas would be required of the electric companies. The Commonwealth would have the authority to see that no company received more nor less than a fair return on its investment.

The report set many people to thinking about giant power. An entire issue of the *Annals of the American Academy of Political and Social Science* was devoted to the subject.[35] The same was true of the *Survey Graphic* magazine.[36] Pinchot, who had the knack of explaining complicated matters in terms easily understood by the general public, used the press and the platform to popularize the discussion. He put his name on a pocket-size pamphlet on the subject, for example, which was widely distributed both in and outside Pennsylvania; Pinchot himself paid for printing the 30,000 copies.

During a trip to Portland, Oregon, to talk to a group of young people on "Christian Citizenship," he stopped off in Denver, San Francisco, and Los Angeles to explain giant power and to proclaim the "control of the electric monopoly" as the "most pressing economic question" in the United States.[37] He told Cooke that if they both lived to be a hundred, they would never be associated with another piece of work "of larger significance and importance" to the American people.[38]

It was hardly surprising that the electric utilities furiously opposed the whole giant power concept as a system of unwarranted regimentation. When the Administration introduced in the 1925 General Assembly 19 bills to carry out the recommendations of the Giant Power Survey Board, the utilities trained their biggest guns on every one of them; all died in the House committee. Three of the most effective opponents of giant power were a former Congressman, a financial writer, and a Harvard professor, all of whom, according to Pinchot, were later found to have been lobbyists for the "power crowd."[39]

Throughout most of his four years in office, Pinchot had a running fight with the state Public Service Commission, which had the primary duty of regulating various kinds of utilities, including electric power and transportation. Probably the major function of the agency, and at the same time the most difficult and controversial, was the regulation of the rates which the utilities charged. The Commission, like those in other states, was charged with seeing that a utility received a fair monetary return on a fair valuation of its property. Once a fair value was set, it was a relatively easy matter to determine what rates had to be charged to yield a fair return, say 7 per cent, on that value (or "rate base"). Although there were various formulae, some of them more or less scientific, for arriving at the fair value of a large utility, the determination of such a figure inevitably entailed a good bit of personal judgment. If the Commission's estimate of the value of a company's property was too high, the rates charged to customers would be correspondingly high; if the property was valued too low, the income would be low and investors in the utility would suffer.

Since 1915 the chairman of the Public Service Commission had been W. D. Ainey, a respected public official, a pillar in his own community, a Y.M.C.A. leader. Pinchot referred to him, in a letter of introduction to his sister, as an "old and good friend" and a "delightful gentleman."[40] But the more the Governor saw the Public Service Commission in action, the more he became convinced that the chairman and the rest of the members saw their problems through "public utility glasses." He became especially irked when the Commission approved an increase in fare from five to seven cents for the subways and trolleys of the Philadelphia Rapid Transit Company. Pinchot believed that the Commission was failing in its duty by sitting back and waiting for complaints to come to it and then settling disputes in court-like fashion on the basis of the evidence presented before it. Contending that such a governmental agency was obligated to take positive steps, "courageously" and "vigorously," to protect the public, he insisted that "A public service commission which is not ready and willing of its own motion to take up the cause of the public and act as its fighting defender merely cumbers the earth."[41]

About a year later the Philadelphia Rapid Transit Company

asked for a further fare increase to eight cents, and the Commission granted the request on a temporary basis. Especially disturbing to the opponents of the increase was the knowledge that the company, in anticipation of favorable action by the Commission, had obtained a large supply of new eight-cent tokens ready for use on the day that the order was issued. Pinchot was tempted to fire the whole Commission, all of whom were carry-overs from previous Administrations.[42] That he did not do so, he said later, was "a blunder."[43] But he did write and make public a strong letter condemning the Commission for reaching its decision in executive session rather than in a public meeting, and for acting "with unseemly haste" before "the case for the public was fully developed."[44] One member of the Commission, furious over Pinchot's letter, resigned in protest. The Governor acidly replied that he accepted the separation "with genuine satisfaction."[45]

Pinchot always maintained that, although he discussed policies and standards with members of the Commission, he did not try to force votes one way or the other in particular cases. "I have never at any time," he asserted in a public statement, "indicated to any member of the Commission what his decision should be in any individual case, and I never will."[46] It is difficult, however, to take this pronouncement at its full face value. Granted that the Governor did not issue a direct order to a Commissioner on how to vote, the Commissioner was made aware in all sorts of ways of what Pinchot wanted. The Transit Company dispute is a case in point; certainly the Governor forcefully "indicated" to every member of the Commission that he did not believe the Transit Company's eight-cent fare should be made permanent. A letter to Cooke showed the way the Governor worked, "I had a talk with some members of the Commission recently, and I think Ainey is going to behave. If he doesn't, I have got plenty more rods in pickle and the disposition to use them."[47]

By the spring of 1925, enough vacancies had occurred on the Public Service Commission to enable Pinchot to appoint four of the seven members. Ainey was still chairman. The two other members inherited from previous governors, James S. Benn and Sidney R. Shelby, had consistently voted in such a way that in the eyes of

Pinchot they were "tools" of the utilities. The Governor, accordingly, dismissed both of them from office.

Although Pinchot made two appointments, including his favorite lieutenant, Clyde King, to fill these new vacancies, both Benn and Shelby refused to leave their posts. The dispute was finally settled, late in 1925, by a unanimous opinion of the state Supreme Court that the Commission was not really an executive agency but an administrative arm of the legislature, and that the Governor therefore had no power to fire its members.

Despite the reinstatement of Benn and Shelby, Pinchot's four appointees still comprised a majority of the Commission. Six weeks after the Supreme Court had spoken, however, by a vote of four members, they made permanent the temporary order for an eight-cent fare in Philadelphia. Such a vote was possible only because one of the Governor's appointees, John L. Stewart, voted with Ainey, Benn, and Shelby. Since Stewart, having been appointed while the legislature was in recess, still needed approval by the Senate before he could serve a full term, Pinchot, admitting his "mistake," attempted to recall the name.[48] But the Senate, refusing to return the papers, handed the Governor a sharp rebuff by ratifying the appointment for a full ten-year term. Two other Pinchot appointees, moreover, never received the necessary Senate ratification.

When the Governor had completed his four years in office, he included in his final message to the General Assembly a bitter denunciation of the majority of the members of the Public Service Commission as "speaking tubes for the public utilities" and as "the catspaw of the corporations."[49] Although careful here and elsewhere not to denounce the courts in public, he also expressed his confidential opinion that the Supreme Court had "shown itself to be completely under the thumb of the utilities."[50]

Since January 1920, the eighteenth amendment to the United States Constitution had prohibited the manufacture, sale, or transportation of intoxicating liquors. Although Pennsylvania had ratified the amendment, the state legislature, before Pinchot became Governor, had not yet seen fit to enact legislation for effectively halting the liquor traffic.

The federal government had a prohibition unit in the United States

Treasury Department which was far from adequate to carry the enforcement load alone. If prohibition was to become a reality, complete cooperation between the national government and the states was needed. Many observers, of course, doubted whether liquor control laws ever could be adequately enforced in the face of the unwillingness of a substantial portion of the population to accept the amendment.

Gifford Pinchot firmly—almost fanatically—believed in the wisdom of prohibition, and promised repeatedly to enforce it rigidly. No governor of any state ever tried harder to keep a pledge. When he entered office, flagrant violations of the liquor laws were common occurrences in Pennsylvania. One of the most difficult problems of enforcement concerned the breweries. Although the law allowed no beer having an alcoholic content of more than one-half of one per cent, the breweries produced legal near beer by first brewing full strength beer and then removing the excess alcohol. In the absence of tight government inspection, some of the 156 breweries in the state were allowing the real beer to leave their premises before it was cut. Equally difficult to control was the fraudulent distilling of whiskey, principally in Philadelphia, by concerns which had permits to obtain alcohol for the alleged manufacture of toilet waters, hair tonics, and tobacco sprays. Moreover, in many areas bars licensed by the state to sell near beer were dispensing, openly and without being disturbed, all kinds of stronger drink.

The new Governor, with his customary flair for the dramatic, quickly made it clear to everyone that law enforcement was a subject uppermost in his mind, and that he meant business. From his first day in office he demanded of each person appointed to a state post a special pledge, broader than the customary oath of office, that he or she would personally obey the United States Constitution, *including* the eighteenth amendment and all state and national laws enacted to give it effect. Although there were some protests against the principle behind this procedure, it is doubtful whether the strategy kept from office more than a handful of persons who might have been appointed if there had been no pledge. Most persons who were asked to make the pledge did so without question.

Further relying on the pledge technique, Pinchot refused to discuss common problems with representatives of the state brewers association until he had extracted from its president a published promise that its members would obey the law. In this case, however, the Governor was disillusioned; admitting that there were a "few honest" members of the profession, he later charged that "as a whole" they persistently violated the laws.[51]

Early in the 1923 session of the legislature, the Administration introduced three enforcement bills. In colorful appeals to the public, Pinchot solicited support for his legislation. One of the bills, designed to put more teeth in the drive to outlaw the saloon, passed the Senate handily, but ran into exceedingly rough weather in the House of Representatives. In his campaign to propel the bill through the second chamber, the Governor personally talked to every member whose vote was in any way doubtful. Needing 105 votes from the 208 members of the House, he finally gained the support of 107. It was a mixed victory, however, since the two companion bills—regulating the breweries and distilleries—fell by the wayside.

Pinchot was highly pleased to obtain the one piece of legislation, but he received another severe setback when the General Assembly refused to appropriate the $250,000 that he had proposed for enforcement purposes. The Women's Christian Temperance Union of Pennsylvania, however, set out to raise money to fill the vacuum left by the legislature. In due course they turned over almost $150,000 to Pinchot to use as he saw fit for enforcement purposes. The Governor was forever grateful to the W.C.T.U. and especially to its president, Ella George; near the end of his term he called her "one of the best and boldest fighters" he ever knew.[52] Indeed, in his second term as Governor, Pinchot made no political appointments in her home county without first clearing them through her,[53] an arrangement that helped to create a quarrel within the W.C.T.U.

Armed with his new enforcement law and the W.C.T.U. cash, Pinchot set out in earnest to "close the saloons." For the first time in Pennsylvania the state police became active prohibition officers; during the four-year term they made 13,368 arrests for liquor law violations and padlocked a sizable number of saloons. Pinchot, maintaining a close watch over such operations, insisted on a daily report from the state police of the number of arrests and the quantities of liquor confiscated.

Pinchot's sincerity of purpose in matters alcoholic was demonstrated by some of the firm stands that he took on appointments. The Governor wrote a special letter to the chairman of the voting registration commission in Pittsburgh, which had authority to appoint some 3,000 district registrars throughout the city, expressing his hope that every man appointed was "absolutely right on the dry question."[54] An illustration of both courage and forthrightness was his reply to a letter and telegram from the secretary-treasurer of the United Mine Workers strongly advocating the appointment of a particular judge in one of the counties in the anthracite coal region. "The reason I cannot consider [this man]," Pinchot wrote, "is that his appointment would be . . . a very severe blow at the dry cause in this State, and that I will not do." Adding that he had been told this appointment would bring him "great political value," he refused to "do what I believe to be wrong for the sake of getting votes." "Please remember," he advised, "that the kind of a man who would be disloyal to the drys under pressure from the miners might also be disloyal to the miners under pressure from somebody else."[55] His stand apparently appealed to the union's president, John L. Lewis, who wrote a letter of assurance that it would not hurt the members' feelings of friendship toward him.[56]

Pinchot's heart and soul were so deeply in enforcement that he had no sympathy with lukewarm administration of the prohibition laws. Highly critical of Washington's efforts at enforcement, he summarized his feelings in a confidential letter written in 1927 describing a talk with Wayne Wheeler, the noted lobbyist of the dry forces, "I said the whole atmosphere of Washington was wet (which Wheeler admitted); that obedience to the law among members of Congress, of the Cabinet, and of the Government, was at a very low ebb; that the President could fix it if he would, but that he had never shown any real interest in doing so."[57]

In his public declarations while Governor, Pinchot was cautious about directly blasting Coolidge for the "indifferent" enforcement. His sharpest barbs—and there were many—were aimed at the Secretary of the Treasury, Andrew W. Mellon. As Pinchot told the

World Congress Against Alcoholism, in a speech delivered a few months after the end of his term, "The thing which hampered me beyond all else was the refusal of Mr. Mellon to have the law enforced."[58]

Mellon and Pinchot were always poles apart in their economic and social philosophies; to Pinchot, Mellon represented the "magnates," against whom he fought so assiduously. Mellon was also very powerful in the Republican political machine which had done its best to defeat Pinchot in the 1922 primary. Pinchot's impatience with Mellon in this instance, however, was based primarily on their differing attitudes toward the liquor laws. Mellon, neither by inclination nor conviction, was an advocate of prohibition. When offered the post of Secretary of the Treasury he had not relished assuming responsibility for liquor law enforcement; he had been assured the prohibition unit would be transferred to the Department of Justice. This, however, was not done. Mellon was particularly vulnerable because of his substantial holdings in the Overholt distillery; on taking office, he disposed of his shares.[59] Mellon adopted the attitude that the law of the land had to be enforced, but he scarcely put his heart into it in the way Pinchot wanted.

In a running fire of open letters to Mellon, Pinchot charged in effect that the Treasury Department was making no effort to enforce prohibition in Pennsylvania. In a kind of preaching tone he explained to the Secretary what was needed to repair the "breakdown of Federal enforcement" and to stop the "reign of disorder."[60] Mellon's answer, in the form of a press release, emphasized the enormity of the task and the limited amount of money which Congress had appropriated for enforcement.[61]

In spite of all the setbacks that he encountered, Pinchot by the end of 1923 had some real success in enforcement in Pennsylvania. Alcoholic beverages still flowed, but not so freely. The Law Enforcement League of Philadelphia, for example, wired him their appreciation of the fulfillment of his pledges, and praised God for such a Governor.[62] Philadelphia, however, was the most difficult area in which to achieve enforcement. Pinchot charged before a state convention of the W.C.T.U. that the state got little help from the Philadelphia police. "In one saloon," he told the ladies, "the law-breaking drinkers surrounded the illegal bar four deep . . . there was as little secrecy about it as there is about the Washington Monument. . . . A policeman stood at the very door."[63]

It brought great joy to the Governor, therefore, when the mayor of Philadelphia at the end of 1923 borrowed from the United States Marines General Smedley Butler, to fill the post of city Director of Public Safety. For two years this colorful figure, acting independently of political bosses, conducted a spectacular campaign to clean up the city—during his first five days in office, the doors of 973 saloons were closed. This was the kind of enforcement that the Governor had wanted from the outset. "Every good citizen in Pennsylvania," he proclaimed in an open letter to Butler, "will be delighted with the vigor and earnestness with which you are going at the difficult problem of cleaning up Philadelphia. May you have every success."[64] At the end of 1925, as Butler's leave from the Marines drew to a close, Pinchot traveled to Washington to intercede personally with President Coolidge for a two-year extension. But it was not granted. "Lord," moaned Pinchot a few months later, "how I wish he was back here in the war! It would change the whole complexion of things."[65] Perhaps partly as a result of Butler's help in Philadelphia, Pinchot was feeling optimistic over prohibition early in 1924. "The booze hounds," he confidently wrote a minister friend, "will die out pretty soon and the liquor question will pretty much disappear with them."[66]

Among the many problems that Pinchot faced during his first year as Governor, he believed his "severest test" was the anthracite coal strike. In his 1914 campaign he had toyed with the idea of advocating federal government ownership of at least a part of the anthracite industry. Although modifying this drastic position, he remained convinced that this "monopoly" was reaping inordinately high profits by charging consumers too much for their coal; he favored designating the anthracite business a public utility and regulating prices by a government commission.[67]

The mine workers' union in the 1920's, under John L. Lewis, was pressing hard for increased wages in both the bituminous and anthracite coal fields. The operators were resisting with equal vigor. Disagreements between the anthracite miners and operators in 1922, before Pinchot was in office, had closed down the mines for a five-month period. The contract that finally was hammered out at the end of this suspension was scheduled to expire on September 1, 1923.

When President Harding died in the summer of 1923 and Coolidge entered the White House, there were indications that another anthracite strike was imminent. The union was requesting an eight-hour maximum day, a closed shop, and a 20 per cent increase in wages. Conferences between management and labor had broken down; intervention by a United States Coal Commission, appointed by Harding, brought no agreement. The new President did not believe the emergency was serious enough to warrant drastic action by the government. Coolidge had soared to national prominence as a result of his part in handling a strike of Boston policemen a few years before. Now, however, he was moving cautiously.

Upon seeing the new President in Washington on the day after Harding's funeral, Pinchot offered his cooperation. But as the strike deadline of September 1 approached, he grew restless. Picturing how Roosevelt might have reacted in the same situation, he was certain that Coolidge suffered seriously by comparison. On August 15 he urged the President to recommend arbitration and at the same time to announce the names of the arbitration board which he would appoint.[68] Finally, on August 23, with only a week to go and with no solution in sight, Pinchot could contain himself no longer. Telephoning the President's secretary, he announced that if the President was going to do nothing, it was the duty of the Governor of Pennsylvania to act. Within a few hours he had an invitation to lunch next day at the White House with Coolidge and with John Hays Hammond, the chairman of the federal Coal Commission.

Pinchot was disdainful of the familiarity of both men with labor problems; neither of them, he said later, really knew what was needed to handle the dispute. Their only solution, he complained, was the same as that of the operators—to use substitute miners to get the coal out.[69] Pinchot had a clear impression, as a result of his White House conference, that Coolidge was not interested in the federal government's taking any further action in the matter, and that he was therefore free to try to find a solution entirely on his own. He was nettled, therefore, to read in the news release from the White House that Pinchot was going to act in "co-operation" with federal authorities.[70] As he told a friend, "The talk of my being the President's agent in this matter is pure nonsense."[71] Fourteen years later, still resentful, he wrote to William Allen White that the inference he was acting as the President's agent was "a lie out of the whole cloth" and "left me with no respect for him whatsoever."[72]

Following his conference with the President, Pinchot quickly jumped into the dispute by asking both sides to meet with him on August 27 in Harrisburg. As one newspaper columnist put it, the Governor was "quoting Roosevelt precedents and following them."[73] Placing the spokesmen for the miners in one room and the operators' representatives in another, while he himself acted as a roving mediator shuttling back and forth between the two groups, Pinchot promised each group that anything it said to him would be held in confidence. Within two days the Governor had a plan for settlement, which neither side immediately accepted. The proposed agreement provided for an eight-hour day for all miners (most of them already had it), and a 10 per cent increase in wages. When the existing contract expired on September 1 the strike of 150,000 miners began as planned, but a week later both sides accepted the Pinchot terms.

Pinchot was proud of his achievement. "It is one of those things," he wrote, "that happened to work out just exactly right. Of course I am perfectly delighted."[74] Congratulatory letters came from a host of his friends and from national leaders. Coolidge also sent "heartiest congratulations," and assured the Governor he could not commend his service too highly; making an effort to be friendly, the President added a handwritten note reminding him that he and his wife were invited to visit at the White House soon.[75] But the Governor fumed at Coolidge's persistence in seeming to look upon him as an agent; "It was a very difficult situation," the President said, "in which I invited your cooperation."[76]

Pinchot's opponents were inclined to explain his actions in the anthracite dispute entirely as a play for political support by the coal miners. Undoubtedly, politics played a part; Pinchot's concern over who got the credit for the settlement tended to support this conclusion. Although the miners did not get all they asked for, they did have some feeling of appreciation toward Pinchot for their fairly substantial pay boost. It is not belittling the political side of his actions, however, to say that more than a bid for votes was involved. Once again Pinchot's concern for the underdog was showing itself. He sincerely believed that as a matter of justice the coal miners in Pennsylvania deserved a better life.

William Allen White, who enthusiastically congratulated Pinchot on his coal victory,[77] seemed to see more readily than the Governor that strong repercussions were inevitable. He reported that the big newspapermen did not like either the wage increase or the eight-hour day. "The red-baiters have so thoroughly scared the people, with the bogie of Bolshevism," admonished White, "that any public man who takes any public attitude in favor of . . . labor . . . does so at his tremendous peril politically." Calling Pinchot's efforts "a righteous act," he warned, "you certainly did put the trimmings on your presidential boom if you ever had any."[78]

Although there were complaints over Pinchot's handling of the strike, the criticism multiplied when the operators raised the price of coal to cover their increased costs resulting from the settlement. Despite Pinchot's insistence that the figures showed the coal companies could absorb these costs, the general public was not convinced. Some of the 40 million anthracite users throughout the country found it easy to blame the Governor of Pennsylvania for their larger fuel bills. The price increase only helped to reinforce Pinchot's determination to have tighter government supervision over the operators.

The anthracite settlement that Pinchot engineered in 1923 ran for two years. In 1925, labor and management were again unable to agree; a strike, which began in September, lasted six months. This time the Governor was not in as much of a hurry. As the end of November approached, however, he informed President Coolidge by letter that he had invited the miners and operators to meet with him in Harrisburg on the very next day. Representatives of the miners arrived at Pinchot's office at the appointed time for the conference; the operators, now distrustful of the Governor, stayed away.

At the end of his term, Pinchot did not hesitate to state his feelings about labor and management in the anthracite industry. The 1925 strike, he recorded in his final message to the legislature, "confirmed my opinion of the anthracite operators as hard-boiled monopolists, whose sole interest in the people is what can be got out of them." His relations with the miners, on the other hand, "have given me confidence in their integrity and public spirit."[79]

Pinchot had been remarkably successful in 1923 in getting from the General Assembly the legislation that he wanted. As 1925 approached, he was aware that his victories in the next session of the legislature were bound to be fewer. By this time, of course, he had made his political appointments and no longer could hold a patronage club over the heads of reluctant legislators. The provision of the state constitution prohibiting a governor from serving two terms in succession was an added handicap. "[The] second session of a Governor who can't be reelected," Pinchot admitted, "is not exactly huckleberry pie."[80] Moreover, Messrs. Grundy and Vare, who had gone along with much of his program in the first session, were now part of the opposition; and the Mellons of Pittsburgh had no more friendship for Pinchot than he had for them.

An indication of the way the wind was blowing was the decision by leaders of the opposition to support Thomas Bluett, a Philadelphian in the Vare camp, as speaker of the House of Representatives. Pinchot had been assuming that the former speaker, Jay Goodnough, whom he admired so sincerely, would be re-elected without opposition.

In the face of the solid forces for Bluett, the Republican state chairman suggested in the interest of harmony that Goodnough withdraw. But Pinchot, fighting to the very end, urged the people of Pennsylvania to press their representatives to support Goodnough. The Philadelphia machine, he charged, "has undertaken to force a wet Speaker upon the Commonwealth. . . . Mr. Bluett is the wet candidate, and a rubber stamp for Mr. Vare. The thing to do with him is to beat him."[81] But the strength of the opposition was revealed in the caucus of the Republican members of the House when 58 voted for Goodnough and 133 for Bluett. "[The] old bunch all got together," Pinchot told his sister, "elected a wet speaker, and set out to run the Administration off its feet, play horse with the Budget, and generally have a hot time."[82]

Some months before, the Governor had planned his strategy for the session, "[The] position I propose to take . . . is that the Administration secured from the last session practically everything it wanted and, therefore, can afford to sit still and let the other fellow walk the floor." He planned, therefore, to recommend only three or four items "and rather put them up to the people than demand them as Administration measures."[83]

The Governor advocated only two major measures. The first, as has been seen, was a series of bills to pool electric power into a scheme of giant power. The second was legislation to permit the state to regulate "illegal drink" at the source, through the control of alcohol distilleries and breweries. The General Assembly's answer in both cases was complete rejection. Despite these failures, Pinchot fared rather better in the 1925 session than might have been expected. Not only did the legislature adopt a number of the Governor's relatively minor suggestions but, more important, it gave him appropriations of money, which, for the most part, were not drastically changed from the suggestions he made in his budget at the beginning of the session.

After the General Assembly adjourned in mid-April the Governor might have concentrated on avoiding controversy, and used the remaining twenty months of his term to consolidate his gains. But tranquility was rarely associated with Pinchot. It soon became apparent that in 1926 he planned to run again for the United States Senate.

CHAPTER 19

THE ELUSIVE SENATE SEAT

IN THE FALL of 1923 the Pennsylvania Republican state chairman, in accordance with the customary deference shown toward governors, invited Pinchot to run as a candidate for one of the state-wide delegates to the 1924 presidential nominating convention. Inasmuch as the slate of candidates picked by the state organization usually won without question, Pinchot did no campaigning. A month before the election he had no doubts of victory.

Pinchot's gaze tended to rest, however, on a point beyond the office of delegate. Once again his presidential ambition was quietly asserting itself. The wish was there, but not the necessary organization to back him. Knowing that his chances were "exceedingly small,"[1] he stood in the rain hoping that lightning just possibly might strike. Courting only the Republican brand of lightning, he took no part in the progressive movement of 1924 which nominated Robert La Follette and gave him almost 5 million votes in the election. Pinchot's feeling of hopefulness sprang from his confidential conviction that, partly because of the Teapot Dome oil scandals, neither Coolidge nor any other conservative Republican could possibly defeat a strong Democrat.[2] If any Republican could win, he reasoned, it would be one, like himself, disassociated from the party's old guard.

Secretary Mellon was willing, if Pinchot ceased his attacks on federal prohibition enforcement, to have the Pennsylvania delegation at the Republican convention vote for Pinchot on the early ballots as a favorite son.[3] But Pinchot persisted in his criticism and showed little restraint in lashing at Mellon directly, and at President Coolidge indirectly, for lax enforcement.

Although Pinchot was not one of the leading potential candidates, his name sometimes appeared on the lists of "dark horses." There was some gossip that he might be nominated for second place on a ticket headed by Hiram Johnson.[4] William Allen White wanted to support him for President despite the poor chances of winning.[5]

When Pinchot received from Governor Neff of Texas a gift of a ten-gallon hat, he promised that "the hat will appear at the Republican Convention if I do, and no mistake." Perhaps he was looking forward to the possibility of his own candidacy for a national office when he added the comment, "Your kind of Democrat and my kind of Republican can appropriately wear the same hat, for our agreements are infinitely more than our differences."[6]

The Republican organization leaders in Pennsylvania, however, decided to teach the Governor a lesson. Determined to demonstrate that the Pinchot criticism of the national Administration amounted to disloyalty that could not be countenanced, they decided, contrary to precedent, that the Governor should not attend the convention in Cleveland. Shortly before election day, therefore, they quietly passed around the word to vote for Strassburger instead of Pinchot for delegate. Informed of the plot, the Governor did all he could over the final weekend to counteract the opposition. It was too late. Although he accumulated a majority of the votes in most of the rural counties, he was smothered in the urban areas. Grundy and Vare had openly withdrawn their support. Vare, resenting the attacks on Mellon, and irked at the zeal of Pinchot's prohibition forces, delivered 225,000 Philadelphia votes to Strassburger, as opposed to Pinchot's meager 38,000.[7]

Pinchot blamed the whole debacle on his prohibition stand. "[The] wets have elected Strassburger," he announced. "This . . . is merely proof that the old alliance between liquor and gang politics in Pennsylvania remains in full force and effect."[8] The whole performance made him fighting mad; "damn poor politics, a rotten trick, treachery"—were some of the bristling words he used to describe it.[9] The Governor was in error, however, in attributing the defeat entirely to the wets. Pennsylvania's United States Senators—Pepper and Reed—announced publicly that it could be traced to disloyalty toward Coolidge and Mellon. Unquestionably, part of the explanation was the feeling of the state organization leaders that the Governor was a maverick who, for the sake of unity within the state, had to be corralled.

The ten-gallon hat from the Governor of Texas did not, therefore, reach the nominating convention in Cleveland. When Coolidge was renominated, however, Pinchot stuck by the party's decision. In a lukewarm statement he promised that Pennsylvania (presumably including himself) would "get vigorously behind the nominees of the Cleveland convention."[10] But when Coolidge won handily, Pinchot was disheartened. "[It] is perfectly clear," he wrote to friend Plunkett, "that this country is at the moment falling back under a more complete domination of the plutocracy than for many years past, and eventually something has got to be done about it."[11]

Pinchot was positive that the Republican party and the country needed a leader of Theodore Roosevelt's stripe, who could bring the nation back to "true progressivism." Inner whispers kept telling him that perhaps some day he might become that leader. Despite his election setback, some people both inside and outside Pennsylvania gave him enough encouragement to keep his aspirations alive. Making the most of his appearance in Coolidge's inaugural parade, he borrowed his uncle's thoroughbred horse, donned his picturesque Texas hat, and waved to the admiring crowds. It must have buoyed his spirits to read in the Harrisburg paper that he won more applause than Coolidge himself.[12]

Within a few weeks, some politicians were prophesying that Pinchot's political ambitions would carry him toward the 1926 election for the Senate. When a reporter asked in the middle of May whether he would enter the campaign, he coyly countered with "What was the color of George Washington's white horse?"[13] But the Governor's intentions became more evident in the summer when he blasted George Wharton Pepper, the incumbent Senator, who was certain to run for re-election. Pinchot's accusations that the Senator had recommended an unqualified man for United States Marshal, and Pepper's indignant replies, had all the earmarks of the opening guns of a political campaign.[14] If there still remained any doubts that Pinchot had his eye on the election, they were largely dispelled in August when, on his sixtieth birthday, he began a tour of inspection of some 350 state-owned and state-aided hospitals, asylums, and homes throughout Pennsylvania. Such an expedition was a worthy project for a Governor interested in learning at first hand of conditions in the institutions and the efficiency of the managers. At the same time it served neatly as a vehicle for furthering

Pinchot's political fortunes. Carefully planned by his secretary and past campaign manager, Stahlnecker, the group of automobiles in the entourage formed a kind of political parade across the state. The Governor's car, even at night, had the top lowered. Received in many towns and the rural areas by crowds of people on flag-bedecked streets, Pinchot had plenty of opportunity to proclaim the accomplishments of his Administration and at the same time to castigate the big city bosses. The "gang controlled majorities in the great cities," he would say, "is the most dangerous factor in American public life today."[15]

While it was generally known that many elections in Pennsylvania, especially in the large cities, were crookedly run, little had been done to correct the situation. There was probably some truth in Pinchot's claim that he had been robbed of at least 50,000 votes in the gubernatorial election of 1922. If he were to have any chance whatsoever in a contest for senator, he reasoned, elections had to be cleaned up. In order to dramatize the issue for the people, he organized a Committee of Seventy-six, composed of both Democrats and nonorganization Republicans, to investigate the situation and make recommendations. This Committee reported "brazen" election scandals which included "falsified" returns and outright "theft of votes on a wholesale scale"—especially in Philadelphia, Pittsburgh, Scranton, and a few other places.[16] As remedies, they suggested twelve clean election laws.

Although the General Assembly had been adjourned and would not regularly meet again during Pinchot's term of office, he considered calling it into special session. Some of his close friends, fearing that a series of rebuffs by the legislature would hurt him politically, advised against the call.[17] But the Governor saw this as a last chance to obtain not only stricter regulation of elections but also other legislation which the General Assembly in its two regular sessions had declined to enact. Taking a calculated risk, therefore, he called it back for the first extra session in twenty years. With no lack of persistence, he asked for legislation on eight subjects, including prohibition enforcement, giant power, and the designation of anthracite as a public utility.

The 1926 extra session was a five-week battle staged before the backdrop of the coming senatorial election. Pinchot limited his opening address mainly to an appeal for the bills on ballot reform. In addition, by entreaties on the radio and a letter mailed to 30,000 representative citizens, he asked public support for the legislation. Of the even dozen election reform bills, however, ten met defeat in the Senate. One was so emasculated that it drew a veto from the Governor; another, a constitutional amendment to permit the use of voting machines, was permitted to pass.

At the beginning of the special session, the Administration introduced a total of thirty-six bills. Only four survived, but one of them gave the persevering Governor a highly prized victory. From the early days of his term, he had been agitating for legislation giving the state the power to inspect and otherwise control both distilleries and breweries. His continual campaign finally had its effect when both the Senate and House, with comfortable margins, passed the alcohol bill regulating distilleries. Although the wet forces would not yield on breweries, the court approved a construction of the distillery law which gave the new Alcohol Permit Board some control over breweries as well.

Some three weeks after the General Assembly adjourned, Pinchot announced his candidacy for the Senate. Labeling himself as "a Republican, a supporter of President Coolidge, and an enemy of the gang," he declared that the "plain people" of Pennsylvania ought to have some one to represent them in the Senate—"They have no one there now."[18] The incumbent Senators were David A. Reed of Pittsburgh, and George Wharton Pepper of Philadelphia, both elected with the support of the Republican organization. Pepper, with his middle of the road liberalism, was now up for re-election. He and Pinchot, of course, had known each other as far back as their not entirely happy relationship as lawyer and client in the Ballinger-Pinchot dispute. Through the years the two men had maintained a meticulous courtesy toward each other, but found themselves at odds on a good many public issues.

Pepper was classed with the drys. Not an ardent dry like Pinchot, he believed that since prohibition was written into the law it should be enforced. Pinchot regarded him as a "damp" rather than a true dry, but to a good many ministers and members of dry organizations he was as acceptable as Pinchot. Much consternation was thrown into the ranks of the dry forces, therefore, when boss William Vare entered the senatorial race the day after Pinchot. Vare, an avowed wet who promised to work for the modification of prohibition, later claimed he would have become a candidate whether or not Pinchot ran,[19] but it was apparent that his chances of winning were materially improved by the possibilities of a split in the dry vote.

Pinchot's campaign strategy was to pound away far more relentlessly at Pepper than at Vare. He did not ignore Vare; he repeatedly pointed with scorn at the "wet" candidate of the Philadelphia "gang." When the Pinchot forces learned that a good many of the names on the petitions that Vare filed to enter the primary were obviously forged, they covered the state with photostats of some of the fake names.[20] The Governor surmised, probably correctly, that the kind of voter who might support Vare could not be persuaded by any amount of campaigning to switch to Pinchot; a good many of those, however, who would have nothing to do with Vare might cast their ballots for either Pepper or Pinchot. His approach, then, was to try to convince voters that he was the only man who could beat Vare.

Pinchot did not have the money to match his opponents in paid newspaper advertising, but by the use of speeches, circular letters, and press releases he pictured Pepper as a straddler who "stands for nothing." "If you want to throw your vote away," he wrote to all county chairmen, ". . . vote for the colorless candidate, the milk and water candidate . . . who is on every fence in sight—the perfect compromiser, George Wharton Pepper."[21]

Mrs. Pinchot once again came to the aid of her husband with all the vigor of which she was so capable. Working long hours at the Pinchot headquarters in helping to organize support by the women of the state, she wrote thousands of personal and form letters. On one speaking tour, she delivered as many as nine speeches a day for her husband. As the campaign progressed it developed into a furious battle for political power by such Republican titans as Grundy, Vare, and the Mellons—not one of whom supported Pinchot. Nor did Pinchot have an alliance of any kind with candidates running for the office of governor in the election.

When the campaign opened, Pinchot had felt that the support of the drys was his "almost by right."[22] He was shocked and disillusioned, therefore, when the Anti-Saloon League did not give him wholehearted support and some of its leaders preferred Senator Pepper. Nothing aroused his ire more than the intermittent request from drys that, in order to defeat Vare, one of the two dry candidates should withdraw. Standing firm on his position that there never had been more than one dry in the race, he never considered withdrawing.

The United Mine Workers, including their president John L. Lewis, lent the strongest kind of support to the Governor. Even before Pinchot announced his candidacy, Lewis had lauded him for his "high courage and unselfish devotion to public interest"[23] during the anthracite coal strike. For several days at the end of the campaign Lewis accompanied Pinchot on a speech-making tour of the coal regions and appeared with him on the platform.

When the ballots were counted the race for governor proved to be nip and tuck but the vote for senator was not nearly as close. Vare won only two counties, but the spectacular control that he exercised over Philadelphia—338,000 for Vare, 114,000 for Pepper, and a scanty 27,000 for Pinchot—was sufficient to give him the nomination with a total of 597,000 votes. Pepper trailed with 516,000. Pinchot received handsome pluralities over both other candidates in the hard coal regions and showed strength in several rural counties. Altogether he was first in 23 counties, but in total votes ran a poor third with 339,000. A good many people believed that in a two-man race Pepper would have defeated Vare. But Pinchot held to the conviction that his own withdrawal would have increased Vare's margin of victory.

"The man who won," Pinchot wrote his nephew in England, "is a wet gangster who represents everything that is bad in Pennsylvania."[24]

Pinchot personally spent $44,000 in the primary; Mrs. Pinchot spent $40,000. The total expenditure by him and on his behalf from all sources, including $50,000 from his aunt (Mrs. Charles B. Wood) and $10,000 from his brother, was reported as $187,000. The rumors of deals and sky-high expenditures were so prevalent, however, that immediately after the primary the United States Senate voted an investigation. Although the investigators were not able, in the opinion of their chairman, to uncover every single expenditure, they found $1,805,000 had been spent for the ticket headed by Pepper and $796,000 for Vare and his allied gubernatorial candidate.[25]

The sequel to the primary attracted national interest. Pinchot could not bring himself to vote for Vare in the November election. "I am a Republican," he affirmed, "but I cannot stand for Vare. He is not fit to represent Pennsylvania in the Senate. . . . I shall take no active part in the campaign. . . . As a Republican, I shall vote for a majority of Republican candidates."[26] Vare won handily, however, although he did not overwhelm his Democratic opponent. When it fell to Pinchot's lot, as Governor, to certify to the Senate his opponent's election he refused to use the customary phraseology that the candidate was "duly chosen." He stated instead that "on the face of the returns . . . Vare appears to have been chosen by the qualified electors." And further, as if to make certain that no one misunderstood his implication, he added in a note to the Senate, "I am convinced . . . that his nomination was partly bought and partly stolen. . . . [The] election returns do not in fact represent the will of the sovereign voters of Pennsylvania."[27]

Vare eventually was denied a seat in the Senate, primarily, it was said, because of excessive expenditures.

CHAPTER 20

NEW APPROACH IN STATE GOVERNMENT

DESPITE all the difficulties associated with his first term, Gifford Pinchot repeatedly declared that his two terms as Governor of Pennsylvania were the most interesting years of his life. Buoyant in any case, the exhilaration that came from his accomplishments seemed to add an extra spring to his step. "The Governor is a very active man," testified a member of his staff who served with several governors, "and is always stepping and it keeps us stepping too."[1]

As he had in the U.S. Forest Service many years earlier, Pinchot engendered a strong sense of loyalty in most of his immediate staff. Quick to recognize and acknowledge work well done, he wrote brief personal notes of appreciation to deserving members of his Administration. To an employee who estimated within one-half of one per cent the amount of income that the Highways Department would receive over a two-year period, he sent "Heartiest congratulations."[2] Just as ready, however, to call attention to shoddy work, he was frank in grumbling about some publicity pictures taken by photographers in the same Department, "[If] one good man . . . could not beat the work these men did, I miss my guess. I think you need one good man instead of three duds."[3]

Annoyed by letters which clung to "outworn formalities and bungling phrases,"[4] he regarded many government letters as so cold and formal that they amounted to "rebuffs."[5] Members of his office staff who prepared letters for his signature were kept constantly aware that he did not sign his name perfunctorily. The assistant who proposed using a sentence such as "I am glad indeed to have the suggested plans for the rehabilitation of the coal industry and will refer same at once to my committee of coal operators," was almost certain to find it returned with a circle around the word "same," and a notation written with a broad stub pen, "How could you approve? G P," or "I want this to stop *now* and once for all. G P." A memorandum to his office staff illustrated his almost fastidious standards, "Ants, bees, and wasps, with commas between.

That is right. Ants, bees and wasps, with no comma before the 'and.'
That is wrong. . . . [The] order for this office is to use the comma
in this way—ants, bees, and wasps."[6]

Pinchot's personality shone through many of his letters. He liked
to say what he thought, and on occasion to adopt a "go-to-hell"
attitude toward his critics. Persons preparing letters for him frequently had difficulty in anticipating his exact mood. When a Philadelphian wrote the Governor, for example, criticizing his appointments to the city registration board, Pinchot found on his desk a
mild suggested reply, "I am somewhat surprised at the tone of your
letter. . . . It has been my aim since I became Governor to select
the best possible person for each position. . . . I hope time will convince you how greatly you have erred." Unable to bring himself
to sign such "un-Pinchotian" prose, the Governor drafted a revision that sounded far more like himself, "Either you are totally
out of touch with public sentiment, or you decline to believe what
you hear. . . . To say that I was not attempting to do right when
I made these appointments is nonsense. I was doing the best I knew
how, and my confidence that I did so is by no means impaired by
your letter."[7]

When the Governor, in his movements around the Commonwealth, came across state employees on the job, he often showed
a personal interest in their activities. On one occasion he got out
of his car to suggest to highway workmen that they fix a fence;
another time he stopped employees from burning brush too close
to living trees. Now and then he visited some state institution completely unannounced.

Around the capitol he sometimes casually dropped into department offices to see conditions for himself. Appearing at the Department of Health early one morning during his first year in office,
he found only four girls at work at 8:10.[8] His biting statement to
the press brought a complaint from the head of the Department
that he had hurt the employees. Pinchot's reply was brusque, "a
situation in which a considerable percentage of the employees of
a Department are absent twenty minutes after opening time, and
a very small percentage of those present actually at work, calls for
open comment." Strong measures were needed, he insisted, to im-

prove morale "in a service which has degenerated as much as that of the State of Pennsylvania."[9]

As soon as the first General Assembly adjourned in the summer of 1923, Pinchot gave more thought to job patronage. Because Pennsylvania had no civil service system, the Governor had wide authority to replace existing employees with persons of his own choosing. The strong pressure placed on him to appoint "deserving" supporters was in a way disillusioning. "One curious and decidedly embarrassing difficulty," he confided to a British friend, "is that almost all the original Pinchot primary people are now insisting that the patronage of the State should be handled for their benefit in exactly the same way as they and I have denounced the machine politicians for handling it." But he vowed to hold the line, admitting that "I am going to make a great many enemies and lukewarm friends out of hearty supporters by my refusal . . . to treat jobs I can dispose of as pure spoils."[10]

At the outset Pinchot's policy was to dismiss incumbent employees actively hostile to him and his policies, but to keep many of those who, while unsympathetic, assumed a neutral attitude. By the end of his term, however, he acknowledged his mistake in leaving so many enemies in office where they could sabotage his policies.[11]

The Governor's frankness and his willingness to resist pressures from politicians and other influential citizens, endeared him to a good many Pennsylvanians. Some of them relished the tone of such letters as the one he sent to a state senator who, peeved because Pinchot had not helped him get a new road for his district, told the Governor he could not support him for the Senate. "I don't know whether I am going to run for the Senate or not," exploded Pinchot, "but you may be perfectly sure of this: that I will not vary my course by one hair's breadth from what I believe to be right, whether I run or whether I do not, for the sake of getting your support or anybody else's support. That is not the way I play the game."[12]

Like any man willing to work hard for change and to take stands on highly controversial questions, Pinchot was the object of a great deal of criticism. His remarkably thick skin served him well. He could see the humor, for example, in a chain of insulting letters that he received on stationery of the Union League Club in Philadelphia, all in the same angry handwriting but signed with a variety of names. He frequently boasted of the ease with which he could shed denunciation by his enemies. There were exceptions, but, in general, he hit his opposition hard and expected to be hit hard in return.

Throughout his first four years as Governor, but especially during the 1926 primary election, the gossip and violent attacks on him reached such proportions that Pinchot, or sometimes Mrs. Pinchot, found it necessary to answer. A few of the widely circulated stories were: the Pinchots served alcoholic beverages to guests in their home; the enforcement fund raised for Pinchot by the Women's Christian Temperance Union had been spent improperly; the Governor was not a church member. Occasionally some critic tried to link him with the Communists.

The rumor that the Governor was not a church member came closest to the truth; he rarely attended church services. In contrast with his younger days at Yale and in North Carolina, he had drifted away from regular church attendance. No one, however, could deny that as Governor he showed a concern for public morals that was in harmony with the beliefs associated with a good many religious leaders in the state. In addition to his celebrated attitude toward prohibition, which he regarded as a moral question, he was unalterably opposed to gambling. When the legislature appropriated money to help subsidize some of the county fairs in the state, Pinchot vetoed the measure because it did not specifically prohibit payments of grants if a fair allowed gambling or immoral shows.[13] He likewise branded as "the most absurd suggestion that has been brought to my attention in many a moon"[14] a proposal that the state use a lottery for the purpose of raising money.

The Governor on more than one occasion made clear to the state's board of censors that he wanted motion pictures kept rigidly clean. After witnessing a picture in Harrisburg one afternoon, he protested most emphatically to the board's chairman against the failure of the censors "to eliminate one scene in which a girl appeared to all intents and purposes entirely naked above the waist." Demanding that "this sort of thing" must stop, he reiterated that he wanted censorship conducted "on the basis . . . of what is proper and not proper to be shown to boys and girls of fourteen and fifteen."[15]

Pinchot also was sympathetic with the Pennsylvania "blue laws" regulating the observance of the Sabbath. During his second term as Governor, he was placed in an embarrassing position when the General Assembly passed a bill to allow individual localities to vote on whether they wanted Sunday baseball. The huge amount of mail that he received on the subject was so heavily on the side of opposition to the law that he feared he would be letting down many of his strongest supporters if he signed it. Upon finally deciding to approve the bill, he personally drafted, after many revisions and much labor, a radio broadcast explaining his position. Affirming his emphatic opposition to the commercialization of the Sabbath, he piously explained that he had reached his decision only after "long, anxious, and prayerful consideration." Thinking perhaps of the tennis that he himself frequently played at his home in Milford during restful weekends, he reasoned that Sunday baseball would "not seriously change" conditions in a state which already had Sunday trains, concerts, golf, and tennis. One of his strongest reasons for signing, he announced, was that the tolerance of "golf with caddies" during church services was an "unjust discrimination in favor of the rich against the poor."[16]

Pinchot revealed his strict attitude at a meeting of the nation's governors—the Governors' Conference—in Indiana in 1923. A show staged at an official session of the Conference offended his sensibilities. Describing it as "coarse and offensive," he "expressed [his] sentiments forcibly and at once" to those responsible including the Governor of Indiana. The next day he prepared a public statement in which he described the incident as an "insult to the wife of the Governor of Pennsylvania" and therefore "an insult to the women of the Commonwealth." After consulting with some of his friends, however, he decided not to release the statement. In a handwritten note scratched across its front, he maintained it was "amply justified," but admitted that "it might seem like a grandstand play."[17]

To some of the hard-boiled politicians around capitol hill in Harrisburg, Pinchot represented many of the things that they scorned. He was a reformer; in their minds he also had the marks of a prude. They could not understand him. Such a man inevitably was the butt of a good bit of ridicule. One of the most vocal of the scoffers was "Charlie" Snyder, the likable state Treasurer, a carnation-wearing, cane-carrying politician who had been around the hill in various capacities for two decades. As a separately elected official, and therefore completely independent of the Governor, he rarely missed a chance to direct his sarcastic humor toward the reformer. "Every Sunday," he told reporters, "the Governor tries to make some change in the universe where the Lord hasn't done it right."[18] Snyder's most famed sneer at Pinchot occurred at an annual banquet of a Republican club in Pittsburgh commemorating the birthday of General Grant. The toastmaster, Senator David Reed, called on him for a few impromptu remarks. With extreme ridicule Snyder urged that the state constitution be abolished because it failed to suit Pinchot; and predicted that in the future the measurement of time would be changed from B.C. and A.D. to B.P. and A.P. (after Pinchot). His little discourse brought gales of laughter from most of the banqueters.

Pinchot refused to let Snyder worry him. "After all," he wrote to a friend, "he is of those whose opposition is more valuable than their support."[19] The old adage that politics makes strange bedfellows was proved once again a few years later when Snyder joined Pinchot's political camp.

It was characteristic of Pinchot that he provided a dramatic finale in his address to the General Assembly in January 1927 just before the curtain fell at the close of his first term. As he neared the end of his long speech, he analyzed what was wrong with Pennsylvania politics and lashed at the opposition he had been fighting for so many months. Speaking as one sure of his ground and sensing that he had won considerable popular support, he obviously was addressing not only the legislators and guests but also the people of Pennsylvania and the nation (he sent thousands of reprints of his remarks throughout the country). "I am going out of office," he declared, "with the most hearty contempt not only for the morals and the intentions, but also for the minds of the gang politicians of Pennsylvania." He named names. Stating frankly that he believed Vare "deserves to be and will be excluded" from the United States

Senate, he decried the buying and the stealing of votes in elections which "have combined to bring upon Pennsylvania a dishonor which will take years to live down." Singling out the Mellon machine in Pittsburgh and the Mitten machine in Philadelphia (the Mittens ran the Philadelphia Rapid Transit), he described them as typical of city organizations spreading "their black hawk-like shadows over the community." And he severely castigated the "respectable element" for joining "organized crime" in supporting these machines.

Describing the politics of the state as having been run in the past by "certain great monied interests," while the "people got little more than the crumbs which fell from the rich men's table," he portrayed his Administration as resisting the "debauchery" and providing for the average citizen, as Roosevelt had so often phrased it, a "square deal." In a ringing conclusion he sounded a call to arms behind the "liberal movement to which Roosevelt gave point and power."[20]

Although Pinchot was far from deafened by the applause at the end of his address, he told his sister that he "really had a great time writing it, and even more fun delivering it. You ought to have seen the opposition squirm!"[21] Obviously delighted, he also wrote John L. Lewis that he "greatly enjoyed rubbing it into the gangsters in the Legislature."[22]

He was proud of his record. No sooner had he left office than he began writing the story of his Administration. Various readers of the manuscript, however, believed it mentioned too many names unknown outside Pennsylvania and that it was weakened by egotism, invective, and personal animosity. After the seventh publisher had turned it down, Pinchot confessed he didn't know whether it was "because it is rotten or because they are afraid to publish it."[23] The historian, Charles Beard, who was not one to pull punches, advised Pinchot that he used unnecessarily harsh language. Pinchot, in retrospect, tended to agree. "My story," he wrote Beard, "was written when my temper was still hot from the four year fight, and I am sure I can greatly improve it by reducing the billingsgate."[24] But he never found time.

Many Pennsylvanians agreed that Pinchot deserved to be proud.

"The Pinchot administration . . . has accomplished much," declared the *Philadelphia Inquirer*.[25] The *Public Ledger*, in the same city, agreed that "Mr. Pinchot has a right to be proud of his record," although it warned that his "vehemence of expression and his bitter denunciation" of his opponents "may tend to obscure in the public mind the sound achievements in his record."[26] His acclaim was not confined to Pennsylvania. On the floor of the United States Senate, for example, Senator Pat Harrison of Mississippi extolled him as "one man whose integrity, honesty, and high purpose the people of Pennsylvania and the country have confidence in."[27]

Hosts of Pennsylvania citizens agreed that Pinchot was the best chief executive the state ever had. A quarter of a century later, there was still considerable concurrence that his first Administration, all things considered, was superior to that of any other governor.

There can be no doubt, on the other hand, that a good many political leaders in the state had been longing for January 18, 1927, the day when Pinchot left Harrisburg for Washington, D.C. For years he had been a source of irritation to them; now they anticipated that the irritant was permanently disappearing. The Governor, after all, had suffered two crushing defeats in the primaries for delegate to the Republican national convention and for United States senator. Wasn't he politically finished?

Pinchot did not perform, however, like a man on his way to oblivion. "[I] am trying . . . to let the gang understand that I am going out of office with my head up and my tail over the dashboard," he wrote to Smedley Butler.[28] Repeatedly he stressed the "fun" of being Governor; he had, he claimed, gained twenty-five pounds and "got rid of my indigestion."[29] Frequently hinting that he would be back, he expressed the hope, at a reception for state employees a few days before his departure, that "during the years that are left to me I may still be of some good to Pennsylvania."[30] At the bottom of many of the personal farewell letters which he sent to members of his Administration he added the sentence, "The fight is not over either for you or for me, or for the other decent minded citizens of Pennsylvania, so long as the present abuses exist. I hope to have my part in doing it."[31]

328

Pinchot was highly pleased two months after he left office when one of his deputy Attorney Generals sent him a clipping from a newspaper in suburban Philadelphia quoting the comment by a dairyman to a local health officer that "Pinchot is no longer Governor. It isn't necessary to be so strict now."[32]

CHAPTER 21

CONSERVATION AND THE
INTERVENING YEARS

WHEN GIFFORD PINCHOT entered politics in Pennsylvania in 1921 some of his conservation friends felt sorry to see him "throw away" his acknowledged talents.[1] Even before his first campaign for governor, while serving as Pennsylvania's Forestry Commissioner, several of his former Washington colleagues urged him to return to the national capital and revivify the National Conservation Association.

Foresters and their friends in Pennsylvania were somewhat disappointed with the limited amount of attention Governor Pinchot gave to their problems. In many little ways he demonstrated his interest in forestry; he appointed an able expert as head of the Department of Forests and Waters. But he did not, as some had expected, place forestry at the top of any priority list. Despite his comment to some of the employees in the Department that he was reluctant to show partiality to his own field of interest, the probable explanation was simply that there were more immediately pressing problems to be dealt with than forestry. The Governor did give earnest support to a proposed constitutional amendment authorizing the state to borrow $25 million for the purchase of forest lands, but the voters eventually rejected it.

Just before running for governor, Pinchot had been voicing vigorous protests against the Snell bill in Congress. Although the aim of this proposed law was to bring about good forestry practices on private lands, Pinchot found it defective because it provided for federal assistance to the states which in turn would exercise forest control. In 1919 he had been chairman of a committee of the Society of American Foresters which had strongly recommended the need for direct federal control of cutting on private forest lands.[2] Far more to his liking than the Snell bill was legislation sponsored by his friend, Senator Arthur Capper, of Kansas, which proposed federal regulation. The fact that the lumbering interests were supporting the Snell bill was, to Pinchot, simply added evidence that they believed the states would be ineffective.

Unquestionably some lumbermen looked on the Snell bill as the lesser of two evils. But there was also support for the bill by sincere "states righters" who believed that control by the federal government was not only unwise but unconstitutional. Pinchot was more than annoyed that W. B. Greeley, the current head of the United States Forest Service, favored the state approach; for this and other reasons, Pinchot regarded Greeley as a pawn of the lumbering interests.

Contrary to Pinchot's best judgment, Congress in 1924 passed the Clarke-McNary Act, a compromise bill which has been described as a "lineal descendant" of the Snell Bill.[3] Providing for federal-state cooperation in the protection of forests, it omitted, however, any reference to government regulation of timber cutting.

Pinchot had a special interest in the Teapot Dome scandals that broke while he was Governor. In line with Roosevelt's conservation policies, the Taft and Wilson Administrations had taken steps to set aside certain oil bearing lands in the West to serve as reserves for the future oil needs of the United States Navy. Pinchot in 1916 had publicly accused Wilson's Secretary of the Interior, Franklin K. Lane, of working for legislation which would destroy these reserves.[4] When it was alleged later that private wells next to the reserves were draining away the government's oil, Congress placed the Secretary of the Navy, Josephus Daniels, in charge of the reserves and gave him authority to conserve the oil as he saw fit.[5] Pinchot's confidence in Daniels allowed him to rest more easily.

Harding had been President less than three months, however, when he transferred the reserves from the Department of the Navy to the Department of the Interior. Pinchot objected violently, but could not undo what had been ordered. Secretary of the Interior Albert B. Fall had already aroused his suspicions. "Don't quote me yet on Fall," he had wired a friend who asked for an opinion just before Fall assumed office, "Want to go carefully over his record. . . . He has been with exploitation gang, but not a leader." And then, with an ominous warning, he concluded, "Trouble ahead."[6]

Just how much trouble was around the corner was not revealed until, shortly after Harding's death in the summer of 1923, the Senate investigating committee headed by Senator Thomas J. Walsh began unveiling the circumstances under which Fall had disposed of some of the oil in the reserves. Without any competitive bidding, he had leased the oil at Teapot Dome to Harry F. Sinclair's Mammoth Oil Company, and that at Elk Hills to Edward F. Doheny's Pan American Company. When it was alleged that Sinclair had given Fall $260,000 in government bonds, and that Doheny had delivered to Fall in a satchel a "loan" of $100,000 in cash (bearing no interest), it was time for the government to prosecute.

Senator Pepper, early in 1924, wired Pinchot asking if he could quote the Governor as favoring Owen J. Roberts of Pennsylvania, future member of the United States Supreme Court, as a special counsel in the oil cases. "If high character and great ability were all that was needed," Pinchot replied, "Owen would be an ideal man." But, referring to the "ignorance" of Secretary Ballinger's lawyer, Vertrees, in the controversy of a decade and a half before, Pinchot maintained that counsel in the oil cases also needed knowledge of "public land law and procedure."[7]

On the same day he wrote Pepper, the Governor sent a letter to Roberts offering to assist in the case in any way possible.[8] Nothing he was doing in Harrisburg was any more important to him than this battle. He revealed his concern when he told his nephew in England that "most" of his time during the past quarter century had been given to "fighting to crystallize" the Roosevelt conservation policy and defending it against attacks, but that "If we get the Naval Oil Reserves back . . . this thing may be worth almost what it has cost."[9]

By the time the participants in the leasing were indicted, Pinchot was out of office. Several times he supplied information and suggestions to Roberts (hired in spite of Pinchot's evaluation) in an effort to help with the prosecution.[10] On one occasion he sent his secretary, Stahlnecker, directly to Roberts in Washington with a list of names of detectives who allegedly were shadowing the jurymen in the Sinclair-Fall trial.[11] When Roberts finally presented affidavits showing that Sinclair actually had employed detectives, a mistrial was declared.

Secretary Fall, as is well known, was eventually found guilty of accepting a bribe, sentenced to a year in prison, and fined $100,000. Sinclair was guilty of contempt of court and also of the Senate. Doheny was acquitted. More important to Pinchot, the courts canceled both leases.

Pinchot's other unhappy experience with Fall occurred early in 1921, shortly after President Harding transferred the Naval oil reserves to the Department of the Interior. Fall thoroughly frightened Pinchot by proposing that the national forests in Alaska be placed under control of the Interior Department and opened for private development. By the use of every device of publicity at his command, Pinchot produced a wave of protest by conservation-minded citizens. The transfer was never made. Harding apparently was impressed. According to Pinchot, the President at a lunch admitted he was opposed to Pinchot's point of view, but recognized that legislation could not be forced through Congress against Pinchot's opposition—"I pay you that compliment," Pinchot quoted Harding as saying.[12]

When Pinchot left Harrisburg at the end of his term in January 1927, he told friends of his plans to continue conservation work and "dry work," and to write the story of his four years in office.[13] Although he wrote the book and delivered many speeches on prohibition enforcement, he gave more attention to conservation. It was as if he wished to make up for lost time. His inability, while governor, to obtain any interest in joint state action for the regulation of anthracite coal or for the promotion of "giant power" had fortified his opinion that the states, neither individually nor collectively, could be depended upon to halt what he called "exploiters" of natural resources.

With more time now to devote to forestry, he began a renewed and ardent drive for direct federal regulation of private forests. Despite some current questions concerning its constitutionality, he threw his support to a new Capper bill which would have compelled careful cutting of trees by laying a tax of $5 per thousand feet on all timber harvested on private lands, with a provision for a rebate of $4.95 per thousand if cut in accordance with federal regulations.

By 1928 Pinchot entered a kind of informal partnership with Major George P. Ahern to alert the nation to what they agreed was a critical forest situation. Ahern, the same man who had sought Pinchot's advice on forestry in the Philippines a quarter of a century earlier, was a fighting Irishman and a graduate of West Point. Not a technically trained forester, he was respected among foresters for the work he had done in the Islands.

Ahern became so agitated over "the present ghastly forest devastation" that he wrote a pamphlet—*Deforested America*—charging the lumber companies with destructive logging practices, and the Forest Service (under the direction of Greeley) with complacency. Pinchot, who probably helped compile material for the pamphlet, added his hearty approval in the form of a foreword in which he pointed out that "the ax holds unregulated sway" over four-fifths of the nation's forest land and urged enactment of legislation, such as the Capper bill, to "control the ax." Pinchot and Ahern mailed several thousand copies of the pamphlet to foresters, newspapers, state legislators, teachers, and others. When more copies were needed, Pinchot arranged with Senator Capper to have the pamphlet printed as an official Senate document; 10,000 additional reprints were then mailed throughout the country, some of them in franked envelopes provided by the Senator.[14] In the midst of the drive to publicize the information in Ahern's pamphlet, Pinchot obtained "great satisfaction" from a letter he received from Secretary of Agriculture Jardine assuring him that the Department of Agriculture was deeply appreciative of the work he was doing to conserve the nation's forest resources.[15]

At a meeting of the Society of American Foresters in Des Moines in December 1929, Pinchot and Ahern, disturbed by some of the items in a report of its Committee on Forest Policy, drafted a vigorous minority report and released it to the press. Once again espousing the Capper bill, they stated that whereas ten years previously the destruction of forests was four times greater than new growth, it now had grown to six times greater. They estimated, moreover, that only one per cent of all the lumber removed from private lands was cut under any plan to insure another forest crop.[16]

Pinchot himself drew an interesting comparison between the current forest situation and that of slavery before the Civil War. The North, he maintained, had refused to face the hard fact that only the abolition of slavery could solve the problem; now, he believed, there was "only one central thing that will meet the situation, and that is to put an end to forest devastation."[17]

Pinchot was of course prepared for the roar of rebuttal that came from the lumbermen. One "forest economist" referred to the Pinchot-Ahern minority report as a "socialistic and destructive document." Others spoke of the "timber famine bogy."[18]

The secretary of the National Lumber Manufacturers Association composed a mimeographed reply to *Deforested America*, which he called *Reforested America*. Forwarding a copy to the ex-Governor, he was highly critical of Pinchot, and labeled the Ahern pamphlet as deceptive propaganda.[19] Pinchot's one sentence reply sarcastically assured the secretary that he would be glad to read it "if I get the time."[20] His anger boiled, however, when he read in *American Forests*, the magazine of the American Forestry Association, an advertisement by the Lumber Manufacturers Association offering free copies of *Reforested America*.[21] The Lumber Association pleaded its case in the advertisement by claiming that the industry was actively promoting good forestry practices and by protesting the new movement to substitute a "Big Stick" of statutory compulsion for the policy of cooperation between the lumbermen and the government. Pinchot, already believing that the American Forestry Association was dominated by the lumbermen, protested vehemently that its magazine ought not "to hold its advertising columns open for the dissemination of propaganda intended to facilitate the continued destruction of American forests."[22]

Although Pinchot expected opposition from the lumbermen, he was keenly disappointed that more foresters did not fully support his views. It was not a complete surprise that Henry Graves, who had more faith in state regulation than did Pinchot, had been unwilling to sign the minority report by Pinchot and Ahern at Des Moines.[23] It was a severe shock, however, when he learned that another of his closest colleagues in the old Forest Service, Dol Smith, was taking a moderate stand which Pinchot described as "the Greeley point of view in the worst way"; he confided to Woodruff that "I got so mad about it that I woke up at two o'clock this morning, and have not been asleep since."[24] It is interesting to note that in this instance Pinchot, who often suspected ulterior motives in those who differed with him, never questioned the sincerity of his two long-time friends.

Unquestionably a majority of the foresters in the nation failed to see a necessity for the Capper bill. Some of them actually believed the lumbermen could do no wrong. A good many, including Graves, honestly believed that the states, under federal leadership, were adequate to perform the desired regulation.[25] Others, recognizing the past and current abuses of commercial timber cutting and discerning that lumbermen as a group may have been exaggerating their accomplishments in real forestry, nevertheless believed that at least part of the industry was slowly changing from a "mining" to a "perpetual crop" system of cutting. Pinchot was a leader of the minority who admitted that a few operators were improving their methods, but maintained that general progress was far too slow to avert an impending famine.

Although there is no way to prove it, it is likely that the Pinchot-Ahern clamor for the Capper bill spurred some lumbermen into employing conservation methods as a means of resisting federal regulation. Pinchot apparently subscribed to this idea for he wrote a forester friend at the end of 1929 that the "lumber crowd" was beginning "to get thoroughly scared," and that he and his group were "in a better condition to make the fight for putting an end to forest devastation than at any time in the last ten years."[26] It is significant that only four years later, under Franklin Roosevelt's National Recovery Administration, the lumbermen inserted in the code that governed their industry a provision requiring cutting methods which would encourage a new crop of trees.

Pinchot's activities in the interest of conservation during the years 1927 to 1930 were far broader than mere concern with forestry. Wherever an undue wastage of natural resources occurred, his presence was likely to be felt. When the Mississippi River overflowed its banks in the late spring of 1927, for example, he was on the spot to view the damage. A few months later he was writing letters to key experts urging them to testify before a congressional committee studying flood control;[27] shortly thereafter he wrote to the governors of all states in the Mississippi drainage basin discussing two plans that were before Congress.[28]

Although active in conservation after he left Harrisburg in January 1927, the issue which concerned Pinchot most deeply for the next eight years was electric power. No sooner had he ended his term as Governor than he began hammering incessantly at the dangers of the "growing electric monopoly."[29] In a letter to the governors of the forty-eight states, copies of which went to 5,500 newspapers, he charged "the electric interests" with fighting to "prevent interference with the extortionate profits they are squeezing from the small consumer." He specifically alleged that in Pennsylvania the small consumer was paying two or three times what it cost the electric companies to serve him.[30]

In February 1927 Pinchot spoke on giant power before the Maine legislature,[31] and in March before the Wisconsin legislature.[32] He was by no means fighting singlehandedly. Influential members of Congress, like Senators Thomas Walsh and George Norris, were equally vigorous in their denunciations of "power," but no individual was more instrumental than Pinchot in bringing the subject to the surface as a major issue.

Senator Walsh, late in 1927, proposed a senatorial investigation of electric and gas utilities. Pinchot, in an effort to help the resolution through the Senate, made public a letter to Walsh containing information on the concentration of control of electric power, and offering to submit additional facts to an investigating committee.[33] The electric lobby, unsuccessful in a campaign to bottle up the Walsh resolution in committee, then concentrated on an amendment to transfer the investigation from the Senate to the Federal Trade Commission. Pinchot, and apparently the utilities, believed that a Commission investigation would probe less deeply and less effectively than one conducted by a Senate committee with Walsh as chairman. Dispatching a personal letter to each of twenty-six senators, Pinchot warned that the "power lobby is trying to pick out its own jury," and that the Commission would not disclose the information the "public ought to know."[34]

To the surprise of many, however, the Commission retained R. E. Healy as chief counsel and he vigorously uncovered financial, lobbying, and propaganda activities by some utilities which tended to give a black eye to the entire industry. The revelations of the methods used by some organizations in the utility industry to influence public opinion—subsidization of authors, reporters, and teachers—were especially damaging.[35] The disclosures of course helped to reinforce some of the statements that Pinchot had been proclaiming far and wide.

Pinchot could not be called an expert on the intricacies of electric utility financing and rate-making. For these and other legal and economic matters he relied to a large extent on a kind of brain trust. Morris L. Cooke was a regular contributor of information; so was Harry Slattery whom Pinchot continued to retain in Washington. Two of the other important advisers were his long-standing associates, George Woodruff and (until he died in 1929) Philip Wells. The extent to which he leaned on the latter two friends was shown by a letter he sent to a Washingtonian who had asked for comments on a proposed power bill; asking to be excused from "expressing judgment on your bill at this time," he frankly stated he had been unable to consult with Woodruff and Wells.[36]

One of Pinchot's chief contributions to the drive against what some persons called the "power trust" was his ability to reduce complicated statistics and explanations into simple English that could be understood by the man on the street. Early in 1929 he published and widely distributed a pamphlet, *The Power Monopoly; Its Make-up and Its Menace.*[37] Nowhere in the sixteen pages did he even hint that such a thing as a good utility existed. Rather he sounded an alarm to the nation that there was actually in operation an electric power monopoly, "organized and financed . . . for ruthless exploitation." Before many years, he warned, "it will be not 'the hand that rocks the cradle,' but the hand that turns the electric switch that will rule the land."

His basic complaint was the common practice of pyramiding one holding company on top of another so that the valuations of the individual electric companies were artificially inflated. When a company was permitted to earn a fair return, say seven per cent, on such an inflated value, it meant that unjustifiably high rates could be charged to consumers. Pinchot estimated that "the" monopoly's total assets, valued at more than $8 billion, were really worth only $5 billion. The ex-Governor drew a parallel between saloons and utilities in a form letter mailed in April 1928. "The saloon," he reasoned, "put itself out of business by its own excesses." In the same way, he forewarned the electric industry, if the "present abuses" continued, people would be driven to public ownership "in self-defense."[38] Pinchot could be almost certain of at least one thing. If he ever ran for public office again, his opponent, whoever he might be, would win the solid utility vote.

As the 1928 elections approached, Pinchot was carefully watching for any sign of a significant movement to run him for elective office. When Coolidge announced that summer that he did not choose to run for re-election in 1928, Pinchot could not help thinking of himself as a possible replacement. But he could find only a tiny trickle of suggestions of Pinchot for President.

The ex-Governor did give serious consideration to running again for United States senator. Certainly the Senate floor would have given him an excellent forum for his campaigns against deforestation and high electric rates. Fearing that the Pennsylvania voters had returned to their old ways, however, he doubted his ability to win, and decided eventually that his candidacy would be unwise.[39]

At least some Pennsylvanians got an opportunity to vote for or against a Pinchot when Mrs. Pinchot announced as a candidate in the Republican primary for Congress. Seeking to represent the rural district around Milford, she had a formidable opponent in Louis T. McFadden who was completing his fourteenth year in Congress. To the Republican state organization and some of its supporters, of course, the mere name of Pinchot was anathema. Many of them were eager to see Mrs. Pinchot defeated as decisively as her husband had been in the primaries of 1924 and 1926. Despite McFadden's victory in both the Republican and Democratic primaries, Pinchot was proud of his wife's showing. She was beaten, he maintained, by "the Pennsylvania Railroad, the Lehigh Valley Railroad, the big bankers, and the Pennsylvania State machine."[40]

A few months later, at the end of the summer, the Pinchots gave a basket picnic one Saturday at their Milford estate for the residents of the three neighboring counties, and on the next Saturday, for those from the two other counties of their congressional district. Letters to some key people and advertisements in the newspapers urged "all our friends" to bring a picnic but to remember that the Pinchots would serve ice cream, coffee, cake, "and a few fixings." The promised attractions were a baseball game, swimming, a band, and dancing. The hosts stressed that the gathering was "purely social" and "in no sense political." Between three and four hundred persons appeared at the first picnic, and almost two thousand at the second. A Pinchot picnic became an annual event, sometimes attracting as many as four thousand guests.

At the beginning of 1928 Pinchot predicted that neither Herbert Hoover nor Al Smith would be nominated that year for President. When they both were, he could muster little enthusiasm for either one. He thought Smith's stand on electric power was "simply admirable," but the Democrat was an avowed wet. On the other hand, he approved Hoover's stand on prohibition and furthermore he was a Republican. Heartily as Pinchot disagreed with the Republican leadership on many issues, he was enough of a G.O.P. supporter to vote Republican if he felt the candidates were equal. By no means a worshipper of party regularity—quite the contrary—he knew the value to the politically ambitious of maintaining loyalty to the ticket of his own party. Although willing to cross party lines when there was a compelling reason, he did not consider Al Smith such a reason. "I am perfectly clear that this is no time for a third party," he wrote to a newspaper friend, "and furthermore that as between the Republicans and Democrats there is no place for me to go but with the Republicans."[41]

Announcing his support of Hoover, he immediately received a letter of appreciation from the Republican state chairman of Pennsylvania.[42] But just as quickly the Democrats began unearthing some of the more extreme comments that Pinchot had made about Hoover in the past. They threw back in the face of the Republicans, for example, Pinchot's statement in 1920 that Hoover was "wholly unfitted to be President" partly because he was "essentially a foreigner, and therefore is neither a real Republican nor a real American."[43]

Pinchot's offer to take the stump for Hoover in some of the western states was not accepted when he frankly told the director of the Republican speakers' bureau that if he were questioned about some of his past criticisms of Hoover's attitude toward farmers and electric power, he would have to answer "that I believed those statements when I made them" and "that I believe them now."[44] Pinchot remained relatively quiet, therefore, during the rest of the campaign. Contrary to the advice of one of his brain trust on electric power, he even delayed the publication of his pamphlet, *The Power Monopoly*, until after the election because it might add to the ammunition of the Democrats against Hoover.[45]

As soon as the election was over, however, Pinchot would feel free to continue his fight. Cautioning a friend to "watch my smoke on the electric question" after the President was elected, he added that "Hoover is just as wrong on that as the devil himself."[46]

It might have seemed to a casual observer in 1928 that Pinchot ate, slept, and dreamed nothing but prohibition, forestry, and electric power. But behind the man with a mission was the man with the dream of a great adventure. As far back as their sophomore days at Yale, Pinchot and George Woodruff had looked forward to the time when they could buy a boat and sail to the South Seas. Through all the years in Washington and Harrisburg, the vision of such a trip refused to dim in Pinchot's mind. He loved the water. He loved to see new things. And most of all he loved to fish.

Of all forms of recreation, none brought him as much consistent pleasure as fishing. Whether he was trying for tarpon in Florida, or tuna at Block Island, or trout in the stream that ran through his own estate at Milford, he found it an easy way to relax. There perhaps was only a little exaggeration in his statement to a magazine that his "greatest thrill in life" came one day when he caught "a good-sized pickerel with a streamer fly on a three-ounce rod."[47] Even in the middle of a Pennsylvania winter, an unseasonably warm day would sometimes make his "right arm twitch."[48] On the jacket of a little book he wrote, *Just Fishing Talk,* a collection of two dozen personal experiences in story form, he was described as "America's premier fisherman."[49]

Aged sixty-three, Pinchot began to realize that it was now or never if he was to realize his long-held dream. If Hoover won the election, which seemed probable, there was no chance of his naming Pinchot to any important post. Moreover, no major elections were scheduled for Pennsylvania in 1929. In October 1928, therefore, Pinchot bought second hand a handsome three-masted, 148-foot, topsail schooner, which he promptly christened the *Mary Pinchot* for his mother. With all the enthusiasm and delight of a small boy going on his first camping trip, he began the task of getting the boat repaired and provisioned, and hiring a crew for a seven-months' cruise. A deep disappointment was the inability of Woodruff to go along. When the boat finally sailed from New York it had about twenty-five persons aboard including the crew. Besides the ex-Governor were Mrs. Pinchot (the only woman passenger, who regularly wore sailor's clothes), their thirteen-year-old son "Giff," and "Stiff" Stahlnecker (the son of Pinchot's regular secretary). Also included among the passengers were three scientists to study and collect specimens of fish, animal, bird, and plant life. One of the results was the discovery of a new species of fish which was named *benthosema pinchoti,* and another *Giffordella Corneliae.*

Basking in the warm sun, Pinchot had time to relax as he had not done for years. He reread Theodore Roosevelt's *Autobiography,* which brought back "the old energetic days."[50] He also had plenty of opportunity to satisfy his curious desire to produce jingles. Such bits of nonsense often brought a welcome light touch in his political speeches. Perhaps it was the tropical air that encouraged couplets with an Ogden Nash flavor:

> There's many a hellion
> I prefer to Andy Mellion.

Or, referring to a Democratic leader from Pittsburgh:

> There are times when Dave Lawrence
> Fills me with abhawrence

But politics was not always the theme:

> Have you heard the sad story of the
> daughter of Mr. Cadwallader?
> A shark swallader.

> It is an interesting fact that not
> many people
> Are able to balance themselves for any
> length of time on top of a steeple.

In contrast with many American tourists of that time, Pinchot remained steadfast to his prohibition principles. He must have caused some glances filled with wonder during his visit to the governor's mansion on St. Andrews Island; his host turned on a recording of the "Star-Spangled Banner" and furnished champagne for all to drink a series of toasts, but Pinchot made a speech explaining that he must follow the prohibition laws as conscientiously in the South Seas as in Pennsylvania.[51]

Both the ex-Governor and his wife took care that their political futures were not harmed by their absence. Mrs. Pinchot sent home a series of chatty articles which were published in some small Pennsylvania newspapers. Pinchot sent a newsy mimeographed letter to two thousand people and added special footnotes to a good many of them asking about the political situation.[52] Stahlnecker, at home, selected a list of persons to receive more personalized letters and postcards.[53]

Before Pinchot left the United States, one of his advisers had been collecting information on the relation of public utility companies to the political control of state government. Because Pinchot earnestly wished the study to be completed by the time he returned, he prodded repeatedly. "The most important thing I have in mind," he wrote to Stahlnecker from aboard the *Mary Pinchot*, "is that description of the POLITICAL CONTROL OF STATES which you are working on with Einar [Barfod] and Harry [Slattery]."[54] It became increasingly clear that Pinchot wanted to continue his attacks on the abuses of power by the public utilities when he returned to the United States. Slattery, to whom Pinchot was paying a salary equal to Stahlnecker's, kept the traveler well informed by letter of the general situation in the nation and the more specific news on power, forestry, and prohibition.

Stahlnecker, on the other hand, supplied the information on the political situation in Pennsylvania. Mrs. Pinchot, apparently without the knowledge of her husband, wrote from Balboa asking his opinion of the prospects of Pinchot's running for office again.[55] Her letter crossed one already sent by his secretary assuring Pinchot of wide support and urging him to run for governor. Reporting that resentment against the Pennsylvania Public Service Commission was intense, he advised the ex-Governor to make utilities the paramount issue and to relegate the dry question to the background.[56] "My interest in what you have written," replied Pinchot, "is so great that I have temporarily lost interest in the trip because of it."[57]

The cruise of the *Mary Pinchot*, including stops at the Galapagos, the Marquesas, and the Tuamotu Islands, and at Tahiti, was the sort of story-book adventure that received generous publicity. Only a few days before it was over, pictures of the trip, including one of Pinchot in a handsome beard, appeared in the rotogravure section of the Sunday *New York Times*.[58] The Plaza Theater in New York City, during the week of July 26, 1930, featured, in addition to Maurice Chevalier and Claudette Colbert in "The Big Pond," an hour-long "talking picture" of "Mr. and Mrs. Gifford Pinchot in their Cruise of the South Seas." At the same time Celebrities Management, Inc., was announcing the availability of Pinchot as a lecturer on his expedition, with motion pictures and colored slides.

Pinchot's book, *To the South Seas*, received favorable reviews. Written with simplicity, charm, and humor, it sold almost 8,000 copies before the end of 1930.

During the cruise Pinchot kept a list of items to take along on the *Mary Pinchot*'s next trip, but the second trip never took place. Maintaining a large boat was an expensive luxury. Not only had the initial trip cost him more than estimated, but the stock market crash and the accompanying depression were hitting him hard financially. Deciding to sell the boat, he spoke of a "sacrifice" price of $75,000. But the market for 148-foot schooners in 1930-1931 was anything but brisk. First reducing his price to $65,000, he finally sold her for $19,000.

Pinchot's sentimental nature was revealed nowhere more distinctly than in reactions stemming from his trip to the South Seas. When he learned in 1937 that the ex-*Mary Pinchot* had sunk near Honolulu, he wrote his informer that he had "great affection" for the boat, but that it was perhaps better to have her at the bottom of the sea than engaging in her recent occupation of delivering fish bait to Japanese tuna boats.[59] Six years after the cruise he saw the motion picture, "Mutiny on the Bounty." Writing a note of congratulation to the producing company, he admitted that he "choked all up over some of the shots of the 'Bounty' under sail."[60]

When Pinchot landed on the west coast, however, sentimentality took a back seat. Uppermost in his mind was Stahlnecker's advice that he run for governor.

CHAPTER 22

RUNNING FOR GOVERNOR ON HIS RECORD

GIFFORD PINCHOT was ready for energetic action soon after reaching the east coast. On his arrival, however, he spent a brief time in an institution in New York City trying to regain some of the twenty pounds he had lost on his trip to the South Seas.[1] Believing that the stock market crash "had taken a good deal of the paint off" Andrew Mellon and the regular Republicans, he thought he could "smell the beginnings of a new Progressive movement" which might burst into vigor very rapidly if an extended period of bad times followed. Optimistically he told one of his political advisers that it looked as if "the haughtiness of the old Gang was going to be quite considerably mitigated in the next few years," and that he wanted to be "present when the mitigating takes place."[2] Within two weeks of the crash, in other words, Pinchot was envisioning the reaction that came to fruition with Franklin Roosevelt's New Deal.

Looking to the future, he could picture himself emerging at the front of such a new movement. Although admitting to a number of persons that he would "like immensely" to be governor again, he was unwilling to run unless there was "a good deal more than an even chance of nomination."[3] Acutely aware that another defeat would be political suicide, he shied away from running for United States senator against Joseph Grundy, an apparently formidable candidate.

Although acknowledging that he found himself "constantly more interested in National work than in State work," he maintained that a second victory for governor over the opposition of "the Gang" would give him "a much wider hearing" than he could possibly have as a private citizen "to carry on the work I am interested in."[4] As had been his custom before plunging into previous election campaigns, he asked the advice of many friends. In the middle of December he frankly saw "very little demand of any sort" that he throw in his hat.[5] But the following month he was encouraged when a group of rural leaders at a Philadelphia banquet gave him an enthusiastic reception for a speech on utilities. "I don't want to make a fool of myself," wrote the wavering Pinchot. "On the other hand, I don't want to miss a chance of having a real pulpit again for four years."[6]

His chances of a possible victory were enhanced by the continued deep cleavage in the leadership of the Republican party in Pennsylvania. The struggle for power between Joseph Grundy and the Vare machine in Philadelphia was still as bitter as it had been when Pinchot ran for governor in 1922. Boss Vare was sponsoring for governor a respected Philadelphia lawyer, Francis Shunk Brown, who some years previously had served as Attorney General of the state. Grundy, determined that the state government must not come under the control of the Philadelphia machine, was backing the former Auditor General, Samuel S. Lewis. Although Grundy himself was running for the United States Senate, he was reported to have said privately that he was less interested in his own victory than in the defeat of the Vare candidate for governor.[7]

As soon as Pinchot on March 10 announced that he would again seek the governorship, the various political factions in the state began lining up their forces for the May election battle. William Vare pledged his support for governor to Brown and for senator to James J. ("Puddler Jim") Davis, President Hoover's Secretary of Labor. Once more, as in 1922, Grundy saw the hopelessness of trying to defeat an organization candidate for governor by running both a Grundy man and Pinchot. Within two weeks after Pinchot's announcement, therefore, Grundy's man Lewis withdrew. The Mellons in Pittsburgh, who could not stomach Pinchot, split their endorsement by backing Brown for governor and Grundy for senator.

Pinchot's electioneering methods resembled those he used in previous contests. Rubbing shoulders with as many voters as possible, he carried his campaign to the people with a man-killing schedule of speeches all over the state, supplemented by a series of addresses on the radio. Mrs. Pinchot campaigned for her husband, often using the film of their trip to the South Seas. Stahlnecker once more was manager.

The one big issue for Pinchot in the campaign was public utilities and the need for replacing the Public Service Commission, which he described as "the catspaw of the utility corporations," or "the sore thumb of Pennsylvania." Charging the Commission with "resolving every question in favor of the public utilities and against the interest of the general public," he pledged to replace it with a Fair Rate Board elected by the people.[8] The utilities, naturally, lined up solidly behind Brown and threw everything they had into the effort to defeat Pinchot.

The primary battle was fought with bare knuckles rather than padded gloves, and each side was willing to abuse the other. Mrs. Pinchot, for example, in personal letters to women all over the state, reported such rumors as Brown's cursing of a minister of the gospel. The Brown-Davis committee, on the other hand, accused Pinchot of responsibility for the scalding to death of two men; his "parsimonious program" as Governor, they reasoned, resulted in the explosion of an inadequate boiler at the state capitol. Neither Brown nor Pinchot, however, personally engaged in defamation of character. Pinchot, in addition to his constant pounding at utilities and the Public Service Commission, appealed to the voters to save Pennsylvania from the Vare "gang" which had picked Brown.[9] Pointing to his own record as Governor, he covered the state with the slogan, "One good term deserves another."

The striking difference from his earlier campaign for governor was his assignment of the liquor issue to the background. Advisers whom he trusted, sensing a cooling by the nation toward prohibition, told him that bringing the dry issue into the campaign might mean defeat.[10] He must have anticipated that some of his dry supporters would decide he was too easily influenced by the winds of public opinion. But as a politician interested in being the next governor, he could see no use in stirring up unnecessary antagonism by voters who liked Pinchot but detested prohibition. After all, he argued, he had a clear record on the issue, and the drys knew it.

Pinchot was disappointed at his inability to win support from some of the principal labor leaders in the state. Although John L. Lewis and other mine workers had helped him in his futile efforts to become United States Senator in 1926, they were not enthusiastic over what he had done for them in his first term as Governor. Notwithstanding his friendship toward labor, Pinchot had concentrated not on labor legislation but on prohibition, budgets, and reorganization. Now he was focusing his attention on utilities, an issue which did not have strong appeal to the workers. Brown, on the other hand, had delighted labor as Attorney General by his effective leadership in bringing workmen's compensation into Pennsylvania. Officers of the United Mine Workers like John L. Lewis and Philip Murray, therefore, although not hostile to Pinchot, supported Brown. The recently retired president of the Pennsylvania Federation of Labor took the more extreme position that Pinchot had actually double-crossed labor.[11] Perhaps partly as a result of his influence the Federation officially endorsed Brown over Pinchot.

Although there is no direct evidence to prove it, it may be that some labor support for Brown stemmed from a desire to back a winner. With both candidates more or less acceptable, there might have been some doubt about supporting a man who had been defeated twice in seven years. Be that as it may, the ex-Governor's strategy was to appeal to workers directly, regardless of the positions of their leaders. The results of the primary seemed to show that a good many rank and file union members voted for Pinchot.

There were two situations in the primaries which did much to strengthen Pinchot's position. One was the assistance from Grundy who was campaigning for the Senate. Although there apparently was no formal hook-up between the two candidates, Grundy's "sixteen-inch shells," as Stahlnecker called them, leveled against the Philadelphia city organization did Pinchot an immeasurable amount of good.[12] The Grundy forces had money, and they used a sizable amount of it in state newspapers to picture the Vare machine as a sordid outfit which was conspiring with General W. W. Atterbury, the president of the Pennsylvania Railroad and a member of the Republican national committee, to control the state. Pinchot, too, singled out Atterbury for strong attack. Hearing that the Pennsylvania Railroad was encouraging its employees to vote for Brown, he bluntly wired the General that "as [president of the company], you have no business in politics in this State." In addition, charged Pinchot, Atterbury "violated the rules of decency," as a Republican national committeeman, by interfering in a party primary.[13]

The second situation which arose was perhaps even more beneficial to Pinchot—the filing of a third Republican candidate for governor, Thomas W. Phillips, a representative of the wet forces. Because Brown supported the calling of a referendum to reconsider the prohibition question, he was unacceptable to strongly dry adherents, who were therefore certain to flock to Pinchot. It seemed likely that whatever votes Phillips could attract from the two major candidates would otherwise have been mainly for Brown.

When the voters cast their ballots on May 20, they nominated Davis by a three-to-two vote over Grundy. With one exception, the entire slate backed by Vare was successful. The early returns also showed Brown winning, but when the slowly counted votes in the rural areas were reported the lead shifted to Pinchot. True to form, Philadelphia buried Pinchot by giving him only 55,000 votes to 245,000 for Brown and 116,000 for Phillips. Brown won 5 other counties and Phillips won 1 county; Pinchot captured the other 60, including even the Pittsburgh area where he gave much of the credit for his victory to a friend on the county governing board who stayed on watch in his office to protect the ballot boxes and tally sheets against fraud.[14] Pinchot's total vote was 633,000 to 613,000 for Brown and 281,000 for Phillips. The ex-Governor frankly admitted, at least in later years, that he probably would have been defeated if the wet Phillips had not been a candidate.[15]

Still trying to recover financially from the unexpectedly heavy cost of his South Seas cruise, Pinchot found his campaign expenses a severe burden. The Pinchots themselves contributed almost all the money received by the Pinchot for Governor State Committee—Pinchot's share was $94,000 and Mrs. Pinchot gave $15,000. Each of them, in addition, gave $5,000 to the Pinchot committee in Philadelphia.[16]

Pinchot soon got the disturbing news that the Brown forces were not ready to concede his victory. In Luzerne County in the anthracite coal region, which had given Pinchot 26,000 more votes than Brown, the official ballots had been perforated in order to thwart the stuffing of boxes with bogus ballots. Brown's supporters, on a technicality, asked the court to throw out the entire county vote. Since Pinchot had won the state by only 20,000, an adverse court ruling could make Brown the victor. To prepare for the worst, Stahlnecker, with the greatest secrecy, had Pinchot's supporters file papers simultaneously in all counties in order to permit Pinchot, if he lost the case, to run in November on a new Square Deal party ticket. After several anxious weeks, however, the state Supreme Court late in August decided for Pinchot. By that time the incident had attracted enough attention to rate front-page stories in the nation's press. Pinchot had boasted that he could win in November, even on an independent ticket, and therefore claimed to be almost sorry to lose the chance to battle Brown again. "It's going to be a lot easier since the Supreme Court decision," he wrote, "but not half as much fun."[17]

Meanwhile, the Pinchot organization was retaliating by demanding a recount of the votes in 550 ballot boxes from seven wards in Philadelphia. In 75 voting divisions, not a single vote had been reported for Pinchot. To obtain a recheck the law required a deposit of $50 per box, which the court would refund only if substantial errors were discovered. The recount uncovered 122,889 errors in the 550 boxes; Pinchot gained 4,805 votes over Brown, and Phillips gained 5,405 over Brown.[18] All of the deposits were refunded. Eighty-five election officials were indicted. Such was the state of affairs in Philadelphia under the Vare machine.

Now that he was successfully nominated, Pinchot entered the election campaign fully confident of victory in November. His assurance was reflected in a letter he wrote asking to be excused from writing an article because the election, the inauguration, and the ensuing legislative session would take all of his time.[19] In September, moreover, it was reported that his Washington home was for rent. After all, Democrats never won state-wide offices in Pennsylvania. How was it possible, with only 676,000 registered voters compared to the Republicans' 2,660,000?

Once again, as he had eight years before, Pinchot attempted to supplant the current Republican state chairman with one of his own supporters. Chairman Edward Martin, a brigadier general in the National Guard, was too conservative and too much an organization man to suit Pinchot. Popular with the Pennsylvania voters, he was a strong believer in loyalty to the Republican party. Having been elected twice to state-wide positions, he subsequently served both as governor and United States senator. Although Grundy joined Pinchot in the effort to unseat the chairman, the two dissenters received only limited support and the state committee re-elected Martin by a vote of more than two to one.

The Democrats had chosen as Pinchot's opponent John M. Hemphill, aged thirty-nine, a Philadelphia attorney who was a leader in the movement for repeal of the prohibition amendment. He did not appear to be a strong candidate, although it was rather certain that the wet forces of the state would line up behind him.

Not many weeks went by before it was clear, however, that what one newspaper called the most exciting election campaign in Pennsylvania in more than a generation was beginning.[20] Pinchot and Stahlnecker began to realize that a rebellion was taking place within the Republican party. Representatives of Vare's powerful Philadelphia machine, backed by utility executives and other businessmen, and by wet Republicans, decided that they preferred Republican defeat to Pinchot as governor. Because many of them could not bring themselves to marking an "X" for a Democrat, they created a new Liberal party and placed Hemphill's name in a second space on the ballot. Pinchot still saw victory for himself, but realized he had a fight on his hands. Appearing for speeches in every county, he estimated at the end of the campaign that he had personally met 225,000 voters. A week before the election his tired voice was reduced to a whisper.

One by one during the campaign some Republican leaders deserted their party candidate. The chairman of the Baldwin Locomotive Works stated that "The utilities of the State will not tolerate [Pinchot] to become Governor."[21] General Atterbury even announced he was resigning from the Republican national committee because he could not support Pinchot;[22] signs were posted in his Pennsylvania Railroad shops advising, "Safety First—Play Safe—Vote for Hemphill." Indeed, a good many utilities, determined to rid the state of "Pinchotism," bent every effort in both the primary and general election to convince their stockholders and employees that Pinchot's election would be detrimental to business and result in fewer jobs.

Other business leaders—some executives of the Westinghouse companies, for example—spoke against him.

Martin, willing in the interest of harmony to overlook Pinchot's efforts to oust him, had the difficult task of trying to hold the party together. Since all the Republican nominees except Pinchot seemed certain of easy victory, the chairman's appeals to the voters concentrated on the need for voting a straight ticket. Especially disturbing to him was an analysis showing that in the primary 85 per cent of the registered voters in Philadelphia had gone to the polls, but only 46 per cent in the rest of the state; he therefore stressed the importance of a heavy vote outside Philadelphia to offset the city revolt.[23] Martin stepped into the middle of the biggest issue, moreover, by insisting that "There is nothing in the personal policies advocated by Gifford Pinchot . . . to which any fair public utility can object."[24]

Side by side with Martin in trying to hold the line for Pinchot stood Grundy. To help counteract the charges that the election of Pinchot would be "dangerous" for business, Grundy, as president of the Manufacturers' Association, spoke, for example, in Harrisburg before 300 businessmen summoned from all over the state by Martin.[25] Because many of the ex-Governor's ardent supporters were markedly antagonistic toward Grundy, Pinchot found his support embarrassing as well as helpful. Labor had no use for him. Pinchot himself had not hesitated on occasion to voice aversion to him; when a newspaper in the anthracite region of the state had editorialized that Grundy was the greatest enemy of organized labor on the continent, Pinchot sent a letter congratulating the editor for "hit[ting] the nail on the head."[26]

After Grundy's bad defeat in the primary, some of Pinchot's advisers urged him to cast off the "dead duck," and not run the risk of losing votes from his many friends who were dissatisfied with Grundy.[27] But Pinchot took the position that, once his platform was announced, he "could accept the support of anyone who was willing to endorse" him. He maintained, furthermore, that not many people "think that I am in any way under the influence of Grundy or anyone else."[28]

Be that as it may, "Grundy" became a campaign issue. Little cards were distributed around the state saying only:

G	O	P
r	w	i
u	n	n
n	s	c
d		h
y		o
		t

Grundy and his state-wide organization did in fact work hard for Pinchot. And the *Pennsylvania Manufacturers' Journal* rebutted the charge that Pinchot was an enemy of business by asserting that "The manufacturer, the mine owner, the store-keeper, were all in the end benefited by Pinchot's efforts" in his first term.[29]

This aid for Pinchot did not mean that Grundy had deep admiration for the ex-Governor. There probably was some truth in Pinchot's observation years later that Grundy had supported him "Because at that moment he hated someone else more than he hated me!"[30] Grundy's bitter attacks on the Philadelphia machine and on Atterbury for trying to take over the state lent support to this comment. But one can speculate that Grundy also was influenced to some extent by Pinchot's record of economy and good management in his first term. At any rate, the "Grundy group" cooperated effectively with Pinchot's manager—although not always in the open.[31] It was also interesting that the Mellon machine in Pittsburgh remained loyal to the entire party slate.[32]

Although the defections from Pinchot were heavy, there were also some counteracting defections from Hemphill to Pinchot. John McSparran, the Democrat who ran for governor against Pinchot in 1922, refused to support a man as wet as Hemphill and campaigned for the ex-Governor. By election time, indeed, at least three former candidates for governor on the Democratic ticket had bolted their party's candidate. President Wilson's Secretary of Labor, William B. Wilson, also announced for Pinchot. Similarly pleasing to the ex-Governor was a resolution of support by the Pennsylvania Federation of Labor, which had gone to Brown in the primary.

Pinchot, at the age of sixty-five—a time when many men are embarking on an easy life of retirement—rushed from county to county addressing large crowds. Ruddy and in good fighting trim, he fairly breathed confidence. His two prime targets were the utilities and the Philadelphia machine. Material for his utility speeches, much of it from the records of the Federal Trade Commission's investigation, was supplied by his paid informer in Washington, Harry Slattery. In his attacks he made little effort to pull punches for the purpose of assuring voters that he could be moderate. What he thought, he said. In a letter to every voter in Philadelphia he charged the Philadelphia politicians with all sorts of graft, and challenged Vare to publish his income tax returns. Time and again he accused the city machine of cheating in elections. A number of his friends, agreeing that he was telling the truth, but fearing a possible boomerang, questioned the wisdom of lashing so unmercifully at the Philadelphia organization.[33]

Perhaps more than on any previous occasion, Pinchot did in fact let his enthusiasm lead him into making a few extreme statements. His close associate on utility matters, Morris L. Cooke, pointed out, for example, the lack of any basis for his statement that gas and electric companies sometimes used meters registering too high.[34] While berating General Atterbury he again veered from accuracy when he stated that the Pennsylvania Railroad did "not pay one penny of local taxes on its vast real estate holdings in Philadelphia."[35] Faced with a photostat of a check for the payment of the railroad's tax of $1,442,000 to Philadelphia in 1930, he had to admit that the company was required to pay on office buildings and other real estate not directly connected with the railroad.[36] These deviations from precise truth were more than a little harmful to Pinchot's reputation, for they seemed to add credence to the allegations that his enemies had been making for a quarter of a century —often without justification—that he was inclined to accuse publicly before thoroughly checking his facts.

Pinchot, of course, had other planks in his platform in addition to his insistence on fair utility rates. Before an estimated 40,000 picnickers at a Grange outing he promised that the state would "get the farmers out of the mud" by hard-surfacing and maintaining

20,000 additional miles of rural roads. The wild cheering that followed the announcement assured him that he had a popular issue.[37]

The candidate, as in previous elections, tried to avoid aligning himself too closely with the regular party organization. One ceremony during the campaign from which he was conspicuously, but understandably, absent was the unveiling on the state capitol grounds of a statue of Boies Penrose. Both Governor Fisher and Grundy delivered speeches. All other state-wide Republican candidates (except Davis) were on the platform.[38] Although Pinchot frequently appeared with Martin at political rallies, he preferred where possible to go his own way. His independence was underlined by the active continuation of the Pinchot for Governor State Committee and the various Pinchot county committees. Although efforts were made to synchronize amicably the work of this organization with that of the regular Republican machine, it was probably inevitable, in view of the intense feelings both for and against Pinchot, that the two groups sometimes found it difficult to cooperate. Both Martin and Pinchot had to take time to smooth ruffled feathers among leaders in their respective organizations. It was also significant that Martin, as late as October 1, found it necessary to ask Pinchot for a contribution and to remind him that the usual gift from state candidates was $2,500.[39]

More people voted for the office of governor on November 4 than at any previous time in the history of the state. All the other Republican candidates on the state-wide ticket defeated the Democrats by around 250,000 votes in Philadelphia and a total of 900,000 in the state. Hemphill, however, received 357,000 in Philadelphia against Pinchot's 111,000. But Pinchot ran far enough ahead in 59 of the remaining 66 counties to elect him by a plurality of 59,000. Pinchot's total of 1,069,000 votes included 32,000 by the Prohibition party; and Hemphill's 1,010,000 included 367,000 votes by the Liberal party.

Pinchot's victory in Pennsylvania in 1930, together with Democratic gains which gave them a majority in the United States House of Representatives, might be interpreted as a sign of the rising national dissatisfaction which was to culminate a few years later in the New Deal of Franklin Roosevelt.[40] A more probable explanation of

356

Pinchot's triumph was, however, simply the personal appeal of Pinchot and the unsettled state of Pennsylvania politics. Whatever the significance, it was a fact that Pinchot, whom politicians had tended to discount after his overwhelming defeat for senator in 1926, was once more a force to be reckoned with in the state, and perhaps in the nation. Never before in the twentieth century had a governor come back for a second term in the Keystone State.

Josephus Daniels, North Carolina editor and former Secretary of the Navy under President Wilson, pointed with pleasure to the election of Senators Walsh and Norris on the same day that Pinchot was chosen Governor of Pennsylvania. "Tuesday was a cold day," he wrote, "for the candidates serving the power companies instead of the people."[41]

CHAPTER 23

GOVERNOR AGAIN

GIFFORD PINCHOT's successful campaigns in both the primary and the election attracted the attention of a good many citizens throughout the country. *Collier's* magazine devoted an editorial to "Gifford the Spotless" whom it called "not quite human" and "ascetic." Pennsylvania turns to him, it reported, "as something good for its soul after too much of the Vares, Mellons, Grundys and pious Peppers."[1] Within two weeks after his November victory, he was deluged with fourteen to fifteen thousand letters and telegrams[2] from an impressive and diversified list of Republicans, former Progressives, and Democrats. More than a few of the well-wishers thanked the Almighty for seating him again in the governor's chair.

Subsequent events demonstrated that Pinchot began his second Administration with four subjects uppermost in mind: first, the alleged control by the public utilities of the Public Service Commission; second, the worsening economic situation in Pennsylvania and the nation; third, the desirability of improving rural roads for the farmers; and fourth, the 1932 presidential election. If the Republican party would only heed his warnings and those of other progressives, it could strengthen itself by nominating a liberal candidate. If it did not do so, a third party might be able to seize the reins. In either case, could not the candidate be Gifford Pinchot? He was careful to say nothing publicly on this last subject. Mrs. Pinchot, who was always at least as ambitious as her husband in laying plans for his future, was also cautious; writing to Felix Frankfurter at Harvard for suggestions for Pinchot's inaugural address, she stressed in a handwritten postscript that it should not sound as though he were running for President.[3] But the wish unquestionably was there.

His inaugural address given on January 20, 1931 lasted a brief twenty minutes. At least a third of it dealt with utilities. "The task today," he intoned over a national radio hookup, "is to defeat the attack of the public utilities. Government by utility magnates must

not be substituted for government by the people." Most of the remainder promised to carry out the specific planks in his platform,
including "a Roosevelt Square Deal."⁴ Two features of the inaugural
parade were of particular interest to Pinchot. Contrary to all tradition, there was no marching delegation from the Philadelphia Republican machine. As a kind of balance to this boycott, however, was
a banner in the parade urging "Pinchot for President in 1932."

Compared with the cabinets generally selected by governors in
Pennsylvania, Pinchot's was light on political influence and heavy
on individuals chosen primarily because he believed they had ability.
A political debt was paid to Grundy by the appointment of Samuel S.
Lewis, who had withdrawn from the Republican primary, as Secretary of Highways. Recalling that Theodore Roosevelt had a Democrat in his cabinet, Pinchot chose his Democratic opponent for governor in 1922, John A. McSparran, as Secretary of Agriculture. Mrs.
Alice Liveright became Secretary of Welfare.

Both the Governor and Grundy had deep respect for the Attorney
General from the previous Administration, William A. Schnader.
Pinchot, having brought him into the state government as a deputy,
now asked that he continue as Attorney General. An able Philadelphia lawyer, he was liberal enough to satisfy Pinchot and conservative
enough to please Grundy. Pinchot leaned on him heavily for important decisions. George Woodruff, Attorney General in his first
Administration, continued as one of Pinchot's closest counselors under
the title, "Personal Adviser to the Governor on Public Utility Questions."

Before his term was completed, Pinchot elevated a second woman
to a cabinet post under unusual conditions. Miss Charlotte Carr,
serving in 1933 as Deputy Secretary of Labor and Industry, was an
aggressive friend of labor. The suits which she wore, coupled with
her short, straight hair, gave her a definitely masculine appearance.
Critics of Pinchot sometimes derisively referred to his "long haired
men and short haired women." Miss Carr, in battling side by side
with Mrs. Pinchot against what they referred to as "sweatshop conditions" for women in industry, collided head-on with Grundy who
vigorously denied published accusations against his own company.
The legislature became so antagonistic that they refused to vote funds

for the payment of the salary of the Deputy Secretary of Labor and Industry. But Miss Carr continued to receive her salary checks when Pinchot dismissed the Secretary of Labor and Industry and promoted the Deputy to the higher post.

Pinchot's experience in his first Administration had convinced him he was too lenient in allowing his opponents to continue working for the state. In the second Administration he was determined to weed out all active adversaries. Again requiring new appointees to take a special pledge to obey the Constitution of the United States, he added the clause, "and loyally support the policies approved by the people of this Commonwealth in the election of 1930." A conscientious objector to the battle against utilities, therefore, was not qualified to receive an appointment.

The Governor would not tolerate outright opposition by employees. A mother of thirteen children who pleaded with him to re-employ a son laid off by the Highways Department after eight years of service, received no sympathy from Pinchot. "[Y]our son," he reminded her, not only "worked against me during the 1930 campaign, but also . . . continued to express violent antiadministration views while holding an administration job. A state government cannot function properly when its employees are cursing it behind its back."[5]

Directing, however, that "employees of value to the work of the State Government must not be lightly discarded for political reasons,"[6] he incurred the wrath of a host of job seekers by protecting in their positions the technical employees who had not actively opposed him politically. With the rising unemployment brought on by the depression, the Governor was besieged by applicants for positions; by the middle of April, an estimated 100,000 applications were on file. His orders to his personnel secretary were that "No one must be appointed to any position who is not competent to fill that position."[7] In the face of the strong political pressures put upon the Governor's office, these aims could not always be reached, but Pinchot kept prodding his staff to maintain the higher standards.

Although Pinchot during the campaign did not place the same emphasis on his economy plank that he had eight years before, he did try to cut expenses. All department heads, for example, were ordered to report to the Governor on the number of telephones they could eliminate.[8] His order that state-owned automobiles were not to be used to transport state officials between their homes and the capitol brought an appeal from one cabinet wife for an exception because of her husband's physical condition; but Pinchot stood firm, "It costs at least $3000.00 a year to maintain a Cadillac car with a chauffeur. To put the question whether the taxpayers ought to pay that amount of money to bring any official to and from his work is to answer it."[9]

Marveling at the heavily increased load which was placed on a governor in 1931 compared to his first term, Pinchot estimated that he received twelve times as much mail as before. The job was markedly heavier, but Pinchot reveled in it. "No, it isn't so tough to be a Governor these days," he told ex-Governor Pardee of California. "It is the most interesting job I ever had, and while I could yearn about going fishing, I wouldn't be in private life right now for a raisin and a cookie and a stick of candy."[10]

His vigor amazed both his friends and enemies. Persons who walked beside him still spoke of the difficulty of keeping up. At a departmental picnic the sixty-six year old Governor won a seventy-five yard race with a much younger member of his cabinet. A year later he passed a test for a student pilot's permit. A companion on a hunting trip, not a particular admirer of the Governor, was astonished that Pinchot had more vigor than most men twenty years his junior, and was as "straight as an arrow"; most of the party slept in a cottage, and two of them in tents, but Pinchot "slept out on the ground, all wrapped up in a sleeping bag lined with lynx skins."[11]

Even before the state legislature began its 1931 session, it was certain that Pinchot could count on considerable support in the House of Representatives, but many members of the Senate were opposed to the things the Governor stood for.

Pinchot had to make an early decision whether or not to fight for the Senate's selection of a president pro tem friendly to the Administration. After inviting 32 of the Republican senators to confer with him (all but the 4 Democrats, and the 14 Republicans from the Pittsburgh and Philadelphia areas), he announced his opposition to the re-election of Senator A. F. Daix, of Philadelphia, as president pro tem. The Philadelphia machine, the Governor insisted, had, by bolting Pinchot's candidacy, "forfeited all claim" to put one of its members into this important position of leadership.[12] Republican state chairman Martin, eager to avoid a party fight, disagreed with Pinchot's stand and reminded him that the Philadelphia delegation to the General Assembly had already met in caucus and agreed not to interfere with his program. But the Governor bitingly stated publicly that although Martin claimed the election of Daix would not "menace" the Pinchot legislative program, "The General knows better."[13] The tiff was only one of many skirmishes in a running political battle between Martin the conservative and Pinchot the progressive. As the crucial vote was taken in the Republican caucus, over 400 persons stood outside the room waiting the verdict. Daix won with 24 votes to 22 for Pinchot's man. Most signs pointed to a rough road ahead for Pinchot.

Pinchot's struggle with the public utilities during his second term was one more dramatic chapter in a highly dramatic life. Shortly after becoming Governor, he appealed over the radio for listeners to send him all their complaints concerning utilities.[14] Within a week he received 1,200 replies. When he used some of this information on a succeeding broadcast to support his contention that electric rates were too high, the incensed president of the Philadelphia Electric Company, W. H. Taylor, ran a full-page advertisement charging him with spreading information "grossly in error."[15]

Unquestionably a number of people in Pennsylvania, and throughout the nation, were receptive to suggestions that utilities were not only charging unreasonable rates but engaging in high pressure lobbying in order to resist regulation. The basis for these suspicions could not be laid entirely at Pinchot's door, although he fanned the flame incessantly. Revelations by the Federal Trade Commission and the Federal Power Commission had suggested that some utilities, and the holding companies over them, were at serious fault. The collapse of the Insull empire in 1932 helped to confirm the charges that part of the utility industry was in great measure overcapitalized. Within Pennsylvania, moreover, there was a growing realization that vigorous regulation of the utilities in the state could not be expected from the Public Service Commission as then constituted.

Pinchot soon proposed an investigation of utilities and their rates and practices, to be conducted by a joint committee composed of an equal number of members selected by the president pro tem of the Senate, the speaker of the House, and the Governor.[16] The House quickly approved, but the Senate provided for an investigation by a subcommittee of one of its own standing committees. "As everybody knows," sneered Pinchot, the Senate's inquiry "is intended to white-wash the public utilities."[17]

Unlike the rebellious Senate, the House was ready to follow Pinchot's bidding. By a vote of two to one it provided for a House inquiry into the subject and invited the Governor to appoint three nonvoting observers to sit with its committee. As one of the three, Pinchot chose his standby in utility matters, Morris L. Cooke. The majority of the House committee, as well as its chairman and counsel, were Pinchot supporters. This was, indeed, the Governor's own committee.

While the two committees were investigating, the Pinchot Administration introduced three bills in the General Assembly to do away with the Public Service Commission and replace it with a fair rate board having strong regulatory power. Contrary to the plank in Pinchot's campaign platform specifying that the board be elected, the proposed legislation provided for appointment by the Governor with the consent of the Senate, and for removal by the Governor alone. Some persons, therefore, although professing agreement that a new board was desirable, refused to go along with an agency so subject to control by Pinchot.

The Governor took every opportunity to berate utilities, the Public Service Commission, and the Senate investigators. Appearing in the Senate chamber before the Senate committee, he cited alleged abuses by utilities, to fortify his contention that the Commission was "worse than useless." Flaying the Senate committee, he held that so far it had "done little more than afford the representatives of the Public Service Commission and the public utilities an opportunity to testify to their own virtue."[18] When he finished his twenty-three minute discourse, the visitors in the packed Senate chamber gave him long and hearty applause.[19]

Although repeatedly telling the committee and others that he did "not advocate public ownership" of utilities, he was beginning to waver. "Unless the power people and the other utilities radically change their point of view," he wrote to a friend, "I see no outcome of the present situation except government ownership"; they were, he continued, stupid in their refusal to let regulation work.[20] Two years later he confided to Cooke that he was on the way to becoming "a public ownership advocate."[21]

In an address before a conference of state governors, in June 1931, Pinchot used the word "graft" in describing his charge that the utilities, by the device of writing up their valuations, were collecting in Pennsylvania each year $50 million more than a fair return on their investments. Even among his own advisers there was a difference of opinion on the desirability of citing a figure such as this which had to be based to a large extent on controversial estimates.[22] S. M. Vauclain, chairman of the board of the Baldwin Locomotive Works, quickly telegraphed every governor that Pinchot was misrepresenting conditions in Pennsylvania and making "misleading statements." Pinchot made no immediate rebuttal to Vauclain; "Nobody bothers much about the old boy," he wrote a friend, "and I think we can let the matter rest."[23]

The House investigating committee issued two reports. Signed by five of the seven members and approved by the three observers of the Governor, they supported Pinchot's program. The Public Service Commission, they maintained, had allowed excessive earnings by utilities, and had been "negligent in its duties, indifferent to its stewardship, and a menace to proper utility regulation."[24] Within forty-eight hours of the filing of the preliminary report, the House passed the three fair rate bills and sent them to the Senate. A "great and notable victory," said Pinchot.[25]

The story was entirely different in the Senate where five of the eight members of its investigating subcommittee favored not only retaining the Public Service Commission but also transferring to the Superior Court rather than the Governor the power to nominate and remove its members.[26] The full committee, after holding hearings on the three bills, killed them by a rumored vote of fourteen to eleven. "That's what I call service," exclaimed Pinchot, but made it clear that he meant service to the utilities.[27]

In the face of this defeat Pinchot promised to continue carrying his fight to the people. For the next two years in Pennsylvania there was waged the bitterest kind of a battle between the utilities and Pinchot. By means of the radio, the mails, the press, and personal appearances throughout the state, the Governor pressed his unyielding attack. At no time did he indict utilities with harsher words than in a message to the Senate in the summer of 1932. With no reservations, he stated flatly that "When public utilities are willing to substitute fair play for shameless greed, to stop playing politics for profit, . . . call off their lobbyists, quit their bribery, cease their extortion, . . . and generally act the part of decent and cooperative members of the Commonwealth . . . then the threat of public ownership which they so greatly fear will disappear."[28]

The utilities of course did not take the castigation without retaliating, but were every bit as aggressive in fighting Pinchot and his proposals as he was against them. The public service companies, for example, banded together to publish a thirty-four-page pamphlet analyzing and criticizing the Governor's fair rate bills; "Taking all the provisions together," it concluded, "they reflect a policy of governmental acquisition and of ultimate government ownership." Several utilities denied the accuracy of some of the Governor's figures. The president of a telephone company dispatched a strong letter to the senators objecting to the Pinchot bills.[29] The president of an electric utility sent weekly letters to residents of the Pittsburgh area defending utilities and insisting, as did most of Pinchot's opponents, that the agitation for lower rates was politically motivated; this same executive, quoted in Pittsburgh papers in an advertisement six columns wide, lashed Pinchot for "outdoing" the Soviets.[30]

The killing of the Governor's fair rate bills by the Senate committee was followed almost immediately by the resignation from the Public Service Commission of the member most obnoxious to Pinchot. Moreover, in about six weeks the term of a second commissioner would expire. Pinchot's main strategy, therefore, veered from the effort to install a new fair rate board, to one of gradually gaining control of the existing Commission through appointment of his own

men. Within a few months he filled the vacancies with two of his
followers, including the faithful Woodruff.

The morning newspapers of June 30, 1932, announced that a
bombshell had fallen into the utilities controversy. Two evenings
earlier, in the office of the Attorney General, a man claiming to have
been a former confidential secretary to the late Thomas E. Mitten,
head of the Philadelphia Rapid Transit Company, signed a statement
charging W. D. Ainey, chairman of the Public Service Commission,
with receiving $150,000 in gratuities from Mitten. On June 29 Pin-
chot sent the statement to Ainey with a notation that he would be
"glad to afford you an opportunity publicly to answer these charges"
on July 11 in the Governor's reception room.[31] Ainey vigorously and
indignantly denied the charges, "While I had not always agreed
with the Governor, I had sufficient confidence in him to believe that
he would not countenance or truckle to any blackmailing attempts."[32]

The charges created a furor. Ainey, aged sixty-eight, was probably
the most prominent and widely known public service commissioner
in the nation. He had served on the Pennsylvania Commission for
seventeen years, and as both vice-president and president of the
national association of commissioners. Earlier in the year he had been
re-elected president of the state Young Men's Christian Association.
At the hearing before the Governor, Ainey flatly denied all the
charges. Pinchot thereupon transmitted the reply to the Senate,
which on the same day appointed a committee to investigate the
matter in cooperation with the Attorney General.

Pinchot at first made no allegations himself, but merely passed
them on for study. Within a fortnight, however, he appeared before
the Senate with additional charges of his own. Quoting a letter he
had sent to Ainey that day, he produced photostatic copies of papers
to support his complaint that the chairman had permitted a utility
president to pay a hospital bill of his in 1926 in Baltimore, and
another utility man to finance his passage to Europe in 1927. Charging also that Ainey had acquired wealth not explained by his salary,
Pinchot scheduled a second hearing for August 8 to permit Ainey
to answer the new charges. "This evidence," Pinchot told the Senate,
"drags at last into the light an evil system long suspected in Penn-

sylvania but until now not definitely proved. This system includes the deliberate bribing of public officials as a method of doing business. . . . By this system the utilities succeed in charging excessive rates to the people and in securing huge profits for insiders." The Governor gave wide distribution to his address to the Senate by having it printed in a pamphlet entitled *The Power System Brought to Light.*[33] Reproduced on the cover was his prediction that "We approach the end of a long fight for Justice."

With unconcealed relish, Pinchot wrote on August 1 to Slattery, who was convalescing in South Carolina, "We are having a gay old time up here, and I think we have got Mr. Ainey cold."[34] The next day, however, six days before he was to appear before the Governor, Ainey resigned. Explaining his withdrawal by ill health—he had indeed appeared in a wheel chair before the House investigating committee—and his lack of money to carry on a trial, he categorically denied all the charges against him.[35] But Pinchot was not convinced; the resignation, he announced publicly, was "conclusive proof" that the chairman was "unfaithful and unfit." His acknowledgement of Ainey's letter was brief in the extreme, "Sir: Your resignation is accepted."[36] Only a month later, however, Ainey was dead.

On the same day that Ainey stepped down, the Senate's committee of inquiry was discharged and the investigation brought to a halt. Pinchot, therefore, soon appeared before the Senate again to "demand" (he chose the word carefully) "with all the vigor of which I am capable that the investigation should not and must not stop."[37] In support of his stand he quoted from the strong and widespread editorial comment in the state's newspapers insisting that the atmosphere should be cleared by further inquiry. The Senate, before it adjourned ten days later, created a new committee to investigate the Public Service Commission.

In the midst of the Ainey skirmish, Pinchot wrote to another member of the Commission, who had participated very little in its work, demanding his resignation for inefficiency and neglect of duty.[38] The commissioner unwillingly resigned. Because of the expiration of another man's term, Pinchot on September 1 had three more vacancies to fill.

Once again the Governor looked to his closest associates for candidates, and finally selected Stahlnecker and Clyde L. King; the latter he designated as chairman. Now, for the first time, he had a majority of the Commission. "It will be said," he admitted, "that I have put men in nomination who hold the same views on public utilities that I do. I have, and I make no apology for doing so."[39] Less than a month later he had five members when he nominated speaker of the House Goodnough to the remaining vacancy.

As his thoughts turned back to the hero he was emulating, he proudly stated to the legislature that "The reorganized Commission has put in force the principle of Theodore Roosevelt that it is the duty of a public servant to do whatever the public good requires unless it is directly forbidden by law."[40]

Clyde L. King, all things considered, contributed more than any other person to Pinchot's first Administration and the beginning of the second. Pinchot had the utmost confidence in him, and was extremely laudatory of his work, "You have collected our taxes with an efficiency never before approached, and your knowledge of the finances of Pennsylvania has worked out into estimates of unparalleled accuracy. I congratulate you with all my heart on your fine work."[41] Although King had resisted Pinchot's efforts to name him to the Public Service Commission, he finally was persuaded to assent.

Almost as soon as he assumed his new post, however, minor trouble arose between the two men. Apparently King thought of the Commission as at least a semi-independent agency, which certainly was not intended to be under the direct control of the Governor. Seemingly he had reservations, moreover, about some of the Governor's stronger statements against utilities. But Pinchot, acting as an overprotective mother, kept telling the new chairman what to do. On one occasion he merely asked King to read a particular letter at a meeting.[42] Again, he requested the Commission to clear its decks of business in order to handle a "petition from the anthracite region."[43] In December he asked that one of his bright young advisers be added to the Commission's staff.[44]

King, however, had a mind of his own, and a temper as well. The climax in their relations came when the chairman took a position directly opposite to Pinchot's by telling the Senate committee investigating the Commission that it could accomplish more good by helping to provide a smoothly-working Commission than by digging up "historical facts."[45]

Pinchot could scarcely believe his ears. Slowly his attitude changed from annoyance to full-fledged anger. The break came on March 9, 1933. Pinchot, lamenting a "deplorable change of front" which "pains me more than I can say," insisted that "Anyone who opposes a full investigation of the public utilities and their past relations to the Public Service Commission thereby puts himself squarely on the side of the public utilities and against the people."[46] King's reply accused Pinchot, among other things, of "hypocrisy."[47]

Within a week the Governor formally requested the Senate to withdraw King's nomination, but the Republican leadership, seeing Pinchot's discomfort, took no action. In further bitter correspondence between the formerly inseparable colleagues, each charged the other with false and unfair statements. "The change which has come over you," Pinchot wrote, "is completely beyond my comprehension."[48] It was inconceivable to Pinchot that a right-thinking man could strongly disagree with him on the utility question.

When the General Assembly adjourned early in May without having approved any of Pinchot's appointees to the Commission, their terms presumably were automatically ended. The Governor promptly reappointed all except King. King, however, announcing that what Pinchot wanted "P.S.C." to stand for was "Pinchot Service Commission,"[49] refused to budge from his position until the Supreme Court ordered his ouster at the end of June.

In his two terms of office Pinchot had named a total of seventeen men to the Public Service Commission. The Senate had rejected only two, but approved not a single one.[50] Each time the General Assembly adjourned, Pinchot appointed or reappointed persons who, unless confirmed by the Senate, could serve only until the close of the next session. Finally, on September 19, 1934, less than four months before the end of his second term, the Senate confirmed all five of the Governor's appointees. "Tonight," rejoiced Pinchot, "my long fight for a Public Service Commission owned by the people and not by the utilities has at last been won. I feel like giving not three cheers but five."[51]

Ironically, however, his appointees had but a limited time to demonstrate their regulatory prowess. The Democrats, placed in full control of the state government in Pennsylvania by the elections of 1934 and 1936, promptly abolished the Public Service Commission and replaced it with a brand new agency.

Without even waiting for his election as Governor in November 1930, Pinchot appointed a committee on unemployment, composed of some forty persons ranging from Senator Grundy to the president of the state Federation of Labor, to formulate plans for the relief of the jobless. For chairman he chose Clyde L. King and, for the key post of secretary, Paul H. Douglas, an economist and future senator from Illinois. But when the Governor laid his program before the General Assembly at the beginning of its 1931 session, public utilities took precedence over all other issues.

Within a few months, however, convinced that the economic situation was becoming desperate for a good many Pennsylvanians, Pinchot saw a need for assistance from the national government. The state had its hands tied by a provision in the state constitution setting the debt limit at $1 million. Another constitutional roadblock, according to an opinion of the Attorney General, permitted work relief but forbade the appropriation of money specifically for food, clothing, or shelter (direct relief).

First among all the governors, Pinchot publicly appealed for help from the federal government. In a dramatic speech in Detroit in August 1931, which attracted national attention, he told of little children in Pennsylvania who had "not tasted milk for many months," and reminded that "Communistic leaders are teaching them to hate the Government under which they go hungry." He was forced to the conclusion, he said, that "the only power strong enough, and able to act in time, to meet the new problem of the coming winter is the Government of the United States."[52] Forwarding a copy of the speech to President Hoover, he urged the calling of a special session of Congress to meet the emergency.[53]

Even if the state and local governments were able to do more, he maintained, it was desirable for the federal government to come into the picture, since, with its graduated income tax, it could take bigger bites from the wealthy. After all, he reasoned, the depression was "largely due to the over-concentration of wealth"; why should not the people who brought on the slump "carry at least their fair share of the load?"[54]

Two months after Pinchot's Detroit speech, with Pennsylvania figures showing one quarter of the normal working population out of work, it was evident that no early help could be expected from Washington. The Governor, therefore, called a special session of the General Assembly in November 1931 for the sole purpose of providing unemployment relief.[55]

Pinchot proposed that the wealthy citizens of Pennsylvania lend about $35 million to the state to be used for direct relief, with the understanding that after the passage of a constitutional amendment the money would be repaid, with interest, from the proceeds of prosperity bonds to be issued by the state. Each of several men in Pennsylvania, he told the legislature, was able, without depriving himself of "any comfort or any luxury," to carry the whole burden of direct relief through the winter.[56]

Three days after the General Assembly convened, he was in Washington asking Secretary of the Treasury Andrew Mellon for a loan of $1 million.[57] Pinchot told reporters that the Secretary promised to take the plan under advisement; Mellon announced that he declined.[58]

When Pennsylvania's Senator Davis offered the opinion that Pinchot should lend the million himself rather than run to Mellon, the Governor publicly announced his gross income for 1930 as $52,650.45, and promised to give one-quarter of it for relief.[59]

The members of the General Assembly, hardly enamoured of the Governor's proposals, were inclined to agree with General Edward Martin, State Treasurer and Republican state chairman, that no new taxes should be levied at this time.[60] Nor did they embrace a "mortgage of the future" by the use of prosperity bonds. Eventually they ditched the Pinchot plan and substituted a $10 million appropriation for the payment of direct relief through local poor districts. Pinchot was caustic, "Because General Martin and the Organization have put politics ahead of human need, many thousands of men, women, and children will go hungry and cold."[61] Although believing the bill unconstitutional, he did not veto it, but, on the "remote" chance that it might be upheld, allowed it to become law without his signature.[62] Within four months the state Supreme Court held the law valid and thereby established the authority of the state to spend money for direct relief.

Much of Pinchot's time and energy during the last three years of his term were consumed in efforts to persuade first Washington and then Harrisburg to provide economic relief. He tried first to get every possible cent of federal help, and then to squeeze just enough money from the state legislature to satisfy Washington that Pennsylvania was doing its share. No governor pounded more consistently or vigorously on Washington's door to obtain the various kinds of relief which the federal government made available.

Although the number of unemployed in Pennsylvania reached 1,132,000 in May 1932, many legislators and a large proportion of the general public were unconvinced of the seriousness of the emergency and of the real need for relief. Disgusted with such a "Pollyanna view," Pinchot resolved to dramatize the suffering. From the Governor's publicity office came a story of ten paroled prisoners who voluntarily returned to penitentiaries because of the depression.[63] And Pinchot told reporters how he had wired $17.90 to a justice of the peace to pay the fine of a woman jailed for catching a flicker and feeding it to her hungry children.[64]

Although the General Assembly met in regular session in 1933, Pinchot called it into special session three additional times from 1932 to 1934 to provide money for relief. But the legislature's idea of the best way to find additional money was to cut government expenditures. Inevitably relief became tangled in the running fight between the Governor and the General Assembly.

Those forces in the state in favor of a minimum of government were increasingly vociferous. For some months the *Pennsylvania Grange News* had been calling for a reduction in the cost of state government. *The Right of Way*, an organ of the Pennsylvania Threshermen, which formerly had given Pinchot strong support, now lashed at the "unbearable" taxes; the issue of December 1932 complained of a "528 per cent jump in school costs," and featured an article entitled " 'High Pay Boys' on Capitol Hill Get Same Fat Checks Despite the Depression." The Auditor General of the state

also contributed his piece, "Government has gone hog wild in governing. . . . The effort of the Commonwealth should be to meet the
needs of government, and not the needs plus the whims and foibles."[65]

In its drive to cut costs, the General Assembly, after voting a
decrease in salary for its own members, passed a resolution urging a
reduction for all government employees in the executive and legislative branches. Although the resolution merely recorded the sense
of the legislature, Pinchot vetoed it with a warm blast at the lawmakers. Reminding the public that the General Assembly, if sincere,
could actually have reduced the salaries of its own employees, and
that the judicial branch was specifically excluded, he expressed his
opposition to reductions for executive employees, whose pay level was
only slightly in excess of the rate paid in 1914.[66] Pinchot himself,
however, took a voluntary pay cut of 10 per cent.[67]

As Pinchot and his opponents in the legislature intensified their
fights over economy, utilities, and other controversial matters, one
of the Senate leaders became sufficiently infuriated to complain that
in "Gifford Pinchot are all the arrogance, self-will and danger of
Adolph Hitler."[68] The Governor hurled back one of the same words
when he vetoed a reorganization bill which would have weakened
the authority of the governor and curtailed some of the governmental
activities closest to Pinchot's heart, "This bill was conceived in political hatred and is the fruit of political arrogance."[69]

Throughout the session of 1933 the General Assembly threatened
to chip off portions of the Governor's recommended expenditures.
Each time that the appropriation for a particular department was
menaced, Pinchot sent out a call for help to the people in the state
who would be affected by the reductions. Although in the end his
budget figures were moderately reduced, the final appropriations
represented a victory for the Governor.

After the General Assembly adjourned, Pinchot admitted privately that it was the "toughest" session he "ever knew." The sixty-
eight year old Governor acknowledged that "when I got through
with it I was pretty well all in, but you can bet your boots and my
boots too that the opposition didn't know it."[70]

For about six months in the middle of 1934 the federal government paid practically the whole cost of unemployment relief in the

state. Although Roosevelt personally wrote Pinchot that he felt "very strongly" Pennsylvania should "assume a proper share of the burden," the Governor, pleading state poverty and explaining that the state constitution prohibited any new amendments of any kind before 1938, managed to postpone a showdown.[71] But when Washington threatened to stop its help until Pennsylvania carried more of the load, Pinchot summoned the General Assembly and asked for $20 million.[72] The legislature, in a session of only a week's duration, provided the money without imposing additional taxes. Pinchot had unaccustomed words of praise for the lawmakers, "The General Assembly has done its work promptly and has done it well."[73]

Pinchot unquestionably was sincerely solicitous for the unfortunate. He could not bear to have government stand by and see honest victims of the depression go without food, or clothing, or shelter. It is also fair to conclude that the Governor genuinely tried to keep politics out of relief. The initial state relief funds were turned over to local poor boards for distribution. Although some of these boards were effective, most close observers agreed with Pinchot that much of the money was "wasted or spent for political purposes."[74] In order to provide more state supervision and greater uniformity, therefore, the General Assembly created a State Emergency Relief Board to allocate state funds and to advise the Governor concerning the distribution of federal aid. Pinchot was chairman, but a majority of the board, including General Martin, were stalwarts of the regular Republican organization and unsympathetic with a considerable portion of "Pinchotism." In this instance, however, both sides worked in surprising harmony. While there were some differences, the gravity of the situation seemed to foster moderation, and political feuding within the Board was kept to a minimum. Pinchot, indeed, made a point of expressing before the entire legislature his "high appreciation of the cooperative attitude" of the Emergency Relief Board members.[75]

Of all the accomplishments of Pinchot's second term, perhaps the one of which he was most proud was "taking the farmers out of the mud." Before he came into office the more than 1,500 second class townships of the state were responsible for maintaining 73,000 miles of roads. Few of them were paved; some were little more than widened cowpaths. Carrying out his campaign promise, Pinchot asked the legislature to approve the state's taking over some 20,000 miles of these roads. The state, he reasoned, could purchase both materials and equipment more economically and build highways more effectively than the tiny townships. The General Assembly approved without a dissenting vote.

Promptly the Administration embarked on a program of criss-crossing the state with a network of paved rural roads. Pinchot insisted that frills be dispensed with. Of light construction, consisting of a layer or two of stone covered by an inexpensive bituminous macadam, most of them were built at a cost of less than $7,000 a mile, compared to the usual $30,000 to $35,000. Varying in width from 10 to 16 feet, they generally followed the contours of the land and required little detailed planning. By the standards of the next generation, they were far from impressive, but they served adequately to link the farmer and his market, and to carry the increasing number of rural school buses. "I am," said Pinchot, "for more miles of good road rather than fewer miles of faultless boulevards."[76] Thousands of farmers were eternally grateful for their emancipation from mud. A quarter of a century afterwards the term "Pinchot roads" was still heard in the rural areas of the state.

This road construction program became a significant factor in unemployment relief. In order to provide work for as many persons as possible, the Department of Highways used a minimum of machinery and a maximum of hand labor. To spread the work, each of two gangs was sometimes employed for three days a week, and individuals were limited to 30 hours of work in a single week. The wages paid were those prevailing in the community.

Pinchot directed that priority for work be given to needy persons recommended by the county relief boards. In letters to local government officials he asked to be notified of any instances coming to their attention of the selection of workmen on the basis of politics. His reaction to an application blank that came to his desk demonstrated he meant what he said; noting that the blank required a statement of the applicant's politics and sponsorship by two or more "responsible people" in his voting district, Pinchot called it "the most damnable thing of the kind I ever saw." In a letter to the political leader in the offending county, he reminded him that the Administration was making "every effort" to provide relief through work on the highways "entirely without regard to political considerations." Sharply he ordered that every copy of the blank be sent to him "at once for destruction."[77]

In the winter of 1931, the Highways Department, at the insistence of Pinchot, established several camps for men who could not obtain employment near home or who had no homes. In reply to persons who complained that tents were too cold for winter, the Governor explained that he had "lived in tents, and even without a tent, in zero weather enough to know that it is practicable."[78] Each tent, supplied and erected by the National Guard, contained six cots and a soft coal stove. A total of 85 cents a day was deducted from each man's wages for meals and lodging.

By 1933 the Governor advocated that the state take over the remaining 53,000 miles of township roads. Although the Republican state organization was opposed to assuming this additional burden, the proposal passed the House of Representatives. The Senate, however, blocked the plan. There is no way to ascertain how much the Senate's lack of enthusiasm may have resulted from reluctance to provide the Governor with additional favorable publicity.

During his first term Pinchot had shown a friendliness toward labor that was uncommon in political leaders in Pennsylvania. After four years in office, however, he had not thoroughly convinced the leaders of the labor movement that he was their sincere and unwavering supporter. As if to overcome the doubts that lurked in some of their minds, he seemed to pay increased attention during his second Administration to the needs and demands of the worker. In addressing the annual convention of the Pennsylvania Federation of Labor, for example, the Governor pictured himself as the champion of the workers, and prodded them to "go out and fight for [what you want] until you get it." In a straight bid for political support, he urged them to "stand by" their friends. "I am with you one hundred per cent," he pleaded, "But I can not put it through singlehanded, while you sit on the side-lines and chew gum. It is your fight even more than mine."[79]

Near the end of the 1933 session of the General Assembly, in a letter to 177 members of key legislative committees, Pinchot strongly urged old-age pensions, compulsory unemployment insurance, minimum wages for women and minors, maximum working hours, and more stringent prohibition of child labor.[80] Not only did the General Assembly decline to approve the legislation, but they eliminated or drastically reduced funds for mediation and inspection work by the Department of Labor and Industry.

Pinchot passionately blamed the Republican organization, and General Edward Martin in particular, for the failure to enact his recommendations. Addressing the Amalgamated Clothing Workers in Philadelphia, he charged that "Andy Mellon—the only man in American history to have three Presidents serve under him," was one of the "vicious swarm that sucks the honey from the flower of the labor of other men." His ardor even led him to aver that "The Jews in Germany today are receiving little worse treatment from the infamous Hitler than Jews and Gentiles alike of the working classes have received and are receiving from the Republican Organization of this State."[81]

Renewing his demand for social legislation later the same year, Pinchot received support from Secretary of Labor Frances Perkins, in Washington, who wired of the need for laws to supplement the New Deal's federal legislation.[82] General Martin, however, in addressing a caucus of House Republicans, pleaded for economy rather than "new fields of governmental activity."[83]

Although the General Assembly did pass old-age assistance and pension laws for the blind, other legislation, such as that for minimum wages and maximum hours, died in the Senate. When the session ended, the Governor, who had called Martin the "best helper the Democrats have" in their fight for control of the state,[84] laid the blame on his favorite target, "The special session . . . shows that sweatshops and the money lords still control General Martin and that General Martin still controls the Senate."[85]

The Governor displayed a special concern for the plight of the coal miners. Back in 1928, midway between his two terms, he had charged that the authority of the State of Pennsylvania was being used to break a soft coal strike.[86] Shortly thereafter he contributed $1,000 for the relief of the strikers.

In the early 1930's the coal business was continually beset by labor unrest. A sick industry, its prices, especially in the highly competitive bituminous or soft coal areas, were dropping. Profits were slipping. Wages were notably low. The workers, seemingly caught on a treadmill, commonly lived in company-owned homes and bought their supplies on credit at company-owned stores.[87]

Faced with a strike of the soft coal miners during the first year of his second term, Pinchot emphasized what he called the need for recognizing human rights and not merely property rights. Convinced that the use of the Pennsylvania state police by prior governors in strike areas had worked to put the state on the side of the employer, he proposed, instead, to place it "squarely on the side of justice and human rights."[88] Demanding neutrality, he directed that, except in cases of violence, the state police should "take no position, either for or against either side, in any strike."[89] To insure impartiality, the Governor also forbade any state policeman from receiving any "meals, stabling, gasoline," or other favors from either side in an industrial controversy.[90] When he learned that one officer stopped a group of marchers, he "called him down good and hard," and explained to the commander of the police that this man had "of course, no business whatever to prevent men marching peacefully."[91]

In spite of the state police, however, the 1931 strike developed at a few points into an armed battle which resulted in several injuries and at least two deaths.[92] Part of the disturbance unquestionably could be traced to the county sheriffs' practice of appointing as deputy sheriffs in the strike areas men employed by the coal companies. In addition, as Pinchot admitted in an off-the-record interview, a portion of the trouble was fomented by Communists who came into Pennsylvania and "shifted their men from one mine to another in trucks."[93]

Through representatives of his own office, Pinchot kept in close touch with conditions in the mining areas. When, late in 1932, they and union officials informed him that in some instances the very low pay of the miners was being cut still further, he issued a scathing attack upon some of the soft coal companies. Carefully refraining from damning them all as a group—a precaution he usually did not take when flaying utilities—he admitted that a minority of the producers treated their employees fairly. He alleged, however, that "Many coal companies" were "deliberately making matters worse" by "grind[ing] the miners to a level of poverty and despair never before known in the industry."

Charging further that these companies were making excessive charges for rent and for provisions in their stores, he gave the press an example of an actual miner's pay envelope which he called "not exceptional" (it was, in fact, similar to a number of others in his files). The period covered was the first half of September 1932:

Credits				Deductions	
7 wagons coal @	.77	$5.39		Rent	$5.25
9 " " @	.34	3.06		Tool sharpening	.25
2 " " @	.47	.94		Lamps	.60
3 " " @	.21	.63		Doctor	.75
				House lights	.50
		$10.02		Powder	.57
				Insurance	2.10
					$10.02
				Balance due—ooo	

"For 12 days," commented Pinchot, "this man got . . . nothing at all for food or clothing."[94]

In spite of some violence in the 1931 strike, the situation did not get seriously out of hand. By 1933, however, all signs pointed to real trouble in the bituminous areas. The industry was so depressed, Pinchot wrote President Roosevelt, that he saw no hope for its salvation unless the federal government stepped in to supervise it.[95] Describing conditions as "simply horrible," he told the President that even some of the miners who were working six or seven days a week had to go on relief.[96]

The United Mine Workers, encouraged because of a new friend in the White House, were bent on organizing the miners and winning the right to bargain collectively with the operators. Federal law now required such collective bargaining in all industries covered by the NRA and its blue eagle, but most of the mine operators were determined to stand firm against all inroads into their industry by unions. The core of the resistance was in the "captive" mines associated with the United States Steel Corporation.

In the summer of 1933 a strike at one of the captive mines, the Frick Company, began to spread. Soon thousands of Fayette County miners were marching, armed with pool cues, baseball bats, lead pipe, and some firearms. The county sheriff quickly enrolled a band of deputies armed with guns and tear gas. In a threatened civil war, there were shootings and clubbings on both sides. A request from the sheriff for a force of state police met with Pinchot's demand that he first agree to withdraw his deputies. After the sheriff, refusing to recall his men, issued a proclamation banning picketing, Pinchot at two o'clock in the morning ordered national guard troops to the strike area. Calling this a "new kind of martial law," the Governor issued the same kind of neutrality order to the troops that he had given the state police. Picketing was allowed if it was peaceful, but violence by either side was to be suppressed. At the same time, Pinchot obtained a written agreement by the union leaders to limit the time, place, and nature of their picketing.[97] Although sporadic incidents of rioting continued to occur, the general disorder declined. The president of the Frick Company, however, protested that his employees were still being prevented from working by outside violence and intimidation.

About 300 troops handled the situation for two weeks, and about 150 state police afterwards. Meanwhile, the Governor's efforts to bring management and labor together for discussion went for naught when the Frick president declined to sit down with the president of the union.[98]

On August 2, without saying a word to anyone, Pinchot flew from Harrisburg to Washington with General Hugh S. Johnson, who was attempting to mediate the dispute for the federal government; for several hours the state police and some other state employees were frantically trying to learn of the Governor's whereabouts.[99] Two days later the President, complimenting Pinchot as one of the intermediaries, optimistically announced that the strike had ended by an agreement to submit all disputes to a board of three appointed by Roosevelt. After some persuasion, including a formal proclamation by Pinchot,[100] most of the miners, temporarily at least, returned to work.

But peace still did not reign, and soon the strike was partially resumed. A number of the mine operators were, by Pinchot's standards, acting reasonably, but the captive Frick Company was refusing to recognize that any such organization as the United Mine Workers existed. Pinchot's wrath at United States Steel now matched his feelings toward electric utilities. A "private and confidential" letter to Slattery was bitter against what he held was the wish of the corporation to settle the strike by violence.[101] Associating himself with the ever-present image of Theodore Roosevelt, he intimated he was about ready to declare "full martial law" and, as TR was prepared to do in the early part of the century, to take over the mines and see that coal was produced.[102]

Speaking in the rain to several thousand miners in the center of the soft coal area, Pinchot complimented them on their behavior during the strike and lauded the union for the gains it had won for them. He was firmly convinced, he said, that "90 per cent of the shooting and head-cracking that [occurred] was due to the brutality of company-owned deputy sheriffs." The Governor nevertheless made a ringing appeal for peace. "Whatever else you do," he pleaded, "keep the peace. . . . I am your friend. . . . If you resort to violence then I am against you. I mean exactly what I say."[103]

The next day Pinchot wrote Roosevelt a detailed account of the rally, "You would have been deeply touched to see how these people believe in you. They had a parade four miles long, and it was dotted all over with pictures of you as the miner's friend."[104] Not until a month later did Pinchot get the news that pressure from high Washington levels had brought agreement by the captive mines to accept collective bargaining. The Governor immediately asked all miners to go back to work.[105]

Pinchot's animosity toward United States Steel and its subsidiaries, however, was not soothed by their concessions. "The miners have been simply wonderful," he wrote to his sister a few days later. But the "swine of a Steel Trust" acted "like nothing so much as a vicious small child . . . cheating, lying, and doing its level best not to prevent trouble but to create trouble."[106]

Pinchot now had a little more time to devote to a less thorny problem. It was obvious that the thirty-sixth state would soon approve the twenty-first amendment to the Constitution of the United States and thereby bring an end to national prohibition. To be ready for the change, Pennsylvania needed a new set of liquor laws. Two days after the 1933 election, accordingly, the Governor called a special session of the General Assembly to convene in the middle of November.

One of the major ways in which Pinchot's second term differed from his first was his relegation of prohibition enforcement to the background. Continuing to identify himself with the drys he accepted election in 1931 as a member of the board of trustees of the Pennsylvania Anti-Saloon League, and the following year as a member of the Allied Forces for Prohibition. He still wrote letters of encouragement to federal and state officials fighting their uphill battles to enforce prohibition.[107] But the old zeal was gone.

Six months after Congress legalized 3.2 beer in early 1933, the Governor prepared an address on "What Shall a Dry Do Now?" for delivery on the Pennsylvania State College campus. The extensive scratches and revisions on his original draft showed with what difficulty he found the precise words to explain his current stand. Although many persons believed his widely-heralded remarks made sense, some of the die-hard prohibitionists were sadly disappointed. He began by assuring his audience that "I am not only A dry, but I am dry." Citing his record, and his deep conviction that liquor was "a moral wrong and an economic mistake," he held that "Prohibition at its worst has been infinitely better than booze at its best." The gist of his position now, however, was that since the people of thirty-three states had already recorded their approval of the twenty-first amendment, repeal was inevitable; and the "business of the sincere drys from now on" was not to fight the decision of the American people but to work with others, including "sincere wets," to "keep down the evils of liquor."[108]

In accordance with his own formula, Pinchot consulted extensively with both drys and wets, Republicans and Democrats, and obtained some basic agreement on the principles that should be embodied in the new liquor legislation. The final proposals for a state monopoly system were presented by Pinchot to the General Assembly in the form of drafts of bills on November 13.[109] Only three weeks later, on the very day that the repeal amendment became effective, the legislature listened to laudatory remarks by the Governor of a kind they had not heard during his entire second term. Spirited opposition, especially on the part of a segment of the wets, had developed in the General Assembly to some of the Governor's proposals. But his basic suggestions, generally speaking, had survived. Moreover the General Assembly had acted with unusual dispatch. "I congratulate you upon an unprecedented achievement," said Pinchot. "You have . . . adopted . . . the best system of liquor control yet devised in America . . . you have earned the respect and the gratitude of your constituents."[110]

The Governor's sincerity on the subject of alcoholic beverages was occasionally questioned by his enemies. Both he and Mrs. Pinchot were aware of the rumor that liquor was stored in the executive mansion and on occasion felt obliged to deny it. Early in 1933 the gossip reached the floor of the state Senate—a member questioned the sobriety of Mrs. Pinchot at the time of an incident which took place in Newark, New Jersey. Although the attacks on both the Governor and his wife were stricken from the record, Pinchot made a surprise appearance the next day before the Senate. White-faced, and with tightly drawn lips, he branded the accusation as utterly false and demanded that the Senate "require the slanderer to produce his proof or make public reparation." Recognizing that the law did not permit him to take the matter into his own hands, he lamented that "I cannot properly horsewhip a senator, however much I may desire to, and however much the senator may deserve it." Completing his remarks within two minutes, he strode out from a hushed assembly. Following a brief recess, the senator rose to say he regretted the remarks about Mrs. Pinchot and "tender[ed] the Senate" his apologies.[111]

Partly because of these experiences, Pinchot was extremely careful to keep his slate clean with the new Liquor Control Board. Learning, for example, that the Board might be asked to purchase champagne from one of his distant cousins, he wrote the chairman urging that they buy from no one "even remotely connected" with the Governor.[112]

Throughout his term, Pinchot showed deep concern for the underdog and for the rights of minorities. An appointment to the State Athletic Commission gave a Negro the highest position ever held by a member of his race in the state government. When Pinchot was criticized, as he not infrequently was, for appointing a Jew or a Catholic to some high post such as the Supreme Court, he lustily defended himself by quoting Theodore Roosevelt in a similar situation.[113]

He was a particularly ardent champion of freedom of speech, even when it took high courage to defend it. After the University of Pittsburgh had dismissed a faculty member, allegedly for liberal political activities (although the head of the University denied this), Governor Pinchot, as an ex officio trustee of the institution, protested vigorously against "this denial of constitutional rights."[114] Since the University depended partially on appropriations by the state, Pinchot pointedly reminded the Chancellor that "academic freedom is a necessary condition for obtaining State aid. . . . If the Mellons want a school to teach their ideas, then let them support it."[115]

Some months earlier he had shown his attitude on academic freedom to be consistent in his reply to a suggestion that a professor at the University of Pennsylvania be removed because he was allegedly a Nazi propagandist, "We cannot put an end to intolerance by becoming intolerant ourselves . . . if academic liberty has been destroyed in Germany it is not for us to destroy it here."[116]

The Governor stood firmly on the same ground when dealing with Communism. He brought down on himself the protests of some Pennsylvanians, for example, when he granted clemency to Lazar, who had been convicted of violating an antisedition law. The defendant admittedly had voiced the Communist line in a speech advocating the election of the Communist party candidate for President in 1932. Believing that further imprisonment beyond the six months that Lazar had already spent in jail would have been "unwarranted persecution," Pinchot commuted the sentence. "I have no apologies to make for my action," he wrote the state head of the Patriotic Order,

Sons of America. "One of the fundamental tenets of our government has always been the right of free speech shall not be abridged. To imprison a man for publicly expressing his views on a political subject does not repress communism. It encourages opposition to the government, breeds hatred and disloyalty, and is thoroughly un-American."[117] Writing a letter on an entirely different subject, he once expressed the opinion that the "surest way to spread any doctrine" was to forbid people to mention it in public—"Even the savages, who perpetuate the names of their dead chiefs by forbidding the speaking of their names, have learned that fact."[118]

The Governor was annoyed by the occasional epithets of "Communist" that were directed his way. "A lot of people in this country seem to believe," he complained "that any time anyone stands up for one's rights that in itself makes him a Communist." He acknowledged that he got "frightfully sick" of the insinuations that because he supported the rights of strikers and the rights of free speech, "therefore I am trying to make this country into a dependency of Russia."[119]

Pinchot had to withdraw from the battlefield before the final legislative session of his term was completed. Struck by a severe case of shingles, he was in a New York hospital for almost three months. Experiencing considerable distress—"I felt as though I were wearing a strait-jacket made out of a red hot wire waste-basket"[120]—he lost twenty pounds.

While he was away, Mrs. Pinchot, to the consternation of some of the Pinchot opponents, took over much of his job. Although in frequent communication with her husband by telephone, Pinchot said later that it was she "who was running the State of Pennsylvania when I was laid up."[121] During his entire Administration, indeed, she worked closely with her husband and made innumerable suggestions concerning his speeches, appointments, and general activities.

In his final message to the General Assembly in the closing days of his term, the Governor voiced "special thanks" to his wife, "whose advice in this emergency was indispensable. Indeed throughout both my terms Mrs. Pinchot's assistance in dealing with the human side of government has been invaluable. In her the people of the Commonwealth have had an ally impossible to duplicate or replace."[122]

While in the hospital, sometimes signing bills or issuing statements for the press, the Governor received a great deal of publicity throughout the nation. *Time* magazine, for example, ran a picture of the large board which he received as a Christmas card bearing the inscription, "Shingle Bells! Shingle Bells! Shingles all the day! Merry Christmas!"[123] Flowers from President Roosevelt brought a wire from Pinchot saying that they and the thought behind them had "done me more good than all the medicines."[124]

With time to kill during his stay in the hospital, he returned to his avocation of writing light verse. Labeling them "Shingles Jingles," he composed, for example, the following verse at three o'clock in the morning: "I do not sing the flowing bowl,/Because the flowing bowl is cold./But I sing that which I had orter;/Good hot Croton drinking water."

During this period of enforced loafing, the Governor made a major decision—to run a third time for the United States Senate.

CHAPTER 24

ONE EYE ON WASHINGTON

BUSY AS Pinchot was at the beginning of his second term as Governor of Pennsylvania with utilities and relief, he still found time to look longingly toward Washington. Indeed his activities in both these fields were woven into a definite bid for a presidential nomination.

For two decades, on and off, he had heard his name mentioned in connection with the White House. Sometimes his hopes had risen a little, but for one reason or another the time had not seemed opportune, and his small trial balloons had been quickly deflated. But as 1932 approached, he went to strenuous lengths to call himself to the favorable attention of the voting public. Since he was sixty-seven years old in 1932, he must have realized that this was his last chance of running for President of the United States. He was convinced, moreover, that the American political pendulum was on the verge of swinging away from Hoover and conservatism toward more liberal candidates. As he said upon the death of ex-President Coolidge, ". . . he typified an era. That era is passing or has passed."[1]

Scattered suggestions of "Pinchot for President" began immediately after his nomination for Governor in May of 1930. As a good presidential candidate should, he belittled these early expressions of confidence. "Don't let anybody fool you about my having a chance for the White House," he wrote a friend.[2] "I have no political ambitions," he kept telling correspondents who sent encouraging comments. But there was no question that he had high hopes.

More than a little pleasing to the unannounced candidate was a national news release that appeared in a number of newspapers a few days after his election as Governor of Pennsylvania in November. Under the caption, "Mentioned as Presidential Candidates in 1932," were individual pictures and comments on: Franklin Roosevelt (re-elected Governor of New York); Gifford Pinchot; Dwight W. Morrow (newly elected Republican Senator from New Jersey);

and Herbert Hoover.[3] Less than a month later, however, Frank Kent, a political columnist, threw chilling water on the Pinchot "boom." Calling "this 'Pinchot-for-President' business" a "joke," he reminded his readers that Pinchot was too old, that since his enemies were in control in Pennsylvania he could not win his own state's support at the Republican national convention, that the most delegates he could hope for was 90 out of 1,100, and that he was too strongly anti-public utility and anti-big business to be nominated by the Republicans.[4]

The Governor, unable to deny that much of what Kent said about the Republicans was true, began to waver. Perhaps his best chances, after all, lay with a third party. To his friend Plunkett in England he admitted the general public's opinion that a third party in 1932 was "impossible," but, he argued, "I am not so sure about it myself." There was the chance, he believed, that the West and the South would combine in revolt against "the utility owned politicians" on both sides. Significantly he added, however, that "This presupposes that Franklin Roosevelt will not be the Democratic nominee. My own opinion is that he will not, but I have only limited confidence in my own judgment."[5] Six weeks later he reported to Plunkett his resistance to the efforts of his "enemies" to have him become an open candidate for the presidency; "you and I know what would happen to a man of my stripe in the Republican National Convention, and I am not in the least deceived."[6]

But hope would not down. Beginning in June 1931, although still professing no presidential ambitions, there was no doubt that he was in the pre-convention scramble. At the annual Governors' Conference that month, in French Lick Springs, two of the governors—Franklin Roosevelt and Gifford Pinchot—held the publicity limelight because they were recognized as presidential possibilities. Pinchot in fact threw away his prepared speech on "Timber Needs of the Future," which had been mimeographed for release to the press, and spoke instead on utilities. "We are facing a new threat to the rule of the people established by the founders of this Republic. The Public Utilities underlie that threat."[7] The *New York Times* gave Pinchot top billing over its own state governor the next day in a three-column headline which read: "Pinchot Attacks Utilities for 'Graft'; Urges Federal Rule before Governors; Roosevelt Hits 'Passive' Government." Nearby on the front page of the *Times* was a second headline: "Norris Hails Pinchot for '32; Prefers Him to Hoover 500 to 1."[8]

The *Pittsburgh Post-Gazette*, editorializing that the speech was "an attempt to appeal to the insurgent Middle West," labeled it as a "keynote" for a campaign—"His intention to challenge President Hoover's leadership of the Republican party is plain."[9]

Within the next few months Pinchot found time to deliver a series of major addresses from coast to coast. Probably the most dramatic and widely read of the speeches was the one already described which he delivered in Detroit in August 1931, on the subject of federal aid to unemployment relief. To mention only two others, he assured the Missouri Farmers' Association of his eagerness to have the ignored farmer get "his fair share of the pudding";[10] and before the League of Women Voters in Washington, D.C., he demanded that tax rates in the upper bracket incomes be increased.[11]

Envisioning himself, on a nation-wide radio hookup, as a kind of instructor in a brief course in economics, he explained that the basic cause of the current economic depression was the "selfish and short-sighted" failure of big business "to share with labor and with the consuming public the tremendous profits of mass production." The federal government, he demanded, should take active measures "to guide the economic affairs of this nation."[12] Businessmen shuddered, and further resolved that Pinchot was a menace. Each speech was printed in pamphlet or flyer form and distributed nationally to editors and other key citizens.

The Governor's personal files showed to what extent he was preparing for any political eventuality. In a folder labeled "Speech Material, Presidency" he had a proposed platform for a presidential candidate and a collection of slogans. In another folder were notes dated October 11 and November 4, 1931, which he had penciled on a scratch copy of a platform that began "If elected I will use the full power of my office. . . ." In addition he had listed the date of the primary in each state, the delegates to the previous Republican convention, and all Republican state chairmen.[13]

The Governor's staff enlivened their Christmas party by presenting him with a black sombrero and a large wooden ring in which to throw it. "A dark horse with a darker Stetson—/Will be the one a wise man bets on," they wrote. Earlier in the month he was enough of a national figure to be invited to the annual Gridiron Club (newspaper correspondents) dinner in Washington where he sat at a long head table between the Secretary of the Interior and the Secretary of Commerce.

Although encouraged by some 350 voluntary letters received from 44 different states and the District of Columbia (125 of them from Pennsylvania) backing him for President,[14] Pinchot was aware of his lack of support among the Republican party hierarchy. In a Lincoln's birthday address at Springfield, Illinois, he sounded bitter. If Abraham Lincoln was currently a candidate for President on his platform of human rights, he asked, "Where would he get with the controlling powers of the Republican Convention in Chicago?" Supplying the answer himself, he snarled, "He wouldn't get to first base."[15]

About this time the Governor decided to take a sounding of public opinion. Drafting a letter boosting himself for President, he asked his old friend Harold L. Ickes of Chicago to sign and mail it to an assorted list of Republicans throughout the nation. Pinchot agreed to pay all the costs. Ickes, who had tried to persuade Hiram Johnson to run, later said he was not enthusiastic over Pinchot's letter, but nevertheless agreed to send it.[16] The first half of the letter made the point that Hoover could not win, "not one Republican voter in ten wants President Hoover renominated and hardly anyone believes he can be re-elected." Then the "Ickes-Pinchot" letter continued, "I can see no reason why the Republican Party should deliberately run into a smashing defeat merely to satisfy one man's ambition. Why not replace a man who is certain to lose by a man who is certain to win? In my judgment Gifford Pinchot as the nominee of the Republican Party would carry the next Presidential election just as surely as Hoover would lose it . . . Pinchot offers the best chance for Republican victory next fall."[17]

Pinchot waited expectantly for the first batch of replies which Ickes sent him. But the results were far from encouraging. "They are so unanimously antagonistic," he wrote Ickes, "that it seems to me we might call a halt."[18] Not for another six weeks, however, did he make a definite decision. By that time the Pennsylvania primaries had come and gone, and Pinchot's candidate for United States senator, as will be seen, had been soundly beaten. Although it did not show in his everyday work around Harrisburg, Pinchot was downcast. A large number of the people replying to Ickes believed he had no chance whatever for the presidency. An analysis of some of the letters could be summarized roughly as follows: of the 168 Republican delegates canvassed almost all were solidly against Pinchot's candidacy; 100 college professors were canvassed with the same result; a very small number of businessmen, writers, and ministers favored his candidacy.[19] "I think," he wrote again to Ickes, "that the way things are moving it would be a pure waste of money to send out any more letters"; he requested him to send back the names and "let the thing go."[20]

Pinchot's cynicism concerning the two major political parties was never quite so marked as in the spring of 1932. In a harsh speech to the Young Republican Club of Evanston, Illinois, one month before the Republican national convention, he found little to choose between the heads of the Republican and Democratic parties. "Big business," he maintained, "is holding in its fat hand the reins of the regular organization of both Parties." Turning his attention to the Republican party, he charged that its national leaders were betraying both the American people and the principles of true Republicanism.[21]

As the Republican delegates assembled in Chicago in June, and renominated Hoover almost unanimously on the first ballot, the Governor sat on the sidelines in Harrisburg and explained to a friend how much he marveled at the willingness of the "dear public" to be fooled.[22]

From at least one point of view it was unfortunate that Pinchot was unable to free himself from presidential aspirations before beginning his second term as Governor. After all, he was probably too uncompromising an individual ever to have a chance of being President. In his efforts to attract the nomination he made statements which made many Pennsylvanians unwilling to follow his leadership. The ideas behind some of the things he was saying were markedly similar to those of the Governor of New York, but Governor Franklin Roosevelt made his statements sound more moderate than Pinchot's.

It is not suggested that Pinchot's strong statements against concentrated wealth, and utilities, and big business were primarily made to further his political ambition. They were, rather, in line with sermons he had been preaching for two or three decades. The change that became apparent in 1931-1932 was the lack of restraint he showed in where and how he presented them. Although usually willing to speak out plainly for what he believed, he had made some effort during his first term as Governor to refrain from unduly antagonizing his opponents. Now he appeared to criticize with greater vehemence and less caution. Many men seem to become more complacent with age, but Pinchot, if anything, was growing more harsh and uncompromising in his denunciation of the "rulers" of America. As long as Pinchot followed the will-o'-the-wisp nomination of 1932, those Pennsylvania legislators and politicians whom he attacked could offer a standard and telling rebuttal—that he was motivated solely by political ambition. There is no question, therefore, that his presidential aspirations to some extent limited his effectiveness in the first year or so of his second term.

Moreover, the results of two Pennsylvania elections in 1932 gave the Governor's opponents renewed hope that the Pinchot name had lost some of its political magnetism. In the Republican primary for United States senator, Smedley Butler, the Marine General who had performed so spectacularly during Pinchot's first term in trying to enforce prohibition in Philadelphia, was decisively beaten by the incumbent, James J. Davis. Pinchot, who had taken a strong stand for Butler, was disillusioned by what he thought was a lack of support for the General among the "church people." A comment to Ickes revealed his feeling of frustration, "Some cynic once said, 'The preacher and the pimp finally vote the same ticket.' The way I feel now I am not so sure he isn't right. The hold the over-rich have on the pious is something to make angels weep."[23] Mrs. Pinchot's solid defeat in her second try for a seat in Congress was no less disheartening to the Governor. Characteristically, however, his spirits soon rose again. Replying to a letter of encouragement from a political cohort, he hoped "the people" were beginning to appreciate what he had been trying to do. Optimistically he saw "brighter times ahead for all of us."[24]

Only Pinchot knew positively how he voted in the November election. Although not openly endorsing the Democrats' Franklin Roosevelt, he was in no mood for another term for Herbert Hoover. Reporting merely that he "voted for the majority of the Republican ticket,"[25] there is little doubt that he marked his ballot for Roosevelt. To Pinchot's mind, Roosevelt's resounding victory over Hoover (although Hoover won in Pennsylvania) proved the points he had been making. He publicly announced on the night of the election that the Republicans asked for defeat and got it. Addressing an open letter to all Republicans, he maintained that "You cannot convince the average man that all he deserves of the apple is the core." Pleading for a complete "reconstruction and change of purpose" he described his party as "badly asphyxiated by the poison gas of concentrated wealth."[26]

In view of Pinchot's utter disgust with the leadership of the Republican party, he must have found a letter received in November 1932 very attractive. He was invited to join the League for Independent Political Action which expressed concern over the concentration of "approximately 70% of the nation's wealth in the hands of 2% of the people." But the Governor shied away from political action conducted outside the two major parties. Informing John Dewey, the chairman, that he had read "with keen interest, and with not a little sympathy" the League's invitation to participate, he preferred to wait for two things: one, the "possible reorganization of the Republican Party"; the other, "Franklin Roosevelt['s] chance to show what he proposes to do."[27]

One might have expected that Pinchot, frustrated in his own aspirations for the presidency, would harbor some inner resentment toward the New York Governor who had eclipsed the Pennsylvania Governor. With considerable justification, Pinchot could have resented the fact that for long years he had been advocating many of the very things which Roosevelt was now popularizing under the name of a New Deal. If the resentment actually existed, however, it was kept well hidden. Pinning his hopes for a better America on the new President, Pinchot demonstrated almost surprising cordiality and loyalty. Writing to congratulate "Dear Franklin" on his election, he declared his confidence that the President-elect would render a "prodigious service" to the nation. Eschewing any desire for a "job or anything else except to be of use," he offered to "come a runnin'" to Washington if he could be of help.[28]

The Roosevelts and the Pinchots had been acquainted for a good many years. Cornelia Pinchot and Eleanor Roosevelt had gone to dancing school together as children. Back in 1912, when Roosevelt was chairman of the forest, fish and game committee in the Senate of the New York state legislature, he asked Pinchot to give an illustrated talk in the Assembly chamber. Two slides showing the dire effect of forest devastation in an area of northern China left a deep imprint on the minds of Roosevelt and other legislators in the audience.[29] In 1929 Pinchot felt he knew Roosevelt well enough to ask him to support his application for admission to the New York Yacht Club.[30] A few weeks before Roosevelt's inauguration, the Pinchots entertained Mrs. Roosevelt while she was in Harrisburg to deliver an address to a conference called by the Governor on malnutrition. The press widely publicized a "relief" meal which the hosts purchased at one of the community markets and served to Mrs. Roosevelt and some fifty guests at a total food cost, excluding the dessert, of $2.75.[31] A fortnight later, when Roosevelt escaped an assassin's bullet in Miami, Pinchot wired with feeling, "Thank God you are safe. This Nation needs you right now."[32]

As has been suggested, there was more than a little accuracy in the opinion of one Philadelphia office holder that Pinchot and Roosevelt had practically the same views on most public questions.[33] At a conference of governors called by Roosevelt at the White House two days after his inaugural, Pinchot delivered a speech in which he referred to such matters as increased purchasing power and a huge program of public works—all having a distinct New Deal ring.[34] Shortly after Roosevelt's nomination, indeed, the *Philadelphia Public Ledger*, under the headline, "Parallel Views Cause Alarm," had run side by side a series of strikingly similar utterances by the two Governors.[35]

After the nation had experienced six months of the New Deal,

Pinchot was satisfied that the Administration deserved support for its experiments, and that, if they failed, the country was destined for a more radical departure from its "traditional conservatism." To a New York attorney who was viewing the developments in Washington with alarm, he expressed his "frank opinion" that if the people could not have the right to work, or have enough to eat or wear "under our so-called Constitutional Government, they will have it some other way."[36] In a speech delivered on Pennsylvania day at the Chicago World's Fair, he praised the change taking place in America "from an unlimited monarchy to a really democratic Government."[37]

Meanwhile, Pinchot was conducting a mild flirtation with some of the leaders of the Democratic Party in Pennsylvania. Opposed at almost every turn by many of those in control of his own party, he solicited aid from the expanding minority. At the close of his opening message to the 1933 session of the General Assembly, he took cognizance of the 1932 election which had increased the number of Democrats from 22 to 65 in the House of Representatives which had a total of 208 members. "There are few things this Commonwealth has needed so much," he stated, "as a strong, intelligent, and constructive minority" in the legislature. "I welcome the presence of such a minority in the House."[38]

The future United States Senator Joseph Guffey and the future Governor David L. Lawrence were two of the Democratic leaders with whom Pinchot conferred during the legislative session. In addition, on at least one occasion during the final six weeks of the session, the Governor saw President Roosevelt on matters not divulged by the two participants.

Whatever the reason, an analysis of the votes in the 1933 General Assembly shows that the Democratic members, in controversies between Pinchot and the Republican organization, frequently were counted on the Governor's side. Shortly after the session ended, Pinchot sent an appreciative letter to "Dear Franklin," with a copy to Guffey, thanking him for his "personal help" in winning "several hot fights" in the House. The President, he wrote, "had good reason to be proud" of Guffey, Lawrence, and other Democrats in Pennsylvania.[39] Later, in writing Lawrence, he spoke of working "together for a progressive program," and claimed to have accomplished "a lot of things" that would have been "impossible without your cooperation."[40] The proof of the existence of a kind of alliance was Pinchot's willingness to treat favorably some patronage requests made by Democratic leaders.[41]

Pinchot saw more clearly than a good many of his fellow Republicans the reverse swing of the political pendulum which had already begun in parts of Pennsylvania. When Harold L. Ickes, now a Democratic cabinet member in Washington, expressed surprise at the size and enthusiasm of a Democratic dinner he attended in Pittsburgh, Pinchot wrote, "I think we are all going to be surprised over and over again at the power of the Democrats in Pennsylvania. It is a wonderful tribute to Franklin."[42]

While still in the hospital suffering from shingles, Pinchot early in 1934 announced his intention of running a third time for the United States Senate. His principal opponent in the Republican primary was the incumbent, David A. Reed. "Reed," said Pinchot, ". . . has run the errands and taken the orders of Mellon . . . and the steel interests long enough." Pennsylvania, he argued, needed someone to work with the President to restore prosperity instead of "snapping and snarling at his heels."[43]

After a trip to Florida to try to regain his strength, he formally opened his campaign scarcely five weeks before primary day. "I stand beside President Roosevelt in his fight for the forgotten man," he told the Republican voters.[44] Contrary to his prior campaigns, he had neither the time nor the energy to conduct a whirlwind tour around the state, but instead confined himself primarily to the radio and a series of addresses to larger audiences.

The main theme of the Governor's abbreviated campaign was that the Republican party had been led away from the principles on which it was founded, and that the nomination of Reed—a "breed of reactionary [who] has almost died out"—would assure the deliverance of the state into the hands of the Democrats in the November election. Reed, he kept repeating, was simply Andrew Mellon's messenger boy.[45]

Mrs. Pinchot did her best to compensate for Pinchot's lack of energy. Ardently she proclaimed her husband's cause by letters and speeches. Impulsively she hired a sleigh on rollers—pulled by a brown horse decorated with jingle bells—and rode around the Philadelphia City Hall displaying a placard, "Voters—Don't let Reed take you for another sleigh ride—vote for Pinchot."[46]

The Governor realized that he was fighting against great odds. He was not the type of man who campaigned well by proxy. Furthermore, in this election the Republican organization was solidly against him. Joseph Grundy, without whose support he had never won an election, was in Reed's camp. The *Pennsylvania Manufacturers' Journal*, a Grundy organ, was proclaiming that "Reed in the Senate Spells Prosperity for Pennsylvania—Pinchot Spells Poverty"; it was also claimed that Pinchot was an enemy of industry and not a Republican.

Although the Governor was supported by various labor groups, it must have been disheartening to have the Pennsylvania Federation of Labor at its annual convention table a proposal to endorse him officially. If he believed the Federation to be ungrateful, however, it was not revealed in what he said and wrote. One can only guess that he felt certain the rank and file of the workers would support him.

Senator Reed polled 600,000 votes in the primary to Pinchot's 501,000. Perhaps the most remarkable thing about the primary was the Governor's ability, in spite of the united and determined opposition that he faced, to win as many votes as he did.

In the Republican gubernatorial primary, in which Pinchot maintained absolute neutrality among sixteen candidates, his Attorney General, William Schnader, backed by the Republican organization, won handily.

The Democrats, for their part, nominated for governor George H. Earle, recent minister to Austria and a member of an old Philadelphia family. For senatorial nominee they chose Joseph F. Guffey, a long-time political leader in the Pittsburgh area. Both men had pledged allegiance to Roosevelt and the New Deal, and both won easy nominations.

Pinchot, in a number of letters to friends, blamed his defeat more on his illness than on anything else. Recalling that in one day in his

1930 campaign he made more speeches than in the entire 1934 battle, he declared it a "reasonable bet" that if he had been able to campaign the entire state "the result might have been different."[47]

After the primary, only eight months of Pinchot's term remained. He now seemed to be almost a man without a party. A national magazine concluded that his "exact political position lies camouflaged somewhere East of Democracy and West of the G.O.P."[48] It is clear that at this time some political overtures were made between the Governor and some Democrats. It is not so evident, however, who originated the overtures. Later in the campaign, gubernatorial candidate Earle charged publicly that at Grey Towers, shortly after the primary, both Mrs. Pinchot and the Governor "had the nerve" to offer him the "shameful proposition" of deserting Guffey, "to take on Gifford Pinchot as the Democratic candidate for Senator."[49] In a detailed reply Mrs. Pinchot presented her side of the story—that Earle instead tried to win Pinchot support by offering him a seat in the Senate.[50] Manifestly, Earle and she had discussed a proposal for a possible coalition between the Democrats and the Pinchot-Republicans. Who, if either, advocated it remained a mystery.

Pinchot, in private correspondence with President Roosevelt, threw his light on the charges and countercharges. In a long letter of recapitulation to "Dear Franklin" he recalled that "many months ago you suggested that I should run for the Senate with Democratic support." But, said Pinchot, this plan could not be carried out because, as Roosevelt had told both Pinchots, the Pennsylvania Democrats "were so certain of victory that they declined to consider any coalition."[51] Roosevelt, when he replied to this letter of Pinchot's, did not question the Governor's facts.[52]

Both Pinchots, undeniably, would have been happy to have the Governor change his prefix to Senator. Harold L. Ickes recorded that after the primary Pinchot placed before him on two or three occasions the suggestion of a ticket of Earle for governor and Pinchot for senator; he added that Mrs. Pinchot did the same by letter, by interview, and by telephone.[53]

By early September, however, the Governor apparently came to a partial meeting of minds with some of the Republican organization leaders. First, Pinchot announced he would not run for senator in the November election. Then the Republicans adopted a liberal platform which he hailed as containing "substantially everything I would have put in it if I had drawn it myself."[54] And in a special eight-day session of the General Assembly, uncommon harmony prevailed between Governor and legislators.

When it was announced subsequently that Pinchot would campaign for the Republican ticket in the coming election, some of his most devoted supporters parted company with him; agreeing with the unflattering picture of Reed that Pinchot had drawn in the primary, they could not see how the Governor could now support him for re-election. Unquestionably Pinchot had maneuvered himself into an awkward political position. Having for a year and a half been singing the praises of Franklin Roosevelt, he was now urging the re-election of one of the President's severest critics in the United States Senate.

During the last month of the campaign, Pinchot cheerfully attacked Democrats Earle and Guffey. As if to make up for his lack of vitality in the primary, he spent the latter part of each week stumping the state. He was in rare speaking form. Through his long years before the public he had developed an attractive presence on the platform. Tall, and still handsome, he usually kept his expressive eyes focused on the audience. Although taking few steps as he spoke, his arm and facial movements conveyed a sense of dynamic energy. He was not an arm waver, but frequently drew back his right arm and then snapped out his index finger to emphasize a point. His voice was "clear, ringing, and fairly high pitched"; pronouncing his words crisply, he spoke rather rapidly and somewhat jerkily. He was not a great orator as were Webster or Bryan, but he was unusually effective in holding the attention of his listeners.[55] Preferring short sentences, he maintained that these were all that the audience could grasp—especially in political speeches. His language and style were simple. Many times in his diary he commented on his own speeches; not easily satisfied, he as frequently graded them "poor speech" as he did "good talk." Like most vigorous campaigners, he had his own formula for saving his voice; between speeches he would allow a little vaseline to melt on the back of his tongue.[56]

Mustering all of his best speaking techniques against Earle and Guffey, and adding the spice of a little humor, the "old scout," as he often was called, thoroughly enjoyed going off to the wars. Referring consistently to Guffey as "two-thirds Joe" and to Earle (who was George Earle III) as "George the Other Third," he called the latter everything from "fool" to "greenhorn playboy" to "liar"; he received the same in kind.

More serious about Guffey, he repeatedly criticized the Democratic candidate's alleged past relations with Andrew Mellon, and questioned his "public character." He insisted he was for Reed merely because the Senator was the better of two bad bargains.

In answer to those who criticized him for seeking the defeat of two such strong supporters of the Roosevelt whom he continued to laud, he simply declared that "you do not hurt your dog when you kill his fleas."[57] To set the record straight with the President, he wrote a lengthy letter explaining in detail why he opposed both Earle and Guffey, but reminding that "In every one of my speeches in this campaign I have expressed my admiration for you personally and for your policies. . . . The special point I want to make . . . is that I am not fighting you."[58] The President's reply, however, gently rebuked the Governor for backing a reactionary like Reed.[59] Pinchot's vigorous campaign against Earle and Guffey also brought to an end the rumors that Roosevelt was planning to use the Governor as director of a vast shelter-belt of trees to overcome drought in the West.[60]

Neither Pinchot nor anyone else could hold back the Democratic tide in Pennsylvania. Both Earle and Guffey were seated. Not since the 1870's had Pennsylvania sent a Democrat to the Senate. "The Republican Party," declared Pinchot the day after the election, "must go progressive or stay bust . . . the American people are sick of the Old Deal."[61]

The second term had been a hard and lively battle throughout. Although accustomed to strife during most of his life, probably never before had Pinchot been more consistently bellicose. Usually he had been at odds with both the majority in the Senate and with the leaders of his own party.

In the four years of his term the legislature passed 1,591 bills;

Pinchot issued 430 vetoes, a higher percentage than for any governor since records were kept. Not every veto, of course, represented a serious fight. On one occasion, for example, the Governor found on his desk two different bills, one designating the wild honeysuckle and the other the mountain laurel as the state flower; quipping that presumably the General Assembly wanted "a state flower and not a bouquet," he vetoed the honeysuckle.[62] Generally speaking, however, there was much hostility.

As the final few weeks of his Administration slipped by, however, the Governor seemed to bury the hatchet. He and his wife, he told Pennsylvanians on the day before Christmas, "wish every one of our friends—and our enemies too—the very merriest" holiday.[63] In his final message to the General Assembly, delivered on New Year's Day, 1935, he proudly recounted his Administration's accomplishments, but the tone was definitely moderate. Although suggesting that if the legislature had passed the "progressive" legislation that he had proposed, the next Governor would have been a Republican, he expressed to the members his "very warm appreciation for many courtesies and much cooperation." When he closed by describing the past four years as "the most strenuous" but at the same time "the most fascinating" of his life, it was evident that the sixty-nine year old Governor left the scene with real regret.[64]

Reported to be in "rare good humor" at his final press conference, Pinchot stated that he had no future political plans, but looked forward to writing a book on his early forestry days.[65] On inauguration day, wearing a cutaway coat but insisting on his felt headpiece rather than a top hat like Earle's, he rode in the traditional open Victoria with the new Governor. As soon as Earle took the oath of office, Pinchot left the platform, while someone in the quiet audience called "So long, Giff."

If there were those who expected Pinchot to withdraw at this time and seclude himself from active politics, they did not know their man. The *Philadelphia Evening Public Ledger* realistically predicted that before long he again would make "the political atmosphere . . . sizzle and crackle." In the same editorial this paper, which was not an admirer of Pinchot, acknowledged that the Governor could recite a long list of "practical accomplishments for the good of the Commonwealth." Although Pinchot had made a host of enemies, there were still a good many people who would have agreed—though perhaps reluctantly—with the editorial's conclusion that "Taken all in all, it might have been just too bad if he hadn't been Governor during these last four years."[66]

One week after the inauguration, Mr. and Mrs. Pinchot sailed from New York on the *Stella Polaris* to the South Seas and a six weeks' vacation in Tahiti. While on the island, his political appetite was whetted by a letter from a secretary reporting that some of his intimate supporters believed he could step into control of the Republican party in Pennsylvania. Upon landing in San Francisco in April, he completely ducked all discussion of politics by stating that he felt "like a visitor from another planet."[67] As soon as he reached the east coast, however, he invited the Republican state chairman to lunch at Grey Towers.[68]

PART THREE
Active Last Years

CHAPTER 25

FORESTRY ONCE MORE—AND POLITICS

RETURNING from vacation in April 1935, Gifford Pinchot once again was foot-loose and free from all routine responsibilities. Although it seemed certain that he would devote a substantial portion of his time to matters political, he was eager to return to the battle for the protection of the nation's forests.

Occasionally, during his second term as Governor of Pennsylvania, Pinchot became aroused over some piece of legislation being considered in the United States Congress. Frightened, for example, by a bill proposed in 1932 to transfer to the states portions of land in the national forests, he circularized the newspapers of the country to warn against this "most dangerous attack on the [Theodore] Roosevelt conservation policy."[1] The truth was, however, that he found less time for either forestry or general conservation in his second than in his first term.

Six weeks before Franklin Roosevelt's inauguration, in response to a request from the President-elect for an outline of a forest program, Pinchot advised that voluntary private forestry in America, as everywhere else in the world, had proved to be a failure. "Neither the crutch of a subsidy nor the whip of regulation can restore it." He therefore drafted a detailed plan whereby the federal government would acquire large additional tracts of forest land. Undoubtedly the Governor would have been delighted to help with administering such a program. "If I can be of use," he ended his letter, "blow your whistle and I'll come a running, as I said before."[2] The President-elect apparently was not impressed with the feasibility of the total plan, but replied that the Governor's ideas of what was needed in the forests fit in well with his own plans for helping the unemployed.[3] Here was the germ of the idea of the Civilian Conservation Corps which did so much for the nation's woods.

Only five days after he left the governor's chair, Pinchot showed his yearning for action again in the field of forestry by sending a letter to the annual meeting of the Society of American Foresters apologizing for his recent neglect of the profession, but assuring the members that "From now on I shall have more time for forestry . . . my first love." Using the letter to reiterate his basic ideas about forestry—"the social purposes of forestry [are] more important than private profits"—he announced that he was "happier about the prospects of forestry than I have been for many years."[4]

Primarily responsible for this optimism was the man now at the head of the Forest Service in Washington, Ferdinand A. Silcox, an old-time forester and unusually able administrator, who was on the same side as Pinchot in many of the recurring debates concerning forestry. Since taking office at the end of 1933, Silcox had been in frequent touch with Pinchot. These two, along with a few others, had signed a letter in mid-1934 to the executive council of the Society of American Foresters complaining that the editorial policy of the Society's *Journal of Forestry* no longer represented the broad social ideas of the founders of the Society (i.e., Pinchot and a half dozen others).[5] Pinchot had been disappointed in the two most recent heads of the Forest Service, but saw the bureau under Silcox as "becoming again . . . the aggressive agent and advocate of the public good, and not the humble little brother of the lumbermen."[6]

Admittedly long out of touch with conditions in the field, the Governor, as he was still commonly called, persuaded two of his oldest and closest friends from the early Forest Service days, Harry Graves and Dol Smith, to join him in a six weeks' trip through the national forests of the West. Flying to Montana, they were met by Pinchot's chauffeur who drove them a total of 5,200 miles. The "three ancient derelicts," as Pinchot called them, were literally thrilled by the receptions they received from the Forest Service personnel, and by the condition of the forests. "What I saw gave me the greatest satisfaction," wrote Pinchot. "The service is better than it was when I left it and everywhere the forests are coming back. What more could a man ask?"[7]

Nostalgically he also periodically invited the Washington, D.C., chapter of the Society of American Foresters to meet at his home there and served the famous baked apples and gingerbread just as his mother had in the old days.

Although pleased with the national forests, he was equally displeased and discouraged over conditions in the nation's private forests. He was convinced that most lumber companies were talking more about the practices of good forestry than following them. "A few companies, no doubt, are on the level, but, in my judgment, not many," he wrote to a friend.[8] His vexation spilled over in a letter of 1941 to an official of the National Grange. Recounting that less than 15 per cent of privately owned forests had "any sort of practical forestry applied to them," and that 85 per cent were "still subject to unrestricted devastation, and all the evils which follow," he emphasized that even in the 15 per cent "only a small fraction" of the forest was treated as a crop. In other words, he complained, the efforts to secure a future supply of timber for the United States, "after more than forty years of begging and pleading, has failed. Forty years of urging the lumbermen to practice forestry of their own free will has come to practically nothing." Making his case for government control of cutting on private lands, he took a stand for federal rather than state regulation because it was "more honest, more effective, and fairer. . . . I believe that because I have been a State Governor for eight years."[9]

A sizable number of foresters, holding that Pinchot's accusations against the lumber industry were too sweeping, were inclined to believe that in his last years the ex-Governor was not fully aware of the progress being made in getting lumbermen to provide properly for reforestation. Although lumbermen still did not always follow the best possible forestry practices, the completely unscrupulous cutter of a few decades before was becoming the exception. But as long as more lumber was being cut than produced, Pinchot would never be satisfied—and this was the situation in the early 1940's.

With the advent of World War II, he became concerned, with considerable justification, that the trees were in danger of being carelessly felled in the name of winning the war. Working closely with the head of the Forest Service, he not only accused the Governor of Pennsylvania of allowing "butchery" in the state forests,[10] but sent a letter to the nation's newspapers appealing to their readers to ask congressmen to stop the needless national destruction of forests. Acknowledging that huge quantities of wood were needed to win the war, he pleaded that this was no reason for "killing the goose that laid the golden egg." Private cutters, when they harvested their crop, he maintained, should be required to leave the land in condition to grow more crops.[11]

Pinchot finally came to a parting of the ways with the American Forestry Association (to be distinguished from the Society of American Foresters, which he helped found). Although regularly accepting honorary membership in the Association, over the years he came to the conclusion that it was under the dominating influence of the lumbermen. The last straw, from Pinchot's point of view, was a 1943 issue of the Association's journal, *American Forests*, which not only published an advertisement by the National Lumber Manufacturers Association advocating state rather than federal control of private forest management practices, but also carried an editorial opposing federal control.[12] Pinchot, "mad clear through," privately characterized the editor as a "traitor to the cause,"[13] and sent his resignation to the president of the Association.

In a great many situations in his life, Pinchot displayed unusual perseverance. But never was he more persistent than in his determination that the United States Forest Service belonged in the Department of Agriculture. From the days of Theodore Roosevelt, there were persons who believed that the national forests should be lodged in the Department of the Interior, which supervised the national parks. Others saw a need for a new "Department of Conservation" which would unite all agencies, including the Forest Service, in this general field.

Every chief of the Forest Service from Pinchot on, however, has opposed a transfer from the Department of Agriculture. One of their basic arguments has been that since trees are a crop, they logically belong in the department that deals with farmers. Some foresters have feared, moreover, that their interests would be overridden in the Department of the Interior which administers large water projects. Also important has been the feeling in the Forest Service that as a subdivision of the Interior Department they would have to encounter more hostile congressional committees than under the present setup. Over and above these stated reasons, the Forest Service's satisfaction with the lack of interference in its affairs by the secretaries of Agriculture has been apparent.

To Pinchot, perhaps more than any of the others, it was almost an obsession that the bureau which he had nurtured should remain in the Agriculture Department. Based partly on his experiences in the days of Ballinger, he never trusted the Department of the Interior; even on the few occasions when he believed it was headed by a good Secretary, he felt that it was infiltrated with underlings who had little concern for the general welfare. He had once expressed the view to Senator Norris that the Interior Department had been notorious for incompetence and scandals for a long time. He believed, furthermore, that the Interior Department's "spirit is all wrong"—that it had been trained "to get rid of the natural resources owned by the Government as rapidly, and with as few questions asked, as possible."[14] For some forty years, therefore, he stood guard, ready to fight furiously anyone who threatened the transfer of his Forest Service.

Curiously, the Governor's greatest anxiety over a possible transfer of the Forest Service occurred after his old and good friend Harold L. Ickes, the self-styled curmudgeon, became Secretary of the Interior in 1933. At first the two men had nothing but acclaim for each other. Ickes had been extremely cordial in his congratulations when Pinchot was elected governor in 1930.[15] Pinchot was equally hearty in congratulating Ickes on his appointment. "Hurrah, Banzai. Three times three and nine times nine," he wired; with equal enthusiasm he told Roosevelt that it was a "splendid" appointment "in every way."[16] Even as late as 1936, the Governor was still friendly enough to inscribe in a book which he presented to the Secretary, "To Harold Ickes, whose courage, conscience, and common sense have made him one of the most outstanding servants of his time."[17]

But if Pinchot had an obsession for keeping the Forest Service in Agriculture, it gradually became apparent that Ickes had an equally strong passion to bring it under Ickes by transforming the Department of the Interior into a new department of conservation.

"Saw Harold," noted Pinchot in his diary in June 1935, "who is red hot to get Dept. Cons. I'm again [sic] it strong."[18]

Once more the Pinchot propaganda machine began operating. A letter to newspapers appealed for help "because the National Forests are again in serious danger." Maintaining that the record of Interior was "far and away the worst in Washington," he tried to soften the blow for Ickes by stressing that the Secretary was sincere and honest.[19] Before mailing the letter he warned Ickes it was coming; assuring him that he "hate[d] like the devil" to be against him, he insisted he had to follow his conscience.[20] Meanwhile, he worked closely with the Forest Service which secretly was doing everything possible to prevent its own transfer.[21]

For about a year and a half, while the proposal for the new department made little headway, the two opposing conservationists, crouched ready for battle, confined their combat to intermittent angry growls. Early in 1937, however, the President's Committee on Administrative Management (the Brownlow committee), which had been commissioned to make recommendations for the reorganization of the federal government, proposed the creation of a department of conservation and public works. From this point on, the Ickes-Pinchot feud was bitter.

Pinchot at first was pessimistic. After the President addressed some remarks to Congress on the subject of reorganization, Pinchot noted in his diary that the transfer now seemed certain. "Tough luck," he wrote, "after stopping it so many times."[22] Nor was he encouraged after a talk with Secretary of Agriculture Henry A. Wallace; it was, he wrote, "Perfectly evident he will make no fight."[23]

But even if the odds were against him, Pinchot resolved that the transfer would not be made without a struggle. In April 1937, speaking at the national convention of the Izaak Walton League in Chicago, he opened his attack. Although carefully assailing the entire concept of a department of conservation, he did not stop there. Aligning himself squarely on the side of the anti-Roosevelt groups who were fighting the entire Brownlow committee's report, he charged that the enactment of its provisions would provide an "utterly unjustifiable" increase in the power of the President. By raising the cry of dictatorship he hoped to prevent the transfer by defeating the entire set of reorganization recommendations. In this speech, moreover, Pinchot for the first time openly assailed Ickes. "What is behind all this?" he asked, and then replied, "The ambition of one man . . . [Ickes] has allowed his ambition to get away with his judgment . . . great power has bred the lust of greater power."[24]

The Governor spread the same message in other speeches, in letters, and in magazine articles. In his personal correspondence he referred to his old friend by such titles as "common scold" and "Huffy Harold." Ickes, who himself was no neophyte at name calling, contributed his share to the feud by issuing blasts which in his own diary he described as both "sizzling" and "savage."[25]

The tenacious ex-Governor tramped from office to office in Washington pleading with senators, congressmen, and even the Vice-President, to oppose a department of conservation.[26]

Early in 1938, after Congress decided to shelve the reorganization bill, there was a period of reconciliation between Pinchot and Ickes. The Governor, for example, broke the ice by expressing his delight at a "working over" which Ickes gave Hitler and the German Nazis.[27] Secretary Ickes, when Pinchot became ill a few weeks later, sent him a letter and a bunch of roses, and later paid him a visit.[28] The Governor was touched by the flowers; under his surface display of stoicism, he was actually a sentimental individual. Although too ill to answer his other mail, he dictated a letter of thanks to the Secretary, and asserted that "I am truly glad that, in spite of our disagreement on certain policies, our old friendship of thirty years is to be renewed."[29]

Ickes, however, steadfastly pressed for his department of conservation, and the still smoldering animosity between the two men once more burst into flame.

Meanwhile, President Roosevelt, apparently vexed at Pinchot for soliciting and sending to the White House a batch of anti-transfer letters signed by faculty members of forestry schools, wrote the Governor in January 1940 hinting that he might be leaning toward the Ickes point of view.[30] Pinchot, worried about the "Very sore letter from Franklin," took it to Supreme Court Justice Felix Frankfurter, who agreed that the President was angry but doubted if he would take any action.[31] To make doubly certain, however, Pinchot addressed an anti-transfer letter to every congressman and senator.[32]

After a series of contradictory rumors around Washington that the switch both would and would not take place, Pinchot finally was informed by newspapermen in February 1940 that the transfer was dead. Writing from his heart, he noted in his diary, "If so, thank God. I am profoundly pleased and relieved."[33] Because Ickes still tried to obtain pieces of the Forest Service's domain for his own Department, the feud continued. At one point Pinchot even referred to the Secretary as the "American Hitler."[34] But in the end the Forest Service remained in Agriculture.

Meanwhile, the Governor learned by the grapevine that Ickes was combing old government files in an "attempt to vindicate"[35] Pinchot's adversary of thirty years ago, former Secretary of the Interior Richard A. Ballinger. The bombshell fell in a lead article by Ickes in May 1940 in the *Saturday Evening Post* entitled "Not Guilty! Richard A. Ballinger—an American Dreyfus."[36] Asserting his desire to right a grave wrong, Ickes spoke of the "trumped-up charge" that Ballinger was an enemy of conservation. Maintaining that Pinchot had been moved by "a bitter, personal hostility" against Ballinger, he described the "Pinchot intrigue" as "one of the dirtiest in American history." Ickes, with the help of others in the Department of the Interior, had carefully gone over the records, but his interpretation of the facts was too one-sided to be just. He was correct in stressing that Ballinger was not a crook; but it was equally true that the former Secretary had seriously dragged his feet in conserving natural resources. As was explained earlier, any account of the highly complicated Ballinger-Pinchot controversy which finds all of the wrong on one side and all of the right on the other is bound to be an inaccurate portrayal.

The *Saturday Evening Post*, in its editorial comments on the article, referred to the current grudge fight between Pinchot and Ickes and quoted an appropriate remark by a former editor of the *New Republic*, "the facility with which idealists devise and spread slander is one of the mysteries of idealism."

A more detailed analysis of the Ballinger affair appeared simultaneously in an official government pamphlet, *Not Guilty*, issued by the Department of the Interior. Indicative of its bias was its state-ment that "the congressional investigating committee completely exonerated Ballinger," and its total disregard of the significant minority reports made by the committee.[37]

Pinchot's immediate problem was deciding whether to answer the magazine article. In any event, the details of the story were so intricate that the public was certain to have difficulty in grasping the significant points. Following the publication, moreover, he received only a handful of critical letters. Although he worked on a possible reply, Mrs. Pinchot, Louis Brandeis and others strongly opposed any public answer.[38] Amos Pinchot urged a reply.[39] The Governor eventually confined himself to mailing a five-page rebuttal to a few of his friends and acquaintances.[40]

Almost at the same time that the article appeared, Pinchot re-ceived from Ickes a twenty-eight-page letter packed with sarcasm, ridicule, and vituperation. It is difficult to see how Ickes was able to marshal so many biting nouns and adjectives to describe his former friend. Inferring, for example, that Pinchot had lost his early idealism, he recalled that a good woman, when she slipped off the beaten path, often sank to a state lower than that of a professional prostitute.[41] "[The] man must be almost out of his mind," Pinchot wrote to his brother.[42] Seriously considering releasing the letter to the press, he contented himself with typing a number of copies and sending them to friends.

Pinchot's basic objections to moving the Forest Service, however, applied to the Department of the Interior rather than to Secretary Ickes. As he wrote to Roosevelt in 1940, "If Harold Ickes were in Agriculture and Henry Wallace in Interior, I would still be em-phatically opposed to the proposed transfer."[43]

Although some observers were predicting a transfer of his alle-giance to the Democrats at the end of Pinchot's second term as Governor of Pennsylvania, he remained in the Republican camp. One factor helping to keep him on the Republican side was his continuing political ambition. He well knew that political success at the polls was difficult for irregulars. During these years he had been accumulating a folder of letters from loyal followers who still thought he would make a good presidential candidate in 1936. He knew his chances were extremely remote—a "ten million to one shot," he told a backer—but he continued to hope. He confided, therefore, at the end of 1935 that he was taking steps to get "a little . . . publicity."[44]

Seizing on an issue with wide appeal in the state and nation, he vigorously attacked the politics which he alleged had entered into the Works Progress Administration—the federal work-relief program—in Pennsylvania. Onslaughts against the WPA inevitably led to reflections on the President. Shortly before Christmas, Pinchot wrote Roosevelt, and immediately made copies available to the press, charging that the WPA in Pennsylvania had been "degraded into a Democratic pie-counter." Recalling the President's pledge to keep relief out of politics, Pinchot challenged him "to make the deed match the word" by dismissing the federal appointees managing the program in Pennsylvania.[45] Roosevelt, obviously annoyed, wrote a personal note objecting that the Governor's letter was general rather than specific. And he stated frankly that if Pinchot were not an old friend, the letter, because it was obviously a political play, would never have been answered.[46]

Unabashed, Pinchot dispatched another open letter to the President in January 1936 listing a number of quotations from specific letters in his possession, but declining to give names because it would put needy men "at the tender mercy of the political administrators of WPA." He maintained, moreover, that specific instances were not required, since "to convince a man that it is snowing, there is no need to number and describe each individual flake."[47]

Whether or not Pinchot was primarily seeking publicity, he got it. His charges received featured attention, for example, on the first page of the *St. Louis Post Dispatch*.[48] Anti-New Dealers quoted his letters with relish. On a nation-wide radio hookup, under the auspices of the Republican national committee, he spoke of the mess in Washington. Admitting, as he frequently did at this time, that he liked Roosevelt very much "as an individual," he called him "a frost" as a business executive.[49] "Franklin," he told a friend, "is about as capable of running the Government as I am of teaching Sanskrit."[50]

For a period of a few weeks in the spring of 1936 Pinchot devoted the bulk of his time to assisting his wife. Twice defeated for Congress in the district around Grey Towers, Mrs. Pinchot took the rare step of announcing herself as a Republican candidate for a congressional seat from a district in Philadelphia in which she did not live. Once again, however, the voters denied her a victory.

It is reasonably certain that as the date for the Republican national convention approached, Pinchot no longer was even remotely considering himself as a possible candidate for President. Both he and his wife, however—she perhaps even more than he—were harboring the hope that a turn of the wheel of fortune might point to him for Vice-President. Although he made no direct bid to the Republican convention delegates for their votes, he helped his wife prepare a statement of reasons for supporting him and saw that copies were distributed to a few key friends.

A few days prior to the convention, Pinchot was convinced that Alfred M. Landon would be nominated. Omitting any false modesty in his diary, he noted his belief that Landon could win the presidency in November "if I help him."[51] The next day he had dinner in Topeka with Governor and Mrs. Landon and William Allen White, who had reported that Landon was a Pinchot admirer. Although judging Landon "Not a world beater," Pinchot was pleased with the candidate. "Liked Landon decidedly," he noted.[52]

Despite Pinchot's talk at the beginning of the year of running as a delegate to the Republican convention, he eventually decided against it. Reasoning that it would be "poor business" for a dark horse candidate for Vice-President to put in any appearance, he did not even go to Cleveland in an unofficial capacity.[53] But Mrs. Pinchot was there to do what she could for her husband.

As soon as the delegates began to gather it was readily apparent that there was not the slightest chance that the political wind would blow in the direction of Pinchot; in the end it did, however, strike another Theodore Roosevelt Progressive—Frank Knox. Pinchot, who had realized that his chances were very slim, took it philosophically. The last of many unsuccessful efforts toward elective national office was ended.

Selected as the presidential candidate, Landon appeared to welcome Pinchot's advice and support. On two different occasions Pinchot was on Landon's special campaign train, and in one instance he sat on the candidate's immediate right at dinner.[54] While on the train, however, Pinchot felt a chill in the air emanating from the organization Republicans from Pennsylvania; he felt certain that they were "much put out at my being around."[55] Writing to Landon in August Pinchot reluctantly expressed the opinion that he had better not campaign for him in Pennsylvania.[56]

Pinchot, therefore, did most of his speaking in a half dozen midwestern and western states under the auspices of the party's national speakers' bureau. But even the national organization decided not to send him to Nebraska because he refused to speak there without praising Senator George Norris, a Republican now out of favor with the party's high command. Pinchot's cryptic comment in his diary was simply "How long, O Lord, how long?"[57]

In letters and speeches he hammered at the Roosevelt Administration. Maintaining that the people could "no longer have confidence" in the President, he flayed the "inefficiency," the "reckless extravagance," and the "mess" in Washington. He lampooned the "gay and festive way" in which Roosevelt "flits from flower to flower, starting and abandoning great projects."[58] But he disappointed the more fervent Republicans by periodically explaining that to be a member of the G.O.P. one did not have to attack Roosevelt for everything he did.

Two days after the smashing defeat of the Republicans (only two states for Landon), he jotted down his frank feeling, "I can't be very sorry."[59] Interpreting Roosevelt's re-election as a victory of the "many" against the "few," he felt vindicated in his preachments that the Republican party was out of tune with the times.

No sooner were the 1936 votes counted than Pinchot began to speculate on the coming campaign for Governor of Pennsylvania in 1938. Carefully sounding out opinion, he gradually became convinced that the Pennsylvania Republicans were in no mood to offer serious opposition to a truly progressive candidate in the primary, and that such a nominee would have a better than even chance of winning in November. He realized that he was getting older. His eyes, which had never been especially strong, now tired easily. Because of a touch of "arthritis" in one of his legs, he was ordered by a doctor not to walk more than one mile without a rest.[60] But he still possessed a remarkable amount of vigor for a man of seventy-two; as recently as the year before, he had even played some tennis. He was, indeed, getting bored with his relatively inactive life. Describing 1937 as "a melancholy kind of year," he acknowledged that "A good political campaign would furnish the right kind of medicine for me!"[61]

Announcing his candidacy in January, the Governor did not have to pretend optimism. Heartened by the size and tone of his mail (an "incredible" 10,000 letters, he estimated, in the first ten days), he believed his chances of winning were better than in any one of his past campaigns.[62] Even when a potentially formidable candidate, Arthur H. James, decided to run against him in the Republican primary, he remained unworried.

The results of the vote showed, however, that the former Governor had either overestimated his own popularity, or underestimated the recuperative powers of the Republican old guard in Pennsylvania, or both. Although he won 21 of the 67 counties, including most importantly those containing Pittsburgh and Harrisburg, his total vote of 451,000 was more than doubled by James's 938,000. Pinchot was both surprised and crushed.

The financial drain of the primary, moreover, was a substantial hardship for Pinchot. For the third time since the beginning of the national economic depression he was faced with heavy election outlays. Simultaneously his income had been declining. Since his retirement from the governorship, his own expenses had been paid out of capital. In 1933 he had found it necessary to discontinue his retainer to Harry Slattery in Washington. No longer was Stephen Stahlnecker on his personal payroll. Mrs. Pinchot was carrying much of the load; an itemized list of her contributions to the 1938 primary totalled $87,000.

In the November election campaign James received no help whatever from Pinchot. Indeed, a good many observers interpreted Pinchot's enigmatic statements to mean he was voting for the Democratic candidate. James, nevertheless, amassed a plurality of 279,000 votes and the Republicans were swept back into power in Pennsylvania. Pinchot's calculation that only a progressive candidate and party could defeat the Democrats was badly shattered. His feeling of frustration was very real. His next political move was unpredictable.

But some ten weeks after the election there began a series of events which precluded any intense political activity in the future. On leaving the Cosmos Club in Washington in January 1939, a taxi in which Pinchot was riding was wrecked by a trolley car.[63] Although doing him no bodily injury, the accident apparently contributed to a mild heart attack which he suffered a week later. He was able within ten days to sit up in a chair for twenty minutes, but the heart which had worked so vigorously for more than the allotted three score years and ten was tired. On Lincoln's birthday he had a second heart attack, and before long two other mild ones.

CHAPTER 26

SLOWED, BUT NOT STOPPED

HATING to admit any indisposition, Pinchot, as soon as he could write letters, notified some of his friends of the automobile accident in which he had been involved in Washington in January but did not mention his heart. To others he confessed a coronary occlusion, but insisted that the second attack was "nothing whatever but indigestion."[1] But he was overoptimistic. Not until five months after the original attack was he permitted to walk as much as 250 feet. Shortly thereafter he was driven from Washington to Grey Towers and soon was fishing in his beloved stream.

As it turned out, Pinchot still had seven years to live. They were of course years in which he moved at a slower pace. His eyes still sparkled, and sometimes there seemed to be an almost youthful spring to his step. He was elated when, on occasion, he could defy his age by displaying some of the old vigor. On one day, in 1942, for example, he drove from Washington to Harrisburg to give a radio talk in the afternoon and a speech to an audience of four hundred in the evening; returning to Washington at one o'clock in the morning he bragged the next day that he felt "like a fighting cock."[2]

Although reluctant to acknowledge it in public he was, however, feeling old. Vitamins and injections helped to keep him going. He also complained regularly in his diary of a bad stomach, nervousness, arthritis, eczema, and bad eyes.

While he was still taking it easy at Grey Towers the European situation was becoming more acute. Distressed over Hitler, he guessed, like so many other people, that the dictator was bluffing.[3] But when the war started in Europe he had no trouble in choosing sides. For his friend William Allen White he delivered a national radio talk in October 1939 urging revision of the neutrality law to permit the United States to supply arms to the Allies on a cash-and-carry basis.[4]

So excited did he become over some of the war news on the radio that one doctor thought it was contributing to his nervousness and eczema (although another M.D. thought Harold L. Ickes was a more likely cause of his emotional upset). As was to be expected, Pinchot did not hesitate to express his opinions about the war in letters and telegrams to the Secretary of State and members of Congress. He had only scorn for those isolationists who preached that the United States, being safe from any attack, should allow the Europeans to fight it out on their own. When Colonel Robert R. McCormick took such a stand in his *Chicago Tribune*, Pinchot sarcastically wrote him that "Every now and then in this world of imperfections a man comes across a statement so perfect and rounded in its wrong-headedness as to make it worth preserving."[5]

The day Pearl Harbor was bombed he recorded in his diary, without waiting for the full details, that not only the highest treachery had occurred, but also "the very ultimate in brass-hat dumbness, to be caught utterly napping."[6]

As a patriotic citizen he worried about his country. A month after Pearl Harbor he privately admitted that he was "confidently expecting" Washington to be bombed before the end of the winter.[7] In a six-page letter in March to his old friend Secretary of War Stimson, he analyzed the reasons for what he called the bad morale of the American people, and made suggestions for boosting it.[8] Along the same lines, he urged Secretary of the Navy Knox to appoint a Negro civilian aide to the Secretary and to take other steps to eliminate discrimination toward Negroes in the Navy.[9]

Fretting because he was not playing a more active role in winning the war, Pinchot was almost pathetic in his attempts to find some sort of job in the Roosevelt Administration.[10] When he received no offers, it seemed that the most he could do was to talk, to write, and to cajole.

But his fertile mind soon enabled him to make a useful contribution to the war. Always resourceful, he had frequently contrived to solve a problem by some new invention; while lying in bed after his heart attack, for example, he devised a tube to permit him to drink all the liquid in a glass without raising his head from the pillow.[11] In April 1942, however, he tackled a problem of far greater significance when, on a visit to Lewes, Delaware, he saw the survivors of three lifeboats from ships which had been torpedoed at sea. In one of the boats, which had been adrift for 13 days, 9 of the 20 passengers had died. The survivors attested that the greatest suffering had come from thirst. For several days, Pinchot thought of little else.[12] Remembering that on Tahiti the natives had chewed and sucked the juice from raw fish, he began experimenting with a beef-juice press and a deep sea fish, a red snapper. Succeeding in obtaining 25 per cent of the weight of the fish in juice, he found its taste sweet.[13] The Navy, interested in the idea, conducted tests and found that two men who for 10 days drank no liquid other than fish juice showed no harmful effects whatever.

The Navy also asked Pinchot to make recommendations for the improvement of fishing kits to be placed in lifeboats and rafts for the use of castaways. He and a quartet of other experienced fishermen worked out two versions of a kit which was adopted by the Navy, Army, Coast Guard, and Maritime Commission. Packed with each kit, on waterproof paper, was a set of instructions which Pinchot helped to write. "Fish is Food and Drink," it began.

The realization that, despite his age, he was doing something tangible to "win the war" gave Pinchot an immense mental lift. Proudly he wrote to ambassadors and ministers from the allied nations bringing to their attention the developments in fish juice and fishing kits.[14] The Reader's Digest paid him $1,000 for his story, even though it was rewritten to suit the requirements of the magazine.[15] And on his eightieth birthday, no letter of congratulation gave him greater pleasure than the one from H. H. Arnold, Commanding General of the Army Air Forces, who wrote that Pinchot's pioneer efforts in the field of emergency rescue had helped in developing equipment which not only built morale but aided in saving numberless lives.[16]

Pinchot's frustration and disillusionment over the election of 1938 in Pennsylvania made it difficult for him to make a political decision on the coming campaign for President in 1940. When Harold L. Ickes went to see the former Governor in 1939 after his heart attack, he came away with the understanding that both Mr. and Mrs. Pinchot were willing to get behind some liberal Democrat for President.[17] By the spring of 1940, however, Pinchot seemed to be at sea. The more he thought about "what may happen to the Republican Party," he told Landon, the "sicker" he got. "I wish to goodness that you might be a candidate again."[18] At the same time, he felt "strongly" that Roosevelt would not try for a third term.[19]

After the Republicans nominated Wendell Willkie, and the Democrats chose Roosevelt again, Pinchot described himself as "carefully balanced on the top rail of the fence."[20] From the very first he was skeptical of Willkie, who after all was a utility executive, a breed which he had often delighted in attacking. He found Willkie's acceptance speech "bold" but "otherwise *mediocre*."[21] A Willkie article in the *Saturday Evening Post* sounded to him like words uttered by "another plutocrat, accepting what progress has been made, but no more."[22]

Late in the summer, Pinchot was invited to lunch by Henry A. Wallace, the Democratic candidate for Vice-President, and was told that Roosevelt wanted to see him. Pinchot, in a mood for bargaining, told Wallace that he was interested in three things: no transfer of the Forest Service, the appointment of Earle H. Clapp as head of the Forest Service, and some sort of government job for Mrs. Pinchot.[23] Two weeks later he had his talk with the President. Apparently Roosevelt made no commitments of any kind. Pinchot, indeed, was "pretty angry," since the President, although cordial, talked mostly about the war. "But so far as his bringing up anything," complained Pinchot, "I might just as well not have come."[24]

The following week both Pinchot and his wife talked with Willkie at his home in Rushville, Indiana. Although Pinchot admired Willkie's "courage and great drive," and was pleased by the candidate's position against the transfer of the Forest Service, he had definite reservations.[25] Pinchot did not make his decision easily. For one who never before had openly advocated voting for a Democrat for either the presidency or the governorship of Pennsylvania, it was a hard decision to make. After listening to one more Willkie speech, however, he came away persuaded that "I can't be for him with any satisfaction," and two days later finally "decided for Franklin."[26]

Once again, on October 9, he saw Roosevelt and showed him

the statement that he proposed to issue in support of the President's candidacy. Apparently the President did most of the talking; "As usual," said Pinchot, "[I] had to break in to say anything."[27] As soon as he left the White House, Pinchot sent a wire, marked confidential, to several key friends. "After full consideration," he explained, "have decided to support man with experience and training. Stop. We cannot safely put green hand in charge of ship in this storm."[28]

Warned by a close adviser that he would be booed if he spoke for Roosevelt in Pennsylvania,[29] he nevertheless talked without incident at a large and enthusiastic rally in Pittsburgh and a few other cities. His mail, however, along with a good many letters of commendation, contained an assortment of disapproving messages that ranged from mild expressions of incredulity to abusive attacks against his betrayal of the Republican party. "I hope," wrote "A Good Republican," that "your soul rots in contrition the balance of your living days. Hell will take care of your hereafter."

Voting on election day for Roosevelt and "a majority" of the Republican ticket,[30] Pinchot and his wife wired the President, "May you the best man win."[31] Pinchot never regretted his vote. "The longer I live," he said a few months later, "the more sure I am that what I did in the last election was not a mistake."[32] During the remaining years of his life, Pinchot could not be neatly classified as an adherent of any one political party. Continuing to call himself a Republican, he did not hesitate to cross over to the other side with some regularity.

Pinchot's performance in the 1944 presidential election was largely a repetition of 1940, except that he more quickly came to his decision for Roosevelt. Even before the nominations, he indicated his position by his reply to a form letter, written by a former congressman and celebrated Roosevelt-hater, opposing the fourth term and New Dealers in general. "Apparently," sneered the former Governor, "you have not heard that we are at war." Charging that such people were doing "enormous harm" to the country, he insisted that at such a time "it is false, ridiculous, and unpatriotic nonsense to say that the present Administration is destroying, or permitting the destruction, of the American form of government."[33]

The Republican nomination of Thomas E. Dewey did nothing to entice Pinchot away from Roosevelt. Once again Pinchot visited the White House and pledged his support to the President. Admitting that he did not like everything Roosevelt had done, he asked if this was good reason for "taking out the pitcher who is winning the game for our side?"[34] Gladly he accepted membership on the executive committee of the National Citizens' Political Action Committee which was dedicated to the election of Roosevelt and Truman and a progressive Congress. One of its mailing pieces carried a group picture of four of its "leading liberal figures," including the organization's chairman, union man Sidney Hillman, C.I.O. president Philip Murray, former Governor Elmer Benson of Minnesota, and the seventy-nine-year-old Pinchot. Considering it "unwise" to join the C.I.O. Political Action Committee in Pennsylvania, which had endorsed all the state-wide Democratic candidates,[35] he became chairman of a cooperating organization, the Independent Voters for Roosevelt. In several speeches before political rallies and on the air he hammered home his theme that "Dewey will not do." And with help from the Democrats he wrote some 30,000 "old friends" presenting his case for Roosevelt.[36] After the returns were counted, Henry A. Wallace cheered Pinchot by writing that the former Governor and his wife had played a most important part in carrying Pennsylvania for the President.[37]

When, only five months later, Roosevelt was dead, Pinchot showed the depth of his feeling in a letter to a friend, "What a loss we have had! Or rather what a loss the world has had! For FDR was certainly the leader of the world toward better things."[38] There was no doubt in Pinchot's mind that Franklin Roosevelt's New Deal was the spiritual heir to Theodore Roosevelt's Square Deal.

Pinchot's embrace of Democratic candidates was about to become even more complete in 1946 when two men whom he had fought were nominated in Pennsylvania for United States senator—General Edward Martin by the Republicans, and Joseph Guffey by the Democrats. Less than ten days before his death he was working on the first draft of a statement, never finished, in which he planned to inform the voters that he was as "vigorously" for the election of Guffey as he was opposed to him in 1934. In the same proposed statement, Pinchot threw light on what sort of senator he himself might have been if he had ever been elected. "In practically every case," he wrote, "if I had been in the Senate in his place, I would have voted" as he did.[39]

Two birthdays in 1945 were especially pleasing to the Governor. The first was the celebration early in the year of the fortieth anniversary of the founding of the Forest Service. With great care he drafted a birthday letter for President Roosevelt to send to the Service.[40] Highly gratifying was the presence at the ceremony of Mrs. Roosevelt, who was one of the principal speakers. The Secretary of Agriculture and Pinchot also talked.[41]

The second birthday, his own eightieth in August, was an even more momentous occasion for Gifford Pinchot. A small luncheon party was held. The mails brought an avalanche of birthday wishes. But the most treasured birthday gift he received was a scroll and two large volumes of letters from the members of the Forest Service. Encased in two beautiful binders of material resembling wood, the letters were prefaced by a composite page of photographs and drawings illustrating the high points of his life. The Governor, who knew he had been a controversial figure among foresters, was deeply appreciative of the sentiment expressed in the scroll, "First and foremost American Forester . . . he set in motion those principles which will in no small measure determine the future history of our country. . . . Known affectionately as 'GP' by all foresters." Little wonder that Pinchot called this the "most notable birthday of my life (next to No. 1)."[42]

Throughout the last decade of his life, Pinchot, as always, was ready to battle every action which he considered an onslaught against forestry or the conservation movement. In addition, he continually strove for the attainment of two goals: first, a world conference on the conservation of natural resources; second, writing his book on forestry in the United States. Ever since President Taft had dropped Theodore Roosevelt's (and Pinchot's) plans for such a world conference, Pinchot had periodically tried to revive the idea. Although he presented the plan, directly or indirectly, to Presidents Wilson, Harding, Coolidge, and Hoover, nothing was accomplished.

Not until World War II did he begin to make headway. Then, stressing the slogan "conservation for peace," he argued that every nation's "fair access" to natural resources was "an indispensable condition of permanent peace."[43] After submitting to Roosevelt a proposal for a world conference, his dream seemed nearer to realization when he received a copy of a letter written by the President to Secretary of State Hull suggesting the possibility of such a conference and affirming the President's belief that conservation was indeed a basis of peace.[44] In addition, Roosevelt requested from Pinchot a proposed outline of a conference which he could take to Yalta for his coming discussions with Churchill and Stalin.[45]

Before leaving the country, Roosevelt authorized Pinchot to consult with government experts in preparing a more detailed plan for the meetings during the President's absence. "That was fine! Quite fine!" Pinchot noted in his diary.[46] Immediately he plunged into the job and was therefore well prepared when a White House secretary called to say that the President, now returned, wanted to see a copy of the plan. The next day, March 28, 1945, the Governor and his wife delivered the manuscript to the White House. "I have strong hope for a favorable decision," he wrote in his diary.[47] But only two weeks later, he learned "the dreadful news of the President's death."[48] The following month he was back at the White House discussing the conference with the new President,[49] and in December he personally handed Truman another set of plans for a meeting.[50]

Pinchot in effect got his basic wish, but only after his death, with the calling in 1949 of the United Nations Scientific Conference on the Conservation and Utilization of Resources. Indeed David Cushman Coyle in his book, *Conservation*, pointed out in 1957 that "The World Conference on Conservation, which Pinchot and Theodore Roosevelt planned . . . is now in full and continuous operation in the United Nations and its Specialized Agencies."[51]

Pinchot's second major conservation goal for the twilight of his life—writing his version of how forestry and conservation came to America—was to take the form of an autobiographical book covering

426

the years through 1910 and his dismissal from the United States
Forest Service. For years he had hoped to write such a book with
the help of George Woodruff, but his long-time associate had died
in 1934.

No sooner did the Governor return from Tahiti in 1935 than
he plunged into his self-assigned task with considerable relish. During his career he had done a remarkable amount of writing along
with his other activities; this new book, however, proved to be a
far more arduous undertaking than any of the others. The slow
pace was agonizing. More than once he referred to the "thrice ac-
cursed" book. Harassed with itching and nervousness, he pleaded in
1941 with a reluctant doctor to take him on as a patient. "I do
not feel that I am asking for this special consideration on your part
solely as a private individual," he begged; explaining that he possessed information "which no other man has," he loftily asserted
that the completion of his book would be a "public service."[52]

Although half a dozen people helped him assemble the facts, an
entire decade rolled by before the end of the work was in sight.
Increasingly engaged in a race with time, Pinchot was so engrossed
with his writing in August 1945 that his diary entry on August 6
sounded almost casual, "Atom bomb dropped on Hiroshima today."[53] Of more immediate importance to the author was the occur-
rence noted four days later—one day before his eightieth birthday—
"FINISHED BOOK!"[54]

When Pinchot read the last chapter before a meeting in Washington of almost 100 members of the Society of American Foresters,
it became clear that it was, as expected, a controversial book. Although the Governor believed that a majority of his listeners were
satisfied, he recorded that "some were very much against it."[55]

Although the book still had to be shortened, Pinchot with help
was able to get it practically in final form during the one remaining
year of his life. Published posthumously in 1947 as *Breaking New
Ground*, it was a vigorous defense of his point of view on forestry
and his stand in the Ballinger controversy. The reactions of foresters to the book tended to vary in accordance with their opinions of
the author. Despite a number of sympathetic reviews, the book was

attacked unmercifully in the *New York Times*—the conservationist chosen to write this review was none other than Harold L. Ickes.[56]

Throughout most of his life, Pinchot seemed to be desperately busy, whether or not he held a specific position. At any given time he was certain to be involved in many different projects. His final half dozen years were no exception. To the extent that his age would permit, he devoted many hours of his days to writing his book, protesting every assault that he detected on conservation, doing what he could to help win the war, and plunging into election campaigns.

He was constantly demonstrating, during this period, some of the characteristics which were so distinctly associated with his career. He continued to support with great vigor individuals or organizations that he believed were right. He brought a moral flavor to many of the causes which he chose to champion. "The longer I live," he wrote with apparent sincerity to a clergyman friend, "the more impressed I am with the need for Christianity and the Golden Rule, and the lack of it in our civilization. For that we are paying a tremendous price."[57] Frequently urged by his wife, he associated himself with a number of liberal organizations such as The Friends of the Spanish Republic and the Washington Committee to Aid the Families of General Motors Strikers. He personally signed almost 2,000 letters to newspaper editors urging the need for a permanent United Nations organization.[58]

Refusing to live only in the past, the former Governor showed a lively interest in new developments. So attracted was he to the Tennessee Valley Authority that in the fall of 1938 he made a special trip to see it first hand. Both he and Mrs. Pinchot were agitated over the development of atomic energy. Only a few weeks after the bombing of Hiroshima, a group of "about a dozen atomic scientists" met at the Pinchot home in Washington to dine and to discuss what ought to be done with the dreadful new weapon. Ever fearful of monopoly, the former Governor once more sent letters to a long list of newspaper editors and also wrote forcefully to President Truman pressing the imperative need for government ownership and control of atomic power in peace time as well as during a war.[59]

For more than fifty years Pinchot gave a great deal of thought to government ownership, but he had not been able to work out a precise philosophy on the extent to which it was desirable. Asked by an old Yale crony "just how far public ownership of natural resources and natural monopolies ought to go," he regretted his inability to give a "clear" answer. "That will have to be developed as time goes on," he replied. But he had "no question whatever" that the ownership of both "should go much further than it has yet gone."[60]

On many other questions of the day, however, he had exact and vigorous opinions which he did not hesitate to express with considerable force. Men often mellow with age and tend to grow more tolerant of other persons and other ideas. Only on rare occasions toward the end did Pinchot show any such inclination. One example of this trend appeared when he was asked as one of a group to sign a wire of protest to Prime Minister Attlee of England: he insisted on removing the words "illegal" and "infamous" to describe a British white paper.[61] But tolerance of his opposition was not an outstanding Pinchot trait, and he still seemed to obtain satisfaction from unbridled blasting. Fuming, for example, over an open letter written by a nationally known minister of the gospel opposing a proposal to place a $25,000 ceiling on incomes he notified the pastor that he would do all he could to "prevent the success of your utterly unjustified attempt to defeat the limitation"; he bitingly advised that "A minister of the gospel ought to be in better business."[62]

Pinchot could look back on his life with a feeling of satisfaction; he had indeed earned the wages which society paid him in advance in the form of his inherited fortune. He had contributed a great deal to Pennsylvania and the nation. Almost a quarter of a century after he served as governor, it was a common opinion among Pennsylvanians that, at least during his first term, he was the best chief executive the state had ever had. Any impartial student of government cannot help being impressed by the many steps toward good government taken during his Administration.

America's great debt to Gifford Pinchot, however, came from the zealous energy he expended in the interest of conservation. Had there been no Pinchot to build the U.S. Forest Service into an exceptionally effective agency, it would hardly have been possible to report in 1957 that "most" of the big lumber operators in the nation had adopted forestry as a policy; or that the growth of saw timber had almost caught up with the rate of drain on forest resources from cutting, fire, and natural losses such as destruction by insects.[63] Had there been no Pinchot near Theodore Roosevelt's ear, the Roosevelt conservation movement might never have been initiated. Many other dedicated persons contributed heavily to these accomplishments, but even some of his enemies admitted that Pinchot's efforts were indispensable.

Pinchot liked to quote the old southern minister who said that if the Lord told him to butt his head through a stone wall it was his business to butt and butt, and it was the Lord's business to bring him through. Nothing better illustrated Pinchot's own attitude toward the frustrations and setbacks that he suffered during his persevering "fight" for conservation.

In his great zeal and enthusiasm—for forestry, or prohibition, or regulation of utilities—he displayed on occasion some of the weaknesses common to crusaders. Too often he doubted the honest motives of those who opposed him. Having faced savage fighting early in the century from exploiters who wanted no conservation whatsoever, he was conditioned to suspect his opponents of greediness. Nor did his political campaigning in 1914 in boss-ridden Pennsylvania help to assuage his suspicions. In his mind, usually, a man was either with him or against him—one who was only 60 per cent with him was as wrong as one who was 100 per cent opposed to him.

Crusaders, like prosecuting attorneys, sometimes go to extremes. Pinchot pressed toward his goals so perseveringly and with such fervor that he was willing to sacrifice not only himself, but also on occasion some of his friends. Although a very paragon of charming graciousness and good Victorian manners, he occasionally displayed a combination of impetuosity and acute frankness which bruised both his adversaries and friends. Not always given to observing the niceties of debate, he would hit opponents with such force and in such unexpected places that they sometimes looked upon him as an unscrupulous fighter. He was in fact guilty, on occasion, of making a public charge before fully checking his facts. Prefacing his remarks with some such statement as "I am informed that . . . ," and protecting himself by asserting "If this is true . . . ," he would then launch into an attack on the person concerned. Such procedure sometimes became a case of assuming a man guilty unless he could prove himself innocent.

As has been seen, a long series of disputes occurred between Pinchot and persons with whom he worked. Beginning with his first job in the 1890's in North Carolina where he wrangled with the North Carolinians over the forestry exhibit at the Chicago World's Fair, and continuing through his altercations with Fernow, Sargent, Taft, Ballinger, La Follette, Hoover, Pepper, King, and Ickes— to name only a few—he demonstrated that he found it difficult to work well with others. His quarrels were not confined to persons of a different social philosophy. The dissensions usually occurred when someone seemed to block a goal which he was seeking to reach.

Pinchot worked best with people when he was indisputably the man in charge. His ability as a dynamic administrator was unquestionable. Almost instinctively he could instill in his subordinates a high morale and a fierce loyalty. He probably would have been equally successful at the head of a large military organization or a private corporation. He found it difficult, however, to serve on any rung of the ladder except the top. The one exception to this pattern, of course, was his role under Theodore Roosevelt, where, admittedly, he was given unusually wide freedom and impressive responsibility.

It might well be argued that Gifford Pinchot would have been more successful in politics if he had been less uncompromising. Both Theodore Roosevelt and Franklin Roosevelt were more adept than Pinchot in judging the right moment to make a concession to the other side—a skill Pinchot had difficulty in learning. Partly because of this inability to compromise, Pinchot fought reactionaries more belligerently and openly than either of the two Presidents.[64] Concession and compromise would not, however, have been effective at the turn of the century in dealing with plunderers of the nation's resources: a firm administrator was the need of the hour.

In his ardor Pinchot sometimes had a tendency to exaggerate or read into a man's words something that was not there. On more than one occasion, when someone publicly differed with his point of view, he inaccurately referred to the "attack" made on him. The reverse was occasionally true when he interpreted a guarded statement to mean full support for himself. When Franklin Roosevelt wrote to an anxious Pinchot, for example, that a transfer of the Forest Service to the Department of the Interior was not being considered, the former Governor replied how relieved he was to know that the President felt the Forest Service "ought not to be" transferred;[65] this, Mr. Roosevelt definitely had not said.

Before the break in their friendship Pinchot once acknowledged to Ickes that he knew the world was "full of people who from time to time agree with the objects I have in view, but very much object to the way I am pursuing them."[66] He knew this, if in no other way, from the scurrilous and insulting letters that the United States mail brought after each of the many times that he aroused some segment of society. The older he became, however, the less such criticism seemed to touch him.

Pinchot also realized that he had had a profound effect on many people with whom he associated; this was particularly true in his Forest Service days. In an issue of the *Journal of Forestry* honoring Pinchot on the occasion of his eightieth birthday, a charter member and former president of the Society of American Foresters wrote what some of the others in this group would have sincerely echoed, "I regard him as the greatest soul I have ever known."[67] Sometimes, perhaps, his opponents were too ready to label him a villain, and his friends to think him faultless.

A sizable number of his forestry and conservation friends regretted that he ever decided to run for public office. To them, it was a sad waste of professional talent for the acknowledged leader of forestry in the nation to plunge into the hurly-burly of election campaigning. When he did so, moreover, he became suspect of political opportunism. Pinchot could rationalize his action by maintaining that conservation needed the support of practical politicians just as much as of expert foresters. It was too much to expect that he would remain outside the great game of politics. His years in Washington working closely with Theodore Roosevelt had shown him that high public office was alluring and fascinating and he developed a solid appetite for election to some office of distinction.

Pinchot's sentimental attachment to Yale, which had conferred two honorary degrees on him, remained strong. On few occasions did he obtain more genuine pleasure than at the reunions of his class in New Haven. When in 1944 he attended his fifty-fifth reunion, he was not the last of his class, but many of his old friends were gone. He was not, however, depressed. "I am not so sure," he wrote, "that facing the last things in life is such an unhappy job after all."[68]

Bothered by a stiff leg and shortness of breath, he missed the physical exercise to which he was accustomed. As he wrote Senator Norris, however, the amount of pleasure that he could still get "just from moving around in the outdoors seems almost wicked."[69] Still actively searching for new ideas, he had noticed that he often "felt better" after making a speech. When unable to take long walks or calisthenics, therefore, he would "exercise" by "talking loud and strong for a few minutes," as though he were addressing a meeting out of doors. Insisting that this did him "no end of good," he wrote his son that he hoped the neighbors would lay the noise to "an unruly radio and not to me."[70]

From the point of view of health, the summer of 1945 was a relatively happy period. A doctor's examination in June showed him better than the year before, and surprisingly spry for a man of seventy-nine.[71] Two months later, after turning eighty, Pinchot proudly reported that upon learning of the surrender of Japan he and his wife went to Milford village and, "along with many others, rode the fire truck."[72]

In November he was well enough for Mrs. Pinchot to attend a meeting in Paris. But before she returned a doctor ordered a transfusion to "bring up" his red cells. "Everybody was most kind," he wrote, "looking after me as if I was sick, which I most emphatically was not."[73]

But other transfusions followed to take care of what was referred to as anemia, but which finally was acknowledged to be leukemia.

The last entry in his diary, dated March 3, 1946, told how he remained in bed half the day, after which he lunched with a group of fourteen including his son and family; he admitted he was "Pretty well worn" by the effort.[74] He had a miserable summer in and out of the hospital. For several weeks he was unable to handle his mail or work on his book. On August 10, although too ill to appreciate it thoroughly, he was flattered by an eighty-first birthday telegram from President Truman.

Late in September he became guardedly optimistic. Writing from Milford that he was "making progress toward recovery," he added that he hoped to be in Washington by November 1, "with some punch left."[75]

Ten days later, however, on October 4, 1946, he died. Following the funeral held on the lawn of his home at Grey Towers—outdoors as he would have liked it—he was buried in a Milford cemetery. By proclamation of Governor Martin, all offices of the Pennsylvania state government were closed on the day of the service.[76]

A decade before his death, Pinchot was scoffing at his opponents. Referring to a highly critical letter that was written about him in a California newspaper, he wrote to a friend and former governor of the state confessing that people had been "jumping on [his] quivering frame" for more than forty years. They "may make an impression after a while," he conceded. "But they have got to hurry up, or there won't be any quivering frame to jump on. They will have to jump on my tomb, and I suppose plenty of them will be engaged in that horrid form of exercise when that time comes. It will probably worry me just as much as the jumping does now."[77] Later events seemed to substantiate these predictions.

On the capitol grounds in Harrisburg stands a bronze likeness of Boies Penrose, who defeated Pinchot so decisively in the election for senator in 1914. Pennsylvania has never erected a statue of Governor Gifford Pinchot, but a dozen years after his death it fittingly recognized him by giving his name to a new 2,000-acre state park.[78]

Perhaps an even more impressive memorial to the forester-politician is a huge redwood tree located in the Muir woods in California. Selected because it was considered to be the most perfect specimen in that area, it was dedicated to Pinchot by the Sierra Club.[79] A plaque on a rock in front of the big tree reads:

This tree is dedicated to
Gifford Pinchot
Friend of the Forest
Conserver of the Common-wealth

BIBLIOGRAPHICAL NOTES
TO THE TEXT

In citations I have used GP for Gifford Pinchot. Communications, unless otherwise noted, are from the Pinchot Papers. Items in the National Archives are designated Archives.

PROLOGUE

1. GP to E. W. Scripps, March 27, 1914.
2. GP undated notes, 1936.
3. Gifford Pinchot, *Breaking New Ground* (New York, Harcourt, Brace, 1947), p. 2.
4. J. W. Pinchot to GP, October 15, 1889 (or 1890?).
5. J. W. Pinchot to GP, September 9, 1890.
6. J. W. Pinchot to GP, May 11, 1901.
7. J. W. Pinchot to his father, C. C. D. Pinchot, December 12, 1872.
8. *Detroit News*, January 30, 1910.
9. Mary Eno Pinchot diary, February 21, 1910.
10. *Washington Post*, March 31, 1912.
11. Mary Eno Pinchot diary, September 13, 1910.
12. *Detroit News*, January 30, 1910.
13. *Ibid.*
14. Mary Eno Pinchot diary, December 31, 1909.
15. J. W. Pinchot to C. C. D. Pinchot, July 9, 1871.
16. J. W. Pinchot to C. C. D. Pinchot, October 6, 1872.
17. L. Angelsmith to J. W. Pinchot, September 28, 1880.
18. GP to Mary Eno Pinchot, October 29, 1880.
19. Undated diary note, fall 1880.
20. GP to J. W. Pinchot, December 3, 1882.
21. GP to J. W. Pinchot, May 22, 1883.
22. [W.?] Nutting to J. W. Pinchot, December 4, 1882.
23. GP to Mary Eno Pinchot, November 2, 1883.
24. GP to parents, January 6, 1884.
25. GP to Mary Eno Pinchot, April 27, 1886.
26. GP to J. W. Pinchot, September 27, 1885.
27. GP to J. W. Pinchot, February 27, 1889.
28. GP to Mary Eno Pinchot, January [18?], 1889.
29. GP to J. W. Pinchot, undated, 1889.
30. GP to Mary Eno Pinchot, February 11, 1889.
31. *Breaking New Ground*, p. 4.
32. October 14, 1909.
33. February 16, 1889.
34. GP to Theodore Roosevelt, November 22, 1904.
35. GP to Mary Eno Pinchot, December 11, 1885.
36. William Lyon Phelps, *Rotarian*, March 1943, p. 41.
37. GP to J. W. Pinchot, October 14, 1888.

CHAPTER I

1. GP diary, February 14, 1890.
2. GP diary, November 21, 1890.
3. GP diary, September 20, 1890.
4. GP diary, October 5, 1889.
5. GP to Mary Eno Pinchot, July 20, 1890.
6. GP diary, July 23, 1890.
7. GP to parents, December 8, 1889.
8. GP to Mary Eno Pinchot, April 7, 1889.
9. GP to Mary Eno Pinchot, December 30, 1889.
10. GP to J. W. Pinchot, February 9, 1890.
11. GP diary, May 15, 1892.

12. Detrich Brandis to J. W. Pinchot, March 20, 1890.
13. GP to parents, January 5, 1890.
14. GP to parents, December 23, 1889.
15. GP to Detrich Brandis, August 21, 1893.
16. *Breaking New Ground*, p. 21.
17. GP diary, January 5, 1889.
18. B. E. Fernow, to GP, July 15, 1890.
19. GP diary, August 1, 1890.
20. *Ibid.*
21. J. W. Pinchot to GP, August 19, 1890.
22. GP diary, August 1, 1890.
23. B. E. Fernow to GP, September 19, 1890; GP diary, October 10, 1890.
24. GP to parents, October 12, 1890.
25. B. E. Fernow to GP, October 4, 1890.
26. GP diary, January 11, 1891.
27. GP to J. W. Pinchot, and GP to Mary Eno Pinchot, September 21, 1890.
28. GP diary, February 3 and March 14, 1891.
29. GP diary, June 17, 1891.
30. GP diary, September 6, 1891.
31. GP diary, December 12, 1891.
32. B. E. Fernow to GP, July 7, 1891.
33. GP diary, October 18, 1891.
34. GP to B. E. Fernow, January 18, 1892.
35. B. E. Fernow to GP, February 2, 1892.
36. GP to Maurice Hutton, February 23, 1907.
37. GP to Herbert Smith, August 23, 1919.

CHAPTER 2

1. GP diary, August 19, 1892.
2. GP to George Vanderbilt, August 19, 1895; GP diary, March 9, 1896.
3. May 1941, by E. H. Frothingham. See Technical Note 43 of Appalachian Forest Experiment Station, U.S. Forest Service, January 27, 1941.
4. GP to J. W. Pinchot, March 27, 1893.

5. Mary Eno Pinchot to GP, November 30, 1892.
6. J. W. Pinchot to GP, March 31, 1893.
7. March 16, 1892.
8. GP diary, August 3, 1894.
9. Gifford Pinchot, *The Fight for Conservation* (New York, Doubleday, Page, 1910), p. 38.
10. GP to Mary Eno Pinchot, April 8, 1893.
11. GP to Mary Eno Pinchot, October 20, 1893.
12. GP to parents, October 25, 1893.
13. GP to parents, undated (late 1893).
14. Mary Eno Pinchot diary, February 2, 1894.
15. GP diary, June 18, 1894.
16. GP diary, August 6, 1899.
17. GP diary, March 24, 1906.
18. Notes prepared for GP by Henry S. Graves in 1911.
19. *Breaking New Ground*, p. 72.
20. See general résumé in "The History of Forestry in America," W. N. Sparhawk, *Yearbook of Agriculture, 1949*, p. 702. Also John Ise, *The United States Forest Policy* (New Haven, Yale University, 1920); B. H. Hibbard, *A History of the Public Land Policies* (New York, Macmillan, 1924); and S. T. Dana, *Forest and Range Policy* (New York, McGraw-Hill, 1956).
21. Sen. Doc. 189, 58th Cong., 3d sess., XIII. See E. L. Peffer, *The Closing of the Public Domain* (Stanford, Stanford University, 1951), p. 8.
22. GP to W. H. Taft, October 30, 1906.
23. *American Cultivator*, February 6, 1904.
24. J. S. Morton, Secretary of Agriculture, to GP, December 20, 1894.
25. *Breaking New Ground*, p. 85.
26. C. S. Sargent to GP, March 1, 1890.
27. C. S. Sargent to GP, October 15, 1889.
28. GP to Detrich Brandis, April 25, 1896.

29. GP to Detrich Brandis, May 9, 1896.
30. *Breaking New Ground*, p. 94.
31. GP to Detrich Brandis, May 20, 1896.
32. GP to parents, September 2, 1896.
33. Ise, p. 129.
34. GP reminiscences at meeting of Society of American Foresters in Washington, D. C., February 9, 1911.
35. GP speech at Albany, May 15, 1935.
36. GP, confidentially, to C. D. Walcott, May 6, 1897.
37. *Forest Policy for the Forested Lands of the United States*, Sen. Doc. 105, 55th Cong., 1st sess.
38. GP to Mary Eno Pinchot, June 20, 1897.
39. Detrich Brandis to GP, February 14, 1897.
40. Quoted in Detrich Brandis to GP, August 9, 1897.
41. *Ibid.*
42. GP to C. S. Sargent, April 16, 1898.
43. C. S. Sargent to GP, April 20, 1898.
44. GP to Detrich Brandis, October 2, 1905.
45. Mary Eno Pinchot to GP, August 27, 1890.
46. The report is included in Sen. Doc. 189, 55th Cong., 2d sess.
47. Sundry Civil Appropriations Act, June 4, 1897.
48. GP to Mary Eno Pinchot, June 20, 1897.

CHAPTER 3

1. GP to H. S. Graves, May 12, 1898; GP diary, May 11, 1898.
2. GP to Secretary of Agriculture, May 28, 1898.
3. James Wilson to GP, May 31, 1898.
4. W. B. Greeley, *Forests and Men* (Garden City, Doubleday, 1951), p. 66.
5. *Breaking New Ground*, p. 138.
6. Greeley, p. 82.

7. O. W. Price to GP, June 7, 1898.
8. GP diary, January 23, 1900.
9. J. W. Pinchot to Mary Eno Pinchot, August 30, 1902.
10. GP to Mary Eno Pinchot, July 2, 1905.
11. *Breaking New Ground*, p. 282.
12. GP to W. E. Borah, November 12, 1906.
13. GP to Mary Eno Pinchot, August 7, 1899.
14. GP to J. W. Wadsworth, September 4, 1902.
15. GP diary, January 23, 1900.
16. Theodore Roosevelt, *Autobiography* (New York, Scribner's, 1946), p. 393.
17. GP diary, November 27, 1899.
18. *Breaking New Ground*, p. 145.
19. Theodore Roosevelt to GP, July 27, 1901.
20. GP to Mary Eno Pinchot, October 6, 1901.
21. See, for example, letters to GP signed by Roosevelt's secretary, William Loeb, Jr., asking for his views, April 2, 1906 and January 5, 1907.
22. GP diary, January 28, 1907.
23. GP diary, November 14, 1904.
24. W. D. Lewis, *The Life of Theodore Roosevelt* (Philadelphia, Winston, 1919), p. 251.
25. GP statement, January 18, 1919.
26. Theodore Roosevelt to R. S. Baker, July 4, 1903; quoted in Elting E. Morison (ed.), *The Letters of Theodore Roosevelt* (Cambridge, Harvard University, 1951-54), Vol. 3, p. 510.
27. Theodore Roosevelt to Andrew Carnegie, February 15, 1904.
28. Theodore Roosevelt to GP, March 2, 1909; quoted in 6 Morison 1,541.
29. Theodore Roosevelt to GP, October 18, 1901; quoted in *Breaking New Ground*, p. 194.
30. GP to Theodore Roosevelt, October 19, 1901.
31. GP to Theodore Roosevelt, April 21, 1903.
32. Theodore Roosevelt to GP, September 11, 1903; see 4 Morison 1,183, footnote.

33. GP diary, January 11, 1903.
34. Report dated July 20, 1903.
35. *Breaking New Ground*, p. 246.
36. *Ibid.*, p. 167.
37. Both reports are in Sen. Doc. 189, 58th Cong., 3d sess.
38. GP to Theodore Roosevelt, September 21, 1903.
39. GP to Theodore Roosevelt, September 4, 1903.
40. Peffer, *The Closing of the Public Domain*, p. 22; S. P. Hays, *The First American Conservation Movement, 1891-1920*, unpublished dissertation, Harvard University, 1953, p. 92.
41. Hays, pp. 74, 88, 101.
42. GP to Detrich Brandis, June 7, 1904.
43. January 1, 1905.
44. James Wilson to GP, February 1, 1905.
45. GP to Detrich Brandis, May 12, 1905.
46. GP to D. M. Barringer, June 20, 1903.
47. GP to E. A. Bowers, May 3 and May 12, 1904.
48. Department of Agriculture, Division of Forestry, Bull. 24; H. T. Pinkett, *Gifford Pinchot and the Early Conservation Movement in the United States*, unpublished dissertation, American University, 1953.
49. GP diary, January 1, 1904.
50. GP to W. K. Townsend, October 11, 1905.
51. GP diary, December 28, 1898.
52. GP to Amos Pinchot, October 9, 1902.
53. GP to Mary Eno Pinchot, October 17, 1902.
54. GP to Theodore Roosevelt, October 27, 1902.
55. GP to Theodore Roosevelt, September 16, 1902.
56. GP to W. H. Taft, June 14, 1903.
57. GP diary, January 8, 1903.
58. Lawrence O. Murray, *Elkland Journal* (Pa.), September 7, 1922.
59. GP diary, November 11, 1905.
60. GP to Hamlin Garland, March 27, 1919.
61. GP diary, October 11, 1905. This account of the incident, although varying in a few details from that recorded in *Breaking New Ground* (p. 317), is based on Pinchot's diary notes which were written shortly after the drenching.
62. GP diary, December 26, 1904.
63. GP diary, July 3, 1903.
64. GP diary, October 11, 1905.
65. GP diary, July 3, 1903.
66. GP to William Loeb, Jr., October 31, 1906.
67. GP to Theodore Roosevelt, August 7, 1902.
68. Theodore Roosevelt to George McAneny, June 5, 1900; quoted in 2 Morison 1,320.
69. GP to G. B. Cortelyou, August 15, 1904.
70. GP diary, October 8, 1904.
71. GP diary, November 3, 1904.
72. GP diary, November 8, 1904.
73. GP diary, November 9, 1904.
74. GP to Amos F. Eno, November 15, 1904.

CHAPTER 4

1. Sen. Doc. 189.
2. "The Governor Says," March 1933 (a mimeographed information sheet distributed to newspapers).
3. December 10, 1910 (Archives).
4. Hays, *The First American Conservation Movement, 1891-1920*, pp. 88, 432.
5. J. B. Adams, Acting Forester, to forest officers, March 26, 1907 (Archives).
6. GP letter, November 13, 1906.
7. GP to William Warner, March 13, 1907.
8. U.S. *v* Grimaud, 220 U.S. 506.
9. GP to Mary Eno Pinchot, August 23, 1909.
10. GP speech at Wilkes-Barre, May 11, 1934.
11. *Breaking New Ground*, pp. 326, 359.

12. *Congressional Record*, 57th Cong., 2d sess., p. 3,071.

13. Judson King to GP, June 13, 1935.

14. P. P. Wells, Acting Forester, to Commissioner, General Land Office, October 19, 1909.

15. GP to F. W. Cuttle, May 5, 1908 (Archives).

16. R. M. Saltonstall to G. W. Woodruff, December 21, 1908 (Archives).

17. Pinchot stated the number was 11 in *Breaking New Ground*, p. 303.

18. W. E. Sprott to James Wilson, May 24, 1907 (Archives).

19. GP to J. H. Hutchinson, November 24, 1909 (Archives).

20. GP to F. H. Newell, undated.

21. GP to W. J. Bryan, January 7, 1909.

22. GP to P. P. Wells, March 21, 1908 (Archives).

23. GP to F. Walcott, April 18, 1908 (Archives).

24. Theodore Roosevelt to Chairman, Inland Waterways Commission, March 16, 1908 (Archives).

25. *Congressional Record*, 60th Cong., 1st sess., p. 4,698; *Messages and Papers of the Presidents*, Vol. XVII, p. 7,531.

26. Harold Howland, *Theodore Roosevelt and His Times* (New Haven, Yale University, 1921), p. 143.

27. W. B. Heyburn to GP, June 13, 1905 (Archives).

28. *Congressional Record*, 59th Cong., 2d sess., p. 3,720.

29. James Wilson to GP, February 28, 1907.

30. Summarized in *Congressional Record*, 60th Cong., 1st sess., p. 4,241.

31. GP to Lady Johnstone, April 3, 1908.

32. Pinkett, *Gifford Pinchot and the Early Conservation Movement in the United States*, p. 90.

33. GP to Senator Paris Gibson, March 4, 1907.

34. GP to O. W. Price, August 11, 1905.

35. Theodore Roosevelt to A. E. Mead, March 3, 1907; quoted in 5 Morison 606.

36. *La Follette's Autobiography* (Madison, The Robert M. La Follette Co., 1913), p. 482.

37. Claudius O. Johnson, *Borah of Idaho* (New York, Longmans, Green, 1936), p. 99.

38. October 21, 1908 (Archives).

39. C. S. Thomas to GP, December 2, 1908 (Archives).

40. Calvin Cobb to GP, November 28, 1908 (Archives).

41. GP to E. W. Martin, July 14, 1909 (Archives).

42. S. G. Adams to James Wilson, September 7, 1909 (Archives).

43. L. K. Armstrong, December 22, 1909.

44. *Denver News Times*, June 17, 1909.

45. *Denver News Times*, July 1, 1909.

46. GP to W. G. M. Stone, January 9, 1909 (Archives).

47. GP to O. W. Price, September 7, 1905 (Archives).

48. GP to Theodore Roosevelt, September 22, 1905.

49. J. A. Holmes to O. W. Price, August 22, 1909 (Archives).

50. GP to H. S. Graves, September 24, 1916.

51. GP to F. E. Weyerhaeuser, May 27, 1912.

52. GP to F. E. Weyerhaeuser, March 26, 1907.

53. Norman Wengert, *Natural Resources and the Political Struggle* (New York, Doubleday, 1955), p. 24.

54. GP to H. L. Stimson, June 28, 1911; *Breaking New Ground*, pp. 322-326.

55. Concerning the origin of the movement, see Mark Sullivan, *Our Times* (New York, Scribner's, 1932), Vol. 4, p. 389; GP speech in Altoona, May 3, 1934; GP to Judson King, September 1, 1937.

56. *The Fight for Conservation*, pp. 44-46.

57. Speech by J. M. Phillips to American Game Protective Association,

December 1927 (Phillips papers); GP to E. T. Parsons, August 30, 1909; J. Horace McFarland to GP, March 7, 1908 (Dock papers); Hays, pp. 333-343.

58. Forest Service Circular 157, October 17, 1908.
59. GP to Max Farrand, April 13, 1916.
60. GP to Casper Whitney, February 6, 1909.
61. GP to J. T. Dolliver, September 4, 1908.
62. GP to parents, August 13, 1907.
63. *Denver Republican*, June 21, 1907.
64. GP to Theodore Roosevelt, July 25, 1907.
65. GP to A. J. Beveridge, August 7, 1908.
66. *Congressional Record*, 60th Cong., 1st sess., p. 5,730.
67. *Ibid.*, p. 4,137.
68. *Ibid.*, p. 4,140.

CHAPTER 5

1. GP notes on a meeting with President Diaz of Mexico, January 20, 1909.
2. GP to O. W. Price, August 25, 1905 (Archives).
3. GP to O. W. Price, August 21, 1905.
4. Theodore Roosevelt to C. H. Keep, June 2, 1905; quoted in 4 Morison 1,201.
5. L. D. White, "The Public Life of 'T.R.,'" *Public Administration Review*, Autumn 1954, p. 278.
6. *Washington Evening Star*, March 23, 1906.
7. *Report* of the Committee on Expenditures in the Department of Agriculture, House Rept. 8,147, 59th Cong., 2d sess., p. 17.
8. Preliminary Report, Gunn, Richards & Co., "Forest Service," June 30, 1908 (Archives).
9. Theodore Roosevelt, *Autobiography*, p. 368.
10. Theodore Roosevelt to members, March 14, 1907.
11. *Preliminary Report* of the Inland Waterways Commission, Sen. Doc. 325, 60th Cong., 1st sess.

12. *Breaking New Ground*, p. 344.
13. GP to Theodore Roosevelt, September, 9, 1907.
14. T. R. Shipp to GP, September 29, 1942.
15. *Proceedings of a Conference of Governors*, H. Doc. 1,425, 60th Cong., 2d sess.
16. T. R. Shipp to GP, August 2, 1938; Pinkett, *Gifford Pinchot and the Early Conservation Movement in the United States*, p. 136.
17. Theodore Roosevelt to Governors, November 9, 1907.
18. *Breaking New Ground*, p. 346.
19. C. R. Van Hise, *The Conservation of Natural Resources in the United States* (New York, Macmillan, 1910), p. 7.
20. *Proceedings of a Conference of Governors*, p. 194.
21. GP to C. G. LaFarge, May 16, 1908.
22. Roosevelt, p. 368.
23. Executive Order No. 809, June 8, 1908.
24. *Report* of the National Conservation Commission, Sen. Doc. 676, 60th Cong., 2d sess. (3 vols.).
25. *Ibid.*, p. 1.
26. James Wilson to C. F. Scott, Chairman of the House Committee on Agriculture, January 7, 1909.
27. GP to Theodore Roosevelt, June 29, 1908.
28. GP to Theodore Roosevelt, August 11, 1908.
29. GP to Horace Plunkett, February 8, 1909.
30. GP to W. H. Page, January 15, 1909.
31. Sen. Doc. 705, 60th Cong., 2d sess.

CHAPTER 6

1. GP to J. W. Pinchot, June 15, 1904.
2. GP to C. R. Van Hise, May 5, 1909.
3. GP to J. W. Pinchot, November 30, 1905.
4. GP to Mary Eno Pinchot, July 12, 1904.

5. GP to J. W. Pinchot, July 14, 1904.
6. Theodore Roosevelt to GP, July 16, 1904; quoted in 4 Morison 859.
7. GP to J. W. Pinchot, July 26, 1904.
8. Theodore Roosevelt to C. G. La Farge, August 5, 1904; quoted in 4 Morison 883.
9. GP to Theodore Roosevelt, August 8, 1904.
10. GP diary, December 29, 1904.
11. GP diary, October 22, 1906.
12. GP diary, October 22 and October 26, 1906.
13. GP diary, October 24, 1906.
14. GP diary, November 5, 1906.
15. GP to A. J. Beveridge, November 12, 1906.
16. GP to J. W. Abbott, June 29, 1906.
17. GP to C. L. Pack, November 27, 1908.
18. GP to A. J. Beveridge, November 14, 1908.
19. C. G. Bowers, *Beveridge and the Progressive Era* (Boston, Houghton Mifflin, 1932), p. 236.
20. GP to F. H. Newell, August 29, 1908.
21. GP to J. H. Kellogg, June 29, 1906.
22. Horace Plunkett to Mary Eno Pinchot, January 12, 1911.
23. GP to Horace Plunkett, August 10, 1908.
24. Mary Eno Pinchot to J. W. Pinchot, July 23, 1908.
25. Mary Eno Pinchot diary, February 20 and February 22, 1909.
26. Reproduced in Van Hise, *The Conservation of Natural Resources in the United States*, p. 385.
27. Mary Eno Pinchot diary, February 9, 1909.
28. Mary Eno Pinchot diary, February 16 and February 17, 1909.
29. H. F. Pringle, *Theodore Roosevelt* (New York, Harcourt, Brace, 1931), p. 493.
30. *Breaking New Ground*, p. 382.
31. GP to H. L. Stimson, April 12, 1909.
32. Theodore Roosevelt to GP, Febru-

ary 24, 1909; quoted in 6 Morison 1,535.
33. Quoted in 6 Morison 1,522.
34. A rough manuscript is with the Garfield papers.
35. Theodore Roosevelt to GP, March 2, 1909; quoted in 6 Morison 1,541.
36. GP address at Metropolitan Opera House, February 9, 1919.

CHAPTER 7

1. *Breaking New Ground*, p. 375.
2. *Report* of the National Conservation Commission, Vol. 1, p. 124.
3. *Ibid.*, p. 137.
4. GP to R. E. Prouty, February 14, 1938.
5. J. R. Garfield to GP, May 8, 1909. Also *Investigation of the Department of the Interior and of the Bureau of Forestry*, Sen. Doc. 719, 61st Cong., 3d sess., Vol. 4, p. 1,157. The 13 volumes of this document are hereafter referred to as *Investigation*.
6. J. R. Garfield to Commissioner of the General Land Office, March 2, 1909; *Investigation*, Vol. 4, p. 1,158.
7. *Breaking New Ground*, p. 403.
8. *Investigation*, Vol. 4, p. 1,147.
9. H. F. Pringle, *The Life and Times of William Howard Taft* (New York, Farrar and Rinehart, 1939), p. 479.
10. R. A. Ballinger to W. H. Taft, September 17, 1909; W. H. Taft to R. A. Ballinger, September 24, 1909 (Archives).
11. J. A. Eddy to R. A. Ballinger, January 29, 1910 (Archives).
12. GP diary, April 9, 1940; *Breaking New Ground*, p. 402.
13. GP to J. R. Garfield, April 29, 1909.
14. GP to J. E. Engstad, May 25, 1909.
15. GP to Mary Eno Pinchot, June 10, 1909.
16. *Investigation*, Vol. 4, p. 1,226.
17. *Ibid.*, Vol. 5, p. 1,705.
18. *Ibid.*, Vol. 2, p. 557.
19. *Ibid.*, Vol. 7, p. 4,198.
20. *Ibid.*, Vol. 4, p. 1,230.
21. *Ibid.*, Vol. 4, p. 1,235.

22. GP to Calvin Cobb, July 13, 1909.
23. GP to Mary Eno Pinchot, June 17, 1909.
24. *Washington Post*, June 17, 1909.
25. Rose M. Stahl, *The Ballinger-Pinchot Controversy* (Smith College Studies in History, 1926), p. 88.
26. Fred Dennett to R. A. Ballinger, March 30, 1908, *Investigation*, Vol. 5, p. 1,596.
27. Harold Stein (ed.), *Public Administration and Policy Development* (New York, Harcourt, Brace, 1952), p. 86.
28. Pringle, *The Life and Times of William Howard Taft*, p. 480.
29. GP to William Kent, July 15, 1909.
30. GP to Horace Plunkett, July 13, 1909.
31. *Investigation*, Vol. 6, p. 3,321.
32. GP to W. L. Fisher, February 23, 1909.

CHAPTER 8

1. L. R. Glavis telegram and letter to A. C. Shaw, July 16, 1909, *Investigation*, Vol. 3, pp. 668, 670.
2. *Breaking New Ground*, p. 417.
3. L. R. Glavis to A. C. Shaw, August 1, 1909 (Archives).
4. L. R. Glavis telegram to A. C. Shaw, August 1, 1909 (Archives).
5. GP to Mary Eno Pinchot, August 5, 1909.
6. GP to J. R. Garfield, August 15, 1909.
7. GP speech before National Irrigation Congress, August 10, 1909.
8. GP to *New York Times*, August 13, 1909.
9. G. W. Woodruff to GP, November 16, 1909.
10. J. K. Brilhart, *Gifford Pinchot as a Conservation Crusader in 1909* (unpublished M.A. thesis, Pennsylvania State University, 1957), p. 1.
11. GP to Mary Eno Pinchot, August 16, 1909.
12. *Ibid.*
13. GP to G. C. Pardee, October 26, 1938.
14. *New York Times*, August 13, 1909.

15. *Portland Oregonian*, May 20, 1909.
16. Fred Dennett to H. T. Jones, June 21, 1907, *Investigation*, Vol. 3, p. 47.
17. H. T. Jones to Commissioner, August 10, 1907, *Ibid.*, Vol. 3, p. 321.
18. H. T. Jones to Commissioner, August 13, 1907, *Ibid.*, Vol. 3, p. 323.
19. H. K. Love to Commissioner, August 2, 1907, *Ibid.*, Vol. 3, p. 321.
20. L. R. Glavis to Commissioner, November 5, 1907, *Ibid.*, Vol. 4, p. 811.
21. C. Cunningham to S. S. Birch, December 9, 1907, *Ibid.*, Vol. 5, p. 2,147.
22. *Ibid.*, Vol. 1, p. 168.
23. L. R. Glavis to Commissioner, January 22, 1908, *Ibid.*, Vol. 3, p. 90.
24. L. R. Glavis to Commissioner, January 22, 1908, *Ibid.*, Vol. 3, p. 90.
25. Fred Dennett to L. R. Glavis, February 5, 1908, *Ibid.*, Vol. 3, p. 101.
26. R. A. Ballinger to Fred Dennett, March 31, 1908, *Ibid.*, Vol. 5, p. 1,600.
27. *Ibid.*, Vol. 3, p. 129.
28. *Ibid.*, Vol. 3, p. 108.
29. *Ibid.*, Vol. 3, pp. 109-128.
30. M. C. Moore to R. A. Ballinger, May 24, 1909, *Ibid.*, Vol. 2, p. 72.
31. *Ibid.*, Vol. 1, p. 174.
32. H. H. Schwartz to Commissioner, September 23, 1908, *Ibid.*, Vol. 3, p. 147.
33. *Ibid.*, Vol. 2, p. 469.
34. Fred Dennett to L. R. Glavis, March 10, 1909, *Ibid.*, Vol. 3, p. 201.
35. *Ibid.*, Vol. 3, p. 213.
36. M. C. Moore to R. A. Ballinger, May 22, 1909, *Ibid.*, Vol. 2, p. 71.
37. R. A. Ballinger to M. C. Moore, May 24 and May 27, 1909, *Ibid.*, Vol. 2, pp. 72, 73.
38. Frank Pierce to Commissioner, May 19, 1909, *Ibid.*, Vol. 9, p. 5,107.
39. *Ibid.*, Vol. 9, p. 5,120.
40. *Ibid.*, Vol. 3, p. 262.
41. H. H. Schwartz to L. R. Glavis, July 17, 1909, *Ibid.*, Vol. 3, p. 275.
42. H. H. Schwartz to M. D. McEniry, August 5, 1909, *Ibid.*, Vol. 5, p. 2,114.

43. *Investigation*, Vol. 4, p. 1,218.
44. *Ibid.*, Vol. 4, p. 1,217.
45. R. A. Ballinger telegram to G. O. Smith, August 12, 1909 (Archives).
46. GP to Mary Eno Pinchot, September 6, 1909.
47. GP to O. W. Price, August 25, 1909, *Investigation*, Vol. 7, p. 3,755.
48. GP to O. W. Price, September 1, 1909, *Ibid.*, Vol. 7, p. 3,756.
49. GP to C. L. Pack, August 19, 1909.
50. H. L. Stimson to GP, August 20, 1909.
51. W. H. Taft to R. A. Ballinger, September 13, 1909, *Investigation*, Vol. 4, p. 1,187.
52. W. H. Taft to GP, September 13, 1909, *Ibid.*, Vol. 4, p. 1,220.
53. GP notes on interview.
54. *Investigation*, Vol. 4, p. 1,222.
55. *Ibid.*, Vol. 4, p. 1,223.
56. R. A. Ballinger to Frank Pierce, September 20, 1909 (Archives).
57. GP to W. H. Taft, November 4, 1909, *Investigation*, Vol. 4, p. 1,223.
58. J. R. Garfield to W. H. Taft, November 6, 1909, *Ibid.*, Vol. 4, p. 1,232.
59. R. A. Ballinger to W. H. Taft, November 15, 1909, *Ibid.*, Vol. 5, p. 1,525.
60. *Ibid.*, Vol. 4, p. 1,237.
61. W. H. Taft to GP, November 24, 1909, *Ibid.*, Vol. 4, p. 1,230.
62. GP to A. P. Stokes, Jr., November 23, 1909.
63. *Investigation*, Vol. 4, p. 1,273.
64. GP to G. C. Pardee, November 24, 1909.
65. GP to A. J. Beveridge, December 27, 1911.
66. L. R. Glavis to W. H. Taft, September 20, 1909, *Investigation*, Vol. 4, p. 888.
67. C. C. Regier, *The Era of the Muckrakers* (Chapel Hill, University of North Carolina, 1932), p. 115.
68. *Investigation*, Vol. 2, p. 805.
69. *Collier's Weekly*, November 6, 1909, p. 7.
70. *Ibid.*, November 13, 1909, p. 15.
71. GP to G. D. Seymour, November 18, 1909.
72. GP to G. W. Woodruff, November 24, 1909.
73. Amos Pinchot to GP, November 27, 1909.
74. H. L. Stimson to GP, October 22, 1909.
75. GP to H. L. Stimson, October 25, 1909.
76. GP to H. L. Stimson, November 5, 1909; H. L. Stimson to GP, November 9, 1909.
77. H. L. Stimson to GP, November 15, 1909.
78. GP to H. L. Stimson, November 16, 1909.
79. H. L. Stimson to GP, November 26, 1909.

CHAPTER 9

1. A. T. Mason, *Bureaucracy Convicts Itself* (New York, Viking, 1941), p. 94.
2. Memorandum accompanying Amos Pinchot letter to GP, January 21, 1932; see A. R. E. Pinchot, *History of the Progressive Party*, H. M. Hooker, ed. (New York, New York University, 1958), p. 238.
3. *Breaking New Ground*, p. 442.
4. Amos Pinchot to H. L. Stimson, January 21, 1910.
5. G. W. Norris, *Fighting Liberal* (New York, Macmillan, 1945), p. 109; Alfred Lief, *Democracy's Norris* (New York, Stackpole, 1939), pp. 95ff; K. W. Hechler, *Insurgency* (New York, Columbia University, 1940), p. 64.
6. *Congressional Record*, 61st Cong., 2d sess., p. 282; quoted in Stahl, *The Ballinger-Pinchot Controversy*, p. 125.
7. GP to O. W. Price and A. C. Shaw, December 24, 1909, *Investigation*, Vol. 4, p. 1,275.
8. GP to J. R. Garfield, October 4, 1909.
9. GP diary, January 1, 1910.
10. Archie Butt, *Taft and Roosevelt: The Intimate Letters of Archie Butt*

(New York, Doubleday, Doran, 1930), p. 245.

11. O. W. Price and A. C. Shaw to GP, January 5, 1910, *Investigation*, Vol. 4, p. 1,275.

12. James Wilson to GP, December 29, 1909, *Ibid.*, Vol. 4, p. 1,292.

13. H. L. Stimson to GP, January 5, 1910.

14. G. W. Pepper, *Philadelphia Lawyer* (Philadelphia, Lippincott, 1944), p. 82.

15. GP to H. L. Stimson, January 6, 1910.

16. GP to G. W. Pepper, January 6, 1910.

17. GP to J. P. Dolliver, January 5, 1910, *Investigation*, Vol. 4, p. 1,283.

18. *Ibid.*, Vol. 4, p. 1,295.

19. *Ibid.*, Vol. 4, p. 1,293.

20. *Ibid.*, Vol. 4, pp. 1,297-1,305.

21. GP to Henry C. Wallace, March 8, 1910.

22. GP to W. K. Kavanaugh, January 20, 1910.

23. Butt, p. 253.

24. *Investigation*, Vol. 4, p. 1,453; Bowers, *Beveridge and the Progressive Era*, p. 374; Butt, p. 256.

25. W. H. Taft to GP, January 7, 1910, *Investigation*, Vol. 4, p. 1,289.

26. Mary Eno Pinchot diary, January 7, 1910.

27. *Ibid.*, January 8, 1910.

28. David Hinshaw, *A Man From Kansas* (New York, Putnam's, 1945), p. 121.

29. *Breaking New Ground*, p. 457.

30. Mary Eno Pinchot diary, January 15, 16, 17, 1910.

31. *Investigation*, Vol. 4, p. 1,295.

32. GP to A. P. Stokes, May 22, 1939; *Breaking New Ground*, p. 450

33. GP speech, January 8, 1909.

34. GP diary, January 31, 1910.

35. *Breaking New Ground*, p. 460; GP speech, New Rochelle, December 27, 1909.

36. Undated.

37. GP to Theodore Roosevelt, December 31, 1909.

38. Theodore Roosevelt to GP, January 17, 1910; quoted in *Breaking New Ground*, p. 497.

39. H. L. Stimson to GP, January 7, 1910.

40. H. L. Stimson to GP, February 18, 1910.

41. GP to O. W. Price, December 30, 1909.

42. GP to G. W. Pepper, January 6, 1910.

43. E. H. Abbott, *Outlook*, May 28, 1910, p. 139.

44. Mary Eno Pinchot diary, February 14, 1910.

45. *Investigation*, Vol. 3.

46. H. L. Stimson to GP, February 18, 1910.

47. Amos Pinchot to H. L. Stimson, January 21, 1910.

48. Pepper, pp. 84, 86.

49. G. W. Pepper to GP, February 4, 1910.

50. GP to G. W. Pepper, February 5, 1910.

51. *Investigation*, Vol. 4, p. 1,143.

52. *Ibid.*, Vol. 4, p. 1,144.

53. Theodore Roosevelt to William Kent, November 28, 1910; quoted in 7 Morison 176.

54. GP to J. H. Hammond, October 14, 1909.

55. *Investigation*, Vol. 1, p. 142.

56. *Ibid.*, Vol. 4, p. 1,406, and Vol. 9, p. 4,934.

57. *Ibid.*, Vol. 9, p. 4,933.

58. *Ibid.*, Vol. 4, p. 1,445.

59. *Ibid.*, Vol. 4, p. 1,457.

60. *Ibid.*, Vol. 4, p. 1,443.

61. *Ibid.*, Vol. 9, p. 4,953.

62. *Ibid.*, Vol. 9, p. 4,936.

63. *Ibid.*, Vol. 4, p. 1,383.

64. James Wilson to Comptroller, January 12, 1910, *Investigation*, Vol. 4, p. 1,392.

65. R. J. Tracewell to James Wilson, January 13, 1910, *Ibid.*, Vol. 4, p. 1,392.

66. *Ibid.*, Vol. 4, pp. 1,400-1,406.

67. *Ibid.*, Vol. 4, pp. 1,469-1,491.

68. *Ibid.*, Vol. 9, p. 4,926.

69. G. W. Pepper to GP, March 14, 1910.
70. GP to G. W. Pepper, March 15, 1910.

CHAPTER 10

1. GP to Horace Plunkett, June 5, 1910.
2. *Investigation*, Vol. 2, p. 3.
3. *Ibid.*, Vol. 2, p. 805.
4. *Ibid.*, Vol. 8, p. 4,397.
5. *A Summary of Testimony by the Prosecution in the Pinchot-Ballinger Controversy up to March 18, 1910* (privately printed).
6. Theodore Roosevelt to GP, March 1, 1910; quoted in 7 Morison 51.
7. *Selections from the Correspondence of Theodore Roosevelt and Henry Cabot Lodge* (New York, Scribner's, 1925), Vol. II, p. 361.
8. Theodore Roosevelt to GP (date of telegram illegible).
9. T. R. Shipp to GP, September 15, 1941.
10. Theodore Roosevelt to H. C. Lodge, April 6, 1910; quoted in *Selections*, Vol. II, p. 366.
11. H. C. Lodge to Theodore Roosevelt, January 15, 1910; quoted in *Selections*, Vol. II, p. 358.
12. Theodore Roosevelt to H. C. Lodge, March 4, 1910; quoted in *Selections*, Vol. II, p. 361.
13. GP diary, April 11, 1910.
14. GP to J. R. Garfield, April 27, 1910.
15. G. E. Mowry, *Theodore Roosevelt and the Progressive Movement* (Madison, University of Wisconsin, 1946), p. 125.
16. Theodore Roosevelt to H. C. Lodge, April 11, 1910; quoted in *Selections*, Vol. II, p. 368.
17. Amos Pinchot to GP, April 19, 1910.
18. Mary Eno Pinchot diary, April 8, 1910.
19. O. W. Price to GP, May 2, 1910.
20. GP diary, April 18, 1910.
21. A list of his calls appears in *Investigation*, Vol. 7, p. 4,364.
22. *Investigation*, Vol. 7, p. 3,415.
23. *Ibid.*, Vol. 7, p. 3,631.
24. *Ibid.*, Vol. 7, p. 3,866.
25. G. W. Wickersham to Knute Nelson, May 14, 1910, *Ibid.*, Vol. 7, p. 4,364.
26. *Ibid.*, Vol. 8, pp. 4,452-4,461.
27. *Ibid.*, Vol. 8, p. 4,456. The letter and the memorandum are printed in parallel columns, *Ibid.*, Vol. 8, pp. 4,507-4,521.
28. W. H. Taft to Knute Nelson, May 15, 1910, *Ibid.*, Vol. 8, p. 4,393.
29. C. W. Eliot to T. R. Shipp, May 16, 1910.
30. W. H. Taft to Knute Nelson, May 15, 1910, *Investigation*, Vol. 8, p. 4,393.
31. *Ibid.*, Vol. 8, p. 4,486.
32. *Ibid.*, Vol. 9, p. 5,386.
33. Mary Eno Pinchot diary, May 14, 1910.
34. GP notes of talk with Brandeis on December 30, 1939.
35. Norman Hapgood, *The Changing Years* (New York, Farrar and Rinehart, 1930), p. 190.
36. GP to Theodore Roosevelt, May 16, 1910.
37. R. W. Leopold, *Elihu Root and the Conservative Tradition* (Boston, Little, Brown, 1954), p. 84.
38. GP to Horace Plunkett, June 5, 1910.
39. GP to F. M. Kerby, June 6, 1910.
40. GP to Louis Brandeis, June 14, 1910.
41. *Investigation*, Vol. 1.
42. Elihu Root to Knute Nelson, August 27, 1910 (Root papers); P. C. Jessup, *Elihu Root* (New York, Dodd, Mead, 1938), Vol. 2, p. 161.
43. *Investigation*, Vol. 1, p. 92.
44. *Ibid.*, Vol. 1, pp. 93-147.
45. *Ibid.*, Vol. 1, pp. 149-192.
46. R. A. Ballinger to James Wilson, March 28, 1910 (Archives).
47. Josephus Daniels, *The Wilson Era* (Chapel Hill, University of North Carolina, 1944), p. 304.

48. R. A. Ballinger to James T. Macey, January 12, 1910 (Archives).
49. *Breaking New Ground*, p. 459.
50. GP to J. F. Crawford, June 29, 1910.
51. GP to Theodore Roosevelt, January 21, 1911.
52. GP diary, March 7, 1911.
53. Stahl, *The Ballinger-Pinchot Controversy*, p. 134.
54. GP diary, March 7, 1911.
55. GP statement, March 7, 1911.
56. Gifford and Amos Pinchot to W. H. Taft, November 7, 1910 (Taft papers).
57. GP diary, June 26, 1911.
58. Theodore Roosevelt to GP, June 28, 1911.
59. GP to Louis Brandeis, June 27, 1911.
60. GP to L. R. Glavis, July 16, 1911.
61. GP to Joseph Bristow, July 5, 1911.
62. GP to S. M. Lindsay, March 6, 1921.
63. GP to J. H. McFarland, June 10, 1911.
64. GP diary, May 23, 1913.
65. Pringle, *Theodore Roosevelt*, p. 526.

CHAPTER 11

1. GP to L. B. Anderson, February 7, 1910.
2. J. T. Rothrock to GP, December 1, 1909.
3. Mowry, *Theodore Roosevelt and the Progressive Movement*, p. 118.
4. GP to Mary Eno Pinchot, October 31, 1897.
5. GP diary, February 12, 1904.
6. GP to A. J. Beveridge, November 11, 1904.
7. GP to A. J. Beveridge, October 26, 1905.
8. *Washington Life*, September 30, 1905.
9. GP to J. R. Garfield, June 30, 1910.
10. GP to George Bull, December 30, 1910.
11. Butt, *Taft and Roosevelt*, p. 416.
12. Theodore Roosevelt to GP, June 28, 1910; quoted in 7 Morison 95.
13. Butt, p. 439.
14. Mowry, p. 277.
15. GP to Mary Eno Pinchot, September 6, 1910.
16. Theodore Roosevelt to GP, August 17, 1910; quoted in 7 Morison 113.
17. GP to Mary Eno Pinchot, September 6, 1910.
18. Theodore Roosevelt to GP, August 17, 1910.
19. GP to Theodore Roosevelt, August 18, 1910.
20. Stahl, *The Ballinger-Pinchot Controversy*, p. 132.
21. Mowry, p. 148.
22. GP to R. M. La Follette, September 7, 1910.
23. Theodore Roosevelt to Theodore Roosevelt, Jr., October 19, 1910; quoted in 7 Morison 145.
24. Theodore Roosevelt to Elihu Root, October 21, 1910; quoted in 7 Morison 147.
25. Theodore Roosevelt to William Kent, November 28, 1910; quoted in 7 Morison 176.
26. GP to H. L. Stimson, October 21, 1910.
27. Theodore Roosevelt to Theodore Roosevelt, Jr., October 19, 1910; quoted in 7 Morison 145. H. L. Stimson and McGeorge Bundy, *On Active Service in Peace and War* (New York, Harper, 1947), p. 28.
28. GP statement, October 11, 1910.
29. Theodore Roosevelt to H. L. Stimson, November 16, 1910; quoted in 7 Morison 165.
30. Butt, p. 564.
31. GP to Theodore Roosevelt, December 2, 1910.
32. GP to F. H. Newell, November 28, 1910.
33. GP to Amos Pinchot, February 13, 1911.
34. GP to W. J. McGee, November 28, 1910.
35. GP to P. P. Wells, April 27, 1910.

CHAPTER 12

1. Bela C. and Fola La Follette, *Robert*

M. La Follette (New York, Macmillan, 1953), p. 942.
2. *Washington Herald*, May 13, 1933.
3. GP to H. L. Ickes, February 25, 1933.
4. GP to J. F. Bass, April 27, 1914.
5. H. A. Slattery to C. L. Pack, February 25, 1916.
6. GP to H. A. Slattery, August 23, 1920.
7. Nellie D. McSherry to GP, February 11, 1922.
8. H. A. Slattery to GP, August 31 and September 1, 1916.
9. February 5, 1910.
10. GP to H. L. Ickes, December 11, 1916.
11. GP to G. H. Lorimer, January 2, 1913.
12. GP to W. J. Bryan, December 31, 1912.
13. GP diary, March 3, 1911.
14. GP to Scott Ferris, March 24, 1916.
15. GP to R. M. La Follette, March 12, 1919.
16. GP statement, February 4, 1914.
17. GP to P. P. Wells, June 28, 1920.
18. GP to T. R. Shipp, October 20, 1910.
19. GP to E. L. Worsham, April 27, 1914.
20. *National Conservation Congress, Report of the Minority on Water Power* (undated).
21. GP to Amos Pinchot, November 23, 1913.
22. GP to J. F. Bass, January 29, 1923.
23. GP diary, March 13, 1912.
24. GP to J. F. Bass, January 29, 1923.
25. A. T. Mason, *Brandeis: A Free Man's Life* (New York, Viking, 1946), p. 282.
26. Jeannette P. Nichols, *Alaska* (Cleveland, Arthur H. Clark, 1924), p. 374.
27. *New York Times*, July 27, 1911.
28. *Outlook*, July 22, 1911.
29. *New York Times*, July 27, 1911.
30. GP diary, July 28, 1911.
31. *New York Times*, July 28, 1911.
32. Nichols, p. 381.
33. Mason, p. 288.
34. *Ibid.*
35. James Wickersham to R. A. Ballinger, August 16, 1909 (Archives).
36. GP to Mary Eno Pinchot, September 16, 1911.
37. GP to W. H. Downing, August 6, 1931.
38. *Cleveland Press*, October 25, 1911.
39. Nichols, p. 380.
40. GP to W. H. Downing, August 6, 1931.
41. GP to Mary Eno Pinchot, October 2, 1911.
42. GP diary, October 7, 1911.
43. GP to Mary Eno Pinchot, October 11, 1911.
44. GP to Theodore Roosevelt, October 11, 1911.
45. Mason, p. 288.
46. GP to Daniel Guggenheim, February 9, 1917.

CHAPTER 13

1. GP to O. W. Price, July 12, 1913.
2. GP to J. B. White, September 30, 1912.
3. Mowry, *Theodore Roosevelt and the Progressive Movement*, p. 75.
4. Bela C. and Fola La Follette, *Robert M. La Follette*, p. 316.
5. GP diary, January 21, 1911.
6. GP to Louis Brandeis, March 1, 1911.
7. GP diary, February 23, 1911.
8. Theodore Roosevelt to W. H. Moody, May 18, 1916; quoted in 8 Morison 1,043.
9. Theodore Roosevelt to Robert Bacon and family, January 2, 1911, and to Theodore Roosevelt, Jr., August 22, 1911; quoted in 7 Morison 199, 336.
10. GP diary, February 20, 1911.
11. GP to Theodore Roosevelt, February 28, 1911.
12. *La Follette's Autobiography*, pp. 524, 550.
13. GP diary, May 16, 1911.
14. Bela C. and Fola La Follette, p. 333.
15. GP to Mary Eno Pinchot, May 18, 1911.
16. GP to Horace Plunkett, May 27, 1911.
17. GP diary, June 12, 1911.

18. GP speech at Racine, Wisconsin, October 25, 1920.
19. GP diary, May 30, 1911.
20. "A Look Ahead in Politics," *Saturday Evening Post*, October 7, 1911.
21. GP diary, August 1, 1911.
22. GP diary, July 21, 1911.
23. Theodore Roosevelt to William Kent, September 19, 1911; quoted in 7 Morison 343.
24. Theodore Roosevelt to Theodore Roosevelt, Jr., August 22, 1911; quoted in 7 Morison 336.
25. GP to Amos Pinchot, August 24, 1911.
26. GP diary, August 28, 1911.
27. GP diary, November 12, 1911.
28. J. R. Garfield to GP, November 28, 1911.
29. Mowry, p. 192.
30. GP speech, November 27, 1911.
31. For example, GP speech at Chicago Press Club, December 7, 1911.
32. The passage is quoted in GP to R. M. La Follette, February 17, 1912.
33. William Kent, personal and confidential, to Hiram Johnson, April 6, 1912.
34. Bela C. and Fola La Follette, p. 365.
35. GP diary, December 12, 1911.
36. GP diary, December 17, 1911.
37. Undated (March 1912) statement signed by Amos Pinchot, William Kent, Gifford Pinchot, and Medill McCormick.
38. GP diary, December 26, 1911.
39. Mowry, p. 200.
40. Bela C. and Fola La Follette, p. 374.
41. *Columbus Citizen*, January 1, 1912.
42. *La Follette's Autobiography*, p. 577.
43. GP diary, January 14, 1912.
44. GP diary, January 19, 1912.
45. GP speech, January 20, 1912.
46. Bela C. and Fola La Follette, p. 385; Howland, *Theodore Roosevelt and His Times*, p. 210.
47. GP diary, January 22, 1912.
48. Pringle, *Theodore Roosevelt*, p. 554; *Campaign Contributions*, testimony before a Subcommittee of the Senate Committee on Privileges and Elections, pursuant to S. Res. 79 (1913), Vol. 1, p. 570.
49. GP diary, January 22, 1912.
50. *La Follette's Autobiography*, p. 597.
51. *Ibid.*, p. 602.
52. GP diary, January 29, 1912.
53. Bela C. and Fola La Follette, p. 400.
54. *Ibid.*, p. 403.
55. GP to H. T. Halbert, February 10, 1912.
56. Bela C. and Fola La Follette, p. 420.
57. GP to H. T. Halbert, February 16, 1912.
58. GP diary, February 5, 1912.
59. GP to G. W. Woodruff, February 14, 1912.
60. N. H. Dunn to GP, February 15, 1912.
61. GP to R. M. La Follette, February 17, 1912.
62. GP diary, February 17, 1912.
63. GP statement, February 19, 1912.
64. GP diary, February 18, 1912.
65. Elizabeth G. Evans to GP, February 18, 1912.
66. GP to Elizabeth G. Evans, February 22, 1912.
67. GP to H. A. Slattery, October 26, 1920.

CHAPTER 14

1. GP to J. M. Dixon, March 1, 1913.
2. GP diary, April 9, 1912.
3. GP diary, March 16, 1912.
4. *The Autobiography of William Allen White* (New York, Macmillan, 1946), p. 463.
5. Howland, *Theodore Roosevelt and His Times*, p. 220.
6. Mowry, *Theodore Roosevelt and the Progressive Movement*, p. 249.
7. *New York Times*, June 23, 1912.
8. GP diary, June 22, 1912.
9. GP to W. P. Eno, July 11, 1912.
10. GP to H. C. Wallace, August 2, 1912.
11. GP to G. D. Seymour, August 6, 1912.
12. GP to Horace Plunkett, July 15, 1912.

13. GP diary, August 4, 1912.
14. Mowry, p. 291.
15. White, p. 475.
16. GP to Mrs. J. R. Garfield, January 30, 1911.
17. Mowry, p. 272.
18. GP diary, August 5, 1912.
19. White, p. 487.
20. Lewis, *The Life of Theodore Roosevelt*, p. 374.
21. Bowers, *Beveridge and the Progressive Era*, p. 431.
22. White, p. 489.
23. Theodore Roosevelt to Amos Pinchot, December 5, 1912; quoted in 7 Morison 661.
24. GP to Hiram Johnson, May 30, 1912.
25. GP to Horace Plunkett, July 15, 1912.
26. GP speech at Progressive rally, August 23, 1912.
27. GP to Theodore Roosevelt, October 25, 1912.
28. Theodore Roosevelt to GP, October 29, 1912.
29. GP diary, October 21, 1912.
30. GP to Theodore Roosevelt, August 24, 1912.
31. GP to Theodore Roosevelt, October 25, 1912.
32. GP to Horace Plunkett, October 13, 1912.
33. GP to Mrs. C. B. Wood, November 8, 1912.
34. GP to H. L. Eno, March 12, 1913.
35. GP diary, March 26, 1911.
36. Mary Eno Pinchot to J. M. Foster, October 11, 1911.
37. GP speech at Lincoln Day banquet, February 12, 1913.
38. GP to R. S. Baker, September 15, 1913.
39. Mary Eno Pinchot diary, November 10, 1912.
40. Theodore Roosevelt to GP, November 11, 1912; quoted in 7 Morison 637.
41. GP to J. D. Appleby, August 17, 1938.
42. GP to Theodore Roosevelt, November 9, 1912.
43. Theodore Roosevelt to GP, November 11, 1912; quoted in 7 Morison 637.
44. Theodore Roosevelt to GP, November 13, 1912; quoted in 7 Morison 640.
45. GP to Theodore Roosevelt, November 23, 1912.
46. GP to Amos Pinchot, December 1, 1912.
47. Theodore Roosevelt to Kermit Roosevelt, December 3, 1912; quoted in 7 Morison 660.
48. GP diary, December 11, 1912.
49. GP diary, December 8, 1912.
50. GP diary, December 10, 1912.
51. *Ibid.*
52. Theodore Roosevelt to Amos Pinchot, December 5, 1912; quoted in 7 Morison 661.
53. GP diary, December 12, 1912.
54. GP diary, December 13, 1912.
55. GP to Theodore Roosevelt, December 17, 1912.
56. GP to E. H. Hooker, December 17, 1912.
57. Theodore Roosevelt to GP, December 21, 1912; quoted in 7 Morison 677.
58. GP to Hiram Johnson, December 28, 1912.
59. GP to Theodore Roosevelt, January 1, 1913.
60. Theodore Roosevelt to GP, January 3, 1913.
61. GP diary, February 4, 1913.
62. GP diary, March 29, 1913.
63. GP to Theodore Roosevelt, May 6, 1913.
64. GP speech in New York, October 3, 1913.
65. GP diary, March 30, 1914.
66. GP to Amos Pinchot, April 4, 1914.
67. O. W. Price diary, April 14, 1914.
68. May 23, 1914.
69. GP statement quoted in GP to A. J. Beveridge, June 24, 1914.
70. White, p. 517; Mowry, p. 294.
71. GP diary, April 15, 1913.

72. GP diary, June 13, 1913.
73. GP diary, June 24, 1913.
74. GP diary, July 2, 1913.
75. Theodore Roosevelt, *Autobiography*, p. 394.
76. Mary Eno Pinchot to Theodore Roosevelt (undated).

CHAPTER 15

1. GP to Medill McCormick, April 25, 1913.
2. GP to E. W. Scripps, March 27, 1914.
3. C. O. Gill and GP, *The Country Church; The Decline of Its Influence and the Remedy* (New York, Macmillan, 1913).
4. GP form letter (undated).
5. C. O. Gill and GP, *Six Thousand Country Churches* (New York, Macmillan, 1919).
6. P. S. Stahlnecker to H. A. Slattery, November 3, 1915.
7. GP speech to meeting called by Federal Board of Farm Organizations, August 29, 1918.
8. GP speech, Buffalo, November 20, 1917.
9. H. C. Wallace to GP, November 2, 1922.
10. Leslie Angelsmith to J. W. Pinchot, October 10, 1880.
11. GP to parents, October 12, 1890.
12. GP to J. W. Pinchot, November 9, 1890.
13. GP to Theodore Roosevelt, May 25, 1908.
14. GP to E. A. Van Valkenberg, December 30, 1912.
15. GP to C. O. Gill, January 24, 1913.
16. GP to Horace Plunkett, November 23, 1913.
17. GP diary, January 26, 1913.
18. GP to G. C. Pardee, December 14, 1913.
19. GP to Lady Johnstone, December 8, 1913.
20. GP diary, May [?], 1913.
21. GP to H. L. Stimson, June 5, 1914; H. C. Wallace to GP, December 4, 1913.

22. GP to Theodore Roosevelt, December 10, 1913.
23. GP to A. N. Detrich, February 28, 1914.
24. S. K. Stevens, *Pennsylvania, The Keystone State* (New York, American Historical Co., 1956), Vol. 1, p. 594.
25. GP to E. W. Scripps, March 27, 1914.
26. GP to P. S. Stahlnecker, January 15, 1927.
27. Mary Eno Pinchot diary, May 24, 1914.
28. GP to E. A. Mead, July 21, 1914.
29. GP to Frances A. Kellor, April 15, 1913.
30. GP diary, June 22, 1913.
31. GP to C. B. Pinchot, May 30, 1915.
32. GP diary, August 15, 1935.
33. GP to Amos Pinchot, September 13, 1914.
34. Walter Davenport, *Power and Glory* (New York, Putnam's, 1931), p. 102.
35. *Ibid.*, p. 109; Jean Gould (ed.), *Home-Grown Liberal* (New York, Dodd, Mead, 1954), p. 26.
36. *Philadelphia Public Ledger*, February 9, 1914.
37. *Ibid.*, May 21, 1914.
38. *Philadelphia Inquirer*, October 28, 1914.
39. GP diary, May 20, 1914.
40. Mowry, *Theodore Roosevelt and the Progressive Movement*, p. 300.
41. GP to Theodore Roosevelt, October [?], 1914.
42. O. K. Davis, *Released for Publication* (New York, Houghton Mifflin, 1925), p. 441.
43. GP to H. A. Slattery, October 30, 1914.
44. GP form letter, December 29, 1914.
45. Cable quoted in P. S. Stahlnecker to Amos Pinchot, March 8, 1915.
46. GP to H. C. Wallace, May 5, 1915.
47. GP diary, April 9, 1915.
48. GP to A. K. Fisher, May 5, 1915.
49. GP to H. C. Wallace, January 26, 1916.
50. GP to Hiram Johnson, July 15, 1915.

51. GP form letter, October 25, etc., 1915. See M. L. Fausold, "Gifford Pinchot and the Decline of Pennsylvania Progressivism," *Pennsylvania History*, January 1958.
52. GP to J. M. Dixon, March 3, 1916.
53. May [?], 1916.
54. GP to Theodore Roosevelt, June 4, 1916.
55. *The Autobiography of William Allen White*; Mowry, *Theodore Roosevelt and the Progressive Movement*.
56. GP to W. A. White, July 8, 1937.
57. GP to J. M. Dixon, June 16, 1916.
58. GP to Lady Johnstone, July 1, 1916.
59. GP to H. L. Ickes, July 1, 1916.
60. GP diary, July 21, 1911.
61. GP diary, January 8, 1913.
62. Mary Eno Pinchot to J. M. Foster (undated).
63. GP to G. E. Chamberlain, March 5, 1913.
64. GP diary, March 5, 10, 18, 1913.
65. J. P. Tumulty to GP, May 22 and June 4, 1913.
66. GP to H. D. W. English, April 25, 1914.
67. Theodore Roosevelt to GP, June 22, 1915.
68. GP to F. H. Newell, July 18, 1916.
69. GP form letter, September 20, etc., 1916.
70. GP form letter, September 7, etc., 1916.
71. GP to Lady Johnstone, November 16, 1916.
72. GP to H. D. W. English, December 13, 1916.
73. GP to H. D. W. English, December 20, 1916.

CHAPTER 16

1. GP to Matthew Hale, December 22, 1916.
2. GP statement, December 24, 1916.
3. GP to C. L. Pack, December 19, 1914.
4. GP to G. C. Pardee, January 25, 1917.
5. GP to H. C. Lodge, April 2, 1917.
6. GP to Woodrow Wilson, February 9, 1917.
7. GP to Theodore Roosevelt, May 11, 1917.
8. Theodore Roosevelt to General P. C. March, September 1, 1918.
9. GP to Theodore Roosevelt, May 19, 1917.
10. GP to H. L. Ickes, May 25, 1917.
11. April 26, 1917.
12. GP to A. W. Dimock, May 11, 1917.
13. GP to Theodore Roosevelt, June 21, 1917.
14. GP to J. A. McSparran, August 19, 1917.
15. GP to H. C. Wallace, October 26, 1917.
16. GP to Herbert Hoover, October 25, 1917.
17. GP to H. C. Wallace, October 26, 1917.
18. *Ibid.*
19. Herbert Hoover to GP, October 27, 1917.
20. GP to H. C. Wallace, February 27, 1918; GP to E. M. House, October 20, 1917.
21. GP to J. R. Garfield, September 11, 1918.
22. GP, confidential, to Robert Lansing, October 15, 1918.
23. Theodore Roosevelt to P. C. March, September 1, 1918.
24. M. Churchill to GP, October 29, 1918.
25. GP to W. H. Hays, November 8, 1918.
26. GP to Theodore Roosevelt, November 18, 1918.
27. Lady Johnstone to GP, January 18, 1919.
28. Theodore Roosevelt to C. B. Pinchot, May 13, 1915.
29. GP to Theodore Roosevelt, April 18, 1917.
30. GP to Theodore Roosevelt, January 29, 1917.
31. GP to Lady Johnstone, January 24, 1918.
32. GP to W. E. Crow, June 8, 1918.

33. GP to J. H. Maurer, February 26, 1918.
34. J. H. Maurer, March 6, 1919.
35. Elizabeth Frazer, "Mrs. Gifford Pinchot, Housewife and Politician," *Saturday Evening Post*, August 26, 1922.
36. *East Stroudsburg Press*, August 20, 1919.
37. GP to Boies Penrose, January 25, 1919.
38. *Philadelphia North American*, January 28, 1919.
39. GP to J. R. Garfield, September 27, 1919.
40. GP to G. C. Pardee, October 8, 1919.
41. *La Follette's Autobiography*, p. 593.
42. GP to Amos Pinchot, January 18, 1919.
43. GP to J. R. Garfield, March 26, 1919.
44. GP to H. A. Slattery, December 16, 1919.
45. GP to W. H. Hays, September 4, 1918.
46. GP and others to W. H. Hays, October 8, 1918.
47. GP statement, April 16, 1919.
48. GP notes on interview with Lynn Haines, October 27, 1919.
49. GP to H. D. W. English, February 17, 1919.
50. GP to H. D. W. English, June 24, 1920.
51. GP to H. L. Ickes, February 18, 1920.
52. GP to Horace Plunkett, March 19, 1919.
53. GP speech, March 27, 1920.
54. GP to editor, February 25, 1920.
55. A. N. Detrich to GP, February 9, 1920.
56. GP to H. D. W. English, June 24, 1920.
57. GP to H. D. W. English, July 18, 1919.
58. GP to Calvin Coolidge, November 6, 1919.
59. GP to H. D. W. English, July 10, 1920.
60. GP to H. A. Slattery, August 30, 1920.
61. GP to Lady Johnstone, January 17, 1921.
62. GP to Republican newspapers, October 2, 1920.
63. GP to H. L. Ickes, September 25, 1920.
64. GP, confidential, to S. M. Lindsay, March 6, 1921.
65. GP to Lady Johnstone, March 14, 1921.
66. GP form letter, October 16, 1944.

CHAPTER 17

1. GP to W. C. Sproul, November 8, 1918.
2. GP to Hiram Andrews, August 7, 1919.
3. H. W. Shoemaker and GP to W. C. Sproul, October 31, 1919. Rothrock's annoyance is revealed in a letter to Mira Lloyd Dock, March 4, 1920 (Dock papers).
4. GP to H. W. Shoemaker, December 23, 1919.
5. GP to W. C. Sproul, March 3, 1920.
6. March 11, 1920.
7. *Talks on Forestry by Gifford Pinchot*, Bulletin No. 32, Pennsylvania Department of Forestry, May 1923.
8. GP to W. C. Sproul, March 29, 1920.
9. GP to H. H. Ritter, July 29, 1920.
10. J. T. Rothrock to "Whom It May Concern," April 28, 1922; R. Y. Stuart to GP, July 11, 1922.
11. *New York Times*, January 5 and June 21, 1922.
12. GP to H. M. Chalfant, October 2, 1915.
13. GP to Ernest Lundeen, September 6, 1932.
14. GP to H. A. Slattery, March 23, 1933.
15. T. R. White, "The Philadelphia System," *Forum*, May 1927.
16. *Time*, May 6, 1940, p. 16.
17. GP speech, Philadelphia, March 10, 1922; *Harrisburg Evening News*, March 11, 1922.

18. GP to Horace Plunkett, July 1, 1922.
19. GP to members of Department of Forestry, March 15, 1922.
20. GP to leaders of the Republican State Organization, March 22, 1922.
21. GP to T. L. Eyre, March 24, 1922.
22. *New York Times*, August 27, 1922.
23. GP to Lady Johnstone, April 5, 1922.
24. Form letter, May 9, 1922.
25. GP to L. S. Weaver, April 11, 1930.
26. *Harrisburg Evening News*, July 27, 1922.
27. GP telegram to W. C. Sproul, probably April 14, 1922.
28. *Harrisburg Evening News*, October 27, 1922.
29. May 10, 1922.
30. J. A. Rose to GP, July 3, 1922.
31. "So This Is Politics," Pinchot's unpublished account of his first term as governor. Hereafter referred to as GP manuscript.
32. R. B. Strassburger telegram to C. B. Pinchot, May 2, 1922.
33. *Harrisburg Evening News*, May 5, 1922.
34. GP manuscript, ch. 2, p. 13.
35. *Congressional Record*, 67th Cong., 2d sess., p. 7,911.
36. GP to William Kent, July 1, 1922.
37. G. H. Lorimer to GP, May 18, 1922.
38. GP to Horace Plunkett, July 1, 1922.

CHAPTER 18

1. GP to Horace Plunkett, July 1, 1922.
2. General Asher Miner. GP to Republican State Committee of Pennsylvania, June 7, 1922.
3. *Philadelphia Bulletin*, June 10, 1922.
4. GP to Joseph Grundy, August 28, 1922.
5. GP to editors of Republican papers, August 22, 1922.
6. *Philadelphia Evening Public Ledger*, October 24, 1922.
7. November 1922.

8. GP to G. C. Pardee, December 20, 1922.
9. GP to G. C. Pardee, November 29, 1922.
10. GP to G. C. Pardee, December 20, 1922.
11. GP manuscript, ch. 5, p. 5.
12. GP to Amos Pinchot, November 28, 1922.
13. H. J. Allen to GP, June 3, 1922.
14. W. Brooke Graves, interview, 1955.
15. GP to H. J. Allen, June [?], 1922.
16. GP to George Woodward, June 3, 1922.
17. *Harrisburg Evening News*, January 16, 1923.
18. GP to G. C. Pardee, November 29, 1922.
19. GP to Herman Biggs, December 21, 1922.
20. January 16, 1923.
21. GP to G. C. Pardee, January 27, 1923.
22. GP speech to Manufacturers' Club, Philadelphia, December 9, 1922.
23. GP manuscript, ch. 11, p. 24.
24. Minutes of cabinet meeting, January 29, 1923.
25. October 2, 1923.
26. GP memorandum, November 7, 1924.
27. May 2, 1921.
28. GP to Lady Johnstone, November 28, 1922.
29. GP to H. W. Shoemaker, January 22, 1924.
30. GP to R. L. Jones, August 3, 1940.
31. GP manuscript, ch. 21, p. 15.
32. K. E. Trombley, *The Life and Times of a Happy Liberal* (New York, Harper, 1954), p. 103.
33. *Ibid.*, p. 105.
34. *Report of the Giant Power Survey Board* (Harrisburg, 1925).
35. *Annals*, March 1925.
36. March 1924.
37. GP speech to Commonwealth Club, San Francisco, July 6, 1925.
38. GP to M. L. Cooke, February 18, 1925.
39. GP manuscript, ch. 21, p. 33.

40. GP to Lady Johnstone, June 10, 1924.
41. GP statement, July 30, 1925.
42. GP to P. P. Wells, September 30, 1924.
43. GP manuscript, ch. 22, p. 12.
44. GP to W. D. Ainey, September 24, 1924.
45. GP to S. M. Clement, Jr., October 1, 1924.
46. GP statement, July 30, 1925.
47. GP to M. L. Cooke, November 1, 1924.
48. GP manuscript, ch. 22, p. 14.
49. January 4, 1927, pp. XLIII and XLIV.
50. GP to J. D. Stern, February 3, 1930.
51. GP statement, January 24, 1924.
52. GP to Ella George, November 4, 1926.
53. GP to Ella George, October 27, 1931.
54. GP to C. C. McGovern, August 2, 1924.
55. GP to Thomas Kennedy, March 8, 1926.
56. J. L. Lewis to GP, March 12, 1926.
57. GP to W. B. Wright, Jr., April 13, 1927.
58. GP speech, August 21, 1927.
59. Harvey O'Connor, *Mellon's Millions* (New York, John Day, 1933), p. 236.
60. GP to A. W. Mellon, October 28, 1923.
61. November 2, 1923, attached to A. W. Mellon letter to GP of same date.
62. October 3, 1923.
63. Charles Merz, *The Dry Decade* (Garden City, Doubleday, Doran, 1931), p. 141.
64. GP to Smedley Butler, January 8, 1924.
65. GP to R. J. Beamish, July 8, 1926.
66. GP to E. A. Paddock, January 15, 1924.
67. Gifford Pinchot, "Wages, Margins and Anthracite Prices," *Annals*, January 1924, p. 61; GP to W. D. Lewis, November 7, 1923.

68. GP to H. K. Smith, September 5, 1923.
69. GP manuscript, ch. 19, p. 9.
70. *New York Times*, August 25, 1923.
71. GP to H. K. Smith, September 5, 1923.
72. GP to W. A. White, July 27, 1937.
73. *Harrisburg Evening News*, August 25, 1923.
74. GP to W. D. Lewis, September 8, 1923.
75. Calvin Coolidge to GP, September 12, 1923.
76. Calvin Coolidge to GP, September 7, 1923.
77. W. A. White to GP, September 11, 1923.
78. Quoted in Walter Johnson, *Selected Letters of William Allen White* (New York, Holt, 1947), p. 237.
79. January 4, 1927, p. XLVIII.
80. GP to G. C. Pardee, March 11, 1924.
81. GP statement, December 29, 1924.
82. GP to Lady Johnstone, February 18, 1925.
83. GP to Horace Plunkett, August 13, 1924.

CHAPTER 19

1. GP, personal and confidential, to Horace Plunkett, March 13, 1924.
2. GP to Lady Johnstone, March 31, 1924.
3. O'Connor, *Mellon's Millions*, p. 260.
4. *Harrisburg Evening News*, December 7, 1923.
5. W. A. White to GP, September 11, 1923; quoted in Johnson, *Selected Letters of William Allen White*, p. 237.
6. GP to P. M. Neff, November 1, 1923.
7. W. S. Vare, *My Forty Years in Politics* (Philadelphia, Roland Swain, 1933), p. 145.
8. GP statement, April 23, 1924.
9. GP to H. D. W. English, May 6, 1924; GP to W. A. White, April 24, 1924.
10. GP statement, June 14, 1924.

11. GP to Horace Plunkett, December 2, 1924.
12. *Harrisburg Evening News*, March 6, 1925.
13. *Ibid.*, May 15, 1925.
14. *Ibid.*, July 20, 21, 22, 1925.
15. *Ibid.*, August 28, 1925.
16. Quoted in GP message to General Assembly, January 13, 1926.
17. *Harrisburg Evening News*, November 27, 1925.
18. *Ibid.*, March 13, 1926.
19. Vare, p. 167.
20. GP statement, April 9, 1926.
21. Undated.
22. GP manuscript, ch. 26, p. 17.
23. *Harrisburg Evening News*, February 12, 1926.
24. GP to Harcourt Johnstone, May 25, 1926.
25. See *Senatorial Campaign Expenditures*, Hearings . . . on S. Res. 195, 69th Cong., 1st sess., 3 parts; *New York Times*, December 23, 1926.
26. GP statement, September 14, 1926.
27. *Congressional Record*, 69th Cong., 2d sess., p. 1,338.

CHAPTER 20

1. Richard Heagy, in transcript of "Investigation of Executive Offices of the Commonwealth," February 21, 1933.
2. GP to T. D. Frye, June 30, 1931.
3. GP to S. S. Lewis, July 25, 1931.
4. GP to E. O. Draper, July 7, 1932.
5. GP to department heads, March 24, 1931.
6. GP memo for office force, January 12, 1933.
7. GP to W. C. Goodwin, August 17, 1931.
8. *Harrisburg Evening News*, August 7, 1923.
9. GP to C. H. Miner, August 13, 1923.
10. GP to Horace Plunkett, July 17, 1923.
11. GP to David Hobbs, November 9, 1931.
12. GP to Warren Luckenbill, August 22, 1925.

13. *Harrisburg Evening News*, May 13, 1925.
14. GP to R. W. Beal, March 20, 1933.
15. GP to H. L. Knapp, December 6, 1923.
16. GP radio speech, April 25, 1933.
17. December 5, 1923.
18. *Harrisburg Evening News*, December 13, 1923.
19. GP to C. C. McGovern, May 3, 1923.
20. *Message* to the General Assembly, January 4, 1927.
21. GP to Lady Johnstone, February 5, 1927.
22. GP to J. L. Lewis, January 7, 1927.
23. GP, confidential, to E. J. Hunter, June 20, 1928.
24. GP to C. A. Beard, January 10, 1930.
25. January 5, 1927.
26. January 5, 1927.
27. *Congressional Record*, 69th Cong., 2d sess., p. 5,918.
28. GP to Smedley Butler, January 8, 1927.
29. *Harrisburg Evening News*, January 17, 1927.
30. Typewritten proceedings of reception for state employees, January 13, 1927.
31. January 1927.
32. W. A. Schnader to GP, March 19, 1927.

CHAPTER 21

1. F. H. Newell to GP, April 20, 1921; J. T. Rothrock to GP, March 14, 1922.
2. Committee for the Application of Forestry, "Forest Devastation: A National Danger and a Plan to Meet It."
3. Dana, *Forest and Range Policy*, p. 221.
4. GP statement, June 30, 1916.
5. Naval Appropriation Act of 1920.
6. GP to Walter Darlington, February 24, 1921.
7. GP to G. W. Pepper, February 18, 1924.

8. GP to O. J. Roberts, February 18, 1924.

9. GP to Harcourt Johnstone, March 8, 1924.

10. GP to O. J. Roberts, October 18, 1927.

11. GP to O. J. Roberts, October 24, 1927.

12. GP to H. S. Graves, December 16, 1922.

13. GP to Smedley Butler, January 8, 1927.

14. *Deforested America*, S. Doc. 216, 70th Cong., 2d. sess.

15. W. M. Jardine to GP, January 3, 1929.

16. GP and G. P. Ahern statement, December 31, 1929.

17. GP to Barrington Moore, December 3, 1929.

18. *Santa Cruz News* (Calif.), January 28, 1930.

19. Wilson Compton to GP, January 15, 1929.

20. GP to Wilson Compton, January 17, 1929.

21. February 1929.

22. GP to O. M. Butler, February 8, 1929.

23. GP to H. S. Graves, December 9, 1929.

24. GP to G. W. Woodruff, January 4, 1930.

25. Dana, pp. 213-214.

26. GP to Raphael Zon, November 15, 1929.

27. GP to M. L. Cooke, etc., December 14, 1927.

28. January 26, 1928.

29. GP to governors, March 15, 1927.

30. *Ibid.*

31. February 16, 1927.

32. March 24, 1927.

33. GP to T. J. Walsh, December 2, 1927.

34. GP to senators, February 10 and 11, 1928.

35. Sen. Doc. 92, 70th Cong., 1st. sess.

36. GP to A. S. Goss, December 10, 1928.

37. Milford, Pa., 1929.

38. GP form letter, April 17, 1928.

39. GP telegram to friends, February 22, 1928.

40. GP to Lady Johnstone, May 2, 1928.

41. GP to E. J. Hunter, July 17, 1928.

42. Edward Martin to GP, September 7, 1928.

43. GP to *Los Angeles Herald*, April 13, 1920.

44. GP to W. H. Newton, September 29, 1928.

45. GP to Einar Barfod, October 7, 1928.

46. GP to Alfred Marvin, November 5, 1928.

47. *Sports Afield*, April 1932.

48. GP to A. W. Dimock, January 21, 1916.

49. *Just Fishing Talk* (Harrisburg, The Telegraph Press, 1936).

50. GP typewritten account of trip, p. 792.

51. Gifford Pinchot, *To The South Seas* (Philadelphia, Winston, 1930), p. 36.

52. GP to Mrs. Gladys Wassmann, July 19, 1929.

53. P. S. Stahlnecker to M. E. Gregg, April 30, 1929.

54. GP to P. S. Stahlnecker, July 16, 1929.

55. C. B. Pinchot to P. S. Stahlnecker, July 20, 1929.

56. P. S. Stahlnecker to Mr. and Mrs. Pinchot, June 12, 1929.

57. GP to P. S. Stahlnecker, August 13, 1929.

58. October 27, 1929.

59. GP to C. L. Burke, June 16, 1937.

60. GP to Frank Lloyd, November 20, 1935.

CHAPTER 22

1. GP to H. S. Graves, November 8, 1929.

2. GP to W. W. Long, November 7, 1929.

3. *Ibid.*; GP, personal, to J. H. Gray, January 4, 1930.

4. GP to Horace Plunkett, January 7, 1930.
5. GP to W. W. Long, December 10, 1930.
6. GP to C. L. King, February 17, 1930.
7. T. R. White to GP, May 22, 1930.
8. GP speech to United Business Men's Association of Philadelphia, February 27, 1930; GP to newspapers in two counties, April 5, 1920.
9. GP statement, March 31, 1930.
10. GP to E. J. Hunter, January 18, 1930.
11. J. H. Maurer, *It Can Be Done* (New York, Rand School, 1938), pp. 198-200.
12. P. S. Stahlnecker to W. W. Long, April 3, 1930.
13. GP to W. W. Atterbury, May 13, 1930.
14. C. C. McGovern. See GP to J. J. Coyne, June 26, 1931.
15. GP to W. P. Eno, March 30, 1936.
16. Statement of Pinchot for Governor State Committee, June 3, 1930; P. S. Stahlnecker to GP, May 10, 1930.
17. GP to W. T. Chantland, August 23, 1930.
18. G. W. Woodruff to GP (undated), September 1930.
19. GP to J. T. Faris, June 10, 1930.
20. *Harrisburg Evening News*, November 3, 1930.
21. *Ibid.*, October 8, 1930.
22. *New York Times*, October 10, 1930.
23. Edward Martin form letter to "Fellow Republican," October 27, 1930.
24. *Harrisburg Patriot*, October 15, 1930.
25. *Harrisburg Evening News*, October 23, 1930.
26. GP to editor of *Wilkes-Barre Sunday Telegram*, December 19, 1929.
27. W. W. Long to GP, June 29, 1930.
28. GP to W. W. Long, July 3, 1930.
29. October 1930, p. 10.
30. *Philadelphia Record*, August 11, 1945.
31. P. S. Stahlnecker to GP, September 12, 1930.

32. *Harrisburg Evening News*, October 24, 1930.
33. O. M. Deibler to P. S. Stahlnecker, October 6, 1930.
34. M. L. Cooke to GP, September 29, 1930.
35. GP form letter, October 18, 1930.
36. P. S. Stahlnecker to Ellen Potter, October 23, 1930.
37. *Harrisburg Evening News*, August 28, 1930.
38. *Ibid.*, September 23, 1930.
39. Edward Martin to GP, October 1, 1930.
40. A. M. Schlesinger, Jr., *The Age of Roosevelt; The Crisis of the Old Order* (Boston, Houghton Mifflin, 1957), p. 224.
41. *Raleigh News and Observer*, November 6, 1930.

CHAPTER 23

1. July 19, 1930.
2. GP to Gertrude Broyles, November 18, 1930.
3. C. B. Pinchot to Felix Frankfurter, January 4, 1931.
4. GP inaugural address, January 20, 1931.
5. GP to Mrs. S. A. DeWitt, February 10, 1932.
6. GP to D. C. McCallum, August 6, 1931.
7. *Ibid.*
8. GP to department heads, May 6, 1931.
9. GP to Mrs. Maud Beamish, March 6, 1931.
10. GP to G. C. Pardee, February 6, 1933.
11. Leon Holtsizer in *Philadelphia Evening Public Ledger*, November 21, 1932.
12. GP to G. T. Weingartner, December 15, 1930.
13. GP statement, January 4, 1931.
14. GP radio speech, February 10, 1931.
15. *Harrisburg Evening News*, February 16, 1931. Reproduced in the advertisement was W. H. Taylor letter to GP, February 13, 1931.

16. GP message to General Assembly, February 10, 1931.
17. *Harrisburg Evening News*, February 10, 1931.
18. GP speech before Senate committee investigating public utilities, March 2, 1931.
19. *Harrisburg Evening News*, March 2, 1931.
20. GP to Horace Plunkett, April 27, 1931.
21. GP to M. L. Cooke, August 21, 1933.
22. Stephen Raushenbush to GP, October 29, 1931.
23. GP to Harold Evans, May 15, 1931.
24. *Legislative Journal*, April 27, 1931, p. 2,514; Final Report (mimeographed), undated.
25. GP statement, April 29, 1931.
26. *Legislative Journal*, April 14, 1931, p. 1,926.
27. *Harrisburg Patriot*, May 13, 1931.
28. GP message to Senate, August 10, 1932.
29. Enclosed with L. H. Kinnard to GP, May 8, 1931.
30. *Pittsburgh Press*, May 18, 1931.
31. GP to W. D. Ainey, June 29, 1932.
32. *Philadelphia Inquirer*, June 30, 1932.
33. Message to Senate, July 25, 1932.
34. GP to H. A. Slattery, August 1, 1932.
35. *Harrisburg Evening News*, August 3, 1932.
36. *Ibid.*
37. August 10, 1932.
38. GP to Emerson Collins, July 19, 1932.
39. GP speech to Senate, August 10, 1932.
40. GP message to General Assembly, January 3, 1933.
41. GP to C. L. King, October 1, 1932.
42. GP to C. L. King, October 27, 1932.
43. GP to C. L. King, November 21, 1932.
44. GP to C. L. King, December 15, 1932.
45. *Pittsburgh Press*, February 22, 1933.
46. GP statement, March 9, 1933.
47. *Harrisburg Evening News*, March 9, 1933.
48. GP to C. L. King, March 17, 1933.
49. *Harrisburg Evening News*, May 6, 1933.
50. Except one whose nomination Pinchot had tried to recall.
51. GP statement, September 19, 1934.
52. GP speech to Mayor's Unemployment Committee in Detroit, August 13, 1931.
53. GP to Herbert Hoover, August 18, 1931.
54. GP to G. C. Pardee, November 30, 1932.
55. Proclamation, October 31, 1931.
56. GP message to special session, November 10, 1931.
57. *Harrisburg Evening News*, November 12, 1931.
58. O'Connor, *Mellon's Millions*, p. 350.
59. *Harrisburg Evening News*, November 18, 1931.
60. *Philadelphia Bulletin*, November 25, 1931.
61. GP statement, December 18, 1931.
62. GP statement, December 23, 1931.
63. "Clip sheet," August 18, 1932.
64. GP statement, August 8, 1932.
65. C. A. Waters, "Reduction in Cost of Government," *The Right of Way*, December 1932, p. 20.
66. Veto of S. Res (May 2, 1933), June 3, 1933.
67. *Harrisburg Evening News*, June 5, 1933.
68. *Ibid.*, April 19, 1933.
69. Veto of H. 22, June 3, 1933.
70. GP to G. C. Pardee, May 29, 1933.
71. GP message to General Assembly, September 12, 1934, quoting F. D. Roosevelt letter to GP.
72. H. L. Hopkins to GP, August 31, 1934; quoted in message.
73. GP statement, September 19, 1934.
74. GP message to General Assembly, February 14, 1933.
75. *Ibid.*
76. GP to S. E. Gable, May 20, 1931.

77. GP to W. J. Burchinal, October 16, 1931.
78. GP message to General Assembly, October 10, 1931.
79. GP speech to Convention of Pennsylvania Federation of Labor, Reading, May 11, 1932.
80. GP to legislators, April 24, 1933.
81. GP speech, September 14, 1933.
82. Mrs. Frances Perkins to GP, December 4, 1933.
83. *Harrisburg Evening News*, November 13, 1933.
84. GP to Edward Martin, December 12, 1933.
85. "The Governor Says," December 27, 1933.
86. GP to Hiram Johnson, January 31, 1928.
87. Stevens, *Pennsylvania, The Keystone State*, p. 470.
88. GP statement, March 24, 1930.
89. GP to L. G. Adams, March 3, 1931.
90. GP to L. G. Adams, March 21, 1931.
91. GP to L. G. Adams, July 1, 1933.
92. *Pittsburgh Sun-Telegraph*, June 23, 1931.
93. Notes, in GP Papers, of interview by reporter of *Kansas City Star*, Sedalia, Missouri, September 1, 1931.
94. GP statement, December 9, 1932.
95. GP to F. D. Roosevelt, April 7, 1933; GP statement, April 26, 1933.
96. GP to F. D. Roosevelt, February 20, 1933.
97. GP statement, August 1, 1933.
98. Thomas Moses telegram to GP, July 31, 1933, quoted in GP statement, August 2, 1933.
99. M. E. Gregg to Richard Heagy, August 6, 1933.
100. August 10, 1933.
101. GP, private and confidential, to H. A. Slattery, August 18, 1933.
102. *Ibid.*
103. GP speech at Uniontown, September 4, 1933.
104. GP to F. D. Roosevelt, September 5, 1933.
105. GP statement, October 3, 1933.

106. GP to Lady Johnstone, October 5, 1933.
107. GP to L. G. Adams, June 25, 1932, and to J. D. Pennington, March 14, 1932.
108. October 27, 1933.
109. GP message to special session, November 13, 1933.
110. GP message to special session, December 5, 1933.
111. *Harrisburg Evening News*, January 11, 1933; *Legislative Journal*, January 11, 1933, pp. 153, 156.
112. GP to R. W. Gawthrop, January 15, 1934.
113. GP to D. H. Curry, September 4, 1931.
114. GP to J. H. Berger, July 25, 1934.
115. GP to J. C. Bowman, July 11, 1934.
116. GP to Sofia M. Loebinger, May 25, 1933.
117. GP to H. J. Farr, January 19, 1933.
118. GP to E. K. Bean, May 22, 1931.
119. GP to C. B. Helms, April 11, 1931.
120. GP to Mrs. R. G. Barckley, January 9, 1934.
121. GP to Miss C. E. Carr, December 18, 1936.
122. GP final message to General Assembly, January 1, 1935.
123. *Time*, January 15, 1934.
124. GP to F. D. Roosevelt, January 10, 1934.

CHAPTER 24

1. GP statement, January 5, 1933.
2. GP to A. C. Dale, August 7, 1930.
3. *Philadelphia Evening Star*, November 8, 1930.
4. *Baltimore Sun*, December 5, 1930.
5. GP to Horace Plunkett, April 27, 1931.
6. GP to Horace Plunkett, June 6, 1931.
7. June 2, 1931.
8. *New York Times*, June 3, 1931.
9. *Pittsburgh Post-Gazette*, June 3, 1931.

10. September 1, 1931.
11. November 30, 1931.
12. December 4, 1931.
13. GP to H. A. Slattery, January 12, 1932.
14. Tabulated by "G.H.W.," January 25, 1936.
15. GP speech to Mid-Day Luncheon Club, February 12, 1932.
16. Harold L. Ickes, *The Autobiography of a Curmudgeon* (New York, Reynal & Hitchcock, 1943), p. 253.
17. For example, H. L. Ickes to M. S. Dietrich, March 12, 1933.
18. GP to H. L. Ickes, March 22, 1932.
19. Notes in GP files.
20. GP to H. L. Ickes, May 5, 1932.
21. May 19, 1932.
22. GP to Smedley Butler, June 15, 1932.
23. GP to H. L. Ickes, May 5, 1932.
24. GP to R. E. Flinn, September 1, 1932.
25. GP to W. A. White, November 14, 1932.
26. December 5, 1932.
27. GP to John Dewey, November 14, 1932.
28. GP to F. D. Roosevelt, December 1, 1932.
29. GP diary, February 19, 1912. Roosevelt frequently referred to this "striking" example; see, for instance, his speech, September 14, 1935, at Lake Placid, N.Y., in Edgar B. Nixon (ed.), *Franklin D. Roosevelt and Conservation, 1911-1945* (Hyde Park, Franklin D. Roosevelt Library, 1957), Vol. 1, p. 429.
30. GP to F. D. Roosevelt, January 19, 1929.
31. *Harrisburg Evening News*, February 1, 1933.
32. *Ibid.*, February 16, 1933.
33. T. E. McDermott to GP, December 20, 1932.
34. March 6, 1933.
35. July 10, 1932.
36. GP to A. G. McCarthy, Jr., August 4, 1933.
37. *Harrisburg Evening News*, September 26, 1933.
38. GP message to General Assembly, January 3, 1933.
39. GP to F. D. Roosevelt, May 15, 1933.
40. GP to D. L. Lawrence, July 3, 1933.
41. For example, GP to J. F. Guffey, July 22, 1933.
42. GP to H. L. Ickes, June 10, 1933.
43. *Harrisburg Evening News*, February 26, 1934.
44. *Ibid.*, April 10, 1934.
45. GP speeches at Scranton and Wilkes-Barre, May 10 and May 11, 1934.
46. *Time*, May 14, 1934.
47. GP to M. L. Cooke, May 29, 1934.
48. *Time*, May 14, 1934.
49. *Harrisburg Evening News*, October 4, 1934.
50. C. B. Pinchot statement (undated, approximately October 11, 1934).
51. GP to F. D. Roosevelt, October 29, 1934; GP, confidential, to R. E. Flinn, October 30, 1934; J. M. Burns, *Roosevelt: The Lion and the Fox* (New York, Harcourt, Brace, 1956), p. 199.
52. F. D. Roosevelt to GP, November 9, 1934.
53. *The Secret Diary of Harold L. Ickes* (New York, Simon & Schuster, 1953), Vol. 1, p. 207.
54. GP, confidential, to R. E. Flinn, November 30, 1940.
55. Brilhart, *Gifford Pinchot as a Conservation Crusader in 1909*.
56. GP telegram to Smedley Butler, March 31, 1932.
57. GP speech at Scranton, October 24, 1934.
58. GP to F. D. Roosevelt, October 29, 1934.
59. F. D. Roosevelt to GP, November 9, 1934.
60. *Scranton Republican*, November 7, 1934, syndicated column, Drew Pearson and Robert Allen.
61. GP statement, November 7, 1934.
62. May 6, 1933.

63. *Harrisburg Evening News*, December 24, 1934.
64. January 1, 1935.
65. *Harrisburg Evening News*, January 14, 1934.
66. January 14, 1935.
67. *San Francisco Examiner*, April 6, 1935.
68. GP to Mr. and Mrs. Harvey Taylor, April 11, 1935.

CHAPTER 25

1. GP form letter, March 23, 1932.
2. GP to F. D. Roosevelt, January 20, 1933.
3. F. D. Roosevelt to GP, February 1, 1933.
4. January 20, 1935.
5. Raphael Zon to GP, June 19, 1934.
6. GP to Raphael Zon, June 26, 1934.
7. GP to A. P. Proctor, October 2, 1937.
8. GP to W. T. Chantland, August 16, 1938.
9. GP to F. C. Brenckman, March 14, 1941.
10. GP to A. H. James, July 13, 1941.
11. GP form letter, June 24, 1942.
12. January 1943.
13. GP to E. H. Clapp, February 22, 1943.
14. GP to O. K. Davis, June 29, 1927.
15. H. L. Ickes to GP, November 6, 1930.
16. Handwritten copy of GP telegram to H. L. Ickes (undated); GP telegram to F. D. Roosevelt (undated).
17. *Just Fishing Talk*.
18. GP diary, June 24, 1935.
19. GP form letter, July 9, 1935.
20. GP to H. L. Ickes, July 18, 1935.
21. F. A. Silcox, personal and confidential, to GP, July 31, 1935.
22. GP diary, January 12, 1937.
23. GP diary, February 28, 1937.
24. GP speech, April 30, 1937.
25. *The Secret Diary of Harold L. Ickes*, Vol. II, pp. 131, 238.
26. GP diary, November 20-26, 1937.
27. GP to H. L. Ickes, December 30, 1938.
28. *The Secret Diary of Harold L. Ickes*, Vol. II, p. 565.
29. GP to H. L. Ickes, April 13, 1939.
30. F. D. Roosevelt to GP, January 15, 1940.
31. GP diary, January 16, 1940.
32. February 3, 1940.
33. GP diary, February 13, 1940.
34. GP to G. D. Seymour, April 2, 1940.
35. GP diary, March 8, 1940.
36. May 25, 1940.
37. By Harold L. Ickes, U.S. Government Printing Office (1940).
38. GP diary, May 22, 1940.
39. GP diary, June 16, 1940.
40. May 23, 1940.
41. H. L. Ickes to GP, May 18, 1940.
42. GP to Amos Pinchot, May 28, 1940.
43. GP to F. D. Roosevelt, January 17, 1940.
44. GP to E. B. Logan, December 5, 1935.
45. GP to F. D. Roosevelt, December 21, 1935.
46. F. D. Roosevelt to GP, December 27, 1935.
47. GP to F. D. Roosevelt, January 4, 1936.
48. January 13, 1936.
49. GP radio address, February 20, 1936.
50. GP to S. H. Fisher, January 27, 1936.
51. GP diary, May 27, 1936.
52. GP diary, May 28, 1936.
53. GP diary, June 5, 1936.
54. GP diary, September 11, 1936.
55. GP diary, August 22, 1936.
56. GP to A. M. Landon, August 30, 1936.
57. GP diary, October 5, 1936.
58. GP draft of letter to L. S. Welch, August 18, 1936.
59. GP diary, November 5, 1936.
60. GP diary, January 18, 1937.
61. GP to D. C. McCallum, November 1, 1937.
62. GP to R. A. Beck, January 27, 1938.
63. GP diary, January 20, 1939.

CHAPTER 26

1. GP to R. W. Huntington, June 8, 1939.
2. GP to A. K. Fisher, January 21, 1942.
3. GP to Raphael Zon, August 28, 1939.
4. October 18, 1939.
5. GP to R. R. McCormick, November 7, 1939.
6. GP diary, December 7, 1941.
7. GP to A. P. Proctor, January 8, 1942.
8. GP to H. L. Stimson, March 27, 1942.
9. GP to Franklin Knox, January 17 and 22, 1942.
10. GP diary, January 29, 1942.
11. GP to G. B. Pinchot, March 24, 1943.
12. GP diary, April 25, 1942.
13. GP diary, May 3, 1942.
14. January 28 and April 24, 1943.
15. J. P. McEvoy, "Survive at Sea by Eating and Drinking Fish!" *Reader's Digest*, April 1943.
16. H. H. Arnold to GP, August 9, 1945.
17. *The Secret Diary of Harold L. Ickes*, Vol. II, p. 625.
18. GP to A. M. Landon, April 10, 1940.
19. GP to R. L. Jones, April 1, 1940.
20. GP to G. D. Seymour, August 30, 1940.
21. GP diary, August 17, 1940.
22. GP diary, June 26, 1940.
23. GP diary, August 13, 1940.
24. GP diary, August 27, 1940.
25. GP, confidential, to G. D. Seymour, September 27, 1940.
26. GP diary, September 28 and 30, 1940.
27. GP diary, October 9, 1940.
28. October 9, 1940.
29. GP diary, October 8, 1940.
30. GP diary, November 5, 1940.
31. GP and C. B. Pinchot to President and Mrs. Roosevelt, November 5, 1940.
32. GP to A. K. Fisher, March 1, 1941.
33. GP to J. J. O'Connor, May 16, 1944.
34. GP form letter to "Dear Friend," October 16, 1944.
35. GP to J. A. Phillips, August 21, 1944.
36. GP to D. L. Lawrence, October 16, 1944.
37. H. A. Wallace to GP, November 14, 1944.
38. GP to S. H. Fisher, April 14, 1945.
39. Rough copy, September 27, 1946.
40. GP diary, January 20, 1945.
41. GP diary, February 1, 1945.
42. Forest Service, Washington Office Information Digest, September 7, 1945.
43. GP speech, Eighth American Scientific Congress, Washington, May 11, 1940.
44. F. D. Roosevelt to GP, October 24, 1944, enclosing copy of F. D. Roosevelt to Cordell Hull, October 24, 1944.
45. GP diary, January 19, 1945.
46. GP diary, January 21, 1945.
47. GP diary, March 28, 1945.
48. GP diary, April 12, 1945.
49. GP diary, May 23, 1945.
50. GP diary, December 13, 1945.
51. D. C. Coyle, *Conservation* (New Brunswick, Rutgers University, 1957), p. 247.
52. GP to Dr. T. D. Spies, February 22, 1941.
53. GP diary, August 6, 1945.
54. GP diary, August 10, 1945.
55. GP diary, May 3, 1945.
56. *New York Times*, November 23, 1947.
57. GP to H. L. Reed, April 3, 1946.
58. April 13, 1943.
59. GP to H. S. Truman, September 15, 1945.
60. GP to E. L. Parsons, January 14, 1944.
61. Freda Kirchwey telegram to GP, October 3, 1945.
62. GP to N. V. Peale, December 18, 1942.
63. Coyle, *Conservation*, pp. 115, 267.
64. Burns, *Roosevelt: The Lion and the Fox*, p. 199.

65. GP to F. D. Roosevelt, April 26, 1933.
66. GP to H. L. Ickes, July 27, 1935.
67. W. L. Hall, *Journal of Forestry*, August 1945, p. 553.
68. GP to W. H. Corbin, July 15, 1944.
69. GP to G. W. Norris, July 22, 1944.
70. GP to G. B. Pinchot, May 24, 1943.
71. Dr. D. W. Atchley to G. B. Pinchot, June 13, 1945.
72. GP diary, August 14, 1945.
73. GP diary, January 11, 1946.
74. GP diary, March 3, 1946.
75. GP to M. E. Gregg, September 24, 1946.
76. *New York Times*, October 8, 1946.
77. GP to G. C. Pardee, February 24, 1936.
78. *Pittsburgh Post-Gazette*, May 5, 1958. The park is located near York, Pennsylvania.
79. H. A. Tolson to Mrs. H. T. Mather, December 20, 1945.

BIBLIOGRAPHY

MANUSCRIPTS

The following collections were used:

In the Library of Congress: Albert J. Beveridge Papers, Mira Lloyd Dock Papers, James R. Garfield Papers, William John McGee Papers, Frederick H. Newell Papers, Amos R. E. Pinchot Papers, Gifford Pinchot Papers, Elihu Root Papers, William Howard Taft Papers, Thomas J. Walsh Papers, William Allen White Papers, Woodrow Wilson Papers. From Anna Jane Phillips Shuman, the John M. Phillips Papers.

BOOKS

Oscar T. Barck and Nelson M. Blake, *Since 1900*, New York, Macmillan, 1947

Claude G. Bowers, *Beveridge and the Progressive Era*, Boston, Houghton Mifflin, 1932

John K. Brilhart, *Gifford Pinchot as a Conservation Crusader in 1909*, unpublished M.A. thesis, Pennsylvania State University, 1957

James M. Burns, *Roosevelt: The Lion and the Fox*, New York, Harcourt, Brace, 1956

Archie Butt, *Taft and Roosevelt: The Intimate Letters of Archie Butt*, New York, Doubleday, Doran, 1930

David Cushman Coyle, *Conservation*, New Brunswick, Rutgers University Press, 1957

Samuel T. Dana, *Forest and Range Policy*, New York, McGraw-Hill, 1956

Josephus Daniels, *The Wilson Era*, Chapel Hill, University of North Carolina Press, 1944

Walter Davenport, *Power and Glory*, New York, Putnam's, 1931

Oscar K. Davis, *Released for Publication*, New York, Houghton Mifflin, 1925

Benjamin P. De Witt, *The Progressive Movement*, New York, Macmillan, 1915

Edward N. Doan, *The La Follettes and the Wisconsin Idea*, New York, Rinehart, 1947

Herbert S. Duffy, *The Private Papers of William Howard Taft*, New York, Minton, Balch, 1930.

Wayland F. Dunaway, *A History of Pennsylvania*, New York, Prentice-Hall, 1948

Joseph A. Falco, *Political Background and First Gubernatorial Administration of Gifford Pinchot, 1923-1927*, unpublished dissertation, University of Pittsburgh, 1956

467

Martin L. Fausold, *Gifford Pinchot and the Progressive Movement: An Analysis of the Pinchot Papers, 1910-1917*, unpublished dissertation, Syracuse University, 1953

Bernhard E. Fernow, *A Brief History of Forestry*, Washington, American Forestry Association, 1913

Louis Filler, *Crusaders for American Liberalism*, New York, Harcourt, Brace, 1939

Charles O. Gill and Gifford Pinchot, *The Country Church: The Decline of Its Influence and the Remedy*, New York, Macmillan, 1913

————, *Six Thousand Country Churches*, New York, Macmillan, 1919

Jean Gould (ed.), *Home-Grown Liberal*, New York, Dodd, Mead, 1954

William B. Greeley, *Forests and Men*, Garden City, Doubleday, 1951

Luther H. Gulick, *American Forest Policy*, New York, Duell, Sloan and Pearce, 1951

John Hays Hammond, *The Autobiography of John Hays Hammond*, New York, Farrar & Rinehart, 1935, Vol. 2

Norman Hapgood, *The Changing Years*, New York, Farrar & Rinehart, 1930

Samuel P. Hays, *The First American Conservation Movement, 1891-1920*, unpublished dissertation, Harvard University, 1953

Kenneth W. Hechler, *Insurgency*, New York, Columbia University Press, 1940

Benjamin H. Hibbard, *A History of the Public Land Policies*, New York, Macmillan, 1924

David Hinshaw, *A Man from Kansas*, New York, Putnam's, 1945

Richard Hofstadter, *The Age of Reform*, New York, Knopf, 1955

Herbert Hoover, *The Memoirs of Herbert Hoover*, New York, Macmillan, 1952, Vols. 2 and 3

Harold Howland, *Theodore Roosevelt and His Times*, New Haven, Yale University Press, 1921

Harold L. Ickes, *The Autobiography of a Curmudgeon*, New York, Reynal & Hitchcock, 1943

————, *The Secret Diary of Harold L. Ickes*, New York, Simon & Schuster, 1953-1954. Vols. 1-3

John Ise, *The United States Forest Policy*, New Haven, Yale University Press, 1920

Philip C. Jessup, *Elihu Root*, New York, Dodd, Mead, 1938, Vol. 2

Claudius O. Johnson, *Borah of Idaho*, New York, Longmans, Green, 1936

Walter Johnson, *Selected Letters of William Allen White*, New York, Holt, 1947

Matthew Josephson, *The President Makers*, New York, Harcourt, Brace, 1940

Bela C. and Fola La Follette, *Robert M. La Follette*, New York, Macmillan, 1953

La Follette's Autobiography, Madison, The Robert M. La Follette Co., 1913

Richard W. Leopold, *Elihu Root and the Conservative Tradition*, Boston, Little, Brown, 1954

William Draper Lewis, *The Life of Theodore Roosevelt*, Philadelphia, Winston, 1919

Alfred Lief, *Democracy's Norris*, New York, Stackpole, 1939

Arthur S. Link, *Wilson: The New Freedom*, Princeton, Princeton University Press, 1956

————. *Woodrow Wilson and the Progressive Era*, New York, Harper, 1954

Rodney C. Loehr, *Forests for the Future*, St. Paul, Minnesota Historical Society, 1952

Alpheus T. Mason, *Brandeis: A Free Man's Life*, New York, Viking, 1946

————, *Bureaucracy Convicts Itself*, New York, Viking, 1941

Alfred Matthews, *History of Wayne, Pike and Monroe Counties, Pennsylvania*, Philadelphia, Peck, 1886

James H. Maurer, *It Can Be Done*, New York, Rand School, 1938

Walter F. McCaleb, *Theodore Roosevelt*, New York, Boni, 1931

Francis McHale, *President and Chief Justice*, Philadelphia, Dorrance, 1931

Charles Merz, *The Dry Decade*, Garden City, Doubleday, Doran, 1931

Messages and Papers of the Presidents, New York, Bureau of National Literature, no date, Vol. 17

Elting E. Morison (ed.), *The Letters of Theodore Roosevelt*, Cambridge, Harvard University Press, 1951-1954, Vols. 3-8

George E. Mowry, *Theodore Roosevelt and the Progressive Movement*, Madison, University of Wisconsin Press, 1946

Jeannette P. Nichols, *Alaska*, Cleveland, Arthur H. Clark, 1924

Edgar B. Nixon (ed.), *Franklin D. Roosevelt and Conservation, 1911-1945*, Hyde Park, Franklin D. Roosevelt Library, 1957, Vol. 1

George W. Norris, *Fighting Liberal*, New York, Macmillan, 1945

Harvey O'Connor, *Mellon's Millions*, New York, John Day, 1933

E. Louise Peffer, *The Closing of the Public Domain*, Stanford, Stanford University Press, 1951

George Wharton Pepper, *Philadelphia Lawyer*, Philadelphia, Lippincott, 1944

Amos R. E. Pinchot, *History of the Progressive Party*, H. M. Hooker, ed., New York, New York University Press, 1958

Gifford Pinchot, *Breaking New Ground*, New York, Harcourt, Brace, 1947

————, *Just Fishing Talk*, Harrisburg, The Telegraph Press, 1936

————, *The Fight for Conservation*, New York, Doubleday, Page, 1910

————, *To the South Seas*, Philadelphia, Winston, 1930

Harold T. Pinkett, *Gifford Pinchot and the Early Conservation Movement in the United States*, unpublished dissertation, American University, 1953

Henry F. Pringle, *The Life and Times of William Howard Taft*, New York, Farrar & Rinehart, 1939

————, *Theodore Roosevelt*, New York, Harcourt, Brace, 1931

C. C. Regier, *The Era of the Muckrakers*, Chapel Hill, University of North Carolina Press, 1932

Roy M. Robbins, *Our Landed Heritage*, New York, Peter Smith, 1950

Theodore Roosevelt, *Autobiography*, New York, Scribner's, 1946

Carl A. Schenck, *The Biltmore Story*, St. Paul, American Forest History Foundation, 1955

Arthur M. Schlesinger, Jr., *The Age of Roosevelt: The Crisis of the Old Order*, Boston, Houghton Mifflin, 1957

Selections from the Correspondence of Theodore Roosevelt and Henry Cabot Lodge, New York, Scribner's, 1925, Vol. 2

Darrell H. Smith, *The Forest Service: Its History, Activities, and Organization*, Washington, Brookings Institution, 1930

Edward J. Stackpole, *Behind the Scenes with a Newspaper Man*, Philadelphia, Lippincott, 1927

Rose M. Stahl, *The Ballinger-Pinchot Controversy*, Smith College Studies in History, 1926

Harold Stein (ed.), *Public Administration and Policy Development*, New York, Harcourt, Brace, 1952

Sylvester K. Stevens, *Pennsylvania, The Keystone State*, New York, American Historical Co., 1956

Henry L. Stimson and McGeorge Bundy, *On Active Service in Peace and War*, New York, Harper, 1947

Mark Sullivan, *Our Times*, New York, Scribner's, 1932, Vol. 4

William R. Thayer, *Theodore Roosevelt*, Boston, Houghton Mifflin, 1919

Stuart R. Tompkins, *Alaska*, Norman, University of Oklahoma Press, 1945

Kenneth E. Trombley, *The Life and Times of a Happy Liberal*, New York, Harper, 1954

Charles R. Van Hise, *The Conservation of Natural Resources in the United States*, New York, Macmillan, 1910

William S. Vare, *My Forty Years in Politics*, Philadelphia, Roland Swain, 1933

Norman Wengert, *Natural Resources and the Political Struggle*, New York, Doubleday, 1955

William Allen White, *The Autobiography of William Allen White*, New York, Macmillan, 1946

Robert K. Winters (ed.), *Fifty Years of Forestry in the U.S.A.*, Washington, Society of American Foresters, 1950

SELECTED GOVERNMENT DOCUMENTS

The National Archives of the United States Government: Forest Service
Section, Department of the Interior Section

Congressional Record

Legislative Journal, Pennsylvania

Department of Agriculture, *Yearbook of Agriculture, 1949*, Washington,
1950

———, Division of Forestry, *Primer of Forestry*, Bulletin 24, Washington,
1899

Campaign Contributions, Testimony before a Subcommittee of the Senate
Committee on Privileges and Elections, Pursuant to S. Res. 79, Washington, 1913

Report of the Giant Power Survey Board, Harrisburg, 1925

Senatorial Campaign Expenditures, Hearings . . . on S. Res. 195, 69th Cong.,
1st sess., 3 parts, Washington, 1926

U.S. Senate and House Documents:

    Sen. Doc. 105, 55th Cong., 1st sess., *Forest Policy for the Forested Lands
of the United States*, 1897

    Sen. Doc. 188, 58th Cong., 2d sess., *Message from the President of the
United States Submitting the Preliminary Report of the Public Lands
Commission*, 1904

    Sen. Doc. 189, 58th Cong., 3d sess., *Report of the Public Lands Com-
mission*, 1905

    House Rept. 8147, 59th Cong., 2d sess., *Expenditures in the Department
of Agriculture*, 1907

    Sen. Doc. 325, 60th Cong., 1st sess., *Preliminary Report of the Inland
Waterways Commission*, 1908

    House Doc. 1425, 60th Cong., 2d sess., *Proceedings of a Conference of
Governors in the White House—May 13-15, 1908*, 1909

    Sen. Doc. 705, 60th Cong., 2d sess., *Report of the Country Life Com-
mission*, 1909

    Sen. Doc. 676, 60th Cong., 2d sess., *Report of the National Conservation
Commission*, 3 vols., 1909

    Sen. Doc. 719, 61st Cong., 3d sess., *Investigation of the Department of the
Interior and of the Bureau of Forestry*, 13 vols., 1911

    Sen. Doc. 216, 70th Cong., 2d sess., *Deforested America*, 1929

INDEX

(In the subheads, GP is used for Gifford Pinchot, FDR for Franklin D. Roosevelt, and TR for Theodore Roosevelt.)

Abbott, M. F., 206, 207, 210
academic freedom, 384
Addams, Jane, 235, 237, 251
agriculture, interest in, 100-02, 243, 244, 265, 269, 270. *See also* U.S. Department of Agriculture
Ahern, George, 62, 64, 334-36
Ainey, W. D., 300-02, 366, 367
Alaska, coal lands in, *see* Cunningham Claims; Controller Bay; trip to, 208-10; national forests in, proposed transfer, 333
Alaska Syndicate, 134, 136, 206
alcohol, *see* prohibition
Alcohol Permit Board, 317
Allen, Henry J., 290, 291
Allied Forces for Prohibition, 382
Alter, George E., 280, 284
American Conservation, 200
American Forest Congress, 60, 61
American Forestry Association, 4, 37, 59, 62, 335, 408
American Forests, 335, 408
Angelsmith, Canon L., 9
Annals of the American Academy of Political and Social Science, giant power issue, 299
anthracite, *see* coal
Anti-Saloon League of America, 265, 382
Army, U.S., forest protection by, 39, 41
Arnold Arboretum, 24, 37
Arnold, Henry H., 421
atomic power, government ownership, 428
Atterbury, William W., 278, 349, 352, 355

Bacon, Robert, 66, 108
Bailey, L. H., 101
Baker, Ray Stannard, 55, 233
Baker, W. Harry, 286
Baldwin Locomotive Works, 352, 364
Ballinger-Pinchot controversy, 120-89; background, 120-54; charges by Glavis, 127-29, 132, 133, 135, 151-53; criticism at Irrigation Congress, 129-31; investigations by Glavis, 133-43; Ballinger's contacts with claimants, 139, 140; reports to Taft, 143-45, 148; attitude of Taft, 146, 147, 149, 150; Ballinger's statement, 148f; congressional investigation, 155, 156, 164-75, 178-83; GP as witness, 169-73; attitude of TR, 169,

177, 183, 186; final reports 183-86. *See also* Cunningham claims
Ballinger, Richard A., 88, 89, 118-37, 139-52, 155, 156, 162-66, 168-71, 173-75, 178-89, 206, 208, 209, 412, 413, 427
Barfod, Einar, 343
Beard, Charles A., 327
Benn, James S., 301, 302
Benson, Elmer, 424
Beveridge, Albert J., 89, 106, 151, 177, 190, 191, 194, 198, 217, 235, 246, 251
Biltmore Estate, 26-31, 34
Bliss, Cornelius N., 41, 44, 45
blue laws, 325
Bluett, Thomas, 311
Bonaparte, Charles J., 213
Boone and Crockett Club, 53
Borah, William E., 51, 81, 82
Bourne, Jonathan, 214
Brandeis, Louis D., 155, 156, 165, 166, 170, 173-76, 178-83, 207, 208, 210, 214, 216, 222, 237, 258, 413
Brandis, Sir Detrich, 19-25, 34, 42, 61
Breaking New Ground, 196, 425-28
Bristow, Joseph, 188
Brown, Francis S., 347-51
Brownlow Committee, 410
Bryan, William J., 77, 97, 202
Bull Moose Party, *see* Progressive Party
Burton, Theodore E., 95
business men, attitude toward GP, 352, 353
Butler, Smedley D., 307, 328, 392
Butt, Archie, 160, 195

Camp, Walter, 13
Canada, trip to, 107
Cannon, Joseph G., 51, 156
Capper, Arthur, 330
Capper Bill, 333, 334, 336
Carnegie, Andrew, 55, 97
Carr, Charlotte, 359, 360
Chamber of Commerce, Pennsylvania State, 283
Chugach National Forest, 119, 206
Churchill, Winston S., 426
civil rights, 384, 385
Civilian Conservation Corps, 405
Clapp, Earle H., 422
Clapp, Moses, 251
Clarke-McNary Act, 331

INDEX

paign for governor (1922), 279-88;
Governor (1923-27), 291-329, 429;
candidate for delegate to Republican
National Convention (1924), 313, 314;
primary campaign for U.S. Senate
(1926), 315-20; campaign for Governor (1930), 347-57; Governor (1931-
35), 358-402; primary campaign for
U.S. Senate (1934), 396-98; Schnader-
Reed campaign (1934), 399, 400; Lan-
don campaign (1936), 415, 416; cam-
paign for governor (1938), 416, 417;
presidential campaign (1940), 421-23;
(1944), 423, 424
Pinchot, Gifford Bryce (son of GP), 254, 342
Pinchot, James W. (father of GP), 3-5, 48, 49, 60, 62
Pinchot, Mary Jane Eno (mother of GP), 4, 6-9, 51, 52, 97, 107, 161, 166, 205, 233, 240, 241, 249-51, 267
Pinchot, Warren & Co., 3
Pinchot roads, 375
Pisgah Forest, 30
Platt, Orville H., 68
Plunkett, Sir Horace, 100, 101, 178, 238; correspondence with, 107, 183, 232, 246, 279, 315, 388
Poindexter, Miles, 207, 209
political machines, 326. *See also* Mellon organization; Vare organization
Potter, Ellen C., 292
power, water, conservation of, 73-78. *See also* public utilities
Power Monopoly; Its Make-up and Its Menace, 338, 339
Price, Overton W., 47, 65, 84, 87, 92, 128, 145, 151, 156-59, 162, 177, 199, 202, 205, 206, 216, 239
Primer of Conservation, 88
Primer of Forestry, 62
Princeton University, 103
Proctor, Redfield, 51
Progressive movement, 192, 193, 213, 214. *See also* Progressive party
Progressive party, campaign of 1912, 227-33; Chicago conference, 235, 236; cam-
paign of 1914, 246-53; convention (1916), 255, 256; La Follette campaign of 1924, 313; Pennsylvania, *see* Wash-ington party
prohibition, 244, 245, 265, 283, 288, 302-07, 315, 316-18, 324, 343, 348, 350, 382, 383
Prohibition party, 356
Public Lands Commission, 58, 69, 70, 118
Public Lands Convention, 88, 89

Public Service Commission, Pennsylvania, 300-02, 344, 347, 348, 358, 362-70
public utilities, 297-300, 337-39, 343, 344, 348, 352, 353, 355, 357-59, 362-67, 370, 388
Puerto Rico, trip to, 49

radium, conservation of, 202, 203
Raker Bill, 205
Reader's Digest, 421
Reclamation Service, 123, 124
Reed, David A., 286, 293, 314, 317, 326, 396, 397, 399, 400
roads, *see* highways
Roberts, Owen J., 332
Roosevelt Club, 190
Roosevelt, Edith Kermit, 178
Roosevelt, Eleanor, 394
Roosevelt, Franklin D., 374, 379, 380, 386-88, 392-96, 398-400, 405, 411, 413, 414, 416, 420, 422-26, 431, 432
Roosevelt, Kermit, 235
Roosevelt Memorial Assn., 269
Roosevelt, Theodore, advice to GP, 265, 266; appointments by, 104, 105; Bal-linger controversy, attitude in, 169, 177, 183, 186; conservation advocate, 53, 60, 61, 74, 77-81, 86, 87, 92, 94-100, 107, 108, 114, 116, 117, 123, 184, 193, 204, 210, 233; correspondence with, 64, 162-64, 182, 265; death, 268f; differences with GP, 55, 191-96, 214, 216, 217, 233-39, 431; emulation by GP, 56, 57, 69, 111, 293, 308, 309, 327, 384; friendship with GP, 53, 54, 65-67, 106, 109, 191, 218; ghostwriting by GP for, 54, 55, 114, 193; influence of GP on, 430; political career of GP initiated by, 67f, 111, 190; presidential aspirations and intentions, 162, 163, 190, 215, 216, 219-22, 224, 225; presidential candidate (1912), 224-31; presidential candidacy (1916), efforts of GP on behalf of, 255f; regard for GP, 54-56, 67, 97, 105, 107, 109-11, 124-26, 176, 240, 241; regard for Mrs. Gifford Pinchot, 250; rural life, interest in, 100-02; sup-port of GP in 1914 senatorial campaign, 246, 247, 252, 253; Taft, growing dis-illusionment with, 115, 116, 160, 188, 192, 217; World War I efforts, 260, 261, 264
Root, Elihu, 54, 64, 67, 153-55, 160, 183, 184, 188, 214
Rothrock, Joseph T., 273, 276
Rural Electrification Administration, 199
Ryan, Richard S., 206

479

Weyerhaeuser, F. E., 84
Weyerhaeuser, Frederick, 57
Wheeler, Wayne, 305
White, William Allen, 161, 177, 230, 309, 310, 313, 415, 419
Wickersham, George W., 120, 141, 142, 145, 151, 174, 175, 178-81, 185
Willkie, Wendell, 422
Wilson, James, 45, 46, 60, 61, 75, 80, 90, 93, 103, 104, 106, 115, 116, 128, 157, 159, 160, 172, 187
Wilson, William B., 354
Wilson, Woodrow, 103, 223, 232, 244, 257-61, 264, 426
Wisconsin, University of, 103, 161
women, suffrage movement, support of, 243; support of GP, 285; appointees of GP, 292, 359, 360
Women's Christian Temperance Union, 304, 306

Wood, Charles B., Mrs., 319
Wood, Leonard, 65, 188, 270
Woodruff, George W., 46, 74, 105, 129, 130, 152, 199, 203, 224, 275, 292, 298, 336, 338, 341, 343, 359, 366, 427
Works Progress Administration, 414
World Congress Against Alcoholism, 306
World Conservation Conference, 108, 425, 426
World's Fair, Chicago (1893), 27, 30-32
World War I, 259-64
World War II, 407, 408, 419-21

Yale Forest School, 48, 49, 55
Yale University, 11-15, 22, 433
Yosemite National Park, 87
Young Men's Christian Assn., GP offered position with, 13

Zurich, Switzerland, 20